Children and Media

Children and Media

A Global Perspective

Dafna Lemish

WILEY Blackwell

To Lia Margaret Lemish,
her future siblings and cousins,
and their parents –
who give meaning to it all

Brief Table of Contents

Contents

Preface

Can one book fully and completely cover such a wide and complex terrain as the intersection of children and media, and do so from a global perspective? Obviously it cannot.

What it does seek to do is to provide you with one scholar's account of the landscape, a map, if you will, of the typography of the field of children and media, highlighting favorite places, mountain peaks, and hidden valleys from the point of view of an individual who has been engaged in this global trek over an extended period of time. Thus, by definition, this book is by no means inclusive, and should not be depended upon, solely, for your specific research project or thesis. But if you are looking for a mapping of the field, then I hope you will find this to be the right book for you. If so, it can serve as a takeoff point for your own journey.

Accordingly, this book organizes and analyzes the accumulated literature developed over the past 50 years by scholars studying relationships of children and media, with a view to assisting students, media producers, policymakers, educators, and parents in understanding key issues in relations of media, society, and culture that have been and should be studied, discussed, and confronted in terms of research, public policy, education, and production.

The general structure and content of the book follows an earlier version entitled *Children and television: A global perspective* (2007), which was based, originally, with permission, on a textbook I wrote for the Open University in Israel (*Growing-up with television: The little screen in the lives of children and youth*, 2002, in Hebrew) and updated in 2013 (*Growing up with television and the internet*). I continue to be indebted to the Open University of Israel for their generous permission to expand on that excellent experience. However, this book moves beyond the emphasis on television, including my own earlier work, to present a broader, integrative analysis of what we know about research conducted all over the world on the inter-relationships between all forms of media and children as a global phenomenon.

Expanding the discussion means a lot more than just "adding" all media to the previous analysis of children and television. Indeed, many of our assumptions and concerns about television use have been turned on their head with the introduction of digital media. Take, for example, the preoccupation of much of the public discourse with the passive and isolating nature of television viewing. Over the last decade, the rapid growth of social media has led us to discuss how children's active participation in media production and online social networking are changing the nature of sociability. Thus, integrating new scholarship generated over the last decade in the vast area of children and media challenges us to reconsider many previous understandings of the roles of television.

I have been studying children and media for 30 years in the USA, Europe, and Israel, as well as its complementary implications for the development of media literacy. I have read, taught, conducted research, written about it, and presented my work in numerous scholarly as well as professional settings. I take pride in being in a unique position to bridge two complementary research traditions to children and media, stated very roughly as: The American tradition of developmental psychology with a general emphasis on the individual child, effects studies, and quantitative methodologies; and the European tradition of sociology of childhood and cultural studies with its general emphasis on sociological and cultural issues, and the application of qualitative methodologies. My education and experience in both traditions allows me the privileged position of sharing with you my integration of these traditions into a more holistic view of the field, which is neither limited to nor biased by either tradition.

I bring with me to this work, as to anything else in my professional and personal life, a feminist worldview and set of values. What I mean by this is a special concern for and interest in issues of equality and diversity, a critical view on the constructed nature of all social life, and an ethics of care. Within the framework of my own research, the feminist worldview has stimulated a rethinking of traditional binary oppositions related to children and media: The distinction between childhood and adulthood; the separation of children's public and private lives; rational and emotional reactions to media; formal schooling and leisure activities; cultural constructions and developmental theories; consumption and production of media content. I have also taken very seriously an understanding of the power hierarchies that characterize relations between adult researchers and children investigated, and my own privileged position as a middle-class, educated, white female academic.

A major characteristic of all feminist work is the commitment not only to contribute to research and social theory, but also the commitment to being a catalyst for deep social change. Indeed, the feminist perspective often criticizes contemporary social science for differentiating rather than integrating knowledge and action and highlights instead the emancipatory potential of their co-joint workings. I am, therefore, deeply involved with making academic knowledge accessible to the public through efforts at teacher training, development of media literacy curricula, appearances in the media, advising grassroots organizations, and participating in exchanges with producers. What I have gained from these efforts occupies an important place in the following pages as well.

The task undertaken here is enormous and very ambitious. I approached this challenge with deep gratitude to many, many people who have contributed to my professional development and life throughout the years. While there are too many to even attempt to name individually, I am indebted to them all. A few who stand out as important "mile-stones" on my intellectual way have my deepest gratitude. Therefore, I want to offer special thanks to David Buckingham, Linda Renée Bloch, Akiba Cohen, Máire Davies-Messenger, Kirsten Drotner, Nelly Elias, Shalom Fisch, Maya Götz, Amy Jordan, Barbara Kolucki, Sonia Livingstone, Rivka Ribak, Michael Rich, Chava Tidhar, Barbara Wilson, and Patti Valkenburg – from whom I learned much about children and media as well as about the intricacies of cross-cultural research; to Aletha Huston, Mabel Rice, and the late John Wright who assisted me in understanding the child developmental traditions; and to Ellen Wartella, with whom I first started on this trek in my first course in the field, over three decades ago, and who has continued to fuel my interests since.

To my colleagues and friends from the Feminist Scholarship Division of the International Communication Association (ICA), and especially Carolyn Byrely, Cynthia Carter, Marian Meyers, Lana Rakow, Karen Ross, and Angharad Valdivia, I give thanks for constantly reminding me of the meaning and responsibility of being a citizen of the globe, and the value of our daily work in attempting to make a difference within it.

I owe a great deal to Elizabeth Swayze, Senior Editor of Wiley Blackwell, who believed in this project and in me from our first exchange; to Julia Kirk, Senior Project Editor, Fiona Screen, copy editor, as well as to the production staff at Wiley Blackwell for their professional, efficient, and friendly collaboration. I am also deeply grateful to Jim Bigogno, our Dean's Office administrator in the College of Mass Communication and Media Arts, Southern Illinois University, for his administrative assistance and dedicated, personal, year-round support; and to Jennifer Sigler, a talented doctoral student and graduate research assistant, for her valuable assistance. Finally, I am in debt to my colleagues Sun Sun Lim, Cristina Ponte, and the anonymous reviewers for their valuable comments and contributions to the book proposal and the final draft.

I hope all of these colleagues and friends will find something of themselves resonating in the following pages.

To my children – Leeshai, Noam, and Erga – who were fortunate to enjoy consuming media in several places around the globe, and who never fail to challenge, inspire, delight, and surprise me. I thank them for stimulating my research following their own development from infancy to adulthood.

And finally, I am grateful to Peter Lemish, my lifetime partner and the most critical, yet loving, reviewer and editor, for keeping me intellectually and personally on the tips of my toes.

Above all else, this book is for the betterment of children's lives around the globe.

References

Lemish, D. (2002). *Growing up with television: The little screen in the lives of children and youth*. Tel-Aviv: The Open University (in Hebrew).

Lemish, D. (2007). *Children and television: A global perspective*. Malden, MA: Blackwell.

Lemish, D. (Ed.). (2013). *Growing-up with television and the internet: The screens in the lives of children and youth: A reader*. Tel-Aviv: The Open University of Israel (in Hebrew and English).

Companion Website

Please visit the companion website at www.wiley.com/go/lemish/childrenandmedia to view additional content for this title.

Freely Available:

Meet the author introductory video
Key terms
Questions for discussion and evaluation
Web links

Available to Instructors Only:

Assignments for each chapter
Sample syllabi for undergraduate, graduate, and professionally
    oriented courses

Introduction

Why study the role of media in children's lives? Why a specific concern with the audience of children? And why are children and media a global issue? Let us start our joint journey into the exciting field of the study of children and media by engaging the three central challenges embedded in this book's title.

Why Media (Now, More than Ever)?

The study of children and media relations is an enormously important topic for a variety of compelling reasons. First, children of both genders and all ages, races, religions, classes, and geographical regions of the world use media on a regular basis, enjoy them tremendously, and learn more about the world from them than from any other socializing agent. A phenomenon so pervasive and central in children's lives is bound to be of great interest to anybody involved in and/or concerned about their world – students, parents, teachers, scholars, politicians, professionals, policymakers, and concerned citizens; in short, all of us.

Indeed, there is very little else that can so confidently claimed to be an experience shared by most children in the world today? At the beginning of the third millennium, children are being raised in a variety of social arrangements: by dual parents, single parents, divorced parents, same-sex parents, communal parents, no parents. Furthermore, regarding the existential nature of their lives, we can say that not all children are literate or, for that matter, go to school. They speak hundreds of different languages, eat different foods, play different games, wear different clothes. They face very different challenges in their daily lives, and have different dreams and aspirations for their future. Yet almost all of them spend time with media on a regular basis.

Children and Media: A Global Perspective, First Edition. Dafna Lemish.
© 2015 John Wiley & Sons, Inc. Published 2015 by John Wiley & Sons, Inc.
Companion Website: www.wiley.com/go/lemish/childrenandmedia

In short, media are one of the most shared and homogenizing mechanisms engaged in by children throughout the world, such that today we can barely think of childhood void of media. Whether they have a television or computer in their bedroom, share the family set in the living room, play computer games on their tablet while riding in the car to school, text on their mobile phone in the playground, or use media in the classroom or the community center, for most children today media are part of their taken-for-granted everyday experience. They may be watching television while playing on the rug, texting while eating their dinner, emailing while doing homework, or listening to music while surfing the internet – but still, they are using media. Children around the world are constantly "on" some form of a media experience.

What other cultural phenomena have such a magnitude of penetration, or have even achieved global status? No wonder our vocabulary has been recently expanded with the introduction of the term *mediatization* to refer to the changing nature of our world where media and the institutions that run them are understood to infiltrate all aspects and levels of our personal and social lives.

While relations between children and media are a universal, global phenomena attracting the attention of hundreds of scholars, worldwide, the burgeoning research literature continues to change as we engage a number of significant challenges. For example, as has already become clear from this brief introduction, an individual medium cannot be studied in isolation. It is common nowadays to substitute the discussion of television, for example, with *screen culture*, in order to recognize the trend for convergence of various media that employ screens: television, including cable and satellite connections, video recorder and games, computer games, the internet, movie theaters, hand-held electronic games, tablets and mobile-phone screens. They all share the predominance of the audio-visual system of signification, using similar codes and conventions to convey a rich abundance of contents. Indeed, our discussion of 'television' is deeply integrated with all the above forms.

One result of media convergence is the emergence of new fields of research. Thus, computers in general and the internet in particular, as well as more recently mobile technologies, have become the leading research topics of scholars investigating children and media over the past few years, following quick infiltration and diffusion of such technologies in the lives of children around the world.

At the same time, research into the role of television in children's lives remains quite central in scholarly studies, for a number of key reasons:

First, television remains a dominant medium for young children even in those cultures where computers have reached a high diffusion rate, whether viewed off the air, through cable, satellite, internet downloads, or privately owned discs and DVDs. Mobile media and the internet in particular, while diffused rapidly, are still the privilege of the minority of well-to-do, middle- and upper-class children in both high-resource as well as low-resource societies.

Second, while scholarly study of computer access has been extended beyond the limited focus on ownership of the hardware itself (i.e., who has a computer at home or has access to one in a public place) to questions related to cognitive and motivational access (i.e., who has the knowledge as well as the linguistic and computer skills necessary to access the computer? Who perceives the computer as relevant to their own personal goals and future prospects and thus has the motivation to pursue computer use?).

Third, studying television from a global perspective also provides us with a solid base from which to extend and illuminate the growing fields of digital media studies.

Finally, by way of another example of changes in our research field related to children's use of emergent technologies, we realize that much of our thinking about media consumption has been challenged by the more active role that children are taking today in their leisure culture. As a result, we now understand there is a blurring of the boundaries between consumption and production.

Many of the same questions to be discussed in the following text were investigated over the last century in reference to the place of television in children's lives, and they remain relevant, applicable, and indeed necessary in advancing this field of research. By extension, they can be applied to and compared with evolving research on the convergence of screen media and on mediatization of childhood. Such research is leading to the emergence of new theoretical foundations as new studies lead us into new territories. This constructive tension between continuity and disruption is one reason why the field of children and media is such a vibrant and exciting field of scholarly endeavor.

Why Children (Only)?

Although common discourse suggests that children are living today in a world devoid of what formerly distinguished childhood (i.e., constant blurring of former dichotomies between adulthood and childhood, learning and play, as well as public and private spheres), this book insists on continuing to treat children (somewhat artificially set at the up to age 18 marker) as occupying a very unique time in the human cycle that deserves our special attention as well as the best of our resources and human investment.

Furthermore, scholars of media and children are enriching our understanding of the need for more nuanced approaches to the concept of *childhood*; such as its socially constructed nature, as well as to the various diverse dimensions that it encompasses. Thus, studies of differences of gender, ethnicity, culture, and class are gaining more and more prominence in addition to those related to children's age. All of these add new dimensions for investigation and understanding of the already complex nature of the relationships between children and media.

Similarly, as we map the field today and summarize what we understand about children and media, we find that the theoretical approaches developed to understand the nature and meaning of childhood have deeply affected the kinds of research questions asked and methods employed by scholars in their attempt to answer them.

To a large degree, studies of children and media that dominated the field until the end of the twentieth century were *about* children. For example, children were tested for their understanding of the content of television programs; they participated in experiments that measured the effects of video games on them; surveys were conducted about the amount and kind of exposure they had to digital technologies.

The theoretical assumption of most of this research was to perceive adulthood as the end goal of children's development and the measuring stick of all their performances. Accordingly, children were perceived as deficient: they were unable to understand media content quite as well as adults; they were not yet immunized against its negative effects; and, unlike adults, they were naive and easily persuaded to buy products or to give personal information to strangers on the internet. Furthermore, according to this approach, children were also understood to be inexperienced "subjects" of research who had difficulty accounting for their personal experiences and understandings of the media in their lives. Such research, then, relied heavily on adults – caregivers, educators, parents, researchers – to report about children's inner worlds, their modes of making meaning, and their media-related pleasures.

Recently, the approach known as cultural studies, as well as sociological-oriented research, challenged the assumption that children should be viewed in relation to the process of "becoming" fully grown adults. In its place, they suggested that childhood be assumed to be a form of "being" in its own right. Accordingly, these scholars highlight the need to allow children, in each stage of their development, to be fully recognized as having a unique personal voice that deserves to be listened to and understood with empathy. Such research advances studies that are as much *with* children and *for* children as they are *on* children. This theoretical and ideological turn has led to application of a wide range of methodologies for studying children and media. For example, in addition to the use of surveys and experiments, researchers incorporate a more active role for the children, as participants with an independent voice, such as with in-depth interviewing, participant observation of their media behaviors and spontaneous play, as well as analysis of their artwork and written accounts.

Why Global? (But Is It?)

As we have seen in the preceding text, children and media constitutes a global phenomenon because media are ubiquitous throughout the world, and it is almost impossible to separate media from conceptions of contemporary childhood. In addition, a number of other compelling reasons can be added to the claim that media have global status. First, very similar debates over media's roles in the lives of children have emerged worldwide. On the one hand, the introduction of television and its diffusion, since the middle of the twentieth century, followed by computers, the internet, and mobile devices, have been adopted and integrated into life in all societies. This has happened in conflicted ways, just as was the case with other communication technologies that preceded them (e.g., books, newspapers, radio, films). This process is referred to by scholars as *technological determinism*, according to which technologies determine, to a large degree, the characteristsics of a society.

Accordingly, many writers claim that high hopes and great expectations were expressed that each new medium would enrich children's lives, stimulate their imagination and creativity, widen their education and knowledge, encourage multicultural tolerance, narrow social gaps, and stimulate development and democratization processes. On the other hand, there is also great anxiety that extensive exposure to media can numb the senses, develop in viewers indifference to the pain of others, encourage destructive behaviors, lead to a deterioration of moral values, suppress local cultures, and contribute to social estrangement.

The ambivalent stance with regard to the role of the medium of television in children's lives – as a "messiah" on the one hand and "demon" on the other – has been discussed widely in public debates in every culture that has absorbed the medium. We witnessed the same debates in recent years with regard to the proliferation of the internet, computer games, as well as mobile technologies. The most pronounced concerns are expressed over the effects of media violence on children, as well as the potential harm of exposure to sexual portrayals, effects of advertising on socialization to consumer culture, and more general concerns for children's passivity and social disengagement. Framed by scholars as *moral panic*,[1] public pressure on governing institutions is exerted through discussion and debates in the media, public forums, parents and community newsletters and forums, as well as in expert testimonies offered in legislative hearings by public leaders and broadcasting policymakers.

Countries that can afford to do so allocate public funds to research institutions in search of more definite and conclusive answers to the enduring question: "What are media doing to our children?"

Second, children all over the world use various technologies as they complete their homework or chores to the sounds of popular music on their music devices. As they daydream they may fantasize on love and adventure over blockbuster movies broadcast on their local channels or downloaded onto their computers and mobile devices. They cheer for their favorite sports team across continents and seas; follow the news of armed conflicts worlds apart; admire many of the same celebrities; collect their memorabilia; hang their posters, wear their T-shirts, follow their private lives in magazines and on websites. They share their everyday life experiences via social networks with others worlds apart as well as those next door. They "like" a viral YouTube video and download a popular app on their mobile phone and tablet in the millions.

Indeed, I suspect that if you visit any country in the world today you will be able to strike up a conversation with local children by asking about their favorite programs, video games, movies, songs, commercials, or internet sites. You do not even have to know the language. Hand motioning to pictures and ads, clicking on links and touchscreens, or the mere mention of the names of global celebrities and popular programs and games will stimulate enough cooperation. At least some of the programs or contents are bound to be familiar to you from your own home media offerings or those encountered in the homes of friends, on public transportation, or while waiting in some line.

As part of a global audience, children employ technologies that enable them to access content which transcends local or even regional physical and cultural boundaries in their media experiences. This leads us to ask: Do children live today in a global village as envisioned by Marshall McLuhan? Can we argue that they are living in a shared global culture whose values are learned through the process of *McDonaldization*[2] (i.e., the diffusion of American culture and values around the world)? If so, do they perceive the social world in similar ways? Is their local identity being erased? Are they evolving the same vision of themselves as consumers, individuals, and citizens of the world?

We know that through global technologies children access a largely global fare consisting of cartoons, situation comedies, soap operas, action-adventure serials, as well as Disney-style and Hollywood movies mostly produced in Euro-American cultures in the West. In addition, they also watch programs that come from other parts of the world, such as Latin-American tele-novellas; Japanese and Korean animated series; or local co-productions of the American series *Sesame Street*. Thus, in shifting from a focus on global access to technologies to the contents distributed, we know that children around the world are entertained through technologies that bring them popular culture-style productions, originating primarily in the USA but also in other parts of the world. These productions are diffused through a process theorized as *The Megaphone Effect*.[3] The USA, according to this thesis, collects and adopts cultural artifacts from around the world, adapts them to the American "palate," and then USA-based media conglomerates serve as a megaphone, spreading them to other markets and turning them into a global phenomenon.

The adoption of a new medium in society, initially as technology, is accompanied by the introduction of an entire value system and political economy that can often be quite foreign to the receiving country. As a global phenomenon, media promote mainly what has been termed as *late modernity* values, typified primarily by commercialism, globalization, privatization, and individualization. At the same time, media have also been among the interventions employed in nation building, cultural preservation, and social revolutions.

Third, the field of "media and children" has become a global research interest of scholars, whose primary association is in psychology, media studies, sociology, health, and education. Their varied disciplinary homes make a great deal of difference to the nature of the research; for example, in the kind of theoretical underpinnings used, questions posed, research methods applied, and, therefore, the kinds of findings produced and their interpretations.

Further, in this respect, noting the changes in the influence of the academic disciplines engaged in studying the reciprocal relationships between children and media is crucial to understanding the richness emerging out of this body of research. Psychology, the most prominent of the disciplines applied to this area, continues to focus on the individual child, as well as a host of related issues such as: social learning from media, the effects of media on behavior, development of comprehension of media content, or the uses children make of media and the gratifications they acquire from their related behaviors.

As the body of literature started to accumulate, mainly from the Euro-North American academic institutions, it became clear that the "strong effect" conclusion referred to previously that assumes a unidirectional media effect on children is overly simplistic. Other research approaches demonstrated something that common sense and anecdotal data posited for a long time: children are not the passive, proverbial tabula rasa upon which media messages leave their marks. On the contrary, children are *active* consumers of media. They react to, think, feel, and create meanings. In doing so, they bring to media encounters a host of predispositions, abilities, desires, and experiences. They use media in diverse personal, social, and cultural circumstances that, too, influence and are part of their discourse and interactions with media.

With the exponential growth of digital technologies, the relationships of children and youth with media have taken an interesting interactive twist, with young audiences becoming what scholars came to refer to as *produsers* (producers + users) or *prosumers* (producers + consumers) of media rather being viewed solely as consumers. Thus, it became clear that asking "what do children do with media?" and "how do media and childhoods interact to define each other" are just as important questions as "how do media influence children?"

The impact of this process remains significant as it resulted in what scholars refer to as a paradigm shift. One example of the richness of this impact is that it raised the need for cross-cultural research. Clearly, comparative research of this global phenomenon can illuminate many of the questions at the heart of the field's continually emerging research agenda: Does media violence affect children differently if they are living in a violent urban center in comparison to a tranquil isolated village? Are children more frightened by news coverage of war when they are growing up amidst armed conflict in comparison to children for whom war is a fictitious concept? Do children react differently to actors and actresses of European descent who appear in their favorite programs and movies if they are living in a dominantly Euro-North American society in comparison to African, Latino, or Asian ones? And what about consumerism? Would children raised in rich consumer cultures, amidst an abundance of products from which to choose, interpret advertising differently from those with no financial resources or with limited personal property? Pursuing such questions, as related to children and media, has become a global endeavor for researchers as no single body of knowledge based on contextualized studies in one culture, be it as rich and diverse as possible, can provide us with the in-depth, multifaceted picture necessary to understand such phenomena in their full global manifestation.

Finally, in terms of investment, children and media represents a global business of enormous proportions and value. For huge entertainment corporations, children are first and foremost current consumers, rather than future citizens. From such a point of view childhood is not a distinct period in the life cycle, one that should be attended to with compassion and responsibility. On the contrary, it is a distinct market opportunity. Televisions sets are hooked to cable and/ or satellite dishes, receiving programs fed by huge international commercial corporations over dozens of channels, and the battle over the quality of the local channel is a battle over the quality of one drop in the ocean. Thus, any attempts to develop or lobby for change in the content of television programs for children, for developing policy guidelines for internet sites or the video games developed for them, for restricting advertising and marketing to children or for fostering media literacy skills in the educational systems, cannot be undertaken in isolation. Concern for the quality of the relationship between *children and media* is a global issue and only global cooperative efforts are likely to make a substantial, enduring difference.

About this Book

The intellectual journey offered you, the reader, in this book begins at the place of the regular, lived experience of children's television viewing, namely, in their home settings.

Chapter 1, "Media and Children at Home," examines the changes in the role of media in the lives of families worldwide, and in particular the place media have come to occupy in children's leisure. This discussion addresses such issues as: How are media integrated in the everyday lives of children? What are the various roles that parents and siblings play in intervening in media consumption habits: for example, in controlling amount of time devoted to media as well as type of contents consumed; mediating the messages; incorporating media in family conversations?

Just as family types and the social contexts in which children are growing up are extremely diverse, so are their individual personalities, cognitive skills, and life experiences. Thus, in Chapter 2, "Media and Individual Development," we explore the importance of such individual differences for understanding children's media uses, through such questions as: What can we learn from the literature on various dimensions of children's development and their relevance to the consumption of media? For example, how are children's attention and comprehension of media developed? What roles do the *formal features* of audio-visual texts play in these processes? How do children learn to distinguish between the reality and fantasy dimensions of media content? How does the development of genre recognition, comprehension of narratives, characters, and moral issues progress? What are the forms of children's identification with media characters? What kind of emotional responses to media content do children display? Further, we will ponder the issue of how much of what we know from research can be generalized to children as a homogenous group, across cultures and age groups, versus how far their relationships with the media change as they grow and develop within particular contexts.

The potential of media for formal and informal learning has been recognized by institutions and educational systems around the world, particularly with regard to those less privileged. Televised "schooling" and educational media challenge many of our conventional assumptions regarding proper pedagogies. In this regard, Chapter 3, "Media Learning and Literacy," will include discussion of the relationship between media and various forms of learning. In doing so, we will engage such questions as: What are the inter-relationships between viewing television, school performance, and reading–writing literacy? Is television viewing related to language – as well as second language – acquisition? Prominent cases such as the worldwide research conducted on *Sesame Street* are one of the foci of analyses shared. This chapter also includes discussion of the integration of new media – particularly the internet – in schooling and the role of digital culture, including gaming, in learning, cognitive skills, and literacy.

With the understandings gained in the first three chapters, we will be ready to tackle the much-debated issue of the behavioral effects of media on children in Chapter 4, "Media and Health-related Behavior." Grounded in the branch of the research literature that regards children as a special audience, because of their vulnerability, particular attention will be devoted to research traditions and hypotheses seeking to explain short- and long-term effects of media violence. The effects of media advertising on consuming behaviors, as well as on family dynamics and emotional wellbeing, will be followed by a consideration of the research on the role of media in promotion of unhealthy behaviors, such as smoking and consumption of alcohol, as well as implications for obesity and eating disorders. In addition, the chapter will address the debate over the effects of media on sexual behavior of adolescents, and discuss pornography.

While Chapter 4 is primarily engaged in studies of the more negative effects of media on children, we will remind ourselves that the same mechanisms that explain negative effects can also be applied to promote positive pro-social behaviors. Finally, when reviewing the full range of educational initiatives, we will also be concerned with other important methodological questions, such as: How valid are the methodologies commonly employed in studying these effects? How relevant is this full range of questions to non-Anglo-European societies? What are the issues of study that we have neglected?

The study of the behavioral effects of media is only part of the story. Many questions posed in our field are concerned with influences of media on children's identity formation, and their evolving worldviews, values, and stereotypes. Accordingly, Chapter 5, "Media and Perceptions of Self and Society," focuses on the role of media in the cultivation of perceptions of self and others. We will ask ourselves how media contribute to the construction of gender identities, sexuality, and body image as well as socialization to sex-roles. Do media foster a perception of the world as a mean and dangerous place in which to live? And, what is the media's role in teaching us about "others" (we all have different "others," depending on who we are) – be they racial minorities in our society, persons with physical and/or mental disabilities, older people, etc. What is the place occupied by media for displaced and immigrant children in facilitating integration into their host countries? Do media play a role in helping children "know thy enemy" or in socializing them to the political world and becoming engaged citizens? Are media part of the formation of a global youth culture that transcends cultural and geographical borders?

Chapter 6, "Media, Sociability, and Participation," is devoted to the relatively new, but what now appears to be the rapidly changing and highly attractive, research field of the social aspects of children's current media use. We will discuss social networking and the relationship between children and youth's offline and online social relationships. While risk-taking is part of growing up, including in virtual worlds, there are now several more dangerous forms of risk-taking that involve media use, such as cyberbullying and sexting. And, as a contrast, we will relate our discussions to other studies that focused on various forms of creative participation online, including civic engagement and activism. Thus, Chapter 6 summarizes what we know to date about young people's online involvement.

Chapter 7 discusses the application of all of the above to the area of "Media Literacy Education." The rationale for incorporating such education now, more than ever, as well as the debates surrounding it, will be summarized, and will serve as the foundations for the presentation of various models of media education employed around the world as well as a discussion of several practical aspects related to the development of curricula, pedagogy, and assessment of effectiveness. The continuing inadequacies of research that evaluates the effectiveness of media literacy education, particularly long term, will be pointed out.

Chapter 8, "Media, Policy, and Advocacy," examines a host of interventions worldwide on behalf of children and the media in their lives. We will review the development of media policy and regulations around the world, particularly regarding historical concerns with issues related to television such as broadcasting hours, inappropriate content for children, advertising practices, exposure of children on the screen, and sponsorships of quality programming. We will then explore the vibrant discussion on attempts to regulate the internet, monitor children's usage, and look at the technological tools for access restriction. Various forms of public activism and advocacy efforts at improving children's media and fostering global cooperation will be reviewed. These efforts highlight the value of cooperation between the worlds of academia and activism, both with their unique accumulated bodies of knowledge and experience devoted to the betterment of the lives of children worldwide.

The book's concluding chapter – Growing Up with Media – pulls together the major themes woven throughout the book to provide an overview of the field. In the process of doing so, it also engages the study of children and media in the discussion of the changing nature of childhoods.

Admittedly, these chapters map the field of media and children according to just one of many potential approaches. For example, we could have decided to focus on several central substantive topics (e.g., violence, advertising, fiction, news) and discuss each one of them from various angles. Or, we could have followed age groups separately (e.g., babies, pre-school, elementary-school, middle-school children). Finally, we could have studied each medium independently. Thus, what is offered here is but one way to organize the vast amount of accumulated knowledge available.

Indeed, any approach adopted would have to recognize that the domains and issues are deeply interwoven and cannot be discussed independently of one another. After all, children are holistic human beings and need to be viewed as such. Thus, their cognitive development and learning do not develop or function independently of their social context or of their behaviors and worldviews. Therefore, the book artificially fragments the field to facilitate the acquaintance of readers with this exciting field of study.

You will note that discussion of different media dominates different chapters. For example, the extensive discussion of the integration of television in the family in Chapter 1, and discussion of the internet and sociability in Chapter 6. This imbalance is due not only to the unique opportunities that each medium prioritizes, but also to the availability of existing research. While we have some 60 years of accumulated research on television and children, research activity on the internet and mobile media only emerged over the last two decades. Thus, a new version of this book, issued in the not-too-distant future, might present us with a different format and findings.

Overall, I can say that I have tried to address the issues from as diverse a theoretical and methodological point of view possible, drawing upon studies conducted by scholars from all over the world. This is no small undertaking, as much of the work is not accessible to English speakers, myself included. This having been noted, I recognize that much important work published in professional and academic media in Spanish, Portuguese, French, German, Chinese, Japanese, and Arabic, among other languages, is unavailable to those of us whose main research language is English. Overall, the field suffers from very little exchange between these isolated academic enclaves. One of my primary professional goals – as researcher as well as in my capacity as founding editor of the *Journal of Children and Media* – is to initiate such intellectual dialogue. I acknowledge, regretfully, that the "global perspective" is still a highly Anglo-perspective, as it relies almost in its entirety on research published in English.

Finally, in terms of reading experience, I have used the proverbial "wide-brush strokes" in writing this book, thus giving the "global perspective" an additional meaning, that of a general overview. As a result, specific details of research studies are not included in order to attain a more general, integrative view and to maintain the flow of the argument. Accordingly, bibliographic references are often cited together at the end of the discussion of each theme and appear as footnotes. Beyond their function to give appropriate credit to the authors upon whose work I draw and whose ideas and knowledge are discussed in the book, these citations primarily serve to point out directions for additional readings.

As you read this book you are invited to explore the field on various levels, choosing the ones that fulfill your needs the best. You may choose to read the text alone, in its narrative style. You may want to pause and expand your knowledge and understanding by referring to the more informative referenced readings suggested at the end of the book. In either case, I hope you will get as excited about this field as I am.

Notes

1. Drotner, 1992.
2. Ritzer, 2013.
3. Bloch & Lemish, 2003.

References

Bloch, L.R. & Lemish, D. (2003). The Megaphone Effect: International culture via the US of A. *Communication Yearbook, 27*, 159-190. Mahwah, NJ: Lawrence Erlbaum.

Drotner, K. (1992). Modernity and media panics. In M. Skovmand & K.C. Schrøder (Eds.), *Media cultures: Reappraising transnational media* (pp. 42-62). London: Routledge.

Ritzer, G. (2013). *The McDonalization of society: 20th anniversary edition*. Los Angeles: Sage.

1

Media and Children at Home

Media use, particularly for younger children, occurs to a large extent within the home, in a family context. It is so familiar that it is one of those areas of our life that we take "for granted," as part of everyday routine. Consequently, it is impossible to separate the study of children and media from the context within which it occurs (be it the physical conditions – the kind of media available at home and their location) or the social conditions within which media are used in the midst of engagement in other activities and in the presence of other family members. Further, media use is not necessarily an individual act of choice, but often a result of adjustment, negotiation, collaborations, compromises, and/or imitation of others in the child's environment. What does viewing a particular program or playing a particular video game mean in such a rich context? Is it an active choice on the part of the child to watch television, surf the net, or read a magazine from among all the other activities available at a particular moment? Even mobile media used outside of the home can often be regarded as an extension of the larger context of family and home, as a symbolic "umbilical cord" by which parental control and/or child dependency are negotiated.[1]

Clearly, the growing centrality of home-based media use is culturally dependent. Indeed, many socio-cultural differences may interact to create varied forms and amounts of media use, such as longer or shorter numbers of school hours, warm versus cold weather, safe or dangerous neighborhoods, active social life, child labor, daily chores, availability of media infrastructure, income, and education, which all play a significant role in shaping the centrality media have for children. The larger context of modern family life, too, should be understood. By-products of the transition to a more modernized lifestyle have been, on one hand, the creation of family leisure time and, on the other hand, the growing emphasis on the home as a center of indoor

Children and Media: A Global Perspective, First Edition. Dafna Lemish.
© 2015 John Wiley & Sons, Inc. Published 2015 by John Wiley & Sons, Inc.
Companion Website: www.wiley.com/go/lemish/childrenandmedia

life. The home can be a fertile ground for the gradual growth of the central role media have in family life, given growing urbanization and concern for personal safety in the streets together with exponential technological developments.

The Role of Context

Understanding children's use of media in their everyday life is best analyzed as an interaction not only of individual, contextual, and social characteristics, but also of more general understanding of media as culturally situated.

Let us take, for example, a girl growing up in a society torn by a deep social conflict (such as between ethnic or religious groups) in which there is only one television station, which is owned and managed by the dominant social group. News programs in this country are a central solidifying mechanism that serves to convey a sense of nationality that is highly revered by most viewers of the dominant group. Family members, perhaps some neighbors and relatives as well, may gather around the television set on a regular basis to watch the news programs and argue over the content broadcast. In this particular social context, the girl internalizes an understanding that television has both essential and ideological values, more far reaching than the understanding she gets from watching her favorite cartoon or comedy as a leisure activity.

In comparison, a boy who grows up in a relatively homogenized society that has not experienced overt conflicts, with a multi-channel commercial television and computer in his room, in a culture in which viewing and surfing is regarded as a pass-the-time activity accompanied by a reward system ("No TV until you have done your homework and cleaned your room!"; "you'll get that new video game if your grades improve"), may develop a very different attitude to media use, most likely as a leisure activity. Such cultural differences can be found not only between nations throughout major regions of the world, for example, Latin America in comparison with South Asia, but even within smaller geographical areas that seemingly have a lot in common. For example, a study of European children conducted in the late 1990s found that children growing up in countries that, historically, have been relatively more permissive in parenting style, such as Italy and Sweden, had higher private ownership of televisions in children's rooms, higher individual viewing and less parental mediation. In contrast, in France and Belgium, where parenting styles have been less permissive, television has been found to be a more integral part of the entire family's leisure activities and viewing typically takes place in the presence of other family members. Thus, the contexts of television use and parental educational approaches seem to be part of a more complex and general pattern of cross-cultural differences including general attitudes toward the media, perceptions of the degree of privacy that should be granted children, division of space at home, and availability of additional media.[2]

Another social dimension of interest regarding media use has to do with diversities within each society itself, such as class or sexual differences. Unfortunately, much of the available research has been performed by – and on – middle-class populations, as these are the ones most familiar and accessible to most researchers operating within academic institutions worldwide. Therefore, studies conducted on other populations are of particular interest. For example, several studies of working-class families in Anglo-European countries found that beyond income, education, and occupational differences typical of such comparisons there were also significant class differences in many aspects of family lives, including their experiences in and approaches to child rearing, different roles parents assume in socialization of their children, and the like. Thus, while blue-collar families in the USA were found to emphasize conformity, obedience, and adoption of conservative values in their children's education, middle-class families emphasized motivation, affect, creativity, and self-control. Such differences can have significant consequences for the role media occupy in the family, for example, in parental supervision, time schedules, ideologies regarding uses of time, and desire to limit or advance media use.[3]

Earlier research on television viewing and communication patterns in the family has distinguished between two central orientations – *social* and *conceptual*, with each family located on a continuum between low to high in orientation. Accordingly, families with *high* social orientation are characterized by encouraging their children to get along with other family members, to withhold as much as possible from engaging in confrontations, to depress anger, and to stay "out of trouble." The importance of preserving peace and quiet at home and avoiding hurting others' feelings are central values in the socialization processes of children growing up in these families.

In contrast, families with a *high* concept orientation encourage an atmosphere of open communication, free expression of ideas and conceptual debates. Children in these families are exposed to different sides and perspectives on controversial issues and their parents encourage them to voice their opinions and to argue about them. The central emphasis in such families is on ideas, rather than on feelings.[4]

Interestingly, a family's orientation was found, in the USA, to influence children's viewing habits. As a general rule, socially oriented families viewed television more, but were lighter consumers of news and current affairs programs. They perceived television to be primarily an entertainment medium and means of producing family solidarity. In contrast, children from high concept-oriented families used television more as a source of keeping up-to-date with the news and much less for entertainment purposes. They were lighter television viewers, used it less for social purposes, and their parents were more involved in regulating their viewing behaviors.

Obviously, children who grow up in a variety of combinations of the two family orientations create varying types of communication patterns, including in the use of media. Thus media use habits and preferences are clearly not only an individual choice or personality trait, but are greatly affected by family characteristics.

In turn, the fact that families are also formed within a particular cultural setting must be taken into account. For example, in collectivist-oriented cultures, or those deeply divided by a conflict, where cooperation and conformity to the collective is more highly regarded and children are discouraged from expressing individuality and encouraged to fit in, we may expect social orientation families to be more of the norm and, as a result, stronger emphasis to be placed on the social roles of media. In contrast, valorization of academic achievement in children in several Asian countries, such as Korea and China, complicates mediation of media use, particularly computer and internet use. Hence, while these technologies are perceived as key to academic success, they are also deemed by parents to be time-consuming and frivolous forms of engagement.[5]

Another example that illustrates this argument comes from a comparative analysis of children and media in China and Australia. Differences in levels of modernization, social development, regulatory systems, and nationalism, among others, all make for variation in media flows and availabilities in both local content generation and families' everyday media practices.

Thus, we cannot apply theoretical frameworks and empirical results from one region to another uncritically and non-reflexively.[6] This is true not only across regions and countries, but also within them, as illustrated by comparisons between rural and urban children or along class, wealth, and gender divides.[7]

The analysis of another study, based on in-depth interviews with members of diverse families,[8] found two typical patterns of media use in the USA: Middle- and upper-class families demonstrated an *ethic of expressive empowerment* according to which parents encourage media use that promote their children's education and personal accomplishments. They respect their children's need for independence and privacy, and trust their media-use related judgments. Interestingly, many of these children continue to use media (such as mobile phones) and maintain a strong tie to their parents as they physically expand their activities away from home, while their parents are afforded the possibility of surveillance over them and even the option of intervening in their lives (on social networks, for example). The researcher argued that such *helicopter-parenthood* contributes to a narcissistic environment of self-focus.

In contrast, lower-class families (including those whose life circumstances deprived them of middle-class privileges) were characterized by an *ethic of respectful connectedness*, in which parents encourage use of communication technologies in ways that maintain and respect the centrality of the family and parental authority. Given that, on the whole, children in the lower-class families have fewer options for structured activities outside of the home, they spend more time with other family members in close quarters and develop a stronger sharing orientation of resources and activities. Thus, family needs override individual ones in making media-related decisions. Here, too, the researcher noted that some children raised in such families rebel against the restrictive forms of parenthood, especially those with more advanced technological skills than their parents. Such children walk the thin line of combining approaches and so balance individual needs and personal empowerment with concern and consideration of collective needs, which is a complicated task.

Sociological research dealing with changes taking place in the modern family suggests that children's media use increases in those cases in which they are left on their own for extended periods of time because both parents are working and are less able to supervise their children's activities. This is also often the case for other familial contexts, such as single-parent, immigrant, or working class. Understandably, worrying about children's media use may not be high on the list of concerns when parents are busy providing for their family's basic needs and striving to survive daily difficulties. Even when parents wish to be more involved in their children's media habits they are forced, increasingly, due to their work schedule, to handle such supervision via "remote control" – leaving clear instructions for the children, placing them in the care of family members, employing caretakers and babysitters, or supervising them via phone calls.

Thus, what seems to be clear from the research is that today's families deal more than ever before with conflicting pressures regarding the permeation of communication technologies in their children's lives. In doing so, many encourage use of the media in order to offer their children the best opportunities possible, in the hope that media will assist them to solve problems and strengthen family connectedness. At the same time, they are anxious about the many threats they perceive media to have for their children's wellbeing, and thus look for ways to supervise media use more closely. While they may hope media will ease their parenting tasks, and save them time and effort, in practice the exponential growth of technologies and options only raise expectations for more intense communication and supervision, incurring additional parental work.

Media Diffusion in the Family

The rapid diffusion of television reached saturation point in many places in the world toward the end of the twentieth century. For example, studies have found that 98 percent of US households owned at least one set and 65 percent owned more than one television in the 1990s. Changes in family structures, parenting styles, plus the need to juggle employment and child-rearing missions, all brought about changes at the turn of the century in terms of the place the medium of television played in family life.[9]

Some media critics do not necessarily look at the integration of television in the home as a positive development. They argue that it hurts the unity of family life because of its routine, regular, mechanistic, and ritualistic nature. This forces family members to stay in the same physical vicinity, controls their time together, and, so goes the argument, erases unique family activities such as games, rituals, and conversations.

This perspective assumes that joint viewing of television takes place randomly, without planning. But what about those family events where viewing is a pre-planned activity? What of the bonding of parents and children who view a romantic series together? Or the family members rooting for their favorite sports team? Or the nostalgic, cross-generational viewing of such programs as an old movie, a favorite comedy, a dramatic series, a special holiday event, or a political speech? In such cases, and many others, television has the potential of being as much a stimulator of family integration as it is a barrier.

Furthermore, this situation was complicated by the introduction of smaller, mobile, and better-quality television sets of the late 1960s that enticed middle- and upper-class families to purchase additional sets. This trend resulted in the growing number of children who watch television on their own, often in their bedrooms. Later, the introduction of cable television as well as remote-control devices strengthened the trend of individual viewing. The internet accelerated these processes with the possibilities of downloading programs of one's individual preference for content, schedule, and location. The result of this process is that the multi-channel, multi-device environment produced a situation in which there are very few programs that attract all family members to come together for joint viewing, beyond dramatic special media events and festive occasions.

While these trends are typical of the development of television viewing in Euro-American-oriented societies and the more economically affluent segments in and outside of them, they differ according to society, culture, as well as sub-cultures with lower income levels, dwelling conditions, and a more collective social orientation and value system.

One way or another, screen culture should be perceived as a central force worldwide in the complex social processes involving the many forms of family structures, values, and ways of functioning.

The advent of the internet and the widespread adoption of mobile media, with seemingly unlimited options for surfing, play, creative activity, and networking, have changed family integration around the central medium of television and offered a wide variety of possibilities for re-structuring a family's use of time and space. Indeed, extensive research found that a vast majority of children and youth have online access in many industrialized societies. While data on internet availability are often a function of the method used to measure access and the point in time in which the studies were conducted, overall the findings indicate an exponential growth in internet access and use worldwide, despite differential patterns. For example, access is often facilitated in low-resource countries via mobile phones, due to the absence of terrestrial infrastructure. Indeed, digital divides between the *haves* and *have-nots* across as well as within nations remain a major concern. One general form of categorizing patterns of current domestic media ecologies distinguishes between families that are "media-rich," meaning they own both traditional as well as new media technologies; "media-poor," who have very little ownership of media hardware; and "traditional," where the family relies mainly on broadcast media and limited digital ones.[10]

Furthermore, access in and of itself is conflated with a host of variables related to privilege. Thus, the fact that a child has access to a computer and internet does not mean that she has the motivation to use it, the literacy skills involved in maximizing or employing meaningful usage, or the ability to benefit from it.

The Role of Media in the Fabric of Family Life

Consideration of the concept of *domestication*[11] – the process by which the medium becomes an integral part of everyday family life – leads us to examine the processes of adoption and change in this family context: how does a medium – be it television, computer, game console, or mobile phone – fit within existing gender and age hierarchies (e.g., who owns it? where is it placed? who has access to it?) as well as within family relationships (e.g., its integration into everyday routines, negotiations of access and use, its place in family conversations and in parenting styles)? Overall, it appears that use of the internet and mobile media contribute to blurring external and internal family boundaries, including, for example, the flow of information in and out of the home, as well as blurring the boundaries of work, study, and leisure that happen within and outside the home.[12]

In addition, we can also ask: how do media facilitate the process of reaching out into the wider world that develops with maturation and accelerates during adolescence? For example, the adoption of mobile phones facilitates the dialectic process of "letting go" of children, which contributes to their developing into independent and resilient young people yet keeps parents tethered to them by way of concerns for their safety and growth as they experiment with independence.[13] Similarly, children use media to negotiate this tension. For example, when Israeli-Palestinian girls maintained their secretive use of mobile phones in exploring romantic relationships behind their parents' backs.[14] The medium, in this case, enabled the girls to penetrate through traditional family walls as they reached out to the wider world while physically restricted to their homes, thus negotiating the tension between rebellion and maintenance of cultural norms and expectations.

The rise in children's private media ownership, including those technologies located, physically, in their bedrooms and mobile ones carried with them, so typical of middle- and upper-class children worldwide, present major challenges to parental supervision of media use. Many such media-related activities become private affairs (e.g., phone calls, texting, surfing) of which parents have very little knowledge or control.

In summary, studying media use in its natural habitat, in the home, is by no means a simple task and can involve use of multiple research approaches. Scholars do, of course, ask children – and their caregivers – about media use habits. We use surveys, conduct interviews by phone or face-to-face, and ask children to complete questionnaires in school settings. When we ask them to do so, they may (or may not) do their best to provide truthful and complete responses; they may (or may not) try to guess our intentions and provide what they perceive to be pleasing and socially acceptable responses; they may (or may not) be able to be reflective over their own media-related behaviors and those of other family members. We also use media ratings and marketing data provided by commercial and public companies in order to find out what children like to view, play with, surf and do, when, for how long, and with whom.

While information obtained in these studies provides us with very important data, we are still left with a very incomplete picture of what media use in the home as a routine everyday experience is "really" like for children and their families. To do so, we should probably be invisible investigators, living in the homes of children all over the world, for long stretches of time, and gaining a first-hand, non-intrusive experience with their lives.

Although researchers cannot be invisible, some have been able to become participant-observers of family life over an extended period of time. These researchers have been able to integrate comfortably into the fabric of family routines and so attain first-hand understandings of members' everyday lives, including their media uses. First introduced into the study of television in the 1970s, ethnographies of family lives have slowly gained a following among researchers. These efforts are still disproportionately time-consuming and limited in scope, yet extremely insightful and valuable. While reading the accounts and analyses provided by such studies, one stops to ponder: Is this the way things are happening in my family? Is this true for me as well? Do the issues that emerge resonate with my own reflections? Gained through ethnographic research, many of the findings reported below attempt to answer these questions.

The social uses of television

One of the major contributions of the early work that focused on television was the realization that the medium serves many more functions and roles than simply providing entertainment or information.[15] The social uses of television are surprisingly diverse and can be generally divided into two groups – *structural* and *relational* – and applied to other media as well.

Structural uses of television are non-content related and have to do solely with aspects of medium use. For example, when television is used to provide background noise for routine household activities or to create a feeling that the house is "full" of people when a child is home alone. Originally, television also regulated much of a family's daily schedule: it determined eating and bedtime hours and organized weekly routines. For example, a mother might encourage a resistant preschooler to take a nap with a tempting promise: "When you wake up from your nap, it will be time to watch your program"; or when a teen requests: "Let's have an early dinner tonight so I can see the soccer match." Running errands, or scheduling social appointments and outdoor activities were often affected, directly or indirectly, by the television schedule. This role of television has eroded in multi-device homes with recording capabilities enabling greater flexibility in terms of when favorite programs can be viewed. Yet viewing remains largely intact for special live events in which the experience of engagement in real time is valued highly. Examples are viewing a presidential address, news coverage of a disaster, a cultural or sporting event, or a holiday parade celebration.

Relational uses of television refer to the role of television in patterns of relationships between family members; for example, by facilitating communication between them. Thus, parents might refer to a television character or scene to illustrate experiences, emotions, or opinions in a discussion or disagreement with a son or daughter. Similarly, a familiar television episode can assist a child in gaining access to a conversation as it provides an equalizing and common point of reference to all participants.

Applying social knowledge and behaviors directly acquired from everyday situations portrayed on television confirms television's role as a social role model for imitation and problem solving, as well as for rejection of those same behaviors. "I wish we could have solved our problems just like that …," sighs the girl following a happy ending of the comedy she has been viewing. Or, a father might scold his son by saying: "Where do you think you are, on some TV program?"

The viewing situation provides a common experience that brings the family together – in laughter, suspense, interest, as well as in physical expressions of togetherness, like body contact and hugging a child during viewing. Viewing television together at home can both facilitate conversation as much as it can suppress it, depending on the circumstances and inclinations of family members.

Avoiding interaction, too, is an important function of television for viewers. Television viewing and the attention it demands enables viewers to enjoy privacy and to relieve social pressures for constant participation in family conversations of an unpleasant nature. The child who seeks to unwind after a pressured day at school can watch a cartoon; a teen can wallow in melancholic feelings through viewing a sentimental movie; siblings seeking to separate themselves from the adults can do so by viewing pop music. All of these family members use television viewing to demarcate the boundaries of their personal space.

Using television to demonstrate competence as well as to attain dominance in the family setting is also a common social use. Family members may use television to assert their status in the family as well as to establish areas of expertise: for example, when they preemptively guess the plot's development, shout out the correct answer to a quiz question, or provide a running commentary on the content of a news item. Furthermore, controlling viewing by a parent as well as by an older or younger sibling are means to mark out power spaces and family status hierarchy; as happens in the case of who controls the remote-control and the DVD player, or manages the recording technology.

On the other hand, the struggles over program choices in the main family setting are often a conflict zone representing the power relationships within a family: Do younger children have as much of a say in selecting programs as their older siblings? Research tells us that it is more likely to be the case that children join programs viewed by older family members than vice-versa. Similarly, we can ask: Do female family members have an equal chance of participating in and influencing program choice? Apparently not, as it seems that fathers dominate viewing in many households studied. Does anyone have the power to veto viewing choices at his or her digression? Once again, fathers were found to be more dominate. Is there one person who time and again has to have the final word? Here, too, it was the father.

Thus, as noted previously, we can learn a lot about parenting styles and gender relationships from the way families organize themselves around television viewing. Put another way, television viewing in the family is always contextualized within a particular social environment.[16] Yet family viewing rituals are also grounded in a wider cultural environment and have culturally specific characteristics. In different cultures, families arrange the physical viewing space differently, have different concepts regarding time and its use, and hold different age and gender power structures.

The introduction of additional viewing technologies – originally the video recorder, followed by a host of possibilities for recording, downloading, and controlling scheduling – created new behavioral rituals, such as family viewing times, recording schedules and responsibilities, preparation and consumption of meals, and facilitated individual viewing by family members at their own leisure and according to their own flexible schedule, in their own private spaces. The availability of multiple sets at home also unpacks power struggles around the television set and allows different members to control their own set. However, television sets at home have their own hierarchy of size, functions, and quality and one can learn a great deal from examining where in the home the best set is located, who gets the older set, and who got a new set for a birthday/holiday. Similar questions can be also asked about the availability and placement of computers at home.

We can conclude that children's media habits are not solely a result of their own personal choice, but the product of complicated family constraints and possibilities, and long-term socialization processes. Children learn from their parents, older siblings, friends, and other significant people in their lives a variety of media use habits and appropriate gendered and age-related behaviors, all of which become part of their independent media repertoire.

Parenting Styles and Mediation

What role do parents play as mediators of the media worlds their children inhabit, either through direct intervention (e.g., by setting rules and holding conversations) or indirect influence (e.g., by providing role models for their children)?

The media "rules" that shape the media experiences and habits of families worldwide are often informal and non-visible. When interviewing family members, researchers often find themselves raising issues that operate on a subconscious level in the family, revealing agreements that are embedded deep within everyday life that have never actually been discussed nor even spoken out loud. Therefore, it is not enough to interview just one family member. For example, children may be completely unaware of the media-related rules, followed or violated, that the mother may be explaining to an interviewer. This poses an interesting theoretical issue: since using media is a routine, taken-for-granted activity, any attempt to formalize the norms involved in this may seem overly formalistic. Media "rules" are behavioral directives, based on the family's general value and normative system that can be easily overturned by that family. For example, a family might have a rule of "no computer or TV after 9 p.m." or "no mobile phone use during dinnertime," but parents may actually encourage their youngster to break these rules on occasion and join them for an exploration of an exciting website, the viewing a favorite program well past bedtime, or when asking them to check the weather on their mobile phone during dinner.

Research on parental mediation of television viewing suggests that parents' involvement in their children's viewing may operate on at least three levels. *Awareness and co-viewing* relates to the degree to which parents are around during viewing, are familiar with program contents, offer their children role models of viewing habits, and even view with them. *Supervision*, also termed *restrictive mediation*, relates to the degree to which parents supervise and restrict the viewing times, contents, and amount of their children's television viewing, their use of viewing as a form of reward or punishment, and the degree to which they monitor secondary viewing behaviors (e.g., doing homework or eating while viewing). Finally, *instructive mediation* relates to the degree to which parents mediate between their children and contents viewed – through conversation, explanation, value judgments, processing of emotions, understanding information, application of learning, critical evaluation and the like.[17]

Note that viewing intervention does not necessarily mean *restricting* television viewing, as is commonly accepted. If we operate under the assumption that television has positive as well as negative potential for children, we should expect parental interventions to also include the encouragement of certain viewing behaviors. They can do so by calling their children's attention to valuable programs, applying television content to everyday experiences, using viewing opportunities as a positive socializing force, and the like. Such an approach occurs when parents tell their children: "Why don't you do your homework later – come watch with us this great program about …" According to most research reports parents do not make these types of comments very often.

Overall, viewing television together with children has been demonstrated to be a desirable activity. In doing so, parents help their children to understand the medium of television as well as its content, encourage them to internalize messages selectively and critically, intervene immediately when children are exposed to content which is objectionable in their opinion, and handle emotional reactions of children. Though limited in number, a few case studies explored ways that encourage parental co-viewing and interventions in the early years. One such example was the introduction of the *mommy bar* – subtitles instructing parents on possible forms of mediation.[18] The fact that more and more children are engaged in individual viewing, in the privacy of their own room or when there is no adult supervision at home, denies parents this possibility.

These three dimensions of potential parental intervention – awareness and co-viewing, supervision, and instructive mediation – are intertwined with parents' own attitudes toward television. Some perceive television to be a destructive force in their children's lives, even to the point of believing in the addictive power of the medium, and so take a protective stance toward it. Others see the positive sides involved in viewing television, and its role in providing entertainment, relaxation, and information to their children. Yet another group of parents finds that television assists them in the task of raising and socializing their children, while others allow children almost total freedom to determine their own viewing habits.

The research on parental mediation of digital media use is still very preliminary. However, one large European study did distinguish between five forms of such mediation: (1) *active* mediation included parental participation in activities and discussion; (2) *specific active* mediation promoted internet safety; (3) *restrictive* mediation monitored amount of time and nature of activities; (4) *digital* mediation monitored children's activities with digital media; and (5) *technical* mediation of their activities[19] by uploading censoring technologies on computers restricted access to some content or supervised the computer's history. Most of the findings in this and other studies suggested that parents engage mostly in conversations about and impose restrictions on internet use. Parents may restrict the amount of time children are allowed to spend on the internet or provide the child with a mobile phone minutes-budget and limited data package, as well as the specific time of use (e.g., curfew hours at night, or during family meals). While some restrictions can be easily monitored, others, particularly those related to strategies of content supervision, have been deemed by scholars to be relatively ineffective.[20] A study in Hong Kong, for example, found that families with a more authoritative parenting style, who spend more time together and have better family communication, and at the same time hold positive attitudes toward the role of the internet in their children's lives, were more satisfied with the effectiveness of their mediation practices.[21] Mediating new media use, so it seems, is not very different from mediating other dimensions of children's lives.

This kind of research emphasizes the importance of understanding the place of media in the lives of children as an integral part of socialization processes taking place in the family as a social unit. For their part, parents derive their attitudes toward media from a broader public discourse related to children's developmental processes and their own role as parents and educators. The attempt to find a delicate balance between the desire to protect children from what they deem to be undesirable aspects of reality, such as violence, on the one hand, and the desire to prepare them to handle the complexity of adult life, on the other, creates a dilemma for parents lacking an easy solution. Setting clear media use rules and guidelines is not going to resolve such a dilemma, as this issue is negotiated on a daily basis between children and their parents, and between the parents themselves. Parents are aware of their inability to completely control their children's media use and its influence on them. Many are not interested, willing to and/or able to assume responsibility for deciding what is good or bad for their children to be exposed to or use, and what kind of media experiences are desirable for their children.

Clearly, such attitudes cannot be viewed independently from the surrounding environment and other leisure options available to children. Whether television viewing or internet surfing is perceived as "good" or "bad" for one's children is always a relative matter and highly contextualized, hence, the question is – compared to what? Compared to hanging out on the street in an urban slum area? To helping out in the fields or at home? To getting into trouble with armed soldiers or guerilla fighters? To taking guitar lessons in the community center? To playing soccer in the neighborhood playground?

Thus, media-related middle-class values of what is "good" or "bad" can be completely irrelevant in one setting, or can be a luxury in another social setting.

A child of a lower income family with limited leisure options may do well spending time in front of television or a computer. An ethnographic case study of families in Saudi Arabia demonstrates this argument well.[22] Media content that violates Islamic cultural values and religious rules was deemed to be unwelcome by families who stress that it is their role to transfer cultural traditions and values. Thus, perceptions of the value of media use as "good" or "bad" for children are clearly relativistic, can be one-sided, and all too often highly culturally laden. In fact, it would seem that the mere posing of the question in a binary manner between good or bad needs to be understood not in absolute terms but from the point of view of a specific culture.

This having been noted, there is some evidence that the authoritative, yet respectful and positive approach taken by US parents toward communication technologies and their central role in children's lives does offer a solid basis for families to integrate them into their own in a constructive manner.[23] The following suggestions were offered to parents who wish to adopt such a strategy:[24] monitor child-activities based on clear rules; be familiar with the media texts children are consuming and converse about them regularly; serve as role models in parental media-related behaviors; prioritize family time devoted to joint activities; let children take the lead by following their expertise and preferences; use media for empowerment of all family members; change the conversation about media from a focus on *moral panic* and anxieties to discussion of active involvement and positive potentials; be actively engaged in creating positive opportunities for children; and become involved in activities that promote policy change, including reducing economic exploitation by mega-corporations.

Media-related conversations

Conversation is one of the main means employed by parents in attempts to be involved with their children's media use and to mediate its consequences. Just as understanding media consumption requires its contextualization, so research of media-related conversations must be studied within the social and physical surroundings: the physical setting, the presence of other family members and their composition, the activities in which all are engaged, and the social norms of behavior in place. Naturally, individual characteristics also influence the nature of interaction: the degree of parent or child fatigue or alertness, involvement and excitement from over-stimulation, as well as personal tendency for talkativeness or introversion. Finally, the nature of the content the child is experiencing affects interactions, as some programs, games, or websites are better facilitators of talk than others. Thus, as with other issues discussed, a comprehensive account of any aspect of media experience has to take into consideration characteristics of the context, viewer, and medium.

Studying naturally occurring conversations in the family is a difficult task, as it involves intrusion in homes by a researcher, recording equipment, or a combination of both. The existing literature focuses almost exclusively on television, as most other screens are used more privately, and conversations focused on their use is less predictive and thus less studied. As a result, we know very little about how parents and children talk about these experiences, except for anecdotal renderings. Thus, the following discussion of the research literature regarding television can serve as a basis for inference, until a rich research literature about discussions generated by screen use can come into existence.

Most television-related conversations reported in the research can be divided into content and behavior categories. Often the two types are intertwined in the natural flow of talk.

Content-oriented conversations develop due to the fact that television often presents an unfamiliar world to children that stimulates them to ask questions and seek more information. For example, the following excerpt documented a conversation between an eight-year-old boy and his mother in the USA over the death penalty, which occurred as they were viewing an action-adventure drama:[25]

SON: Is there still an electric chair?
MOTHER: In some states. They want to vote on it.
SON: What is it?
MOTHER: It's a chair where they strap you down like this. [She demonstrates.] And
                then they pass an electric current through you so you die. It's not good.

In addition to being informative, conversations such as this expose moral and political dimensions of parent–child interaction.

Parents' comments can expand the child's informative world and/or reinforce knowledge gained from other sources, including school. This is demonstrated when a 12-year-old girl in the aforementioned study asked for information about England's King George III, following a viewing of a theater production (*Masterpiece Theater*). When her mother explained to her that he was the king of England during the American Revolution, the child recalled learning about him in class. Thus, verbal intervention of parents has a very important role in reinforcing intended learning from other sources, as is often the case with educational and informative content. Furthermore, it was found that children remember information presented on the news much better when their parents elaborate on the information presented.

Indeed, research has found that even making limited comments while watching a program with children can advance learning. Mothers who were observed watching the preschool educational program *Sesame Street* with their children were found to be more attentive to the program, be more efficient learners, as well as to have much more fun watching it!

Interestingly, the mere presence of adults during viewing, without any form of intervention, is apparently very valuable for young viewers. An adult viewing together with a child conveys a message of interest in and respect for the program, as well as the pleasure gained from a social sense of "togetherness." Thus, even "passive" adult participation encourages the child to pay more close attention to the program, so increasing the chances for better learning. For example, research conducted in Israel found that the presence of mothers during the child's viewing not only increased viewing time, but encouraged and stimulated the child to be actively involved with it. In the USA, children demonstrated better learning of letters and numbers following viewing with mediating adults who called their attention to these messages and gave them feedback during viewing. Adults' verbal interventions, such as – "this letter is called B"; "let's read this word together"; or "look, the Giraffe is a vegetarian, he only eats plants" – have very positive influences on children's learning from television, just as they would if parents were engaging children about other stimuli in their environment. Clarification points regarding television content made by parents during viewing times, such as "what she means is that ..." or "he was referring to ...", improved children's ability to understand and make inferences from television content, and thus compensate for young viewers' lack of knowledge and complement their viewing experience. Similarly, parental verbal intervention contributed to children's abilities to make better comparisons between televisual reality and their understanding of everyday life.[26]

It appears, then, that a substantial amount and wide range of information, some trivial, can be acquired through television viewing and discussion. Occasionally, joint viewing can also induce conversations on very fundamental and sensitive topics, such as sexual relationships, death, suicide, prejudice, and religious beliefs, and create opportunities to elaborate on ideologies and value systems that do not arise during everyday family routines or that otherwise are uncomfortable for some family members to discuss. While a statement such as "Let's talk today about homosexuality" does not sound like a natural conversation opener around the dinner table, the topic might be discussed quite naturally following the viewing of a comic stereotype or a news item discussing the debate over gay marriage. Like their children, parents differ greatly in their capabilities and desire to engage children's queries or in the opportunities presented to discuss sensitive or complicated issues; from inability or reticence to eagerness to seize nearly every opportunity to engage the child in deep and serious conversation.

Behavioral, the second type of conversation engaged in during television viewing, refers to situations in which family members discuss behaviors observed on television related to their own or to others' real-life experiences. For example, when a parent tells a child: "In our family we don't hit each other like that"; or a child says to a parent: "See! Why can't I have that too?" In conversations such as these, the content viewed on television provides a basis for comparison with the child's real-life experiences, often presenting the latter as preferable. An illustration of this was related to me in a focus group of pre-adolescent girls in Israel: "Let's say we are watching *Beverly Hills*. My mother immediately will go: 'see how she has no shame at all!' My parents really like to teach me a lesson from movies. For example: 'see how she behaves; how would you have been in that situation?' Those kind of questions."[27] A similar exchange in a study in the USA was observed while a five-year-old boy and his mother were watching a soap opera with a divorced mother as a character. In responding to her son's inquiry about divorce, the mother reinforced her faith in their family's loving relationship and remarked on the pain involved in divorce.[28]

In addition, television-related conversations can also play a significant role in helping children understand the constructed nature of the television world and to distinguish it from life in their own social environment. Parents comment to their children about the reality of television in a variety of ways: "This is (or is not) how things happen in the real world"; "This is (or is not) real." A particular case in point is reference to "television families," such as those depicted in situation comedies and dramas, since often they deal with a realm of life relevant to children who are members of any sort of family. This viewing situation raises questions, such as: How much do children perceive these families to be similar to families with which they are familiar, including their own family? How do parents' comments facilitate children's ability to be critical consumers of portrayals of family life on television?

As explained here, as well as in Chapter 2, we see that it is a very complicated developmental task for children to come to understand the nature of "real" on television, as this process is dependent to a great degree on the child's stage of cognitive development, as well as on his or her accumulated experience of everyday life inside and outside of the television world. Parents' comments can greatly facilitate development of their children's critical abilities by reinforcing, expanding on, as well as negating television content; by exposing the unique audio-visual means by which television represents the world; as well as by providing additional sources of information and knowledge as the basis for comparisons.

Television as a talking book[29]

Even babies and toddlers at the stage of initial language acquisition were found to benefit from active, joint viewing with a caring adult. For example, we know that while viewing educational programs geared to their needs, such as *Sesame Street*, they learn vocabulary and concepts (e.g., geometrical shapes, colors) and are better able to identify letters and numbers. This process can be aided by parental interaction, as one North American mother of a 15-month-old baby girl reported: "She learned to count from *Sesame Street* and we reinforced it. I say: 'one' and she would say: 'two-three-four' and then I say 'five' and she would say 'six.'"

Parents of babies and toddlers are more active in employing television content as "a talking book," perhaps because this age group requires both closer supervision and more intensive investment in language development. Participant observation studies of parents caring for their young ones revealed at least three types of interrelated verbal exchanges: designating, questioning, and responding.

- *Designating*: This practice involves naming the objects and characters appearing on television, as we see in this example: "What is this?" a 2-year-old toddler asked her mother. "Look, it's a flashlight. You see, it gives light," responded the mother. Such a process has been found to help language acquisition as well as conceptual development. Similarly, mothers correct their children's vocabulary, as was the case when a 20-month-old toddler watching a cartoon pointed and said: "Dog!" "No," responded the mother, "it's a rabbit, and also a cat." Parents also encourage their children to practice new vocabulary. For example, during viewing of *Sesame Street*, a father asked his 15-month-old baby daughter: "What is this?" "A frog," responded the baby. "And what's that?" continues the father in calling her attention to the screen; "hop, hop, hop," responded the baby. "What is it?" The mother continues to challenge the baby. "Ball" she responds. "Ball," mirrors the mother. "Three balls. One, two, three."

- *Questioning*: Parents have a variety of reasons for directing questions to their children during viewing, such as trying to direct their attention to the set, expressing their own involvement in the viewing, or posing a rhetorical question, one to which they are not really expecting an answer. For example, they commonly say: "Do you want to watch …?" as they place the child in front of the television set and turn it on. Often the questions are not really intended to start a conversation, as they are behavioral directives, a form of viewing supervision and mediation.

- *Responding*: Parents respond to their children's viewing behaviors by way of mirroring back their verbal utterances, expanding and/or correcting them, as in an exchange between a 25-month-old toddler-girl and her mother while they were viewing *Sesame Street*: Girl: "Boy." *Mother*: "Boy." Girl: "Yellow boy." *Mother*: "Yellow boy." Girl: "Boy." *Mother*: "Another boy. What kind of a boy is this?" Girl: "Brown boy." *Mother*: "Brown boy. And what is this?" Girl: "Girl."

  Parents also respond to children's behaviors in a directive manner: "No, turn this on again!" or "Here is your song! Do you want to dance?" as well as answering direct questions. For example, in response to a 23-month-old toddler-girl's question: "Is she going to preschool?" the mother said: "No she is not, although she wished she could." Girl continued: "Am I going back to pre-school?" "We just got home," answers the mother.

Aside from illustrating types of parent–child interactions during viewing, these examples demonstrate the unique contribution of studies collecting observational data within the natural environment of viewing television in complementing other studies that are based on parental reporting of their children's behaviors. These studies provide us with unique insights into questions about the dynamics of interactions occurring around an operating television set, such as: What is the meaning of these kinds of conversations for parents and their children? How are they being integrated within the patterns of behavioral norms prevalent in their families? How consistent are the parents in their reactions to behaviors on television? How prevalent are such interactions in cultural contexts outside of the North American ones observed? These questions are of great importance in evaluating the influence such conversations may have on children's behaviors. Future research may do well to examine similar conversations taking place around toddlers' use of tablets, for example. We will return to the specific question of media and language acquisition in Chapter 2.

From what we know about children's viewing of television around the world, it seems that joint viewing is quite a rare occurrence. Parents are usually over-extended, overly tired, and if they happen to be at home, they may well use children's viewing as a quiet time to attend to another task or to re-charge their own batteries.

In such cases, the most common type of parental intervention is likely to be an incidental comment as they walk in and out of the room, often of a negative nature, such as: "turn the volume down," or "what is this nonsense you are watching, don't you have anything better to do?" Even if these comments may be appropriate, they do little to encourage critical viewing of television and rather convey a general negative message toward the medium that may inhibit potentially positive learning experiences, when such are available. We can, therefore, conclude that while parents can potentially play many important roles in mediating television viewing, they differ greatly in their aptitude, motivation, skills, and the circumstances that facilitate doing so.

Finally, we should note that while the research reported here is television specific, there is very little accumulated research-based knowledge on parental conversations around other forms of media use, which are more individualistic in nature, such as video-game playing or internet surfing. While the same issues and possibilities can be applied in study of parent–child conversations related to other media platforms and contents, we should also be seeking to determine if there are issues that are medium specific, such as: To what degree and in what ways are parents involved with their children's website choices? Online or video-gaming? Social networking activities? How often do they engage in conversations about the content and values available to children through these media, about making choices and being critical of what they offer? The accumulating research about digital technologies and young people, to which we will return in the following chapters, suggests that in most cases, the answer is not very much.

Conversations with siblings and peers

To date, very little attention in research has been directed to joint viewing by children with siblings and friends, or to their engagement in media-related conversations. This is quite surprising given that, first, this is the most common viewing situation among children who grow up in the same household; and, second, we should be interested to learn about the role such significant-others play in children's social, emotional, and cognitive development. From the little we know, it appears that children enjoy talking while viewing, as do many adults. They talk about the program, they talk about the logistics involved in the viewing, and they often embark on conversations stimulated by the viewing, although they may meander a long way away from it.

Here, too, data collected during a few observational studies in the USA provide us with some insights as to how this process operates in its natural habitat. For example, typically, children were found to ask older siblings for explanations and clarifications: "What is it?" "Why is he doing it?" "What does she mean?" Other questions might relate to understanding the codes and conventions of the audio-visual language. For example, questions that relate to trying to understand uses of the "flashback" ("how come he is back there?"), "re-runs" ("how did she do it again?"), "slow-motion" ("how can they run so slowly?"). Similarly, older children can facilitate younger siblings' understanding of the structural characteristics of the broadcast schedule. For example, here is an interaction between two brothers age nine and six concerning the concept of a television "promo" following the viewing of one for a *Pacman* cartoon.[30] The younger boy asked: "Can I see something for a second? (changes channel for a few seconds) not yet." *Observer*: "What do you want to see?" *Child*: "They're showing *Pacman*." The older brother shouted: "They said this fall ... Tell me, is it fall yet?" The exchange between the two brothers clearly served to help the younger one learn the meaning of a "promo" for a program that is intended for broadcast at a later time.

Other "why?" "how?" and "what will happen now?" types of questions relate directly to understanding the narrative. Older children were found to provide explanations and express tastes and preferences during viewing. In doing so, they may contribute to the viewing habits and understandings developing in their younger siblings. For example, while viewing a new series, the elder of three brothers declared: "No way are we watching this goofy show – it's for dummies." The two younger brothers agreed and the channel was switched.

Thus it appears that older children's responses during viewing can facilitate understanding, allow the younger child to keep up with the narrative, acquire some basic television-literacy skills, as well as help shape more general attitudes toward television, just as is the case with the responses of adults. Similarly, when children watch with other children, be they siblings and/or friends, they are socially attentive and influenced by their behaviors, attention level, and interactions. Joint viewing is sometimes just that – a fun way to spend time together.

Mediating fear reactions

A much-debated public concern is the important issue of parents' ability to mediate frightening images on television, movies or the internet, particularly those dealing with the negative sides of human existence – wars, disasters, poverty, atrocities, and famine. Today, children are exposed, increasingly, to such phenomena due to their high media presence, even in homes where parents actively try to shield them from such events. In an increasingly global world, even crises and catastrophes that take place in countries thousands of miles away become relevant issues for children's daily lives. Children must cope with these frightening, worrying events that were once the preserve of adults alone. They must endeavor to assimilate fragments of information received via the media and try to make sense of them. They have to deal emotionally with the suffering of others and with gruesome portrayals of atrocities.[31] Clearly the picture they develop of such events is a function of their developmental stage, life experiences, and the media offerings available to them.

Adult mediation at home and in children's educational systems was found to be particularly important in such situations.

Clearly, frightening audio-visual content can be fictitious, based on real events, or even be "real," as occurs during a direct but still mediated broadcast of events happening in real time. Scary or non-scary content is not an absolute concept, as children may react very differently to such content, depending on their age, experiences, context of viewing, and relevancy of the threat to their own lives. Here, as in other situations we have examined, age, gender, and cultural context are crucially important. For example, a preschool-age child may feel very threatened by make-believe monsters, sudden noises, close-up shots of snakes, or even dark scenes, but will be completely indifferent to a video footage or news discussion of weapons of mass destruction. On the other hand, a child living in Afghanistan, Syria, Chechnya, or Iraq may react in a completely different manner to a scene depicting tanks and soldiers compared to a child living in New Zealand, Italy, or Uruguay where there are relatively fewer incidents of military violence. North American children may react very differently to news about terrorism following the events of 9/11 or the bomb explosions that disrupted the 2013 Boston Marathon than before these events took place. And South African children may be particularly sensitive to discussions of high mortality rates associated with diseases such as AIDS and the large number of children living in orphanages in their country in comparison to those growing up in the Nordic countries.

Similarly, parental strategies necessary for handling fear reactions can differ significantly. More than by any verbal strategy, younger children can be more easily comforted by physical strategies such as holding, hugging a security object (e.g., favorite blanket or stuffed toy), or snacking. They have a hard time understanding the concepts of "rarely" or "very low chance" which may be used in attempts to distance children from threatening messages. "Earthquakes rarely happen"; "the chance of an airplane crash is very low"; "these kinds of catastrophes usually take place in other parts of the world" are not very efficient with children below school age. Indeed, it is very difficult to convince young children, verbally, that something that looks visually to be scary may not really be dangerous at all, while something that looks very appealing is indeed dangerous. However, as children grow older, the approach needs to be a more cognitive, rational one, rather than emotional, if we are to help them learn to recognize real threats, while gradually reinforcing their sense that things are "under control"; that the adults in their lives and in their society are working hard to protect them.[32]

Studies conducted following traumatic events that affected children in many countries of the world, in various manners – such as the 1993 Gulf War, the September 11, 2001 events in New York, or the war in Iraq that began in 2003 – reveal that an "ostrich" strategy, which assumes children are unaware and/or not concerned, is simply wrong. Research into children's reactions suggests that their media-related questions need to be attended to and answered honestly, when appropriate to do so, and that their fears and concerns should be respected and legitimized. They need to know that their feelings and fears are being taken seriously and not dismissed by statements, such as "you're still too young to understand" or "you shouldn't be watching this." If the child has already begun to watch a program, it is too late to tell him or her that "there is nothing to worry about." What children need in such a situation is to be offered the means to express their anxiety and to share their thoughts about what to do about the situation, as minor as it may seem.[33]

Disturbing news that relates to the emotional wellbeing of children, too, has been a focus of research and educational concern, and has led media producers and educators to seek ways to help children cope with fearful elements of the mediated world. However, little attention has been directed to the role played by such portrayals on television in developing in children a sense of social responsibility, civic awareness, empathy, compassion, and ethical issues related to the pain and suffering of others. Parents all over the globe who are raising their children within such perspectives can find media content to be an immensely important resource for discussing social issues and developing a humanitarian understanding in their children.

Concluding Remarks

Our discussion of media use as an integral part of the home ecology highlighted the centrality of understanding everyday media behavior as contextualized within family patterns and, in turn, how such behaviors are shaped by a host of other social processes. We can conclude by saying that media are an important force due to their central place in a family's daily routines and the many social and personal roles they play for all members of the family. The concept of mediation allowed us to replace the commonly asked question of how television affects children with a very different one: how family life and the reciprocal relationships within it shape the experiences different family members have with the media. This approach emphasizes the important role of understanding everyday life and routine behaviors as part of an ecological approach to the study of media.[34]

We have pointed out that such phenomena require research methodologies that can problematize and investigate the depth and nuances of children's media in everyday life. To do so requires a shift from *functionalist theories* of human behavior to *cultural theories* that when applied to media in the family, assume that media serve specific functions that contribute to the family's stability. Most of the time such theories include the application of quantitative measures to study media functions, through surveys and experimental designs. What such a shift requires is inclusion of theories that posit that a negotiation process is used by children as active media users and that consider the contents of their media consumption as a form of meaning making grounded in specific contexts. Consequently, it also calls for different methods of inquiry: Integration of qualitative approaches that employ participant observation and in-depth inter-views were found to be extremely valuable in documenting and analyzing the dynamics of the very act of media use and meaning making.

We have also argued that discussion of families and everyday life needs to be rooted in an understanding of the complexity of cross-cultural differences including the different values attached to media use and diverse social practices. The way media fit in family routines is shaped by the wider culture, its values, traditions, and history. The concept of "family" itself, as the social context of media use, has a wide variety of meanings in different societies, as does the term "domestic" and its relationship to the "public." Furthermore, societies change over time. While some societies seek to entrench norms, societies that allow flexibility see social norms grow and accommodate change, including significant changes that are taking place in home entertainment technologies.

This is why it is so important to study the meaning of media in the family longitudinally, as it changes over time, and so be able to follow typical developmental milestones. Doing so would enable us to answer such questions as: What are the roles of media in family life during the early years of child rearing? When children grow up? When they leave the home? When the parents are in retirement? Recent changes in the structure of both traditional and modern families have seen the emergence of many forms of family arrangements. At the same time, the media available to families, too, have changed dramatically. All of these changes lead us to understand that the study of media in the family is a dynamic, meaningful, and fascinating field of inquiry. Children, too, are a diverse and complicated group of people who undergo significant changes as they grow up. As they do so, we are interested in studying such questions as: How do children of various ages understand media content? What is the relationship between their development and the meanings they acquire from their media engagements? We will turn now to Chapter 2 to explore these questions.

Notes

1. Ribak, 2009.
2. Livingstone & Bovill, 2001.
3. Jordan, 1992.
4. Chaffee & McLeod, 1972; Chafee, McLeod, & Wackman, 1973.
5. Lim & Soon, 2010.
6. Hemelryk Donald, 2008.
7. Hemelryk Donald, 2010.
8. Schofield Clark, 2013, pp. 201–212.
9. Andreason, 2001.
10. Livingstone, 2007.
11. Silverstone, Hirsch, & Morley, 1992.
12. Mesch & Talmud, 2010.
13. Ribak, 2013.
14. Hijazi-Omari & Ribak, 2008.
15. Lull, 1980a; 1980b.
16. Gray, 1987; Livingstone, 1992; Morley, 1986; Walker & Bellamy, 2001.
17. Buerkel-Rothfuss & Buerkel, 2001; Valkenburg, Krcmar, Peeters, & Marseille, 1999; Warren, 2003.
18. Fisch, 2007.
19. Livingstone, 2011.
20. Nathanson, 2013.
21. Wong, 2012.
22. Al Qurashy, 2008.
23. Schofield Clark, 2012.
24. Schofield Clark, 2013, pp. 218–225.

25. Quotes taken from Messaris, 1983, pp. 295-296.
26. For a review see Fisch, 2004, Chapter 9.
27. Lemish, 1998.
28. Messaris, 1983.
29. Based on Lemish & Rice, 1986. Excerpts republished with permission © 1986 by Cambridge University Press.
30. Quotes from Alexander, Ryan, & Munoz, 1984, p. 358. See also Haeffner & Wartella, 1987.
31. Smith & Moyer-Guse, 2006; Smith & Wilson, 2002; Walma van der Molen, 2004; Walma van der Molen, Valkenburg, & Peeters, 2002.
32. Cantor, 1996; Cantor, 2002; Smith, Moyer, Boyson, & Pieper, 2002.
33. Lemish & Götz, 2007.
34. Vandewater, 2013.

References

Al Qurashy, F. (2008). Role of the family in forming the rational interaction with mass media: A case study of a Saudi Family. In U. Carlsson, S. Tayle, G. Jacquinot-Delaunay, & J.M. Perez Tornero. (Eds.), *Empowerment through media education: An intercultural dialogue.* (225–234). Göteborg University, Sweden: The International Clearinghouse on Children, Youth and Media.

Alexander, A., Ryan, M.S., & Munoz, P. (1984). Creating a learning context: investigations on the interaction of siblings during television viewing. *Critical Studies in Mass Communication, 1*(4), 358, 446–453.

Andreason, M.S. (2001). Evaluation in the family's use of television: An overview. In J. Bryant & J.A. Bryant (Eds.), *Television and the American family* (2nd ed., pp. 3–30). Hillsdale, NJ: Lawrence Erlbaum.

Buerkel-Rothfuss & R.A. Buerkel. (2001). Family mediation. In J. Bryant & J.A. Bryant (Eds.), *Television and the American family* (2nd ed., pp. 355–376). Hillsdale, NJ: Lawrence Erlbaum.

Cantor, J. (1996). Television and children's fear. In T. MacBeth (Ed.), *Tuning in to young viewers: Social science perspectives on television* (pp. 87–115). Thousand Oaks, CA: Sage.

Cantor, J. (2002). Fright reactions to mass media. In J. Bryant & D. Zillmann (Eds.), *Media effects: Advances in theory and research* (pp. 287-306). Mahwah, NJ: Lawrence Erlbaum.

Chaffee, S.H. & McLeod, J.N. (1972). Adolescent television use in the family context. In G.A. Comstock & E.A. Rubenstein (Eds.), *Television and social behavior* (vol. *13*, pp. 149-172). Washington, DC: US Government Printing Office.

Chaffee, S.H., McLeod, J.N., & Wackman, D. (1973). Family communication patterns and adolescent political participation. In J. Dennis (Ed.), *Socialization to politics: A reader* (pp. 349-363). New York: Wiley.

Fisch, S.M. (2004). *Children's learning from educational television: Sesame Street and beyond.* Mahwah, NJ: Lawrence Erlbaum.

Fisch, S.M. (2007). Educational media in the twenty-first century. *Journal of Children and Media, 1*(1), 55-59.

Gray, A. (1987). Behind closed doors: Video recorders in the home. In H. Baehr & G. Dyer (Eds.), *Boxed-in: Women and television* (pp. 38–54). London: Pandora Press.

Haeffner, M.J. & Wartella, E.A. (1987). Effects of sibling coviewing on children's interpretations of television programs, *Journal of Broadcasting and Electronic Media, 31*(2), 153–168.

Hemelryk Donald. S. (2008). Children, media and regional modernity in the Asia Pacific. In K. Drotner & S. Livingstone (Eds.), *The international handbook of children, media, and culture* (pp. 299-313). Los Angeles, CA: Sage.

Hemelryk Donald. S. (2010). Introduction: Why mobility matters: Young people and media competency in the Asia-Pacific. In S. Hemelryk Donald, T. Anderson, & D. Spry (Eds.), *Youth, society and mobile media in Asia* (pp. 3-12). London: Routledge.

Hijazi-Omari, H. & Ribak, R. (2008). Playing with fire: On the domestication of the mobile phone among Palestinian teenage girls in Israel. *Information, Communication & Society, 11*(2), 149–166.

Jenkins, H. (1990). "Going Bonkers!": Children, play and *Pee-wee*. In J. Jenkins (Ed.), *Camera Obscura* (pp. 169–193). New York: Johns Hopkins University Press.

Jordan, A. (1992). Social class, temporal orientation, and mass media use within the family system. *Critical Studies in Mass Communication, 9*, 374–386.

Lemish, D. (1998). Spice Girls' talk: A case study in the development of gendered identity. In S.A. Inness (Ed.), *Millennium girls: Today's girls around the world* (pp. 145–167). New York: Rowman and Littlefield.

Lemish, D. & Götz, M. (2007). *Children and media in times of war and conflict.* Cresskill, NJ: Hampton Press.

Lemish, D. & Rice M. (1986). Television as a talking picture book: A prop for language acquisition. *Journal of Child Language, 13*, 251–274.

Lim, S.S. & Soon, C. (2010). The influence of social and cultural factors on mothers' domestication of household ICTS – Experiences of Chinese and Korean women. *Telematics and Informatics, 27*(3), 205-216.

Livingstone, S. (1992). The meaning of domestic technologies: A personal construct analysis of familial gender relations. In R. Silverstone & E. Hirsch (Eds.), *Consuming technologies: Media and information in domestic spaces* (pp. 113–130). London: Routledge.

Livingstone, S. (2007). Strategies of parental regulation in the media-rich home. *Computers in Human Behavior, 23*(3), 920–941.

Livingstone, S. (2011). Digital learning and participation among youth: Critical reflections on future research priorities. *International Journal of Learning and Media, 2*(2-3), 1–13.

Livingstone, S. & Bovill, M. (2001). *Children and their changing media environment: A European comparative study.* Mahwah, NJ: Lawrence Erlbaum.

Lull, J. (1980a). The social uses of television. *Human Communication Research, 6*(3): 197–209.

Lull, J. (1980b). Family communication patterns and the social uses of television. *Communication Research, 7*(3), 319–334.

Mesch, G. & Talmud, I. (2010). *Wired youth: The social world of adolescence in the information age.* London & New York: Routledge.

Messaris, P. (1983). Family conversations about television. *Journal of Family Issues, 4*(2), 293–308.

Morley, D. (1986). *Family television: Cultural power and domestic leisure.* London: Comedia Publishing.

Nathanson, A. (2013). Media and the family context. In D. Lemish (Ed.), *The Routledge international handbook of children, adolescents, and media* (pp. 299-306). New York: Routledge.

Ribak, R. (2009). Remote control, umbilical cord and beyond: The mobile phone as a transitional object. *British Journal of Developmental Psychology, 27*(1), 183-196.

Ribak, R. (2013). Media and spaces: The mobile phone in the geographies of young people. In D. Lemish (Ed.), *The Routledge international handbook of children, adolescents, and media* (pp. 307-314). New York: Routledge.

Schofield Clark, L. (2012). Digital media and the generation gap. *Information, Communication & Society, 12*(3), 388-407.

Schofield Clark, L. (2013). *The parent app: Understanding families in the digital age.* Oxford, UK: Oxford University Press.

Silverstone, R., Hirsch, E., & Morley, D. (1992). Information and communication technologies and the moral economy of the household. In R. Silverstone & E. Hirsch (Eds.), *Consuming technologies: Media and information in domestic spaces* (pp. 15-31). London: Routledge.

Smith, S.L. & Moyer-Guse, E. (2006). Children and the war on Iraq: Developmental differences in fear responses to TV news coverage. *Media Psychology, 8*(3), 213-237.

Smith, S.L., Moyer, E., Boyson, A.R. & Pieper, K.M. (2002). Parents' perceptions of children's fear responses. In B.S. Greenberg (Ed.), *Communication and terrorism* (pp. 193–208). Cresskill, NJ: Hampton.

Smith, S.L. & Wilson, B.J. (2002). Children's comprehension of and fear reactions to television news. *Media Psychology, 4*, 1–26.

Valkenburg, P.M., Krcmar, M., Peeters, A.L., & Marseille, N.M. (1999). Developing a scale to assess three styles of television mediation: "Instructive mediation," "restrictive mediation," and "social coviewing." *Journal of Broadcasting and Electronic Media, 43*(1), 52–66.

Vandewater, E.A. (2013). Ecological approaches to the study of media and children. In D. Lemish (Ed.), *The Routledge international handbook of children, adolescents, and media* (pp. 46-53). New York: Routledge.

Walker, A.J. & Bellamy, R.V. (2001). Remote control devices and family viewing. In J. Bryant & J.A. Bryant (Eds.), *Television and the American family* (2nd ed., pp. 75–89). Hillsdale, NJ: Lawrence Erlbaum.

Walma van der Molen, J.H. (2004). Violence and suffering in television news: Toward a broader conception of harmful television content for children. *Pediatrics, 113*, 1771–1775.

Walma van der Molen, J.H., Valkenburg, P.M., & Peeters, A.L. (2002) Television news and fear: A child survey. *Communication: The European Journal of Communication Research, 27*(3), 303–317.

Warren, R. (2003). Parental mediation of preschool children's television viewing. *Journal of Broadcasting and Electronic Media, 47*(3), 394–417.

Wong, T.C. (2012). Cyber-parenting: Internet benefits, risks and parenting issues. *Journal of Technology in Human Services, 28*(4), 252–273.

2

Media and Individual Development

Television consumed much of viewers' time when in the 1950s it entered the lives of children in many Euro-American societies and gradually spread from there. Coined by scholars as the *displacement effect*, this intervention in children's leisure culture aroused public and academic debate over the question: Does watching television displace other important activities such as reading, doing homework, or playing outdoors? Notably, at the time, this and associated questions were stated primarily in negative terms: Does watching television take away important time that should be better devoted to activities that foster cognitive development (e.g., reading, homework); physical development (e.g., outdoor activity, sports); and social development (playing with other children, participating in social events)?

Today, it is almost impossible to study even the possibility of such displacement effect, as television has become a fact of life and an integral part of children's lives worldwide. This situation is all the more the case with the spread of the internet and the dramatic growth in access by even very young children to mobile media.[1]

Several comprehensive studies examined the initial introduction of television in the UK, USA, and Canada as well as under special conditions, such as during major television strikes or while voluntarily giving up television for a while.[2] These studies arrived at similar conclusions: the introduction of television was found to lead to significant changes in children's allocation of time and the organization of activities outside the home. However, following a short period of a "novelty effect" of television, most of the changes in children's daily schedules where not related to time devoted to homework, playing with friends, reading, or sleeping, but to use of other media.

Children and Media: A Global Perspective, First Edition. Dafna Lemish.
© 2015 John Wiley & Sons, Inc. Published 2015 by John Wiley & Sons, Inc.
Companion Website: www.wiley.com/go/lemish/childrenandmedia

Why were some media-related activities affected more than others? This question can be answered by the following four *principles* of the *displacement effect*:[3]

1. *Functional similarity*: According to this principle, children only give up activities that basically fulfill similar but less effective television functions (e.g., viewing cartoons replaced to a large degree reading comic books and going to the movies, especially for younger children). This was not the case for older children, as going to the movies gratifies many social needs that television cannot fulfill for them. Similarly, activities perceived to have functions that differ from television were not affected by its introduction. For example, most children studied preferred playing with other children to watching television (n.b., this finding was repeated 40 years later in another comprehensive study of 12 European countries).[4] And, reading newspapers did not diminish among older children, as it was perceived by them to be a source of information, while television mainly served entertainment needs.

2. *Marginal fringe activities*: Activities perceived as marginal and unstructured are replaced by organized and structured activities. This principle assumes that children make time to watch television at the expense of activities without set time boundaries and those perceived by them to be incidental, such as "hanging out" or "going out" for no particular planned reason. In short, television seems to replace idle time, when the child feels they are doing "nothing." On the other hand, free playtime was not replaced by television; perhaps because it was perceived by children to be central and meaningful in their lives.

3. *Transformation*: The use of other mass media is transformed into more specific, goal-oriented uses with much less overlap with television. This principle assumes that instead of competing with television, media that preceded it needed to readjust in order to survive. In turn, succeeding in such adaptation provided them with a renewed right to exist. For example, radio found new ways to satisfy listeners' audio needs in ways that differ from those provided by television (e.g., an emphasis on music and news, interactive call-in programs, and more specialized programming directed to different audiences). While central in children's lives before the advent of television, radio became secondary for some, as it faded into the background. Yet in doing so radio became a more personal medium, providing a pre-teen girl or teenage boy with a source of comforting solitude during moody times and time/space to be with their personal thoughts. Similarly, print media changed significantly for children. Many fiction books reproduced or even imitated stories that appeared on popular television programs; there was growth in consumption of non-fiction books; and new magazines designed for audiences with specific interests came into being.

4. *Physical and psychological proximity*: Activities are more likely to be displaced if they occupy the same physical space (e.g., living room) as television, but provide less satisfaction than viewing does (e.g., doing homework). This principle is probably the weakest of the four, as it is based on very little empirical evidence and lacks well-established theoretical foundations.

Contrary to expectations and common belief, there is no substantial evidence that television has displaced reading books. We can only speculate why this should be so. One line of reasoning proposed is that books fulfill a wide variety of functions for children beyond the content and process of decoding the written text. Indeed, reading involves a different context of use that allows for privacy, personal pacing, lingering, and provides a very different mental and emotional experience to watching television. Furthermore, some argue that just as children really did not read a lot before the age of television, they continue not to read a lot today. While this may be true for childhood in general, some children read more than others and girls read more than boys. Neither trend seems related to television. The phenomenal success of the *Harry Potter* books, as well as other series such as the *Twilight Saga* and the more recent adaptation of children's print culture to technological changes (e.g., e-books, digital apps, multi-media storytelling) suggest that reading maintains its unique place among leisure activities, one that has not been eroded by screen culture.[5]

Above and beyond these conclusions, television may be providing a satisfying alternative when children feel the approach of boredom, as a television set allows for zapping between various channels and pre-recorded programs, with the option of viewing this or another program. This leads us to ask if children today are more impatient and, if so, does this state of mind affect their behavior? Though we lack substantial empirical evidence, the advent of the internet and extensive use of mobile media suggest that studying these questions is even more acute as media content and activities are constantly available at the touch of the fingertips, and children seem to be always "on." One such study included an extensive survey of adolescents, and was conducted in the large cities of Hong Kong, Singapore, Seoul, Taipei, and Tokyo. It revealed a complicated relationship between media use and three types of internet connectedness: Adolescents using the internet mainly for communication (e.g., IM, email) and entertainment (e.g., gaming, downloading music) were watching television more than peers who used the internet more for information and school-related research. The latter, as well as a third type of internet connectedness, for expression and group participation (e.g., blogging, online shopping), read newspapers more frequently. Radio listening, on the other hand, correlated with a higher level of internet connectedness for all three types. Thus, this study suggests that internet use does not necessarily displace other media, rather, complicated uses evolve, depending on the adolescents' main internet use.[6] Similarly, another analysis based on the same survey data found that Asian adolescents used their mobile devices as an extension of rather than replacement for internet activities. This finding provides additional evidence for the "more-the-more" dynamic, according to which newer media complement uses of older media in the same content area.[7]

Answering additional questions regarding "displacement" could provide us with important insights into the place and impact of digital culture on children, as well as adults: Are media displacing social life? Is family life affected by their constant use? And what about formal schooling – does constant media use displace some or even many important formal learning activities?

While children's media-related enjoyment is taken for granted by many people, including parents, its use remains a source of anxiety for many. Are they spending too much time with media at the expense of other activities? Are they exposed to harmful content? Are they wasting their time? Television, for example, has been referred to, pejoratively, by such provocative names as "gum for the eyes," "talking wall paper," "electronic babysitter," and "boob tube." Similarly, children are often described as "addicted" to television, to the internet, or to Facebook activities. The metaphor of addiction is employed by some critics to describe common character-istics of children's media activities: they use media as a way to reduce tension, pain, or anxiety; media-related activities encourage more media-related activities; they lose sense of self-control and time while engaged with media; they arrange their daily schedule around their constant media use; and they miss them when they are taken away. As much as this metaphor seems to encapsulate the essence of the populist argument, there is no research evidence to support such claims, particularly none that present any of the physical consequences of addiction to substances or habits. Furthermore, just as other psychological and behavioral addictions (e.g., gambling, shopping) affect but a small proportion of society, so, too, is addiction to media a rare phenomenon, and when present it is probably related to other mental disorders. As a metaphor, the term "addiction" refers to heavy media consumption. However, even heavy media use is not necessarily addictive, particularly according to approaches that understand children's media use to be an active process motivated by needs and interpreted according to personal abilities and capacities.[8]

Nevertheless, television viewing, internet surfing, and video-game playing are often portrayed as mindless activities by some critics. According to this perspective, children sit in front of a screen of some sorts and expect to be entertained. No one challenges them, so goes the argument, to remember what they access, to analyze it critically, or even to pay full attention to it. However, as we will demonstrate in this chapter, children are not the passive media users claimed in the populist notion. Rather, research confirms that even when they are "only" consuming (and not pro-ducing) media content, they choose to engage with it in a variety of active ways, including managing their attention to the various contents; making meanings out of their messages; analyzing and criticizing what they are exposed to; and selectively remembering bits and pieces of it.

Developmental Theories

"Reading" audio-visual texts, a concept borrowed from the cultural studies approach to media, refers to the process of making meaning of mediated messages and relating them to various other meaning systems available in everyday life. This activity requires users to employ a variety of cognitive strategies related to thought and perception. Thus, in this regard, researchers direct their studies to questions such as: What attracts children to a particular medium? What do they understand in such reading experiences? How do they make sense of information? What do they remember? How do they relate these experiences to their everyday knowledge?

The underlying premise of various approaches that focus on the interaction of the individual child with the media is that children's cognitive, emotional, and social skills develop over time. This premise is based on an assumption adopted from developmental psychological theories: Children make meaning out of media and engage in production activities with the skills and tools acquired with age and experience.[9] As children grow and mature, their interests, tastes, as well as interactions with the media, change dramatically, and so does what they take with them from the experience. Accordingly, the "meaning" children, as well as adults, make of media content can be understood as residing neither in the particular program, website, or game nor as an independent creation in the child's head, but rather it is produced in the interaction between the child and the medium.

A sub-set of this general field of study asks what change over time means for children's development and how can it be studied appropriately? Here we understand that age differences in and of themselves are but a descriptive variable: Surely we can notice that 10-year-olds have a much better understanding of a televised narrative or a Wikipedia entry than do five-year-olds, but why is this so? What are the psychological, physiological, social, environmental, and other processes that explain the meaning of age differences?

Various psychological theories that deal with human development are based on the concept of *stage*. The key to stage theories is the understanding of stage as a unique period of development, with each stage typified by its own special behavioral and cognitive characteristics. According to psychological research, all individuals progress through the same stages in a fixed chronological order, although genetic and/or environmental factors can accelerate or slow down the speed of transition from one stage to another. Stages are perceived to be hierarchical, as well as integrative. What this means is that more advanced stages are based on earlier ones and advancement results in a "re-organizing" of the various cognitive skills. Furthermore, these stages are also perceived as universal: though children grow up in very different cultures and environments and possess very different genetic maps, they seem to proceed through the same stages in the same order. In other words, such a development process has been found to hold true, at least in general terms, for Charudet who is watching television in his house-boat on the Chao Phraya river in Thailand, for Manuel who is watching it in a community center in the Cordillera mountains of Peru, and Dominique who is watching television in a small apartment in Paris, France. In summary, the concept of stage is a theoretical means of organizing, in an integrative manner, various characteristics of children's thinking and behaviors within particular age groups, above and beyond individual and cultural differences.

Jean Piaget's psychological stage theory has been applied the most widely in studies of media and children, as it focuses on cognitive development.[10] Piaget demarcated four major stages, each characterized by development of different mental structures called *schemas*. An overview of Piaget's theory can be stated as follows: During the first two years, the baby-toddler matures through the *sensory-motor* stage, during which time mental schemas are shaped by the infant's senses and actions. Applying Piaget's stage theory to television, for example, suggests that a baby learns about the television-mediated world through such actions as touching the screen when a favorite puppet appears, clapping hands to the music, or by playing with the power button. These sensory-motor experiences are gradually integrated within the child's developing understanding of television and social reality. Thus, the child understands that puppets on television feel very differently when touched on a screen compared to a favorite stuffed animal cuddled in the crib; that a screen can be turned on and off at will, yet a caregiver who returned to their home does not return at the press of a button.

The *pre-operational* stage, which occurs between two to seven years of age, is characterized mainly by the acquisition of language. No longer dependent solely on sensory-motor experiences of the "here and now," the youngster is allowed the space to develop representational thought. For example, the child is able to think and talk about experiences both viewed on a screen and occurring outside the viewing situation.

During the *concrete operational* stage, around seven to 12 years of age, schemas develop that enable the child to engage in mental transformations in interactions with the concrete world. Now a child is able to see, mentally, an object from the perspective of another person and to understand, for example, that the amount of liquid does not change when placed in containers of a different shape and size. Such mental transformations are crucial for understanding many of television's codes and conventions that require filling in gaps in storylines (e.g., what happens after seeing the driver lose control of the car and the quick camera cut to the next scene when the driver is lying unconscious in a hospital bed); or to understand the meaning of close-ups (e.g., the ability to understand that the quivering mouth on the screen is part of the face of the driver's daughter sitting by his hospital bed).

Finally, according to Piaget and his followers, from about the age of 12 and upward, a young adolescent maturing in the stage of *formal operations* develops capabilities of abstract, logical thought, unrestricted by mental operations related solely to the concrete world. From now on, youths are assumed to be able to understand television content from a mature cognitive point of view, in a manner similar to adults, although clearly their life experience, interests, and emotional world continue to differ greatly from those of adults.

Cognitive skills developed through these stages are applied by children to the mediated worlds just as they are to other aspects of their lives. These skills shape the meanings children make of the content and forms of what they see and hear in various media texts. In turn, accessing media content becomes an opportunity, like other experiences in the child's everyday life, to develop and practice a variety of cognitive skills, some of which are specific to each medium, though many are applicable to all realms of life.

While the application of Piaget's cognitive stage theory has made significant contributions to the study of children and television, the tremendous growth in the area of neuroscience and brain research is also starting to inform research in the area of cognitive processing of information from media. We fully expect that these studies will enrich our understanding of the meaning of age-related development and its application to the study of children and media.

At the same time, it is important to point out that the implications of media use for the emotional, social, and moral aspects of children's stage development continue to be studied, as we shall see later in this book. What is appropriate for us to say at this time is that some child development researchers are challenging the explanatory power of the key Piagetian concept of stage, with its emphasis on cognitive development, and proposing the inclusion of a greater emphasis on the social contexts in which children grow up and the different ways in which they interact with their environments over time.[11] For example, the UNICEF *Communicating with Children* project[12] focuses on three major age groupings, while acknowledging fluidity between and variability within each. In summarizing the literature in this area in general terms, the authors suggested that a child's *early years* (which occur from birth until the start of formal schooling – around the age of six in most societies) are characterized by potentially very positive interaction with loving adults and siblings. In addition to the development of cognitive skills and language described above, there is also gradual awareness of one's own and others' emotions, and learning to express and control them; the gradual development of separation and autonomy; and development of collaborative play, helping, and pro-social behaviors. These earliest years are considered one of the most critical times in human development as they establish the foundations of all learning that comes after.

Continuing on with this more inclusive stage theory, the authors argue that during *middle years* (roughly age seven to 11), children gradually develop into more independent human beings with an emerging sense of their own self and capacities to explore and make sense of the world around them. In addition to using more sophisticated language and learning a tremendous amount of new information and skills, they also acquire knowledge about the world and the people in it. They gradually break free from an egocentric perspective of life in which they assume they are at the center of the world, and learn to put themselves in the shoes of others. They are curious and develop social skills and friendships, as well as become more prone and receptive to a host of exclusion practices, such as gender and race stereotyping, bullying, and victimization. They explore their environment in a more independent manner but continue to be prone to accidents. They can assume more responsibility for their behavior, gradually delay gratification, and learn tasks that develop self-confidence and independence.

The *early adolescent* years (from around age 11 to 14) and, indeed, the full *adolescent* period that follows are believed by many to be a potentially stormy and stressful period when young people are handling simultaneously physical, social, emotional, and cognitive changes. This is the time of transition to adulthood when adolescents may experience frequent mood swings and aggressive emotional outbursts. They are often torn between rational thought and irrational risk taking, between adult responsibility and childish mischief. Hormonal and physical changes associated with puberty, as well as a growing attraction and interest in sex and intimate relationships, bring about the development of couples and the onset of sexual experiences in societies that permit it. Depending on their culture, adolescents may rely more on friends than family. Friends can help define their identity and enable them to engage in a variety of connecting and separating behaviors. We will explore in Chapter 6, for example, how this development is manifest in adolescents' social networking. Peer pressure plays a central role in decision making and behavioral patterns. Expectations of autonomy, individualism, and self-reliance are often encouraged in Euro-American societies, but can also be a source of conflict between adolescents and their families. In contrast, in more traditional societies, where a more collective view of society and conformity for adolescents is the norm, such values are less likely to be in place, and as a result adolescence may be a less turbulent, stressful period of life for both the adolescent and his or her family.

We can see, then, that the nature of childhood and adolescence is very much culturally constructed and that growth into adulthood takes different forms in different societies. Cultural differences play a very significant role in constructing what it means to be a child and an adolescent at different stages of development and requires that our understanding of the role of media in their lives be culturally specific too.

What is clearly shared by all cultures, though, is the fact that while growing up, children and adolescents continue to need loving and empathic adults who provide guidance, serve as positive role models, set clear boundaries and expectations, and guide them to make the best choices. All children and adolescents need to feel loved and safe, to develop positive feelings about themselves and others, to feel good about new experiences and learning, to develop resilience, and to have the entire range of their emotions understood and respected.

Despite these current trends in the study of children's development, the rich tradition of applying cognitive stage theory to the study of children and screen culture, specifically, requires that we focus some attention to it. Many of the findings can be easily transferred to a discussion of accessing other forms of televised content, regardless of its delivery form: on the screen of a television, computer, tablet or mobile phone; as a broadcast program, downloaded video, or on YouTube. We refer in this book to all of these by the generic term "television" or "screen." Let us turn now to consider some of these specific skills.

Attention to and Comprehension of Screen Content

What do children attend to on the screen and how is this attention related to content comprehension? Clearly, the child needs to demonstrate some form of attention to television as a necessary condition for the initiation of any thought-related processes. However, understanding this process is complicated, as "attention" to television is not easily defined. Is attention to television measured by the visual orientation of the child's eyes toward the operating screen, even if he or she may be daydreaming or otherwise disengaged? Does it require a visual fixation on a particular element on the screen to indicate active interest? And what about the preschooler who is playing with building-blocks on the rug in front of the television and who glances occasionally at it following an audio cue, such as a loud siren, a familiar commercial, or a child's giggle?

One leading research approach applied to study these questions assumes that attention to the screen is fundamentally reactive; that is, attention is controlled by external elements of the medium to which the child reacts. According to this research approach, younger viewers are particularly attracted to television's formal features, such as visual elements (e.g., camera movements, sharp cuts from one angle to another, slow or fast motion, and the like), as well as audio ones (e.g., unusual noises, music, sound effects). Accordingly, this approach assumes two central characteristics: First, the direction of influence is from the screen to the child; and second, motivation for viewing the programs themselves and the viewing experience of children are of minimal interest as children are perceived as passive reactors attracted to the television set due to the nature of its appealing audio-visual language.

While there is very little empirical evidence for this approach, it has been adopted wholeheartedly by many anti-television advocates, is cited extensively in popular publications, and assigned provocative titles.[13] Such writers see television viewing as a terribly dangerous, addictive "drug" that should be eliminated from children's lives, a passive, reactive behavior devoid of active cognitive processes.

In contrast, the alternative approach – *active attention* – applied by other researchers assumes that attention to the screen is an active form of behavior undertaken by children.[14] Instead of viewing attention as a passive reaction to the screen, they argue that children's attention to television can be understood as an active cognitive integration between the viewer, the television content, and the environment within which it is viewed. It is shaped by existing cognitive schemas based on past experiences in the world, including those gained from television. Thus, understanding content at any given moment involves an active process of applying strategies needed to comprehend that content.

Development of attention to audio-visual content

Attention to television develops from birth. Newborns of a few weeks have been observed reacting to sounds coming from the television set by stopping their feeding and turning their heads toward it. Babies continue to be dependent mostly on audio cues in directing their attention to television for few seconds at a time during their first few months of life. Particularly attractive content, such as commercials, peppy musical openings of programs, and programs designed for the very young, are capable of holding their attention for much longer stretches of time. This fact has not escaped the eye of entrepreneurs and, consequently, there is a booming market of video programs, computer games and mobile applications designed for viewing and interacting by this very, very young audience of "viewers in diapers."[15]

Home observation of babies as well as reports from caregivers suggest that from the age of a few months babies will often stop their activities, move to the music, clap their hands, make happy gurgling sounds, toddle toward the television set, and point at objects and characters on it. Preference for familiar content, viewed with pleasure over and over again, intensifies during the second year of life. In a relatively short span of just a few years at the beginning of the new millennium, we have become accustomed to seeing infants and toddlers in high chairs and car seats playing skillfully with mobile technology, fully attentive for relatively long stretches of time.

Attention to the screen continues to grow as a function of the child's development, personality, and environment. The ability to sustain interest in screen content for longer stretches of time and the capacity to manage attention to the screen as well as to competing activities is gradually strengthened and modified. By the age of six, attention to the screen can be sustained for long periods of time and remains so until adolescence, when a decline in television viewing occurs as part of the many changes taking place in youth's physical, social, emotional, cognitive, and environmental realms of life.

Television channels specializing in preschool audiences offer multi-platform content and activities to complement their programming and engage young children and parents. More specifically, the tablet is thought to have revolutionized the market of infants and toddlers as manipulating it through touch is both intuitive and simple, even for clumsy little fingers. This has created an interesting situation. On the one hand, in 2013 the American Academy of Pediatrics reaffirmed its recommendation, made in 1999, that there should be no screen time for children under two years of age. At the time this book is being written, several researchers have stated that, at a minimum, babies under the age of two do not benefit from screen media, while other researchers have argued that screen media are potentially harmful to babies' cognitive and physical development.[16] On the other hand, it appears that parents' views and behaviors are quite different from those of the American Academy of Pediatrics, as its recommendation seems to be very unrealistic in today's screen-saturated environment, with early use of mobile media undergoing a dramatic rise.[17]

The extant research on various aspects of early exposure to screens will be discussed throughout the book, but there is still very scarce research on the effects of mere exposure to screens on the development of the very youngest of our children. Despite the passion with which both sides of the argument present their pro or con positions in various public discussions over the impact of audio-visual stimulation on brain development, motor-development, or long-term deficiencies (such as attention and autistic disorders), these have yet to be supported by systematic research.[18]

Relationship between attention to television and comprehension

As noted above, the *reactive* approach to television assumes that attention to the screen is an antecedent condition to any process of comprehension of its content; that is, attending to television leads to its comprehension. Critics of television argue that attention to the fast tempo of television is mostly reflexive and immediate; it does not allow children the necessary conditions to reflect over contents or organize mental processes. Thus, comprehension and memory of screen content is understood to be superficial in nature, according to this approach.

In contrast, the *active* approach to children's attention to television understands relationships between attention and comprehension quite differently. Children are assumed to be active viewers whose attention to the screen is motivated by attempts to understand it. Researchers have found that children are able to devote selective attention to television, inquire about the content viewed, decode new information with the assistance of the cognitive skills available to them at the time, and use television content to refine and develop new skills. This approach assumes that television content contributes to two key processes important in children's development, defined by Piaget as *assimilation* and *accommodation*: They assimilate comprehensible television knowledge into existing mental skills and accommodate these skills by refining them according to knowledge newly acquired via television. Thus, the active approach sees relationships between children and television as reciprocal. Attention does not necessarily cause comprehension, but comprehension can shape to a large degree attention directed to the screen. While television conveys particular messages, understanding them (or ignoring them) is dependent to a large degree on the particular social, cognitive, and emotional needs of the individual child's personality and their personal development.

Thus, it seems reasonable to claim that the more viewing and social experience attained by the child the greater the chances that he or she will be attentive to and gain more from viewing television. This interactive process between child and television content has been conceptualized through the acronym AIME (Amount of Invested Mental Effort).[19] AIME portrays a process through which the child evaluates television content as easy or difficult for understanding, as familiar or novel, as important or negligible. In assessment of this process, the child determines the amount of mental effort needed to process the information. For example, if the child perceives a particular behavior or situation to be very familiar to him or her, the amount of AIME as well as attention to television will be lowered. However, if it is perceived as new and intriguing, the amount of AIME will increase. Furthermore, when children are offered challenging and appealing television content to view, they demonstrate active involvement and a higher degree of AIME.

As children grow older they learn to associate particular formal features of television with specific genres, and their viewing expectations develop according to their interest in a particular genre. They learn to distinguish between programs directed to adults and those aimed at children; between commercials and programs; between comedies and action-adventure programs. And, they learn to allocate their attention according to their interests and to activate those thinking schemas that are more appropriate to the particular genre.

Further, children develop clear distinctions between "boys'" and "girls'" programs or commercials and attach clear gender meanings to them, based on formal features alone, regardless of program content or product advertised. They distinguish commercials aimed specifically and stereotypically at boys by the fact that they are typically characterized by loud music, sharp "cuts" from one camera shot to the other, special audio effects, intensive activity level, and blue and metallic colors. In contrast, commercials aimed at girls have soft background music, female voices, pastel colors heavy on the "pink" side, photographic features such as *fade outs* (pictures fading out into blackness) and *dissolves* (pictures dissolving into other pictures), and gradual changes between camera shots rather than sharp "cuts".[20]

Individual children differ in attention and comprehension, but such differences also exist within each child's varying viewing experiences, in different social contexts due to the availability of alternative activities, and according to their internal motivations at different points in time. Clearly then, attention to television programs is not a mechanistic, casual process dictated by a mesmerizing screen that is received by a passive manipulated child-viewer. Rather, viewing screen content by children is a much more complex, active, and reciprocal process.

Development of Viewing Preferences

The worldwide availability of particular television program genres, on the one hand, and the generally universal course of development of children, on the other, result in quite predictable viewing preferences of children that change as they move from one stage of development to the next. As beginning-viewers, babies and toddlers seem to attend more closely to programs designed for them, through features that can include peppy music, sound effects, animation, lively pacing that is not overwhelming, humor and noises of laughter, as well as female and children's voices. They also seem to react to content that makes immediate sense to them: short verbal outputs, smiling faces, loveable animals, as well as pleasing colors and shapes. *Teletubbies* is a good example. Produced by the BBC and first broadcast in 1997, the program quickly became a hit among young viewers and has been marketed in over 60 countries. The four colorful, cheerful, and energetic characters move and behave like toddlers, use minimalist language, repetitive behaviors, and utterances. They are situated in a world that combines open green natural spaces and a modernistic dwelling. Research conducted in Australia, Germany, Israel, Norway, the UK, and the USA found evidence of the program's popularity among babies and toddlers that included high levels of attention and active viewing behaviors such as singing, dancing, pointing, imitating, speaking back to the television, and generally reacting enthusiastically with great joy.[21]

As toddlers grow into preschoolers, they gradually become more interested in comprehensible narratives and in diverse magazine-like formats. *Sesame Street*, produced originally by the Children's Television Workshop in New York (later to be re-named Sesame Workshop), is by far the most acclaimed and researched exemplar of programming for this age group, worldwide. Later, in Chapter 3, we will discuss this television phenomenon; for now, however, it is appropriate simply to note that the program's "quilted" magazine format combines segments of animation, puppetry, documentaries, and drama designed with the understanding that preschoolers' attention and viewing preferences develop gradually. Such a format allows each child opportunities to interact with the program according to his or her individual needs and abilities. Many countries have developed special, locally produced programs targeted for this age group with similar considerations in mind.

Children start developing preferences for more fast-paced programs and complicated content around the age of five or six, and gradually disassociate themselves from clearly educational and "safe" preschool programs. Individual preferences start to emerge and take shape for a specific animation series, a favorite Disney movie, family-type comedies, or soap operas (or telenovelas, as they are named in many parts of the world that import them from Latin America). In addition to watching specific channels targeted for them, children gradually move to what has been dubbed by the television industry "family" fare – comedies, dramas, quiz shows, reality TV, sports, music, and movie channels that are aimed at a wide and diverse audience which shares interest in a common denominator. Here, it should be noted that the range of program options varies greatly between different regions of the world, as well as within them, due in large part to economic and technological differences.

The most pronounced differences in taste already very evident at this young age are associated with gender. The development of "gender-appropriate" behavior, typical of socialization processes that take place in most societies, results in behavioral compatibility in relation to media choices, as well. Here, boys seem to outgrow the more slow-paced educational programs at a much younger age than girls, and they demonstrate a growing preference for action-oriented animations that so strongly dominate the screens of children's television around the world. Boys seem to be attracted more than girls to action, aggressive and dangerous fantasies, sports, as well as programs featuring male heroic characters. Girls, on their part, continue to prefer programs with storylines about human relationships, friendships, and feelings that take place in non-aggressive settings. Thus, while transitioning to viewing teen soaps and family dramas and comedies, they continue to watch and enjoy many educational programs for a much longer period than do boys.

This clear gendered division of preferences continues throughout the school years and seems to be resistant to major changes taking place around the world with regard to gender equality and socialization processes of gender roles.[22] We will continue to discuss aspects of gender throughout this book as it interacts with several important aspects of children's media use and leisure culture.

As children move through elementary and middle school years, they gradually experiment with the entire range of television genres, including those specifically not intended for them – such as violent movies and pornographic material. Many remain generally disinterested in programs that are based predominantly on "talking heads"; that is, programs that feature adults talking about issues framed as solely of concern to adults and conducted in a language that is mostly inaccessible and unappealing to children - such as current events, political or cultural discussions, and most news programs (with the exception of particularly attractive news items that include violent or otherwise unusual and stimulating scenes). We will return to a discussion of the role of news in children's lives in Chapter 5.

As in many other areas of their lives, children develop individual tastes based on the variety of content available to them. Furthermore, they are capable of expressing their preferences as well as articulating their reasoning for selecting particular programs, games, or websites. On the other hand, we, the adults in their lives, may not always approve of their selections and tastes or even understand the reasons for their attraction to such programs or contents.

Development of Fantasy–Reality Distinction

The ability to distinguish between fantasy and reality on the screen is one of the primary differences between children's and adults' thought processes. While "television reality" is a complex and multi-dimensional concept, we refer here specifically to the degree of factuality of the mediated reality. Scholars interested in this phenomenon attempt to answer such questions as: When are children able to determine that people and events presented on television exist beyond the screen; that they are real people representing themselves or actors playing a role; that events depicted on the screen are happening in the outside world or created according to a script? When do children understand that television is not a "magic window" to the real world? Studies of social realism focus on children's answers to these as well as other questions: Are the people, places, and events on television similar to the ones familiar to us from the real world? Are they believable? Is it probable that events depicted in fictional programs will take place? Is knowledge acquired through viewing television applicable in real life?

Researchers have found that, in most cases, children are not systematically instructed in developing such distinctions; rather they develop them on their own as they mature, gain experience, and come to understand the real world, and as their knowledge of television expands. As they mature, children's perception of television as a "magic window" is gradually replaced by a growing understanding that television reality is not quite like the everyday reality in which they live. According to researchers, an important turning point in the development of these understandings occurs around the age of eight; that is, at the beginning of the concrete-operational stage, according to cognitive development theories.

More specifically, researchers employ the following five criteria in studying children's ability to make reality–fantasy distinctions:

1. *Constructedness*: The degree to which children understand that the screen world is a product of some sort of construction and that all television content, including news and documentaries, are a fabrication, to some degree, in comparison to reality outside it.
2. *Physical actuality*: The degree to which children evaluate the reality of television based on their perceptions of the person or event actually existing outside of the screen world.

3. *Possibility*: The degree to which children evaluate the reality of television based on their perception of whether events portrayed are possible in the reality familiar to them beyond the screen.

4. *Probability*: The degree to which children evaluate the reality of television based on their perception of whether it is *probable* that it represents something that could happen beyond the screen, even if it is possible. For example, it is possible that one family would experience all the intensive events happening in the life of one television-family and solve them in similar ways; however, our life-experience suggests that it is not very probable that this would be the case.

5. *Formal features*: The degree to which children understand the formal features of television as "cues" to what may be real or fictitious. For example, older child-viewers understand that an unedited series of pictures of a war scene followed by a medium-range camera shot of an adult seated in a studio behind a desk and who seems to be talking seriously indicates a "real" news report, while a colorful, animated scene of talking animals using children's voices and with background music is "unreal."

We can organize the above criteria in a complementary manner, as follows: While internal cues (within the medium itself) direct viewers to evaluate its realism, external cues enable viewers to make comparisons between their knowledge of the world and their experience within it with regard to the television content. Generally speaking, it seems that younger children are more heavily dependent on the internal criteria (e.g., animation is "imaginary" because it is drawn and does not use live actors). As they mature, children learn to incorporate external criteria as their knowledge of the world expands (e.g., a specific animation series can be much more realistic in content then many programs employing live actors). No wonder, then, that by the age of 12, respondents will answer much like adults to research questions, such as: "What do you mean by 'real'"? or, "real in what sense?"[23]

The development of genre distinction

Distinguishing between television fantasy and reality involves capabilities to identify and differentiate between different television genres. Television programs are mostly designed according to well-defined formulas. Each formula has its own production codes and conventions of typified storylines (e.g., characters, locations, photographic techniques, pace, and soundtracks). Such format molds are filled in with content from diverse cultures and with diverse qualities. Furthermore, beyond being an aggregate of common characteristics, genres can also be understood as an aggregate of viewers' expectations. For example, when a program is identified as "news," the viewer will apply a very different set of expectations toward its degree of realism in comparison to expectations applied to a program such as science fiction identified as "fantasy."

Children learn to associate program characteristics with genres along a continuum from those perceived to be the most "real" to the most "unreal": "Real" programs deal with what is happening in the world – such as news and documentaries; "realistic" programs, a median category, are narratives and characters that, potentially, could take place but are being played by actors, such as situation comedies and soap operas; and "unreal" genres are mainly narratives with characters that are not taking place in the world and – to the best of the child's current knowledge – could not happen; such as science fiction, fantasy movies, or animal animation. As children grow older, they learn the formal features associated with each particular genre and develop specific expectations with regard to the degree of realism the program will represent.

Children of kindergarten age, around five to six years, are already capable of defining the two ends of the continuum: News is "real" and animation is "imaginary." An excerpt from an interview I had with Amy, a six-year-old North American girl, in relation to a situation comedy illustrates this developing ability. The series, *Full House*, deals with three girls who lost their mother and who are being raised by their father, his best friend, and their uncle. Amy attempted to explain to me why the news is different from *Full House*, her favorite situation comedy:[24]

AMY:	Because *Full House* comes with real people and they make it up, and the *Full House* is very silly.
INTERVIEWER:	They make it up?
AMY:	Uh, huh.
INTERVIEWER:	So *Full House* is like real people on television?
AMY:	Yeah, yeah. They're like real people, but they are silly. It is almost like the news, but it is not.
INTERVIEWER:	It is almost, but it's not? I see. So the real people are silly and the news are real people and they are not silly? I see. That's interesting.
AMY:	And cartoons are pretend stuff.

According to this young girl, animation programs are at the imaginary end of a continuum of programs. Comedies are located at the center of the continuum, as they include real people who are acting "silly," while the news is about serious real people.

Children in the concrete operational stage come up with alternative ways of dividing programs. For example, there are "good" versus "bad," or programs that are "for children" versus those that are "for grownups." Or, they may organize them according to perceived content. For example, a family situation comedy could be grouped with an educational program, because both convey messages of concern and love for family members. An action-adventure program and an animation program could be understood to be of a similar genre, because both have shooting in them. A commercial for a food product, news program, and math instructional program are perceived as educational, because they all "teach things."

In this regard, commercials are a very difficult genre for children to understand, since they intentionally blur distinctions between real and imaginary and, as well, employ a range of audio-visual means to sell children products. Studies on children in various countries growing up in an environment with commercial television suggest that they can already identify commercial breaks as a separate genre at a very young age, often as early as three years old. The children learn to identify those cues that indicate a transition between a program and a commercial (e.g., a logo, sign, or sound effect that is repeated regularly). However, their ability to explain this genre develops much more gradually, as does their ability to distinguish between their attitude toward the product in comparison with their attitude toward the commercial for that product (i.e., a commercially literate person may like a product, but not the commercial advertising it, and vice versa; that is, enjoying a commercial is not necessarily an indication that the product is enjoyable as well).

As they start elementary school, children may develop an understanding of commercials' "persuasive intent"; that is, while they can discern that the intention is to sell products, they may not identify the tactics of manipulation employed in the text. Thus, they continue to trust commercial statements as being "real," have difficulty identifying indirect advertising present in much of commercial television programs, and do not understand the economic processes that drive the television industry.[25]

Interestingly, research evidence suggests that it is doubtful if many adults understand these complicated issues either. Analyses of what scholars refer to as advertising literacy explain that this is due to the need for use of seven cognitive understandings:[26] Advertising (1) is different from other media content, (2) has a paying source, (3) has an intended audience, (4) has a selling intent, (5) has persuasive intent, (6) makes use of persuasive tactics, and (7) has a bias in comparison to the actual product. Overall, such understandings may be insufficient in and of themselves as advertising literacy also involves the capacities to apply critical skills to the ubiquitous commercial culture infusing children's lives, tens and even hundreds of times daily. We will return to this topic in Chapter 4.

The importance of distinguishing between screen fantasy and reality

Clearly, then, distinguishing between various forms of fantasy and reality on the screen and sorting television programs into genres is not a simple, objective, or clear-cut task. Indeed, children continue to be confused by realistic genres, as do many adults as they mature as viewers. Furthermore, new challenges are posed to viewers as the media environment changes. Consider the following extensive list of examples: Realistic movies incorporate segments of animation or documentaries; news reports include reconstructions of past events and employ dramatization features; docu-dramas combine use of real places and people together with actors and fictitious dialogue; commercials incorporate scientific information to create infomercials; news and entertainment are combined to create *infotainment*; educational programs integrate entertainment features to form *edutainment*; and there are reality shows, talent competitions, police investigations, and matchmaking programs. All these phenomena that appear in many localized forms around the world purposefully blur genres through the use of "reality" formal features (e.g., rough camera moves and the pretense of no editing; no music or soundtracks; "ordinary" people rather than professional actors; out-of studio settings; intimate moments of display of intense emotion).

All these genres continue to challenge the ability of young as well as older and more experienced viewers to define and understand television's "reality." In addition, the ability to access a mixture of genres through personal tailoring of viewing schedules complicates this even further, as the clear characteristics and nature of a certain broadcast or cable channel disappear (e.g., history channel, news channel, or family movies channel). All of these developments require re-examination of criteria used by viewers to evaluate screen reality.

Finally, cultural experience plays an important role in young viewers' socialization as they mature and develop their own particular perspective on reality. Since the development of the distinction between fantasy and reality on television is shaped by life experiences on and outside the screen, the nature of such experiences is bound to shape this skill. Thus, seemingly independent cognitive skills are very much culturally dependent. For example, while animals portrayed with a human soul may be perceived as an imaginary feature of an animation program by Paola, raised in the Catholic culture of Italy, this may seem perfectly reasonable to Kumar of Hindi faith in India who believes in the reincarnation of human souls in animals. Similarly, a dramatic series on the Jewish Holocaust may be understood as imaginary fiction by José in Mexico, but is very real and relevant to Dana raised in Israel, whose grandparents are holocaust survivors. Yuji in Japan may think that life in outer space seems completely in the realm of fantasy, while for Marina in Russia, whose parents are scientists, it may be perceived as quite real. And dramas describing the lives of the very rich make complete sense to Kevin from a higher social class US family but may seem to be completely fictional to Tomaselli from the poor classes of Botswana. These are just a few of the examples that demonstrate the role of cultural context in perception of television reality as similar to or different from actual reality. As with the case of gender, the important role of culture, too, will be addressed throughout the book.

The development of understanding of television characters

Imagine the social world of a child in your own neighborhood. What kind of people and professions does he or she meet on an everyday basis? It is safe to assume that most children around the world have firsthand encounters with family members, teachers, salespeople, perhaps medical professionals, bus or taxi drivers. They may have an occasional encounter with other professionals, depending on their personal life circumstances. But most of the adult professional world is quite inaccessible to them (as it is to most adults, too). Television, thus, becomes a very convenient, non-threatening way to come in contact with roles beyond our everyday lives, particularly in relation to high-status and stereotyped roles that appear in dramatic genres, such as eloquent lawyers, tough law enforcers, brilliant surgeons, glorious celebrities, vile Mafia leaders, promiscuous students, to name just a few of the types of people who become a part of our viewing lives and who most of us never meet in real life.

Meeting these varied characters portrayed on the screen raises many value-related issues for children, as well as adults, as they compare themselves with fictional television characters: Who am I? Am I similar or different from them? Are they good or bad? Am I good or bad in comparison? Do I want to be like them? If so, how, can I change my behavior or appearance to be more like them? Answers to such questions become part of the process of self-definition and learning about one's place in society. Media characters, thus, can serve as role models for identification and imitation, as well as be a resource for learning about the world. It is therefore important for us to understand how children perceive media characters and their behaviors.

We recall from an earlier discussion that a cognitive schema is a structure for organizing knowledge related to a particular idea or term (e.g., criminal, singer). A schema may be shaped by knowledge acquired through firsthand experience as well as through mediating sources, such as other people and the media. In turn, schemas have implications for understanding how new information is processed. For example, schema regarding gender differences shape the ways we attend differently to content that involves female and male characters, the ways we process and remember content, the ways we perceive it to be relevant to us, and our evaluation of and preferences for the characters themselves.

Following what we already know about cognitive development, we can surmise that as children mature their understanding of media characters changes dramatically. Younger children are more dependent on external appearance in evaluating characters. Accordingly, they tend to equate the unfamiliar look of a foreigner as well as unattractive body and facial characteristics with negative personality qualities, thus perceiving an ugly person as mean. However, as they mature, they gradually assign more importance to internal personality traits as well as circumstantial explanations to characters' motivations and behaviors. But, like adults, they remain highly influenced by social expectations and those stereotypes engrained deeply in different societies that are emphasized all too frequently in commercial television. Indeed, many people continue throughout their lifetime to be wary of characters – on television as well as in real life – who look very different from them (e.g., persons of a different race, disabled people, people who wear a non-conforming clothing style), as well as those perceived to diverge from culturally dominant beauty standards (e.g., overweight people, those with non-proportionate facial features, or some manner of deformity).

The development of moral judgment

While very helpful in understanding general trends in the development of human thinking, cognitive developmental theories alone are often unable to provide us with a comprehensive and satisfactory understanding of thinking, behaviors, and emotions. Clearly, many of the issues involved with children's maturing (deficient, according to some approaches) cognitive abilities remain unresolved during adult years. So how large is the gap between adults and children, and are children really as "deficient" as some persons assume? One additional body of theory that can assist us in understanding this aspect of relations between media and children is the adaptation of developmental theory to the realm of moral judgment, in general, and its particular application to children's viewing of television.

Media are a central source for developing moral judgment as they present many tales about human conduct. For example, understanding the motivations for violent behaviors and their implications for victims is crucial in application of moral judgment by viewers. Thus, adults will usually apply moral criteria differently with regard to a person who purposefully aims to hurt others for personal gain compared to someone forced to behave violently in order to save a loved one. That is, we apply different criteria to acts of violence that seem to us to be random and unjustified compared to acts that in other societies might be perceived as justified or even sacred (e.g., acts of violence by military forces in some countries or those committed under the guise of preserving "family honor" in others). Do children apply these same processes and criteria?

The way children judge television characters and their behaviors is central to the development of their understanding. Again, developmental researchers claim that children's moral and cognitive development are similar across the globe, as each child progresses through specific stages in a fixed order, with each stage being fundamentally different from the previous one. Similarly, moral judgment is under- stood to develop through the combined development of skills, cognitive schemas, and experience.[27] As very young children have yet to internalize cognitive standards that define what is "right, good" or "wrong, bad," they are highly dependent on external reinforcements that teach them what their society perceives as "right" or "wrong." Thus, it is through socialization within their social settings, including the media, that children learn from an early age via imitation, as well as by acting on a desire to please their caregivers, the difference between "right" and "wrong." If caregivers respond positively to a child's actions, the child works out that this must mean it was the "right" thing to do. And, as they view a program, they will often seek guidance in this process, as when they ask questions such as: "those green characters – are they good or bad?" in attempting to understand the world in clear "good and bad" terms.

As they move to the concrete-operational stage, around the age of seven or eight, children gradually become more able to exercise moral judgment autono- mously and to use it as a tool to evaluate human behaviors. In doing so, they apply their emerging understanding of behavioral motivation to their judgment. Thus, the same behavior will be evaluated as good or bad according to the motivation behind it or the circumstances in which it occurs. Gradually, they also learn to experience the world in less dichotomous terms. So, television characters, much like real-life ones, are neither good nor bad, but rather complicated beings who behave in appropriate or inappropriate ways in different situations and within complex cultural norms.

Identification with Media Characters

Why is it at all important to dwell on how children evaluate and understand screen characters? Let us start with three related answers: First, screen characters are the focus of identification, imitation, and idolization. Second, screen characters serve as behavioral role models for children to imitate. But above all, it is because screen characters provide children with the raw materials with which to learn, grow, experience, feel, strengthen their inner world and self-image, and just deal with everyday life.[28]

Many viewers, both children and adults, develop emotional relationships with television characters. We care about them, we want to get closer to them, we are curious about their lives. Identification with television characters can take various forms.[29] Viewers (particularly younger ones) may feel a similarity between themselves and a character, due to sharing the same gender, ethnic origin, age, or appearance. The character may manifest the same values and worldview, and, even subconsciously, the child may perceive him to be from the same class and educational level. Younger children may identify with children or animals that are smaller or in subordinate positions, representing their own powerless position. Often the child-viewer shares the same perspective as a television character they admire, and lives "through" the same experiences with the character. In this way the character serves to reaffirm the child's sense of self-worth; manifest similar beliefs, attitudes, and worldview; and serve as a role model for possible suitable (or unsuitable) behaviors in situations relevant to his or her life.

The child may also be involved in a form of wishful identification – when she seeks to be "like" or to "behave like" the media character. The child may imagine exchanging places with the subject of identification and feel, during the viewing, that things that happen to the character are happening, or could happen, to him, too. In this way the child exchanges her role as a viewer with the role of the character in the program, thus becoming someone else for a short, often intense, period of time.

Related to identification – yet not quite the same – is "para-social interaction." Here, viewers feel that they know the television characters so well that they engage in imaginary interpersonal relationships with them. Para-social interactions are often formed during an extended period of viewing (e.g., actor appearing in a multi-year dramatic or soap opera series; a leading role in a magazine television format; a singer on MTV). In forming such an interaction, a younger viewer, as well as an adult, comes to feel that s/he knows the character's personality, behaviors, tastes, and relationships with others, and cares about the character as if s/he was a close friend. The child may seek advice from the character's role, wish to be part of his/her social world, and engage in a close friendly relationship with him/her. Para-social relationships may provide a deep sense of personal and social satisfaction and encourage loyalty to the program. One possible implication of such a relationship is that children (as well as adults) may treat the actors, and the character they play, as one and the same person. Thus, it is not uncommon for actors to receive comments, gifts, reprimands, and requests directed to the character they portray.

Of particular interest is adolescents' involvement with entertainment celebrities. This widely popular and familiar worldwide phenomenon raises interesting questions about relationships or associations between such involvement and attitudes, behavior, self-esteem, and identity development. A study of adolescents in Singapore, for example, found that reporting a sense of intimacy with celebrities was associated with consumption of related media content, much like the development of interpersonal relationships in the non-mediated world. While depending on a host of variables, such involvement was associated with both positive as well as negative consequences for adolescents' wellbeing and level of materialism. For example, low self-esteem was reinforced by such relationships, particularly among adolescents who demonstrated borderline tendencies for various pathologies. Similarly, adolescents with lower academic scores tended to report a higher level of intense personal feelings toward their idols.[30]

Studies conducted in several countries found gender to be the most predictable characteristic of identification – both similar and wishful – as well as of para-social interaction with television characters among children. Boys of all ages almost exclusively identify with male figures, while girls identify mostly with females but also with males, particularly during their earlier years. Two complementary explanations for this finding have been proposed: First, to date, television continues to purvey a much wider range of male roles with which children can identify than female roles. The latter are still restricted both in absolute numbers as well as in diversity of personalities, roles, settings, and plot lines. This holds true for television all over the world, with a general ratio of two male characters for every single female one.[31] Second, as a general rule, our societies are much more tolerant toward girls who adopt more typical "male" styles of behavior and appearance than of boys who adopt a typical "girly" style. Thus, the general rule of thumb supported by research evidence is that there is a better chance of girls watching television programs designed for boys and featuring male protagonists than vice versa. This conclusion is well known – and indeed utilized – in the commercial domain of the children's television industry, where there is a clear desire to invest resources in developing "boy" genres. While this is the case worldwide, several recent successful productions with global appeal featuring independent child-female protagonists have challenged this producers' rule.[32]

The personality traits that determine the degree of attractiveness of television characters to children reflect, in large degree, the norms and expectations from males and females in most cultures. For example, researchers found that children of all ages wish to identify with winners, even when their behaviors were evaluated as negative. For boys, this is expressed mainly through characters that excel physically and are very active. Both boys and girls value intelligence as a central characteristic that singles out male characters with whom they identify. However, unsurprisingly, this is not true when girls are asked to explain the reasons for the appeal of their favorite female characters: The reasons cited refer, primarily, to their attractive appearances. It seems that girls growing up in many societies today have internalized quite successfully the importance of beauty assigned to female appearance in many societies. Indeed, they are unlikely to see many examples of ambitious, intelligent women on programs they watch as such women are deemed to be less attractive and thus are often sanctioned from appearing on television. Similarly, boys still grow up to believe that manhood is defined by action, physical force, and intelligence superiority. We will return to this important finding in Chapter 5.

Based on our discussion so far, it is easy to see how identification with screen characters may be related to imitation of their behaviors. The underlining assumption is that the viewer comes to place herself in the character's shoes – so to speak – playing the character's role, and even internalizing, usually unknowingly, the value system that the character represents. This raises many important questions: Are there any particular personality characteristics that might predict imitation of negative behaviors (e.g., violence, lying) and others that predict imitation of positive behaviors (e.g., mutual aid, sharing)? Do specific personality characteristics lead to particular kinds of behavior patterns (e.g., physical force and violent behavior; physical attraction and sexual behavior)? We will discuss these and other questions related to imitation of behaviors portrayed on television at length in Chapter 4.

Children's Fear Reactions

Media offer children a variety of emotional experiences. Children observe characters' emotional reactions and learn about emotional situations and behaviors, and they experience a whole range of emotions themselves, including excitement, love, thrills, sadness, and longing. Fear reaction is one form of children's emotional involvement with the screen that has been studied systematically (see also the discussion in relation to parental mediation in Chapter 1). Much audio-visual content, across genres, can instigate fear and anxiety in viewers of all ages: dangerous situations, injuries, bodily distortions, characters' own fearful reactions, and more. Children may express their fear not only during the viewing situation, but also way beyond it – in nightmares, distress, and situations that are associated with the televised scene. Some traumatizing screen moments stay with them for many years and may affect their understandings and behavior in the real world.

Investigation into children's processing and reactions to such experiences raises many ethical issues. Since clearly we should not intervene in children's viewing habits by intentionally presenting them with scary material in order to study their reactions to it, we need to find ways to study such influences when they occur spontaneously as a result of children's own viewing – by choice or coincidence. Alternatively, we can study such reactions in retrospect, in reconstructing scenarios whereby, as adults, they recollect memories of exposure to frightening media stimulus and their enduring reactions to them.[33] An international study of young people's recollection of scary memories they carry with them from their childhood television and film viewing suggests that the majority of them have very clear and detailed stories to tell. The most commonly mentioned moments were triggered by viewing scary fiction (animated, realistic, science fiction, horror) that left a lasting impression. Many were able to relate in words and drawings the exact scene engraved in their memories, such that the researchers could identify the original text to which they referred, compare the scene with the memory, and confirm the similarity in great detail.[34] This and the previous studies revealed that the vast majority of adults studied could describe such experiences, relating the effects they had on their bedtime behaviors, for example. The participants also reported on their childhood coping mechanisms – behavioral as well as cognitive – as well as on avoidance strategies from additional exposure.

As in other phenomena discussed so far, children's development is central to understanding their fear reactions. Contrary to what might be expected, children do not become less easily frightened as they mature. Instead, what seems to happen is that some stimuli that bothered them in the past produce less fear, but other stimuli that never elicited reactions in the past become problematic. For example, pre-operational children up to the age of seven to eight are scared of animals; the dark; supernatural forces such as ghosts, witches and monsters; and things that look anomalous or move unexpectedly. These anxieties are largely replaced by fear of personal injury, as well as fear of injury or death of loved ones, in the concrete-operational stage. Adolescents continue to worry about themselves, but also develop fear reactions with regard to political, economic, and global issues. Concrete screen stimuli (what we see and hear on the screen) decreasingly evoke fear as children mature with more abstract concepts gradually taking their place, such as the ability to understand the meaning and implications of dangers.

For example, preschool children might be more afraid of something that looks dangerous, physically, but in fact is not threatening, rather than something that does not look dangerous, but may in fact be so. Such reactions are reversed during school-age years. No wonder, then, that young children react more fearfully to imaginary programs (e.g., cartoons, monsters) than to real dangers (e.g., news reports about an anticipated natural disaster). Such behavior, too, can be explained by applying lessons from developmental psychology: In order to develop anxiety about certain kinds of complicated threats presented on the screen, children require life experience, capabilities to distinguish between what is real and imaginary as well as to think in abstract terms, and knowledge about actual events such as the spread of a new plague, threats of nuclear disaster, or global warming.[35]

However, here, too, we cannot ignore the relevance of social context to children's fear reactions to television content. Reactions to news reports about wars and terror-ist events is a particular case in point. Unfortunately, recent events have provided many opportunities to study this aspect more closely. Reactions to news of the Gulf War in 1991 among children in both Europe and the USA, who felt relatively removed from the situation, were quite mixed. However, reactions to the bombing of the Twin Towers in New York in 2001, the war in Iraq since 2003, as well as to terrorist attacks by suicide bombers in Israel, were both more dramatic and pro-duced stronger reactions. The growing intensity of live news coverage of the events, particularly when the coverage "drives it home" by presenting the danger as more relevant and immediate, seems to result in an increase in fear reactions among children, as well as a host of additional emotions, such as anger, frustration, a sense of helplessness, and despair.[36]

Discussions among scholars and producers of television news for children produced a set of recommendations for production at a time of war. These recommendations call for them to be attentive to children's cognitive needs for information and interpretation, as well as to their affective needs by recognizing their fears and concerns, and assisting them in emotion management.[37] We will discuss other aspects of televised war coverage and children's political notions of the world in Chapter 5.

Television, Imagination, and Creativity

What are the effects of television viewing on children's fantasy worlds? Some critics accuse television of "killing" children's imagination by imposing on them a limited range of narratives, characters, and ideas about the world. Indeed, several early research studies found negative relationships between television viewing and children's scores on a variety of creative tasks (e.g., thinking, problem solving, and writing abilities), thus concurring with the popular belief that heavy television use, particularly of a violent nature, impedes development of children's creative abilities. Furthermore, a series of studies found that children raised in communities without television rated higher on tests of creativity in comparison with children of similar background and life circumstances raised with it. These studies were conducted during a period when researchers were still able to find non-television societies that do not differ from the general population (e.g., those refraining from television for ideological or religious reasons; or the very poor and homeless). Today, however, it is difficult to find such societies and nearly impossible to reconstruct them. Thus, though these findings remain unverified, they continue to fuel and inspire a lively debate about the possibility that a causal negative relationship does exist between television viewing and creativity and imagination (i.e., that television viewing impedes the development of creativity in children).[38]

Another line of investigation focused on how television stories differ in comparison to other forms of stories as stimuli of children's creativity and imagination. For example, one hypothesis claims that a televised version of a story stimulates fewer creative ideas, storylines, and problem-solving solutions than repetitive verbal storytelling (as in audio or print forms). Here the working assumption is that the attractiveness of the visual aspects of television – dubbed *the visual superiority effect* – is confounded by the advantages of the auditory-verbal track for comprehension. Put simply, listening to a story on the radio may better stimulate the ability to create new storylines, characters, and events than viewing it on television.[39] This finding begs the question of universality since these studies have been conducted primarily in the USA and Europe. For example, will children growing up in a more orally oriented culture (e.g., traditional societies, ultra-religious groups, homes that refrain from watching television for ideological reasons) as opposed to visually oriented cultures (e.g., those heavily dependent on screen culture) perform differently on these tasks, simply because they have been raised to prioritize particular sets of mental skills over others?

The role of television as a stimulant of fantasy play (interchangeably termed pretend, make-believe, or imaginative play) is another area of research. Many of these studies assume that television viewing may displace free play, particularly among young children who normally are expected to engage in such play. The accumulated research in this area suggests that, ultimately, the types of content children watch are more important in determining outcomes of fantasy and imaginative play than the quantity of time spent viewing. For example, viewing fantasy-violence on television may inhibit or take the place of imaginative play, while educational programming that encourages pro-social behaviors designed to stimulate fantasy play may actually encourage it. Critics of commercial television argue that most of the programs appearing on commercial stations encourage passive viewing rather than active thinking and imagination, and rarely provide opportunities for young children to engage in creative imaginative play, presumed to be essential for their development.[40]

In contrast, there are many rich descriptions in ethnographic case studies and anecdotal reports that illustrate potential connections between media texts as stimuli for children's imagination and play. Some examples are: Embracing Ernie from *Sesame Street* as an imaginary companion in the USA; playing *Batman* or *Dragon Ball Z* games in Germany; imitating *Power Rangers* or playing out the roles of friends in *Neighbors* in the UK; aspiring to be like a member of the *Spice Girls* pop group or a *Pokémon Master* in Israel; imagining meeting friends from the *Mongol* television series in South Korea; to name just a few.[41] All of these media contents were found to leave *media traces* in children's stories, play, and artwork. They were used by children to construct their make-believe worlds and in doing so to express their desires through imagined play within those worlds. Further, children were found to borrow from settings seen on television (e.g., a space station, a jungle, even a television studio); objects (e.g., a vehicle, a piece of furniture, a building); characters (e.g., an animated super hero, a celebrity, a protagonist), customs (e.g., a cape, a mask, an accessory); narratives (e.g., action-adventure, soap opera, situation comedy); and specific information (e.g., name of places, characters, events, scientific inventions, medical treatments) and integrate them in their imagined and/or wished-for stories for themselves. Take, for example, this story told by Omer, a nine-year-old Israeli boy, in an interview setting. Omer is describing a drawing he has made of his make-believe world:

> This world is only mine … here I am the ruler. I can do whatever I want. Everything is allowed. I am wearing a suit. The red-cloak is like Superman's. The green are my hands so that I can climb on everything like Spiderman, those blue things in my hands are my fire laser-ray weapons. The red is a belt like Pokémon's. The purple are my flying boots, and the horns I took from Batman's mask. I am the master and I also have a sword, like in *Star Wars*.

He continues with his story, combining a host of media sources, unrelated to the original superpowers, including books – new and old classics:

> There is a carpet and a bed and lots of things for training … like in the Olympics. Also Pokémon figures, a huge Pikachu … In this world there are good people and bad

people, and also a school in a castle, like Hogwarts school in *Harry Potter*, that I have already graduated from … In the middle of my world there is a mystery island like Jules Verne's, with lots of whales, like *Moby Dick*. When I am asleep I dream about the powers of television heroes, and I added a bit from my own imagination…

Omer "slips into" the various super powers, as one slips on a dress, including the special skills he possesses as the master (*Star Wars*) and those he has learned at the school of magic (*Harry Potter*). He goes out armed for adventures in a world where the good and the bad co-exist, as on the famous *Treasure Island* or in the fight with *Moby Dick*. Omer adopts the status of the media character (i.e., being a graduate of the school of magic and being the master), as well as the special skills and weapons of superheroes.

Omer's story is but one illustration of the intense inter-relationship between media culture and children's fantasy worlds as expressed in their everyday lives. However, while we recognize that children do use media content in their fantasy play, many questions remain unanswered; for example: What is the frequency of media's contribution to fantasy play? Is play induced from a non-screen-related source more or less imaginative (e.g., a book, a story told by an adult, a theater play)? Does it make sense to deliberate, as researchers, about whether one kind of imaginative play is of higher quality and more desired than the other?

A Conceptual and Methodological Reflection

This is a very good point at which to stop our review and reflect on some of the conceptual and methodological issues involved in studying children and media as discussed in the first two chapters. We will use the recent section on television, imagination, and creativity as an illustration of a much wider debate. The accumulating body of knowledge that claims that, overall, the negative effects of media on children's creativity, imagination, and fantasy play are stronger than its positive effects has largely emerged from the research tradition of media effects. These studies of children and television embrace developmental theories in cognitive psychology that center on the individual child. Accordingly, this approach views children as being in the process of "becoming" an adult. Their abilities and skills are tested and measured in comparison to the ideal model of the adult thinker. This approach has been named "the deficiency model" as it assumes that the child is "deficient" in comparison with the adult. It is a research paradigm with roots in various stimulus-response models whose goal is to find correlations between television content and fantasy activity. Research that applies this approach has been conducted primarily through experimental designs, where children are brought into a study setting and presented with various tasks. In most cases, such studies quantify pre-defined fantasy activities. Thus, the researcher counts the number of times the child behaves in specific manner, for example, says something aloud, sings a song, dresses up, or re-arranges furniture.

The major strength of studies conducted in the effects tradition is that they can isolate and control the issues selected for study and place each child in a comparable situation. For example, they can control the kind of televisual material to which the child is exposed during the experiment, the skills tested, the toys available in the room, and the order of activities. Researchers assume that such a context has a greater chance of attaining more specific as well as causal explanations. For example, they can determine that a specific educational program elicits a certain activity while a violent program does not. Many questions can be raised regarding the type of activities selected for coding and the researcher's value judgments attached to them (e.g., is it "good" when the child dresses up as a princess after having been read a story, but "not good" if she dresses up like a princess she saw on television?). Reservations can also be made regarding the suitability of the unnatural experimental setting for eliciting and observing fantasy-related activities.

In correlational studies, another often applied research format, home-viewing behaviors are measured through responses to questionnaires and correlated with other cognitive skills. The major strength of this research method is its ability to examine long-term, accumulative influences of viewing television on a very large number of children and so be able to offer insights that can be generalized to other situations.

In contrast to these two approaches, naturalistic or ethnographic studies observe children in their own familiar settings as they express or articulate their inner worlds in play, drawing, and/or talk. Such studies are of a smaller scale, but take place in more natural environments, such as children's homes, playgrounds, and schools, where children engage in and reveal fantasy and creative behaviors more spontaneously. Researchers who apply the ethnographic approach do not test the children, rather they observe as well as talk with them, and try to make sense of what they do and say. Rather than seeing children as in the process of "becoming" adults, these researchers focus on seeing children as a "being" in their own right, at each individual stage of their development. Rather than perceiving children as "deficient" in comparison to adults, they treat them simply as different from one another.

These ethnographic studies have emerged from a very different research tradition to the positivist-based approach summarized above. Here children are presumed to act in meaningful ways that express their own perspectives, worldviews, and self-image. This approach argues that children are often underestimated by experimental research that is psychologically oriented, and, more specifically, that the significance that television has for children's fantasy worlds can hardly be encapsulated in studies conducted through experiments in unfamiliar settings. In contrast, scholars working in the naturalistic–ethnographic tradition approach children as socially competent, autonomous individuals who actively make sense of and indeed construct and express meanings as they interact with the world around them. They do not assume that what is perceived as central or important in a television program for adults is not necessarily the same thing for children. Thus the comparison with adults as a central criterion to evaluating children's comprehension or creativity is perceived as misleading. Referred to colloquially as the qualitative method, this tradition focuses on meanings media have for children and what children do with media, rather than on how children's comprehension is deficient in comparison to adults and what media do to children.

Furthermore, qualitative researchers argue that the effects approach is misguided because it assumes that a television story has one clear, true, deep structure that needs to be understood for mature comprehension of the story. This assumption prevents the possibility of exposing alternative interpretations of it. Evaluating characters, judging their morality, or identifying with them is ground, often deeply, in the social context of the child. If we pursue this criticism further, we can appreciate its possible epistemological implications: understanding texts is by definition, a contextualized experience. Any attempt to enforce one "correct" interpretation, one possible "meaning," for example, an imagined adult view, is misleading. Adults, too, just like children, have a gender, a race, a social class, a religion, a culture, a political view. Adults, too, live in very diverse cultures all over the world. Accordingly there is not, nor should there be, one ideal adult-comprehension model.

This brief characterization of various research traditions employed by scholars in studying media and children relations raises a number of questions that we should consider as we assess the studies and discussions of other issues in this book. For example: Is it possible to see these two approaches as complementary rather than competitive? Can we integrate the knowledge gained from both traditions into a fuller and more comprehensible understanding of the role of media in children's lives? Can we accept that children lack the skills and knowledge that adults have developed as they mature and at the same time respect the meaning children produce from media in their own right? Can we consider each child's individual development and at the same time integrate our understanding of this development as embedded in complicated social contexts? Can we employ experimental, correlational, as well as ethnographic methods as appropriate to our research questions, and combine the results of all approaches to create a more comprehensive understanding of children?

Notes

1. Common Sense Media, 2013.
2. In the UK: Himmelweit, Oppenheim, & Vince, 1958; in the USA: Schramm, Lyle, & Parker, 1961; and in Canada: Williams, 1986.
3. Offered by Neuman, 1991.
4. Livingstone & Bovill, 2001.
5. Tilley, 2013.
6. Jung, Lin, & Kim, 2012.
7. Lin, Zhang, Jung, & Kim, 2013.
8. Messenger Davies, 1989; Smith, 1986.
9. Valkenburg, 2004; Van Evra, 2004.
10. Piaget, 1969; Piaget & Inhelder, 1969.
11. Casper & Theilheimer, 2009; Trawick-Smith, 2006.

12. Kolucki & Lemish, 2011, pp. 13-23. Brief excerpts reprinted with permission.
13. Mander, 1978; Winn, 1977.
14. Anderson & Field, 1986; Anderson & Lorch, 1983; Bickham, Wright, & Huston, 2001.
15. Lemish, 1987.
16. Christakis, 2010.
17. Common Sense Media, 2013.
18. Huizinga, Nikkelen, & Valkenburg, 2013.
19. Salomon, 1981.
20. Lemish, 2010.
21. See issue 12(2) of *TelevIZIon*, 1999, devoted to research on the *Teletubbies*.
22. Lemish, 2010.
23. The discussion in this section has been informed by Chandler, 1997; Dorr, 1983; Fitch, Huston, & Wright, 1993; Hawkins, 1977; and Messenger Davies, 1997.
24. From transcripts in Lemish, 1997.
25. Hansen, Rasmussen, Martensen, & Tufte, 2002; Lemish, 1997; Valkenburg & Cantor, 2002.
26. Buijzen, Rozendaal & van Reijmersdal, 2013, p. 275.
27. Theories of moral development are heavily influenced by Kohlberg, 1984, as well as by the feminist critic of his work, originally voiced by Gilligan, 1982. As applied to television, see Collins, 1983, and Rosenkoetter, 2001.
28. Götz, Lemish, Aidman, & Moon, 2005.
29. Hoffner, 1996; Hoffner & Cantor, 1991; Raviv, Bar-Tal, Raviv, & Ben-Horin, 1996.
30. Chia & Poo, 2009.
31. Götz & Lemish, 2012.
32. Lemish, 2010.
33. Harrison & Cantor, 1999; Cantor, 2004.
34. Lemish & Alon-Tirosh, forthcoming.
35. Cantor 1994; 1996; 2001; 2002.
36. See with regard to the Gulf War of 1991, Cantor, Mares, & Oliver, 1993; Hoffner & Haefner, 1993; and Wober & Young, 1993. With regard to the Twin Towers, see Smith & Moyer-Guse, 2006; and Walma van der Molen & Konjin, 2007. With regard to everyday news reporting, see Smith & Wilson, 2000; 2002.
37. International Central Institute for Youth and Educational Television (IZI), 2004.
38. MacBeth, 1996. Most notable opponents of television in this area are the Singers, see for example, Singer, 1993; Singer & Singer, 1976; 1981; 1983.
39. Greenfield & Beagles-Roos, 1988; Greenfield, Farrer, & Beagles-Roos, 1986; Rolandelli, 1989.
40. Valkenberg & Van der Voort, 1994.
41. Quoted in Götz, Lemish, Aidman, & Moon, 2005, pp. 5–6.

References

Anderson, D.R. & Field, D.E. (1986). Children's attention to television: Implications for production. In M. Meyer (Ed.), *Children and the formal features of television* (pp. 56–96). Munich: K.G. Saur.

Anderson, D.R. & Lorch, E.P. (1983). Looking at television: Action or reaction? In J. Bryant & D.R. Anderson (Eds.), *Children's understanding of television: Research on attention and comprehension* (pp. 1–33). New York: Academic Press.

Bickham, D.S., Wright, J. & Huston, A.C. (2001). Attention, comprehension, and the educational influences of television. In D.G. Singer & J.L. Singer (Eds.), *Handbook of children and the media* (pp. 101–119). Thousand Oaks, CA: Sage.

Buijzen, M., Rozendaal, E., & van Reijmersdal, E.A. (2013). Media, advertising, and consumerism: Children and adolescents in a commercialized media environment. In D. Lemish (Ed.), *The Routledge international handbook of children, adolescents, and media* (pp. 271–278). New York: Routledge.

Cantor, J. (1994). Confronting children's fright responses to mass media. In D. Zillman, J. Bryant, A.C. Huston (Eds.), *Media, children and the family: Social scientific, psychodynamic and clinical perspectives* (pp. 87–116). Thousand Oaks, CA: Sage.

Cantor, J. (1996). Television and children's fear. In T. MacBeth (Ed.), *Tuning in to young viewers: Social science perspectives on television* (pp. 87–115). Thousand Oaks, CA: Sage.

Cantor, J. (2001). The media and children's fears, anxieties, and perceptions of danger. In D.G. Singer & J.L. Singer (Eds.), *Handbook of children and the media* (pp. 207–221). Thousand Oaks, CA: Sage.

Cantor, J. (2002). Fright reactions to mass media. In J. Bryant & D. Zillmann (Eds.), *Media effects: Advances in theory and research* (pp. 287–306). Mahwah, NJ: Lawrence Erlbaum.

Cantor, J. (2004). "I'll never have a clown in my house": Why movie horror lives on. *Poetics Today, 25*(2), 283–304.

Cantor, J., Mares, M.L., & Oliver, M.B. (1993). Parents and children's emotional reactions to TV coverage of the Gulf War. In B.S. Greenberg & W. Gantz (Eds.), *Desert Storm and the mass media* (pp. 325–340). Cresskill, NJ: Hampton.

Casper, V. & Theilheimer, R. (2009). *Early childhood education: Learning together*. New York: McGraw-Hill.

Chandler, D. (1997). Children's understanding of what is "real" on television: A review of the literature. *Journal of Educational Media, 22*(1), 65–80.

Chia, S.C. & Poo, L.Y. (2009). Media, celebrities, and fans: An examination of adolescents' media usage and involvement with entertainment celebrities. *Journalism & Mass Communication Quarterly, 86*(1), 23–44.

Christakis, D.A. (2010). Infant media viewing: First, do no harm. *Pediatric Annals, 399,* 578–582.

Collins, W.A. (1983). Interpretation and inference in children's television viewing. In J. Bryant & D.R. Anderson (Eds.), *Children's understanding of television: Research on attention and comprehension* (pp. 125–150). New York: Academic Press.

Common Sense Media (2013). Zero to eight: Children's media use in America 2013. US: Common Sense Media. http://www.commonsensemedia.org/research/zero-eight-childrens-media-use-america. Retrieved December 23, 2013.

Dorr, A. (1983). No shortcuts to judging reality. In J. Bryant & D.R. Anderson (Eds.), *Children's understanding of television: Research on attention and comprehension* (pp. 190–220). New York: Academic Press.

Fitch, M., Huston, A.C. & Wright, J.C. (1993). From television forms to genre schemata: Children's perceptions of television reality. In G.L. Berry & J.K Asamen (Eds.), *Children and television in a changing socio-cultural world* (pp. 38–52). Newbury Park, CA: Sage.

Gilligan, C. (1982). *In a different voice: Psychological theory and women's development*. Cambridge, MA: Harvard University Press.

Götz, M. & Lemish, D. (2012). *Sexy girls, heroes and funny losers: Gender representations in children's TV around the world*. Frankfurt am Main: Peter Lang.

Götz, M., Lemish, D., Aidman, A., & Moon, H. (2005). *Media and the make believe worlds of children: When Harry Potter met Pokémon in Disneyland.* Mahwah, NJ: Lawrence Erlbaum.

Greenfield, P. & Beagles-Roos, J. (1988). Radio vs. television: Their cognitive impact on children of different socio-economic and ethnic groups. *Journal of Communication, 38*(2), 71–72.

Greenfield, P., Farrer, D., & Beagles-Roos, J. (1986). Is the medium the message? An experimental comparison of the effects of radio and television on imagination. *Journal of Applied Developmental Psychology, 7*(4), 237–255.

Hansen, F., Rasmussen, J., Martensen, A., & Tufte, B. (Eds.). (2002). *Children – Consumption, advertising and media.* Copenhagen: Copenhagen Business School Press.

Harrison, K. & Cantor, J. (1999). Tales from the screen: Enduring fright reactions to scary media. *Media Psychology, 1*(2), 97–116.

Hawkins, R. (1977). The dimensional structure of children's perceptions of TV reality. *Communication Research, 4*(3), 299–320.

Himmelweit, H.T., Oppenheim, A.N., & Vince, P. (1958). *Television and the child.* London: Oxford University Press.

Hoffner, C. (1996). Children's wishful identification and para-social interaction with favorite television characters. *Journal of Broadcasting and Electronic Media, 40,* 289–402.

Hoffner, C. & Cantor, J. (1991). Perceiving and responding to mass media characters. In J. Bryant & D. Zillman (Eds.), *Responding to the screen: Reception and reaction processes* (pp. 63–101). Hillsdale, NJ: Lawrence Erlbaum.

Hoffner, C. & Haefner, M. (1993). Children's affective responses to news coverage of the war. In B.S. Greenberg & W. Gantz (Eds.), *Desert Storm and the mass media* (pp. 364–380). Cresskill, NJ: Hampton.

Huizinga, M, Nikkelen, S.W.C., & Valkenburg, P.M. (2013). Children's media use and its relation to attention, hyperactivity, and impulsivity. In D. Lemish (Ed.), *The Routledge international handbook of children, adolescents, and media* (pp. 179–185). New York: Routledge.

IZI (2004). *Children watching war: A few reminders about potential contribution of the media to children in times of conflict & war.* Munich, Germany: International Central Institute for Youth and Educational Television (IZI). http://www.br-online.de/jugend/izi/guidelines/reminders.htm. Retrieved July 25, 2014.

Jung, J-Y., Lin, W-Y., & Kim, Y-C. (2012). The dynamic relationship between East Asian adolescents' use of the internet and their use of other media. *New Media & Society, 14*(6), 969–986.

Kohlberg, L. (Ed.). (1984). *The psychology of moral development: The nature of validity of moral stages.* Cambridge, MA: Harper and Row.

Kolucki, B. & Lemish, D. (2011). *Communicating with children: Principles and practices to nurture, inspire, excite, educate and heal.* New York: Communication for Development Unit, UNICEF. http://www.unicef.org/cwc. Retrieved July 25, 2014.

Lemish, D. (1987). Viewers in diapers: The early development of television viewing. In T. Lindlof (Ed.), *Natural audiences: Qualitative research of media uses and effects* (pp. 33–57). Norwood, NJ: Ablex.

Lemish, D. (1997). Kindergartners' understandings of television: A cross-cultural comparison. *Communication Studies, 48*(2), 109–126.

Lemish, D. (2010). *Screening gender on children's television: The views of producers around the world.* London: Routledge.

Lemish, D. & Alon-Tirosh, M. (forthcoming). "I was really scared": A cross-cultural comparison of reconstructing childhood fearful viewing experiences. In M. Moshe (Ed.), *The emotion industry*. New York: Science Publishers, Inc.

Lin, W.-Y., Zhang, X., Jung, J.-Y., & Kim, Y.-C. (2013). From the wired to wireless generation? Investigating teens' internet use through the mobile phone. *Telecommunication Policy, 37*, 651–661.

Livingstone, S. & Bovill, M. (2001). *Children and their changing media environment: A European comparative study*. Mahwah, NJ: Lawrence Erlbaum.

MacBeth, T.M. (Ed.). (1996). *Tuning in to young viewers: Social science perspectives on television*. Thousand Oaks, CA: Sage.

Mander, J. (1978). *Four arguments for the elimination of television*. New York: Quill.

Messenger Davies, M. (1989). *Television is good for your kids*. London: Hilary Shipman.

Messenger Davies, M. (1997). *Fake, fact, and fantasy: Children's interpretations of television reality*. Mahwah, NJ: Lawrence Erlbaum.

Neuman, S.B. (1991). *Literacy in the television age*. Norwood, NJ: Ablex.

Piaget, J. (1969). *The origins of intelligence in the child*. New York: International University Press.

Piaget, J. & Inhelder, B. (1969). *The psychology of the child*. New York: Basic Books.

Raviv, A., Bar-Tal, D., Raviv, A., & Ben-Horin, A. (1996). Adolescent idolization of pop singers: Causes, expressions, and reliance. *Journal of Youth and Adolescence, 25*(5), 631–750.

Rolandelli, D.R. (1989). Children and television: The visual superiority effect reconsidered. *Journal of Broadcasting and Electronic Media, 33*(1), 69–81.

Rosenkoetter, L.I. (2001). Television and morality. In D.G. Singer & J.L. Singer (Eds.), *Handbook of children and the media* (pp. 463–473). Thousand Oaks, CA: Sage.

Salomon, G. (1981). Introducing AIME: The assessment of children's mental involvement with television. In H. Kelly & H. Gardner (Eds.), *Viewing children through television: New directions for child development* (pp. 89–102). San Francisco, CA: Jossey-Bass.

Schramm, W., Lyle, J., & Parker, E.B. (1961). *Television in the lives of our children*. Stanford, CA: Stanford University Press.

Singer, D.G. (1993). Creativity of children in a television world. In G.L. Berry & J.K. Asamen (Eds.), *Children and television: Images in a changing sociocultural world* (pp. 73–86). Newbury Park, CA: Sage.

Singer, J.L. & Singer, D.G. (1976). Can TV stimulate imaginative play? *Journal of Communication, 26*, 74–80.

Singer, J.L. & Singer, D.G. (1981). *Television, imagination, and aggression: A study of preschoolers*. Hillsdale, NJ: Lawrence Erlbaum.

Singer, J.L. & Singer, D.G. (1983). Implications of childhood television viewing of cognition, imagination and emotion. In J. Bryant & D.R. Anderson (Eds.), *Children's understanding of television: Research on attention and comprehension* (pp. 265–295). New York: Academic Press.

Smith, R. (1986). Television addiction. In J. Bryant & D. Zillman (Eds.), *Perspectives on media effects* (pp. 109–128). Hillsdale, NJ: Lawrence Erlbaum.

Smith, S.L. & Moyer-Guse, E. (2006). Children and the war on Iraq: Developmental differences in fear responses to TV news coverage. *Media Psychology, 8*(3), 213–237.

Smith, S.L. & Wilson, B.J. (2000). Children's reactions to a television news story: The impact of video footage and proximity of the crime. *Communication Research, 27*(5), 641–673.

Smith, S.L. & Wilson, B.J. (2002). Children's comprehension of and fear reactions to television news. *Media Psychology, 4*, 1–26.

The Teletubbies (1999). *TelevIZIon, 12*(2).

Tilley, C.L. (2013). Children's print culture: tradition and innovation. In D. Lemish (Ed.), *The Routledge international handbook of children, adolescents, and media* (pp. 87–94). New York: Routledge.

Trawick-Smith, J. (2010). *Early child development: A multicultural perspective,* 5th *edition.* Columbus, OH: Merrill.

Valkenburg, P.M. (2001). Television and the child's developing imagination. In D.G. Singer & J.L. Singer (Eds.), *Handbook of children and the media* (pp. 121–134). Thousand Oaks, CA: Sage.

Valkenburg, P.M. (2004). *Children's responses to the screen: A media psychological approach.* Mahwah, NJ: Lawrence Erlbaum.

Valkenburg, P.M. & Cantor, J. (2002). The development of a child into a consumer. In S.L. Calvert, A.B. Jordan, & R.R. Cocking (Eds.), *Children in the digital age: Influences of electronic media on development* (pp. 201–214). Westport, CT: Praeger.

Valkenburg, P.M. & van der Voort, T.H.A (1994). Influence of TV on daydreaming and creative imagination: A review of research. *Psychological Bulletin, 116*, 316–339.

Van Evra, J. (2004). *Television and child development* (3rd ed.). Mahwah, NJ: Lawrence Erlbaum.

Walma van der Molen, J.H. & Konjin, E.A. (2007). Dutch children's emotional reactions to news about the Second Gulf War: Influence of media exposure, identification, and empathy. In D. Lemish & M. Götz (Eds.), *Children and media in times of conflict and war* (pp. 75–97). Cresskill, NJ: Hampton.

Williams, T.M. (1986). *The impact of television: A natural experiment in three communities* (pp. 361–393). Orlando, FL: Academic Press.

Winn, M. (1977). *The Plug in Drug.* New York: Viking.

Wober, M. & Young, B.M. (1993). British children's knowledge of, emotional reactions to, and ways of making sense of the war. In B.S. Greenberg & W. Gantz (Eds.), *Desert Storm and the mass media* (pp. 381–394). Cresskill, NJ: Hampton.

3

Media, Learning, and Literacy

Media are among the most significant of the socializing agents of our times. They teach us facts, behaviors, values, norms about how the world works, and they contribute to the formation of worldviews. All these take place even when these media have no formal educational or instructional intentions, a clear curriculum, or a formalized set of educational goals. In many studies, children report that they use the entire range of media content as a learning environment.

This acknowledgment leads us to discuss the comparison between two primary socialization agents – media and the school system, with the latter alone usually recognized as the primary socializing agent designed by societies all over the world to teach and instruct children and youth. Consideration of the claim that media are a socializing agent involves the following questions: What are the advantages and disadvantages of media as an educational and instructional environment in comparison with schooling? In what ways do they compete and complement each other? What are the possibilities of integrating media within school systems and for integrating formal schooling within media? How effective is learning from media? What kind of learning is required for today's world and the foreseeable future?

Media and School – Two Educational Systems

Though many writers see media as an alternative form of schooling, the two are fundamentally distinct as educational systems. The alternative line of argument follows the theoretical claims of technological determinism according to which human civilizations are shaped to a large degree by their technologies. However,

Children and Media: A Global Perspective, First Edition. Dafna Lemish.
© 2015 John Wiley & Sons, Inc. Published 2015 by John Wiley & Sons, Inc.
Companion Website: www.wiley.com/go/lemish/childrenandmedia

opponents argue that aside from differences in content preferences, these two socializers involve dissimilar technologies and, indeed, different cultures.

The following is an integrated list of the major differences between the two educative systems that apply to most societies:[1]

Institutional goals: School systems have been established with the primary aim of functioning as educational and instructional settings. This aim drives everything that happens within the system. As an over-generalization, one can argue that most schools seek to teach the specific skills, knowledge, and values delineated in formal curricula. Most learning, even in the most democratic and open forms, takes place through a process of interaction, primarily with teachers, who are required by society to undergo training in order to qualify for teaching credentials that attest to their having achieved the requisite education, skills, and knowledge. In all societies, the office in charge of education (be it a national or district ministry of education, a community educational board, or a private organization) applies different forms of centralized supervision and testing to ensure that schools operate according to goals determined for them by society.

In contrast, commercial media, the most extensive form of media institution (i.e., as opposed to educational or public media institutions) disavow having any educational aims or responsibilities. Above all else, their *raison d'être* is to make a profit by attracting as wide an audience as possible in order to sell advertisers' products. Accordingly, the sole measure of a program's influence is its "rating," or web page views, clicks, downloads, or "likes" – that is, the size of the consuming audience.

Language: Learning in schools is directed primarily to verbal languages – in spoken, written, and print modes. At their core, all verbal languages are abstract, their signs are social conventions, and their interpretation involves assigning meanings to signs, be they written letters or audio sounds. Verbal languages are linear, as they require expression in a particular word order, according to each language's grammar and syntax; and, their comprehension as well as interpretation requires systematic scanning of either written or spoken texts (i.e., one needs to listen to the sentences or read the lines in order to make sense of the content).

Screen culture, on the other hand, is based on the audio-visual language. Its visual dimension is material with comprehension moving from perceiving the concrete to abstract interpretation (e.g., from perceiving interlocking glances to the abstract concept of love). It is simultaneous, holistic, and non-linear. One interprets the moving pictures (changing in front of our eyes commonly about 24 times per second) as a whole entity, since detailed linear analysis undertaken with verbal texts is impossible, aside from storyline. Internet surfing complicates matters even further, as branching out through hyperlinks creates a collage of many layers of verbal and audio-visual texts.

The fact that the two systems emphasize different forms of expression requires that children apply different cognitive skills in their engagement with the text: dominance of the verbal in the school culture and dominance of the visual and non-linear in the screen culture. Furthermore, while formal schooling focuses on one form of language at a time, media use often entails multi-tasking and multi-modality – moving back and forth from one type of linguistic system to another, be it verbal, audio, visual, or one of their many combinations.

Hierarchy: In curricular terms, schools are linear institutions in that pupils progress via accumulative knowledge and skills, demarked as moving from lower to higher grades. Since schooling is mandatory in most societies, children must progress through a unified course of study from kindergarten, or even earlier in some societies, and continue on in a fixed order (e.g., first grade, second grade, and so forth, with a few exceptions for those who either skip a grade or are held back) to the grade or achievement level mandated, or until the mandated school leaving age. One key organizing principle of the school curriculum is the use of a linear learning progression. For example, curriculum planners assume that it is impossible for most children to learn to multiply numbers without having mastered the basic motor skill required to hold a pencil, visual recognition of numbers, and the complex concept of the function and value of numbers. Similarly, it would have been extremely difficult to learn details of the history of African nations in the tenth grade without having mastered reading and writing skills in the first and second grades, and so forth.

Media, on the other hand, are non-linear in organization and learning progression. One can access programs, internet sites, or games (i.e., equivalent to school "classes," if you will) without skill and knowledge prerequisites, at any age, and without having earned passing grades in previous classes. While many specific media contents have hierarchical characteristics built within them (e.g., playing a game that requires moving through steps of mastering skills), as an institution they do not require that one "graduate" from particular involvement in a website or video game in order to have access to another website or video game. Indeed, the internet is overtly non-linear in design, allowing flexible access to vast fields of information and stimulation through the use of hyperlinks, jumping back and forth from one site to another with no "pre-requisites" or required order of accessibility.

Unity of time and place: Most schools and most of the activities that take place within them are characterized by unity of time and place; that is, most of the pupils in a particular class engage in the same topic during a predetermined time period. For example, the school day starts at a specific hour and pupils are expected to be on time; a math class starts exactly when the bell rings at 9 a.m. in the home classroom of the fifth-grade class; and, from that point on, all students are to be engaged in math-related activities. Any attempt to be involved in another activity (e.g., doodling, drawing, chatting, sending a note to a friend, talking on the mobile phone, eating, reading a book, doing homework for another class, or even daydreaming) can be negatively sanctioned.

In contrast, media use lacks any uniformity of time and place. No one has to view the same program or access the same Facebook page at the same time and at the same place. On the contrary, most media consumption is done independently.

Each child can view, surf, play, text, according to his or her own schedule and preference, can stop in the middle, switch to another "class," delay the activity, and be involved in many secondary activities at the same time.

Compulsion: Formal schooling is a direct intervention into children's lives. They hardly have any say in the matter, certainly not in societies that impose mandatory schooling. Indeed, even parents can have limited involvement, including lack of choice of the schools their children will attend. Furthermore, upon becoming a participant in this system, children are required to assume a host of responsibilities and tasks undertaken through a normalized system of positive reinforcement and negative sanctions (e.g., compliments, grades, punishments). And, throughout their schooling, children are almost completely under the control and supervision of adults – especially during their early years.

Media consumption, on the other hand, is mostly undertaken voluntarily, and involves limited adult supervision. It neither makes demands nor does it involve obligations beyond the social relationships created within it. It does not impose itself, require formal testing of achievement or motivation, and is more often than not very enjoyable for participants.

Peers: In mass schooling contexts, children learn from and are influenced directly and indirectly by their peers, in terms of ideas and experiences, pace of learning, disturbances, and social pressures. Most children in each class are of similar age and often quite alike with regard to other demographic variables, such as socioeconomic status, ethnicity, and religion. Most contemporary schools direct pupils' learning according to non-pupil-specific learning goals, general curricula, and standard achievement levels, without necessarily developing the individual needs, learning style, and abilities of each student. Alternatively, individual tutoring is often undertaken in progressive educational systems, in conjunction with reduced class size, small group work, and division of pupils according to their interests, needs, and/or achievement levels.

In contrast, learning from the media is usually undertaken within a multi-age family unit, in physical isolation from one's peer group, and occasionally in the intimacy of one or two close friends. Media curricula are not tailored individually. On the contrary, producers often aspire to attract as wide and diverse an audience as possible, indeed to be as global as possible. For example, *Angry Birds*, a popular video and mobile game (currently the highest downloaded game of all time) is promoted indiscriminately, to children all over the world. That is, again in comparison with schools, there is no special version of this game for exceptionally bright children in Nepal, Spanish-speaking children who immigrated to the USA, or children of the Islamic faith in Algeria. In conclusion, programs, movies, games, and websites that are popular globally are offered to the entire population of children in the world, regardless of culture, demographics, or socio-economic differences.

We should note, however, that the exponential growth of social networking has re-instated the central role of peers into some aspects of media consumption, so making it highly relationship based. We will return to this important aspect of media consumption and learning in Chapter 6.

Activity: Active forms of learning accompany or are required for many schooling activities; for example, homework, practice, participation in group discussion, field trips, work on projects, and memorization. Here the contemporary assumption of educators is that active learning is more efficient and has the potential to be more meaningful for pupils.

In contrast, learning from television, specifically, is mainly a product of cognitive and affective processes initiated by the child, with occasional reinforcement through face-to-face or mediated interaction. Beyond early childhood, most children are not particularly physically active in front of a screen (beyond some keyboard typing or screen touching), do not consciously practice or memorize what is being learned while viewing, do not process the concepts and skills through writing homework assignments or preparing for tests, and do not go on field trips to places portrayed in favorite programs.

We should note, in this regard, that digital media have blurred these distinctions dramatically, as much media engagement today is also active in nature and children are understood to be part of a *participatory culture*, belonging to social networks that socialize them into the adult world. Gaming, in particular, involves a great deal of practice and learning that facilitate problem solving and access to higher levels of challenges.

Delay of gratification: Studying in school requires an ability to delay gratification. Efforts invested in a language, physics, or geography class are part of a long process undertaken by the child to attain an education and the skills necessary for what is, admittedly, from the child's point of view, a vague and unclear future – often described to be something that will be satisfying and economically sufficient. Even receiving gratification from reading a book, completing an assignment, or earning an award requires long-term investment by the child.

In contrast, much media consumption, be it viewing television, playing games, posting a photo on Facebook, or texting, is characterized by immediate gratification, as well as the chance to derive pleasure and express a variety of emotional reactions – laughter, suspense, identification, excitement, sadness – that do not require self-restraint in favor of some kind of a future.

These and other substantial differences point to the many advantages of media over school as a system of learning preferred by children. From their point of view, the media environment is, indeed, a culture they enter voluntarily. It makes few demands upon them and provides complex gratifications over which they exert much more control. Furthermore, some media offerings include a preoccupation with interpersonal relationships, struggles of good and evil, or love and hate among other themes that seem to many children to be much more relevant, attractive, and exciting than many of the topics studied in school, which can seem irrelevant and removed from their reality. Media, thus, seem to offer young viewers a variety of alternative ways of learning about the world and oneself that challenge the central place that the school system has had in children's education prior to the media revolution that started in the mid-twentieth century.

Note that the list of comparisons above was composed several decades ago, specifically for the purpose of comparing the institutions of television and school, such that the differences blur with regard to several criteria when we add digital media to the mix. Also, this discussion assumes a traditional schooling system, the one with which many of us are familiar around the world, but this system may be changing too. Dramatic changes taking place during the second decade of the twenty-first century with the growth of media-infused online education, for example, may transform many of the characteristics listed above of formal school systems and facilitate individual tailoring of schooling.

Viewing Television and School Performance

In reality, most children spend considerable time in both educational systems – school and media. On most days they pass from one to the other interchangeably, having learned to manage the differing expectations and conventions of both worlds. Yet, most of the criticism levied at television, in this domain, focuses on how extensive media use might affect school-based learning performance. Four main hypotheses regarding this presumed causal relationship are extant in today's research literature. Note that they are heavily ground in television viewing:[2]

1. *Displacement*: This hypothesis claims that television displaces other activities (as discussed in Chapter 2), including reading, doing homework, and completing other intellectually oriented assignments. As a consequence, skills required for achieving satisfactory performance levels in school are neglected.
2. *Information processing*: This claim asserts that accumulated viewing of television affects children's cognitive abilities, as it requires different forms of information processing than those deemed needed for school-based learning.
3. *Gratification*: According to this line of argument, heavy viewing of television affects children's expectations for school-based learning processes. Indeed, the comparison is quite stark as the relatively slow-paced and long-term goal orientation of school learning stands in contrast to children's expectation that school activities will take place at a quick pace, involve constant stimulation, immediate satisfaction, innovation and surprise – as occurs during television viewing. As a result of this gap, children – so the argument goes –have short attention spans, difficulty delaying gratification, and consequentially are bored, impatient, and develop as well as demonstrate negative attitudes toward schooling.
4. *Interest stimulation*: An opposing school of thought to the gratifications hypothesis claims the opposite: namely, television encourages learning as it stimulates curiosity, widens the child's interests, and reinforces a desire for learning. In addition, it enriches the child's world in specific subject areas, including those studied in school (e.g., vocabulary, civic studies, science, geography, culture).

Thus far, research attempts that seek to gather empirical data to support these claims have been limited in scope, short term, and unsystematic. As a result, none of these hypotheses has either accumulated or, therefore, been grounded in a solid empirical base of research findings. Thus, the arguments for one or another of these approaches are advanced using philosophic or even ideological claims.

Many researchers would argue, too, that it is the learning environment of the family that determines the nature of television's effects on learning, not the medium itself, as the *deterministic* approach would have had us believe.

This having been noted, there is some evidence to support the negative association between heavy viewing of television and basic traditional literacy skills (i.e., reading, writing, and math), and school achievement more generally. For example, several large-scale US research projects conducted in the 1980s found that heavy television viewing was associated with lower scores in reading, writing, and math tests in all age groups, regardless of gender and socio-economic status.[3] However, very light television viewing, too, was associated with lower scores! The conclusion offered is that this is a typical "bell-shaped" phenomenon: There is a positive correlation with achievements for up to an optimum number of viewing hours per week, but beyond that number this relationship reverses itself and becomes more negative as the number of viewing hours increases or decreases.

Since these findings are incapable of providing us with answers regarding the direction of causality, we return to our basic questions: Is heavy viewing of television responsible for low achievements in school subjects, or is it the case that increases in pupil viewing hours are a result of low achievement in school? Or, perhaps, both heavy viewing as well as lower achievement are associated with external variables, such as emotional difficulties, social problems, and learning disabilities?

One promising approach argues that perhaps good students are more aware and more in control of their own cognitive processes as well as their allocation of attention and, thus, manage their studies as well as their television viewing more efficiently. Support for this line of argument is derived from studies conducted in the USA and Europe that concentrated specifically on relationships between television viewing, academic achievement, and reading skills.[4] Researchers found that, as a general rule, the number of viewing hours (over two to three hours of viewing per day; numbers fluctuate according to the research method used) were associated in all age levels with the lowest reading grades, while viewing less than two hours per day was correlated with higher scores. Researchers also found that the home environment plays a central role, for example: Children raised in a reading culture at home receive more encouragement and assistance from their family; having a television in a child's bedroom was found to be negatively associated with test scores. Most importantly, several of the studies suggested there are long-term negative effects of early heavy exposure to entertainment television on educational aspirations and achievements.

The reciprocal nature of this relationship suggests that television viewing is particularly attractive to children who find reading to be demanding (perhaps those with learning disabilities or diminished IQ scores). As a result, children experiencing difficulties in school continue to have less enjoyment from reading out of school, engage in it less than others in their class, and spend more time viewing television. Researchers believe that this argument explains the finding that by the time they reach high school, children at the lowest performance level score less on intelligence tests, are from a lower socio-economic level, read less, and view more television. Accordingly, to claim that limiting viewing time alone will improve children's performance is inaccurate. Rather, children whose learning advances in accordance with their capabilities requires parents who are willing and able to encourage as well as to facilitate their reading behaviors.

Complementary studies that support these findings found that it is not necessarily the amount of viewing time alone that is associated with a host of literacy skills, but the kinds of programs viewed, on the one hand, and the kinds of books read, on the other hand. For example, heavy viewers of light entertainment and violent cartoons were found to score lower on a host of tests; and the limited reading they engaged in was found to be television related (e.g., easy-reading books developed around popular television series).

In summary, there is a body of research that points out the possibility of a negative relationship between the amount of television viewed, combined with specific kinds of television genres, and performance in school, including literacy skills. Furthermore, no evidence has accumulated so far regarding the possibility of there being a positive contribution of television to school performance (option 4, above).

Interestingly, evidence coming from the more medically oriented research literature is unequivocal about the adverse effects of television viewing. As discussed later in this chapter, this conclusion is completely reversed when it comes to a discussion of educational programs designed to advance learning. Researchers agree that the relationships are reciprocal, certainly not uni-directional, and are complicated by a host of variables, such as the socio-economic status of the family, media access, family communication, parental mediation, and specific attitudes toward both viewing and reading. In short, viewing television is only one of the many activities that take place in the home environment that have significance for the development of children's cognitive skills and educational achievements. Therefore, negative aspects of children's lives, including low achievement scores, cannot be attributed solely to one of these factors.

The Audio-Visual Language and Cognitive Skills

As mentioned previously, one intriguing hypothesis suggests that various media cultivate different cognitive skills and, therefore, also affect learning processes in different ways. A few central assumptions lie at the heart of this field of research regarding the nature of the different media, and those media in which they converge, as referred to in the concept of audio-visual language: Screens are distinguished from print as they combine or converge various forms of communication – visuals, speech, voices, music, print. Audio-visual language employs systems of signs that represent meaning in a similar way to verbal language. This language has its own codes and conventions that are expressed to communicate various domains of content. For example, the codes and conventions employed in many popular music videos are quite different than those applied in news broadcasts.

This leads us to ask questions regarding the use of different media platforms, such as: What skills are involved in *visual intelligence*? How can they be measured? How do these skills compare with those attained via verbal intelligence? The existing research into such questions has sought to point out the differences in comprehension and learning that can be attributed to the structural components of the dominant languages of each medium. These studies are supported by evidence from neuro-psychological research that suggests that different symbol systems are processed in different parts of the human brain. For example, the left hemisphere processes sign systems, including verbally transmitted information, while the right hemisphere is more active in processing numerical and figurative information.

When we interpret visual images, including those on television, we do so in a manner similar to the way we perceive the reality of the physical and social worlds. More than our acquaintance with the codes and conventions of television, it is our ability to elicit references from representation that forms the basis of our ability to make sense of it. This capability is different from the way we make sense of things in other languages – such as verbal or mathematical, when we are dependent on familiarity with the signification system (e.g., letters, numbers). Put differently, making sense of television content (at least on a basic level) does not require learning pre-requisite skills, as do other languages, as we practice interpreting visual messages in real life constantly. This characteristic helps to explain why, for example, very young babies already show an interest in screens and picture books without any training (i.e., before being able to read), as well as why children – with communication disabilities such as deafness or blindness – have difficulties interpreting other forms of significations, such as those associated with language.

Furthermore, the special characteristics of visual language, which are fundamentally concrete, are assumed to restrict the development of the more complex abstract-type of thought. Visual language is limited in its ability to refer to the non-visual (e.g., a strong smell), abstract terms (e.g., conclusion), and terms of negation (e.g., the absence of something; "never"), although it can arrive at an understanding of the meaning indirectly or through a concrete example. Thus, while the picture on the screen can present specific instances (e.g., a specific house), words can express the systematic regularity of an entire group of incidences (e.g., the concept of "home"). Visual language, according to this line of argument, deals with representing reality, but does not have the ability to make propositions regarding it. The individual viewer is left with the task of bridging between the concrete picture and the abstract idea behind it.

Finally, we can add that while most humans learn not only to understand verbal language as well as to produce it, until recently, such was not the case for the visual language of television: Most children are capable of interpreting television messages, but only few ever had the opportunity to actually produce them in a television program. This has changed dramatically with the advent of digital media, as smartphones, for example, include still and simple video recording mechanisms easily applied by even preschool children.

This having been noted, the central question of concern regarding television viewing remains mostly unanswered: What, if any, cognitive skills are acquired through our experiences with the visual language? Such a determination can be made in at least two different ways: First, by studying cognitive processes activated during screen viewing with a view to seeking to understand how their repetitive use cultivates the skills necessary for making sense of audio-visual content. Second, by tracing the use of skills required and acquired that are applied for other purposes aside from watching televised texts, such as remembering information or using screen content in mental processes independent of the medium.

The development of special viewing skills

Due to the theoretical and methodological complexity of the topic, the study of the cognitive implications of visual language has focused on specific skills and not general thought processes. These skills are understood to be part of *spatial intelligence*, a domain of intelligence that involves the ability to mentally understand spatial relationships accurately and to imagine the implications of changes within them (e.g., the ability to visually represent walking from one place to another).

In seeking to determine whether viewing television cultivates skills needed for spatial intelligence, several studies focused on the capability of television and film to present various points of view (e.g., to observe the same character from different angles). One experiment presented children with video segments in which the camera moved from one point of view to another. This tested the children's abilities to mentally represent such movements by applying the representation to new situations outside of viewing (e.g., in picture-cards). The rationale for this approach was that camera movements on the screen imitate mental processes required by a child engaged in spatial intelligence tasks, thus facilitating them. Indeed, the results supported the hypothesis that viewing such movements improved children's task performance related to spatial intelligence.[5] However, correlation studies produced contradictory evidence that did not support this finding.[6]

The rival explanation offered suggests that due to editing, television does not provide the whole range of visual experience of changing points of view that occurs in reality. It also limits the range of points of view and does not offer the child an open space for active experimentation with all options. This argument is particularly relevant for young children, as visual skills developed at this age are dependent on physical experiences in real spaces. It is possible that following the acquisition of these skills, children can further develop them by mediated experiences, but no evidence has been gathered to date establishing that these visual portrayals can replace actual real-life experience.[7]

A somewhat different but associated concern relates to the investment children make in interpreting television content. Here the argument offered is that mere exposure to screens is a necessary but insufficient condition for gaining control of visual language. Research suggests that screen exposure can only affect cognitive skills when children attempt to interpret and make meaning out of it. That is, the more children invest mental effort in processing information, the more they get out of it. Here, age is a significant consideration, as it is in other cognitive matters: Younger children have limited "channel-capacity" (i.e., the amount of stimuli they can absorb at a time) and, therefore, have less practice in processing television information regardless of the amount of time they spend watching it. Channel capacity is also dependent on competition with other sources of information operating simultaneously. This may explain why children perform better in an experimental situation: They are not distracted by competing sources of information typically available in home viewing, such as the presence of other conversations, music, phone calls, or street noises.[8] This has become an acute question for researchers with the advent of "multi-tasking" with various media simultaneously.

The concept of Amount of Invested Mental Effort (AIME) discussed in Chapter 2 in relation to attention to television is useful in this regard, as well. Here the working assumption is that a greater AIME leads to improved learning skills, such as improvement of memory, comprehension, and ability to deduct conclusions. However, AIME is influenced, among other things, by the way children perceive what is expected of them, difficulty of content level, expected gratifications yielded, and self-confidence in their ability to make sense of the text. Children perceive viewing screens as a much less demanding assignment in comparison to reading books, as it allows for making meaning in a more sensory manner, appears to be "self-explanatory" and "real," and can be enjoyed easily.

Overall, we need to remember that viewing screens is not a uniform experience, and this discussion is an example of the multiple layers and complexities involved in it. For example, differences in program levels include entertainment versus educational, and adult versus children's programming. Children make use of different cues in the programs to estimate its level of difficulty and the AIME required to interpret it. In addition, the level of AIME is affected by environmental factors (e.g., seating arrangements, screen size, noise), social norms (e.g., the way others are treating the viewing situation), or viewing motivation.[9]

In terms of research results, children with higher mental abilities who had negative attitudes toward television and invested less AIME in it were least able to learn from it. However, when children are directed to learn from viewing a particular program (i.e., their perception of the viewing situation is changed), they increase their AIME and the level of their mental functioning improves. That is to say, children are capable of employing skills already mastered in interpreting television content when they are motivated to do so. This conclusion leads us to suggest an intriguing hypothesis: Children taught to treat viewing screens as a serious endeavor will learn more than children who are not given a positive view of a program or television viewing. Here, our working assumption is that television is an easy activity that requires minimal exertion and thus that learning is based, at least in part, on children's prior conceptions of what it means to view television rather than on the nature of the medium itself. However, even if children invested a high AIME in the viewing, the question still remains: Is learning from television different from any other form of learning? And, if so, does learning from television have any advantage over learning from other media, such as books or radio? Is it more – or less – effective? Do different media have relative advantages with regard to particular subject matter? Evidence from research regarding these questions is to date equivocal, and remarkably, quite dated.

Research findings suggest a rival approach might be considered: Rather than regarding visual and verbal cultures as competing with or in contradiction to one another, perhaps learning requires integrating them in various forms of multi-media systems in order to exhaust the possibilities concealed within the use of varied forms of signification systems. In an environment saturated with audio-visual stimuli to which children are exposed from birth, this proposal may turn out to be an extremely valuable line of research to pursue.

Learning from Educational Television

The inability of psychological studies to, so far, provide conclusive explanations with regard to audio-visual language and cognitive processes contributed to the development of another body of knowledge concerned with educational television, and the intentional employment of television to achieve specific educational and instructional goals.

At the core of this endeavor is the claim that the content of popular television does not necessarily exhaust the potential of the medium and that with appropriate professional investment it is possible to use it in significantly more valuable ways, such as to decrease social knowledge gaps, teach diverse subject matter, convey value-laden messages, and develop specific skills.

Interestingly, research findings regarding the negative effects of television actually serve to reinforce this line of argument: If children are capable of learning negative messages from television, it should be possible to use it to teach them some positive ones as well.

Varying cultural needs led to a rise in interest in the educational potential of television. This interest developed in the USA during the educational crisis of the 1950s, spawned then by the alleged deterioration in the ability of American society to compete with the technological and scientific developments of post-World-War II industrialized countries. Proponents of this argument claimed that this situation existed, in part, due to a teacher shortage, low level of teacher training, and outmoded curricula.

Beyond the USA, in developing countries around the world, television is perceived to be a symbol and potential catalyst of national development, modernization, and progress. Furthermore, television is thought to be among the best means available to advance social change through the educational system since it is accessible, democratic, highly attractive, multi-sensual, and its broadcast channels are relatively inexpensive for audience viewing. Hence, many hopes were invested in the ability of television to contribute to the resolution of a variety of social hardships.

At the same time, indeed since its onset, some critics opposed educational television, claiming that its "robotic," non-personalized nature could harm teachers' employment, damage interpersonal relationships between pupils and teachers, prohibit feedback from and interaction with television teachers, and lead pupils to perceive their classroom teachers as boring and inferior in comparison with their television counterparts. Logistic concerns voiced included the financial expense involved in special productions, scheduling difficulties within the school day, the problem of creating programs relevant to children's lives, and the need for continuous updating.[10]

Critics in developing countries showed strong reticence when former colonizers donated, as was common practice at the time, complete infrastructures of educational television along with initial training and supervision of personnel. They argued that educational television would stimulate a process of cultural intervention by outside forces, as well as inspire eventual takeover by commercial television.

Two different styles of educational television emerged amidst the familiar tension between high aspirations and deep fears that characterized the introduction of each new medium: The first style employed excellent television teachers who led the educational process with the assistance of less well-trained teachers in the classes themselves, thus overcoming problems such as large classes and shortage of well-educated teachers. This was particularly the case for many of the developing countries. A second style gradually became the preferred approach in industrialized countries: High-quality, attractive forms of educational television capable of competing with commercial television. This second style serves as a complement to rather than a substitute for the classroom teacher.

Here, early in our discussion, we need to clarify that the term educational television is inclusive of instructional television. The two concepts often overlap or boundaries are blurred: Educational television usually has more general, educational goals, while instructional television concentrates on specific subjects taught in school.

As with many other topics discussed in this book, in-depth analysis of educational television would require discussion of complicated educational/pedagogical issues that are beyond the purview of this volume, such as teaching methods, curricula development, and learning principles. Thus, we will focus mainly on the characteristics of educational television as a medium, as a world of substance, and as a social resource – and on the contribution of research in this area to understanding the role of television in the lives of young children.

Historically, educational television did not soar in its early days. Viewing surveys suggested, repeatedly, that when given a choice, children preferred, unequivocally, to watch commercial over educational television. It became clear that in order for educational television to survive, it needed to undergo a dramatic transformation from its focus on school instruction to programming that broadens children's intellectual horizons and challenges them in enjoyable ways – an approach referred to now as *quality television*. A breakthrough in this transformation came about with the establishment of the Children's Television Workshop (CTW) in New York, best known for its revolutionary educational program, *Sesame Street*.

This dramatic change of approach included the following features: adoption of commercial formats and genres; involvement of psychologists and educational advisors in production stages; addressing unique issues with well-defined and attainable goals; targeting specific audiences; and incorporation of social as well as educational goals. In addition, innovative quality educational programs were designed to employ patterns of standard television programming, including: commercials, quiz shows, suspense movies, drama, and magazine programs. In doing so, they presented educational programming in an attractive and pleasurable manner that also integrated entertainment elements that make learning much more fun (such as, music, humor, rhyming, and animation). The subject matter areas dealt with were limitless: from teaching numbers and letters, to social values such as tolerance, to all forms of "otherness"; from familiarity with the map of the globe to drug prevention programs. They dealt with learning and education in the realms of cognition, emotion, and behavior. The target audience included children and schools as well as for the entire family. In this way, educational television moved from the classroom to the home in order to become part of the family routine.[11]

Formative research was employed throughout this process to guide these efforts so that program developers were provided feedback from children during the production stages, along with summative evaluation research designed to provide feedback regarding the degree of success in achieving program goals. An impressive body of knowledge has accumulated through such studies. In summary, the positive effects educational television had on young audiences were significant in advancing their aptitude and readiness to learn language, to solve logical and mathematical problems, to advance studies in science, technology, social studies, and history, as well as to improve preschool viewers' general readiness for school.

Sesame Street has been researched more than any other television series, with publications numbering in the hundreds of articles, several books, and dozens of theses and dissertations. One might say that while the issue of television violence (discussed in Chapter 4) represents, in a nutshell, the negative potential of television, *Sesame Street* represents, in large degree, the other side of the coin. At the beginning of the twenty-first century, five decades after its inception, more than 120 million children in 140 countries in the world were estimated to view this series on a regular basis. Broadcasting organizations in 20 of these countries collaborated in co-productions, incorporating parts of the original programs side by side with locally produced segments of local flavor, in the spirit of Sesame Workshop and under its supervision.

Given the unprecedented popularity of *Sesame Street*, what can be said about its achievement record in terms of children's learning? The evaluative research involved in the series from the onset provided systematic evidence that regular program viewing helped three- to five-year-olds perform better in tests of skills, such as number and letter recognition and understanding various concepts (such as near–far, wide–narrow). Furthermore, the more children viewed the program, the more their scores improved. These findings were found to hold for all children – both boys and girls, from a variety of ethnic groups, cultures, and geographical areas within the USA and beyond.

Sesame Street also provided a unique opportunity to undertake a comparative examination of questions related to children and television in many other parts of the world.[12] When children in various countries are watching co-productions, they are exposed to a program with the original American features that have proven to be effective but this time embedded in a local cultural context, with a local cast of characters.

In addition, co-productions addressed local educational priorities; for example: The Chinese adapted series included programming related to esthetics, as it was deemed to be missing from the national school curricula; special attention was given to the transition to an open society in Russia; an attempt was made to deal with the Israel–Arab conflict in the Middle East and the "Troubles" in Northern Ireland; and mothers were addressed in an effort to eradicate illiteracy in Turkey. The sensitive topic of children carrying HIV/AIDS was tackled in the South African co-production; and the Panwapa Project, an international multi-media project, which aimed at the development of global citizenship skills and community activism in young children. The approach adopted to achieve local goals by integrating cultural content in the *Sesame Street* format is said to be at the heart of program's unprecedented international success.

While many other original educational projects and education-entertainment (often referred to as *edutainment*[13]) interventions that integrate educational goals with the attractive features of entertainment have been developed worldwide that deserve our attention, few have been accompanied by the systematic use of evaluative research which is integral to the *Sesame Street* production process and which enables us to assess and to discuss their contributions to children's development and pleasure.[14] Evaluating the effectiveness of such interventions is a complicated endeavor as it depends to a large degree on the project's goals, as well as on definitions of effectiveness.

The accumulative evidence suggests that educational television can and does teach. While children from all strata of society and cultures are attracted to successful programs, those living in more culturally enriched environments, who receive parental as well as other types of reinforcement, seem to gain a lot more from sustained viewing. Furthermore, this review suggests that educational television, alone, cannot succeed in place of other socializing agents in closing substantial socio-economic gaps between different populations.

Realizing the potential achievements of educational television requires a substantial investment of economic, technological, and creative resources. The general crisis of public broadcasting worldwide and of educational television, in particular, threatens the continuity of such efforts. Educational broadcasting, which attempts to contribute among other things to the preservation of multiculturalism and local uniqueness, finds itself engaged in a difficult struggle to survive in a world of globalization and commercialization of television. As a result, although it is clear that the potential of educational television is high, its future remains unclear.

Thus, overall, we can claim that educational television can indeed educate, but will it be given the opportunity to do so in the complex world of the twenty-first century? Some observers argue that the need for quality television is all the more acute given dramatic changes taking place in the media environment of children, primarily through the widespread adoption of new media. Major educational broadcasters integrate multi-platform programming in their offerings, and attempt to reinforce their broadcasts with rich websites and mobile applications designed to enhance the educational experiences of children and their caregivers. In doing so, they are also making proactive efforts to compete with the commercial media environment within which children are immersed, and to offer them a quality and commercial-free alternative. This leads us to address the newly emerging domain of research related to the educational potential of new media.

New Media Learning and Literacy

The infiltration of the internet and mobile media into nearly all levels of society has already had a profound influence on traditional schooling. The internet, in particular, has been integrated in many curricular and pedagogical practices of educational systems worldwide, and has become central in discussions about revolutionizing education on all levels.

Many questions have been posed with regard to the goals to be achieved via use of digital technologies in advancing formal learning:

- Are these new ways to learn traditional curriculum subject matter – or new knowledge and skills?
- Is the use of digital technology designed to help the less successful or less advantaged youth – or will the already privileged succeed better here too?
- Should the knowledge produced by creative digital activities be assessed in new ways – or with the tried-and-true means of assessing standardized knowledge developed under the traditional curriculum?
- Should researchers aim to establish the benefits of using technology in traditional curriculum – or in relation to more innovative curricula?
- Does society expect schools to transform their teaching styles and structures to accommodate the radical potential of digital media – or do many parents, employers, and policymakers just want technology to solve present problems with as little disruption as possible?[15]

While these questions are presented as dichotomies, the components could also be conceptualized to be complementary, involving learning via digital media as a process that combines both sides.

Certainly, assessment of the internet's contributions to learning and literacy extends far beyond formal education, to the never-ending process of learning that takes place throughout the life cycle. The internet offers unlimited access to knowledge, with user capability to personalize it according to individual needs, circumstances, cognitive abilities, interests, and learning styles. No wonder that digital literacy is now being considered a third literacy, following linguistic and arithmetic literacies.[16]

Digital literacy is comprised of a host of skills that require learning and practice. The internet's multiple modalities challenge cognitive abilities of processing information from both linguistic as well as audio and visual stimuli. The critical skills involved in the selection of relevant and credible information from among a seemingly infinite number of sources accessible on the net are among those cited most often in the literature. The nature of non-linear surfing of the internet that allows branching out to different links, too, requires capabilities to both focus and integrate sources.

Successful functioning in the rapidly evolving digital culture requires the development and mastery of skills that were not part of traditional print or screen culture literacies. For example, through the internet, many children and youth today are part of a participatory culture,[17] belonging to social networks that play a major role in their learning and socialization into the adult world. The capability to create new knowledge and products, or to re-create them by combining existing sources into something new, requires a host of creative as well as collaborative social skills and social-emotional intelligence.

There are far too many additional, related skills involved in digital culture to enumerate here; it will suffice to note just the following exemplars: gaming skills that cultivate problem-solving experiences; simulation skills that allow interpretation and conceptualization of real-life processes; performativity skills that represent the ability to adopt alternative identities and to improvise, which can lead to new discoveries and insights; multi-tasking and effectively diverting attention from one task to another as necessary; collective intelligence that facilitates the integration of knowledge of many people working on a joint goal; judgment skills for evaluating the reliability and credibility of various sources of information; trans-media navigation through varied forms of presentation and streams of contents; networking skills for searching for information, synthesizing it, and distributing it farther; and negotiation skills to moving seamlessly between various communities differing in social norms and perspectives and adapting to their environments.[18]

What is particularly intriguing about this and similar lists of skills is that they demonstrate that the skills required to function in the current multi-modal media world go far beyond the usual cognitive and technical skills typical of traditional conceptions of literacies. Many of these extended skills are ground in social practices. We will devote more attention to this area in Chapter 6. Here, we note that, given the complexity of this relatively new field of study, we have to date very limited research upon which to draw. Therefore, much of the existing scholarship, while intriguing, is still quite speculative. Undoubtedly, this picture will change thanks to the groups of researchers worldwide who are currently engaged in exploring these challenges.

Gaming and learning

A particularly interesting aspect of digital literacy and learning is related to the rich and developing digital gaming culture and the challenges it poses to our understanding of learning. While most developmental approaches accept gaming to be an effective and pleasurable route for learning in the early years of life, formal schooling has traditionally shied away from incorporating games in formal curricula, and has tended to make a separation between systematic studying required in schools and play activities representing leisure and fun. This distinction is gradually losing its hold, with ever-expanding play opportunities available through screen culture. Digital games, for example, direct goal-oriented behaviors that require practice, development of decision-making strategies, and an ability to handle failure, on the one hand, and positive reinforcement for success, on the other hand, in the form of accumulation of symbolic rewards or advancement to higher levels of the game.[19] Clearly, the content of the games can be anti-social, when teaching violence, racism, and sexism; but it can also – and in many cases does – teach creative thinking, problem solving, conflict resolution, and tolerance. Games are capable of fostering the participatory culture discussed above by encouraging collaboration, identification with other points of view, and compassion toward others. They can, in summary, promote pleasurable and deeply satisfying learning, and, as a result, we can expect that a number of pressing questions will be researched in the very near future about the meaning of "learning" in this context and the ability to transfer gaming experiences to real-life situations.

While digital literacy from a participatory culture perspective is rooted in approaches that do not separate between consuming, creating, and distributing media,[20] it is also very important to remind ourselves, as we conclude the discussion on learning and literacy, of the digital divides still dominating our world. For many low-resource societies around the world that have limited internet access to start with, and therefore lack opportunities to develop digital skills, this discussion is way too futuristic. Those of us living in media-saturated societies often fail to recognize or appreciate the implications of these huge gaps when considering the range of questions addressed in this and other chapters.

Television and Language Acquisition

The last topic to be addressed in this chapter is the concern often raised in public debates about the possible effects of media engagement on language acquisition. Given the dominance of television viewing – among all media activities – during the formative early years of language learning, it makes sense for us to focus on television here. Discussions of possible relationships between viewing television and language acquisition also lack a strong basis in empirical research. Critics of children's viewing of television pose three key arguments: First, the quality of verbal engagement with television is low, since most of its popular programs are linguistically underdeveloped, they employ a limited vocabulary, and present dialogues consisting of short sentences. Second, the visual aspects of television often dominate the viewing experience. Third, the nature of the viewing experience does not allow for reciprocal interactions; that is, language on television is incapable of adjusting itself to meet the needs or interests of each particular viewer or to provide feedback and appropriate reinforcements.

All these traits might lead us to agree with these critics' claim that television is not a valuable source of language acquisition. However, the current literature on the development of language skills consists of an accumulation of research evidence that supports the claim that it is also possible to acquire language through observation of the verbal interactions of others. Such interactions are plentiful on television. They take place in a wide variety of social situations, in formats that become familiar, repeat themselves, and are thus easily learned by the child. In addition, observational studies of young viewers suggest that they are often active during viewing, including with verbal actions, such as talking and singing.[21]

What, then, is the contribution of television viewing to the development of linguistic skills? Do children learn language from viewing television? Does viewing inhibit language development? While the answers to these questions are equivocal at this time, scholars agree, first, that learning is dependent, among other things, on the type of linguistic skill examined. This leads us to an additional set of questions: Is the influence of television viewing on the development of proper grammar different from its influence on vocabulary accumulation and understanding? Second, development is also related to the type of programs viewed: Do programs directed at a wide audience affect language development in a manner different from those aimed specifically at certain age groups and do these programs advance linguistic level differentially? Finally, we need also to distinguish between the child's acquisition of their native tongue and acquisition of a second language.

Acquisition of native language

Several studies conducted in the USA examined relationships between viewing television and native-English-language acquisition in a child's early formative years.[22] Following our discussion of literacy skills, we should not be surprised to learn that the research demonstrated that heavy viewers had poorer language skills, and vice versa. The researchers also learned that the type of viewing is crucial: While children with limited verbal skills tended to watch programs that were verbally limited, children with rich linguistic skills watched programs with rich language. As in previous cases, we understand that these findings are reciprocal: Young viewers with limited verbal skills are attracted to programs that are more comprehensible to them, thus reinforcing their limitations. We can also argue that those children who spend a lot of time viewing television have fewer opportunities to practice social interactions in real life.

However, studies that examined educational programs designed to enrich young children's lives and facilitate linguistic development demonstrated significant achievements. Such programs adopt linguistic styles that facilitate learning: repetitiveness, clear yes and no questions, specific "Wh" questions (i.e., who, what, where, when, and why), verbal descriptions that are synchronized with the visuals presented, and pacing similar to the one often used by parents to read a story. These presentation styles were found to be effective in research situations: Young viewers learned unfamiliar vocabulary (both nouns and verbs) following exposure to television programs, both in short-term experiments (where children were presented with a video segment only once) as well as in longer-term ones (where children were exposed to a series of programs for several weeks).[23]

A longitudinal study of *Sesame Street* is illustrative of this line of research. US researchers examined the vocabulary of three- and five-year-olds by testing the children's capabilities to name objects appearing in test pictures. Following that, parents filled in weekly viewing diaries for the children once every six months (i.e., a diary providing information of all programs viewed by the child, usually in 15-minute intervals) for a period of two and a half years. Every six months the children's vocabulary was tested once again using the same picture test.[24]

For the purpose of our discussion here, one of the most interesting findings from this study is that three-year-olds who viewed *Sesame Street* frequently improved their vocabulary much more significantly in comparison to those who viewed it a lot less. These findings remained valid even when other related variables that could affect both the viewing of *Sesame Street* as well as language development were considered (e. g., parents' education, number of siblings, performance on the first language test). The researchers suggested that this may be an indication of the direction of causality: Viewing *Sesame Street* contributed to vocabulary development, and not the other way around; that is, it was the case that while heavier viewing of the program lead to better scores on the language test, improved language skills did not lead to more program viewing. An interesting corollary finding is that testing of the older group, which started the study at the age of five, did not produce the same evidence. Since the program's linguistic level was aimed at preschool- and kindergarten-age children, it is possible that it did not contribute anymore for older children.

Another longitudinal study was aimed at even younger children.[25] It found that infants and toddlers benefited most from viewing programs – such as *Blue's Clues* and *Dora the Explorer* – that applied specific linguistic strategies appropriate for this target age group, such as: the actors - speak directly to the child-viewer, encourage their participation, engage in object-naming, and provide opportunities for the child to respond. Watching programs that use attractive storytelling formats (e.g., *Arthur*, *Clifford*, and *Dragon Tales*), was also found to be associated with positive language development. In additional studies, television viewing was found to be effective in word-learning by toddlers.[26]

Similarly, anecdotal parental accounts and the few observational studies reported in the literature that followed the language development of babies and toddlers in their home environment concur that parents use television as a "talking book" with their young ones (as discussed in Chapter 1): They practice linguistic skills during television viewing, particularly with programs aimed at the very young. For example, both children and parents designate objects and characters on the screen by name (e.g., balloon, butterfly, Ernie [*Sesame Street*], Po [*Teletubbies*]); they ask questions (e.g., "Where did they go?" "What is she doing?"); repeat messages, including commercials and slogans; and describe what they see (e.g., "He is sad"; "They are playing with the dog").[27] Recall that the *Mommy Bar* discussed in Chapter 1 instructs parents in ways to stimulate such interactions.

In contrast, researchers who employed an experimental design reported a finding they referred to as a *video deficit* phenomenon:[28] They argue that babies and toddlers younger than two years old do not benefit from watching television in comparison to learning the same vocabulary or behavior from real-life situations. Accumulatively, these and other findings suggest, perhaps, that it is not viewing television in and of itself but rather the type of television content, viewing circumstances, and form of parental mediation that determines the nature of television's relationship with language development.

Acquisition of second language

If, indeed, television does have the potential to contribute to linguistic development, even in ways limited to specific skills, it also makes sense to examine it in relationship to the acquisition of a second language. This is particularly relevant to children growing up in small-language communities when imported programs use subtitles (i.e., they are not dubbed into their own language). Second language acquisition is also a very important process for minority groups whose native tongue is different from that of the majority population as well as for immigrant children who move into a different linguistic culture. This has become a common experience for many children today due, on the one hand, to economic and cultural globalization processes of popular culture; and, on the other hand, to growing mobility of populations from one culture to another.

Viewing television at home and accessing websites provide many varied opportunities in a non-threatening, non-demanding social environment to explore new languages that are embedded in local cultural and socio-linguistic contexts. Anecdotal data from around the world suggest that such viewing does assist in the acquisition of a second language. Indeed, English teachers have argued that English as Second Language pupils are much more proficient when there is a dominance of television programs in English in their country's television fare. Similarly, the popularity of Spanish among children has been given an unexpected reinforcement through the popularity of Latin American telenovelas around the world. But what does systematic research suggest?

The few existing studies support the view presented above. Chicano children in the USA (immigrants from Mexico) who had some basic English skills benefited from viewing American television.[29] For example, the series *Carrascolendas* was produced in Texas in the early 1970s for Chicano children starting their schooling in the new culture. The series employed bilingual puppets, skits, singing, and animation to teach English while helping to preserve the Spanish language and affinity for the cultural heritage of Chicano viewers. Research of the series found that viewers improved their knowledge, pride in their cultural and historic heritage, and their Spanish language skills. Similarly, English-speaking children in the USA were found to learn Spanish vocabulary from the many preschool programs that included Spanish-speaking characters. For example, *Dora the Explorer*, the highly popular series on the Nick Jr. channel of Nickelodeon, features a seven-year-old bilingual Latina girl, Dora, who uses both English and Spanish as valuable tools in her adventures.[30] Similarly, children in The Netherlands who viewed American programs with Dutch subtitles improved their English vocabulary.[31] And, research on immigrant children from former USSR countries to Israel documented the role of media in learning the Hebrew host language, as well as maintaining linguistic skills of the home Russian language.[32]

Such incidental learning of second language vocabulary seems to fit well with current theories of second language acquisition. First, research evidence suggests that learning a language does not necessarily require practice. A "quiet" period seems to exist during the learning process within which a child absorbs linguistic inputs without necessarily using them or demonstrating this knowledge. Certainly, the prior existence of language serves as a general infrastructure supporting the learning of any additional languages. At the same time, the following key variables are stimulated and interact during the process during which a child learns a second language, including via media use: cognitive – such as developmental level, intelligence, linguistic awareness, and general knowledge of the world; personality related – attitudes toward learning, self-confidence, verbal ability, openness, and motivation to learn; social variables – opportunities to interact with the speakers of the second language, receiving corrective feedback, difficulty level of the interactions; and general cultural variables – ethnic identity and status of the linguistic community.

Perhaps, under circumstances where the second language and its speakers are perceived to have a high status, the personal benefit of learning that language is perceived as high, and so is motivation for learning. In such cases, media may have a more central role as an effective teacher. Such may be the case around the world with regard to children's incidental English learning through television viewing as well as use of other English-dominated media, as is currently the case with the internet. Systematic exploration of this intriguing possibility has yet to take place.

Concluding Remarks

This chapter highlighted the challenges involved in the complex relationships between media use and learning. We have examined how the concept of learning has changed in the age of television and digital media, as well as the blurring of the traditional binary that views formal learning in school as distinct from informal learning that takes place through leisure activities outside of formal settings. A study of primary school children in an after-school care program in Australia demonstrates this point clearly as it documented how creative media-play and production can be integrated with informal learning.[33]

The review in the current chapter dealt primarily with the accumulated research pertaining to television. This is due to the fact that most extant research has examined that medium, and the fact that media-learning in general has been studied more extensively in relationship to the younger years, at a time when television is still the most dominant medium. However, it is clear that studies which also include the rapidly growing digital media may challenge many of our assumptions about the nature of learning and what is deemed worthy of learning, as well as identify the most effective ways to do so. An example of such a challenge are the current debates over the role of formal schooling in teaching data retrieval skills and critical literacy skills in order to evaluate sources of information and their credibility, rather than in focusing on knowledge itself which is so readily available via technology. We will return to these implications in Chapter 7.

Other questions pertain to the social and collaborative nature of knowledge building and learning rather than the competitive individual model. These matters will be discussed in Chapter 6. Another line of discussion considers the role of media in learning about the social world and our individual place within it. These topics are the focus of Chapter 5.

Finally, learning is also the basis of our next exploration in Chapter 4, where we examine the behavioral manifestations of experiences with the media. Thus, the multidimensional concept of learning serves as a basis for a significant part of this book.

Notes

1. Meyrowitz, 1995; Postman, 1979.
2. Neuman, 1991.
3. Van Evra, 2004.
4. For an integrative discussion see Schmidt & Anderson, 2006.
5. Salomon, 1994 [1979].
6. Lonner, Thorndike, Forbes, & Ashworth, 1985; MacBeth, 1996.
7. Messaris, 1994.
8. This discussion is based on the work of Cohen & Salomon, 1979; Salomon, 1981.
9. Salomon, 1983; Salomon, 1984; Salomon & Leigh, 1984.
10. O'Bryan, 1980.
11. Fisch, 2004; Fisch & Truglio, 2001.
12. Cole, Richman, & McCann Brown, 2001.
13. Singhal, Cody, Rogers, & Sabido, 2004.
14. Lemish & Kolucki, 2013.
15. Livingstone, 2011, p. 9.
16. Livingstone, 2009.
17. Jenkins, 2006.
18. Jenkins, Purushotma, Weigel, Clinton, & Robinson, 2006.
19. Herr Stephenson, 2013.

20. Alper, 2013.
21. Lemish & Rice, 1986; Singer & Singer, 1998.
22. Naigels & Mayeux, 2001; Selnow & Bettinghaus, 1982; Singer & Singer, 1981.
23. Rice & Woodsmall, 1988; Rice, Buhr, & Oetting, 1992; Rice, Oetting, Marquis, Bode, & Pase, 1994.
24. Rice, Huston, Truglio, & Wright, 1990.
25. Linebarger & Walker, 2005.
26. Krcmar, Grela, & Lin, 2007; Vandewater , Barr, Park, & Lee, 2010.
27. Lemish & Rice, 1986; Lemish & Tidhar, 1999.
28. Anderson & Pempek, 2005.
29. Blosser, 1988.
30. Fisch, 2004; Linebarger, 2001.
31. Koolstra & Beentjes, 1999.
32. Elias & Lemish, 2009.
33. Orr Vered, 2008.

References

Alper, M. (2013). Children and convergence culture: New perspectives on youth participation with media. In D. Lemish (Ed.), *The Routledge international handbook of children, adolescents, and media* (pp. 148–155). New York: Routledge.

Anderson, D.R. & Pempek, T.A. (2005). Television and very young children. *The American Behavioral Scientist, 48*(5), 505–522.

Blosser, B. (1988). Television, reading and oral language development: The case of the Hispanic child. *NAEB Journal,* 21–42.

Cohen, A.A. & Salomon, G. (1979). Children's literate television viewing: Surprises and possible explanations. *Journal of Communication, 29*(3), 156–163.

Cole, C.F., Richman, B.A., & McCann Brown, S.K. (2001). The world of *Sesame Street* research. In S.M. Fisch & R.T. Truglio (Eds.) *"G" is for growing: Thirty years of research on children and Sesame Street* (pp. 147–179). Mahwah, NJ: Lawrence Erlbaum.

Elias, N. & Lemish, D. (2009). Spinning the web of identity: Internet's roles in immigrant adolescents' search of identity. *New Media & Society, 11*(4), 1–19.

Fisch, S. (2004). *Children's learning from educational television: Sesame Street and beyond.* Mahwah, NJ: Lawrence Erlbaum.

Fisch, S.M. & Truglio, R.T. (Eds.). (2001). *"G" is for growing: Thirty years of research on children and Sesame Street.* Mahwah, NJ: Lawrence Erlbaum.

Herr Stephenson, B. (2013). New media and learning. In D. Lemish (Ed.), *The Routledge international handbook of children, adolescents, and media* (p. 410–416). New York: Routledge.

Jenkins, H. (2006). *Convergence culture: Where old and new media collide.* New York: New York University Press.

Jenkins, H., Purushotma, R., Weigel, M., Clinton, K., & Robinson, A. (2006). Confronting the challenges of participator culture: Media education for the 21st century (part two). *Digital Kompetanse, 2,* 97–113.

Koolstra, C.M. & Beentjes, J.W.J. (1999). Children's vocabulary acquisition in a foreign language through watching subtitled TV programs at home. *Educational Technology Research and Development, 47,* 51–60.

Krcmar, M., Grela, B., & Lin, K. (2007). Can toddlers learn vocabulary from television? An experimental approach. *Media Psychology, 10*(1) 41–63.

Lemish, D. & Kolucki, B. (2013). Media and early childhood development. In P. Britto, P. Engle, C. Super, & N. Ulkuer (Eds.), *Handbook of early childhood development research and its impact of global policy.* (pp. 329–347). Oxford: Oxford University Press.

Lemish, D. & Rice M. (1986). Television as a talking picture book: A prop for language acquisition. *Journal of Child Language, 13,* 251–274.

Lemish, D. & Tidhar, C.E. (1999). Mothers close to life: An Israeli case study. *TelevIZIon, 12*(2), 39–46.

Linebarger, D.L. (2001). *Summative evaluation of* Dora the Explorer, *Part 1: Learning outcomes.* Kansas City, KS: Media and Technology Projects, ABCD Ventures, Inc.

Linebarger, D.L. & Walker, D. (2005). Infants' and toddlers' television viewing and language outcomes. *American Behavioral Scientist, 48*(5), 624–645.

Livingstone, S. (2009). *Children and the internet.* Cambridge, UK: Polity.

Livingstone, S. (2011). Digital learning and participation among youth: Critical reflections on future research priorities. *International Journal of Learning and Media, 2*(2–3), 1–13.

Lonner, W.J., Thorndike, R.M., Forbes, N.E., & Ashworth, C. (1985). The influence of television on measured cognitive abilities: A study with Native Alaskan children. *Journal of Cross-Cultural Psychology, 16*(3), 355–380.

MacBeth, T.M. (Ed.). (1996). *Tuning in to young viewers: Social science perspectives on television.* Thousand Oaks, CA: Sage.

Messaris, P. (1994). *Visual literacy: Image, mind and reality.* Boulder, CO: Westview Press.

Meyrowitz, J. (1995). Taking McLuhan and "medium theory" seriously: Technological change and the evolution of education. In S.T. Kerr (Ed.), *Technology and the future of schooling* (pp. 73–110). Chicago, IL: The University of Chicago Press.

Naigels, L.R. & Mayeux, L. (2001). Television as incidental language teacher. In D. Singer & J. Singer (Eds.), *Handbook of children and the media* (pp. 135–152). Thousand Oaks, CA: Sage.

Neuman, S.B. (1991). *Literacy in the television age.* Norwood, NJ: Ablex.

O'Bryan, K.C. (1980). The teaching face: A historical perspective. In E.L. Palmer & A. Dorr (Eds.), *Children and the faces of television: Teaching, violence, selling* (pp. 5–17). New York: Academic Press.

Orr Vered, K. (2008). *Children and media outside the home: Playing and learning in after-school care.* New York: Palgrave McMillan.

Postman, N. (1979). The first curriculum: Comparing school and television. *Phi Delta Kappan, November,* 163–168.

Rice, M.L. & Woodsmall, L. (1988). Lessons from television: Children's word learning when viewing. *Child development, 59,* 420–429.

Rice, M.L., Buhr, J., & Oetting, J.B. (1992). Specific language-impaired children's quick incidental learning of words: The effect of a pause. *Journal of Speech and Hearing Research, 35,* 1040–1048.

Rice, M.L., Huston, A.C., Truglio, R., & Wright, J. (1990). Words from "Sesame Street": Learning vocabulary while viewing. *Developmental Psychology, 26*(3), 421–428.

Rice, M.L., Oetting, J.B., Marquis, J., Bode, J., & Pase, S. (1994). Frequency of input effects on word comprehension of children with specific language impairment. *Journal of Speech and Hearing Research, 37,* 106–122.

Salomon, G. (1981). Introducing AIME: The assessment of children's mental involvement with television. In H. Kelly & H. Gardner (Eds.), *Viewing children through television: New directions for child development* (pp. 89–102). San Francisco, CA: Jossey-Bass.

Salomon, G. (1983). Television watching and mental effort: A social psychological view. In J. Bryant & D.R. Anderson (Eds.), *Children's understanding of television: Research on attention and comprehension* (pp. 181–198). New York: Academic Press.

Salomon, G. (1984). Investing effort in television viewing. In J.P. Murray & G. Salomon (Eds.), *The future of children's television* (pp. 125–133). Boys Town, NE: Father Flanagan's Boys' Home.

Salomon, G. (1994 [1979]). *Interaction of media, cognition, and learning.* San Francisco, CA: Jossey-Bass.

Salomon, G. & Leigh, T. (1984). Predispositions about learning from print and television. *Journal of Communication, 34,* 119–135.

Schmidt, M.E. & Anderson, D.R. (2006). The impact of television on cognitive development and educational achievement. In N. Pecora, J.O. Murray, & E. Wartella (Eds.), *Children and television: 50 years of research* (pp. 65–87). Mahwah, NJ: Lawrence Erlbaum.

Selnow, G.W. & Bettinghuas, E.P. (1982). Television exposure and language development. *Journal of Broadcasting, 26*(1), 469–479.

Singer, D.G. & Singer, J.L. (1998). Developing critical viewing skills and media literacy in children. *The Annals of the American Academy of Political and Social Science Special Issue: Children and Television 557,* 164–179.

Singer, J.L. & Singer, D.G. (1981). *Television, imagination, and aggression: A study of preschoolers.* Hillsdale, NJ: Lawrence. Erlbaum.

Singhal, A., Cody, C.J., Rogers. E.M., & Sabido, M. (Eds.). (2004). *Entertainment-education and social change: History, research and practice.* Mahwah, NJ: Lawrence Erlbaum.

Van Evra, J. (2004). *Television and child development* (3rd ed.). Mahwah, NJ: Lawrence Erlbaum.

Vandewater, E.A., Barr, R.F., Park, S.E., & Lee, S.J. (2010). A US study of transfer of learning from video to books in toddlers. *Journal of Children and Media, 4*(4), 451–467.

4

Media and Health-related Behaviors

The concern that media use may have primarily negative implications for children's attitudes and behavior has been the center of much public and academic debate. Yet, there is also increasing interest in the capacities of children for learning pro-social messages from media use. Therefore, questions regarding what is called the *effects* tradition in media studies deserve the separate attention afforded to them in this chapter.

While early studies of television's effects on children were grounded in a variety of theoretical traditions, scholars gradually came to adopt the *strong effects* discourse of theories of mass communication that focused, originally, on studies of public opinion and political campaigns. Dominant since the mid-twentieth-century in research generated in North America, the basic premise of *effects* studies is that consumption of media content results in related behaviors; thus, media critics employ effects research to claim that violence in the media instigates violent behavior; advertisements lead to the purchase of products advertised and a consumerist worldview; and sex in the media leads to sexual permissiveness.

The accusatory assumption has fueled public debates about media's effects on children and has been the cause advanced by researchers seeking funding from governmental institutions for study of these effects. A milestone case in point is the US Surgeon General's Report of 1972. This is a five-volume report of government-sponsored academic studies that focused solely on the issue of television violence, a source of much public anxiety at the time. While the approach taken in this book attempts to present a balanced view of the research on children and media, and to shy away from the *moral panic* approach that cites the negative effects of media on children, we cannot ignore the accumulated research that presents clear evidence of

Children and Media: A Global Perspective, First Edition. Dafna Lemish.
© 2015 John Wiley & Sons, Inc. Published 2015 by John Wiley & Sons, Inc.
Companion Website: www.wiley.com/go/lemish/childrenandmedia

some such effects. We review them in this chapter in a way that allows the reader to weigh into this debate in a measured way.

What exactly is meant by the term *effect*?

As is often the case, the question asked frames, in large degree, what is studied and the methodology applied. Two primary questions have dominated studies of children and the effects of media: First, do media re-enforce existing behavioral tendencies and/or create new ones? Second, what are the immediate and long-term effects?

The first question assumes that media have a powerful role in influencing people's lives and that they have significant implications with regard to the degree of responsibility ascribed to those in charge of their production. Let us take, for example, the aforementioned concern over the effects of televised violence on children. The position that television reinforces existing behaviors would have us predict that, on the one hand, aggressive children will be affected by television violence, while on the other hand, non-aggressive ones will not be so affected. This will place much of the responsibility for children's behavior on other factors, all external to television, such as the child's personality, family background, or earlier violent experiences. However, the *effects* approach hypothesizes that children learn aggressive behaviors from television, even those children without a predisposition to violence (i.e., without a prior record of having aggressive tendencies), and thus assigns a much more powerful role to television viewing and its messages. Here the assumption is that children are exposed to and absorb a host of influences via television, both negative and positive. Consequently, the responsibility for such behaviors lies directly with the creators of television messages, as well as with parents who allow such viewing.

The second question focuses on the temporal dimensions of effects: Are the behavioral effects immediate (e.g., a *copycat* imitation of a soldier firing a rifle on the video-game screen; a child asking for a new type of candy advertised on a website) or are there long-term behaviors that develop over time and that involve a change in the behavioral repertoire of the child? (e.g., a child becomes more aggressive in non-mediated but related situations; a child demonstrates changes in eating habits). While short-term effects can be isolated events that may not have lasting influence, perhaps they are indicators of the beginning of a trend toward long-term effects?

Despite interest in different sets of questions, there does seem to be agreement, worldwide, that children are perceived to be the most vulnerable members of society: they are smaller and physically weaker; they need protection, care, feeding, fostering, and socialization to the adult world; they lack life experience, knowledge, and critical skills; they think differently from adults; and they lack social and economic resources. If, indeed, media have the potential for short- or long-term effects upon behavior, feelings, or thought, whether it be in reinforcing them or creating them, then children are the most prone to these.

In contrast to the *effects' school* of research, the *cultural studies* alternative grew out of European theoretical traditions. While this approach, too, recognizes the fact that children are different from adults, as noted in the previous paragraph, it does not view them as "deficient" in comparison to adults, rather it focuses on how their unique characteristics mediate the effects. The central premise of this approach is that what children bring with them to the encounter with media determines in large degree what they take from the experience. Here, children are not assumed to be passive, defenseless receptors, the proverbial *tabula rasa* on which media "writes" freely. Rather, they bring with them and apply in media use their own accumulated knowledge and experience, needs and sensitivities, meanings acquired in complicated socialization processes, tastes, and preferences. Thus, rather than look solely for immediate or long-term effects, the *cultural studies* approach studies how children, as media consumers, are actively involved in a meaning making that is the result of a complicated process of negotiation that develops over a multitude of viewing encounters, in given social circumstances, over an extended period of time.

The differences between the two schools in terms of understanding and studying television effects are embedded in a fundamental theoretical controversy within the field of mass communication and have significant methodological implications, as discussed at the end of Chapter 2. Furthermore, it should be noted that in certain academic circles even the term *effects* itself has been ostracized as being old-fashioned and misleading, and its study as superfluous. This having been noted, most of the research discussed in this chapter is embedded in the more traditional effects approaches that apply psychological and sociological theories to the study of human behavior, as well as more recent studies coming out of health sciences.

Media and Violent Behaviors

Of all topics related to children and media, and television in particular, the topic of violent behavior has attracted the most attention. The press media in particular are often keen to report cases that stimulate such concern: In Israel, a seven-year-old boy who broke his spine was reported to have shouted – "Look how Superman flies!" – before jumping out of a window. In Norway, a five-year-old girl was severely harassed by her friends following their viewing of a particular television series. In the USA, viewing Oliver Stone's movie *Natural Born Killers* (portraying a series of murders) was blamed for a 15-year-old youth's murder of his parents. In Thailand, a nine-year-old boy hung himself in imitation of a scene from a popular series that depicted a killing by hanging of the victim. Similarly, school shootings in the USA have been blamed on violent video games, and teenage suicides on cyberbullying. Each of us can probably remember the reporting of similar cases. Often, such reports dramatize the news event and target the media as its sole cause.

The predominance of violence in many commercial television programs, movies, video games, and websites is a well-accepted fact. Scholars claim that multiple portrayals of violence in the media occurs because viewers find it to be exciting and easily understood regardless of language and cultural barriers, and thus it "travels well" in the global market of media content. If we choose to define violence as a purposeful hurting of another being or property (and some may extend the definition to include also unintentional injury, such as accidents, as well as violence located in the animal world), we find that there are many violent elements, salient or overt, in most visual genres: war, westerns, crime detective, horror and science fiction genres of movies; news, documentary films, sports broadcasts, cartoons, music-clips, commercials, and video games. If we include verbal violence (a form of intended harm performed through words rather than physical force), then many comedies, talk as well as entertainment shows, online sites, and social media can also be included in the long list of violent content accessible to children of all ages. Studies that measured the frequency and types of various forms of violence in the media in various countries have re-affirmed the global scope of this phenomenon.

A second, undisputed fact is that most children, from a very young age, consume many of these genres and, thus, are exposed via the media to a multitude and wide variety of violent incidents, on a regular basis, over their entire life. While it is virtually impossible to actually count how many acts of mediated violence a child may be exposed to over time, let alone to suggest an "average" number that can hold true for the "average" child, it has been suggested that by the age of 12, children who view mainly commercial television will have been exposed to about 20,000 murders and about 100,000 other acts of violence on television alone. Putting aside the validity and accuracy of such numbers, there is little disagreement that children all over the world are exposed to a lot more violence in the media on a regular basis then they would ever come close to witnessing in real life.

However, it is not only the volume of violence in the media that is of concern with regard to the potential of children to develop a healthy social life, but also the types of violent acts and the circumstances in which they occur. Consider the following example: A comprehensive study that analyzed television programs produced in the USA (and to which children all over the world are exposed) revealed that three-quarters of the violent characters go unpunished for their acts; about half of the representations of acts of violence did not show injury to or suffering of the victims; only about one-sixth presented the long-term implications of violence, such as those of an emotional or economic nature; and only a fraction of the programs (4%) that presented violence used the opportunity to be critical of it or to discuss non-violent options for resolving problems.[1]

Different genres and media, of course, present violence differently. For example, movies tend to show violence in more realistic terms and to include more gory scenes than other television genres. Some websites post extreme, violent scenes that have been censored out of news coverage, and violent pornographic sites present sexual violence as pleasing and normative. Many violent video games include racist and political violence as well as graphic scenes of war, terrorism, and sexual violence. Children's programs, on the whole, hardly ever present the long-term effects of violence and often contextualize violent scenes in humorous situations.

Do children learn moral as well as practical lessons about a *mean world* through such viewing and playing? Do they internalize notions about the role of violence in our society and about certain violent acts that can be committed without punishment? These are just a few of the questions that have been investigated in the research on children and the media reviewed in the following pages. This analysis is organized according to two time-related levels of effects: first, the immediate influence on children's learning specific violent behaviors; and, second, the long-term effects of exposure to media violence. Please note that the effects of such exposure on children's mental worlds, such as fear, were already discussed in Chapter 2.

Learning violent behaviors

Do children tend to imitate violent behaviors they are exposed to in the media, as is often reported in news coverage? We may want to dismiss the cases cited above as highly exceptional ones in which the media is ascribed to serve as a catalyst for a child who possessed an already strong tendency toward aggressive tendencies, or an inability to distinguish reality from fantasy. This notwithstanding, the question remains – do most children, who could be described as possessing the "normal" range of behaviors, the ones we see around us every day, learn violent behaviors from media exposure? This question has been studied most systematically over several decades in relationship to television. In order to establish a causal relationship between television viewing and learning various forms of violent behavior, including chiefly imitation, researchers have presented children with different versions of violent television stimuli in experimental settings and measured their reactions to it. In doing so they sought to understand the conditions under which a child would imitate an aggressive act of hitting following a similar scene on television.

One leading approach to investigating this question, which is grounded in *social learning theory*, argues that children are positively reinforced for learning a repertoire of behaviors imitating the actions of role models. Media offer a rich resource for such learning, in general, and for violent behaviors, more specifically. Violent programs and games supply children with many ideas for specific acts of violence. They also teach viewers the functionality of violent behaviors: those that receive positive reinforcement (e.g., praise, a reward) versus those that are rejected (e.g., scolding, punishment). Justification of violent behavior is important as it increases the chances of children's imitation while positive reinforcement provides added value by suggesting to children what society values. Furthermore, it is argued that an extended process of viewing violence, and more specifically, playing violent games, may serve to remove inhibitions from performing violent acts by desensitizing viewers to the consequences and implications of such acts, and by legitimizing such behaviors as being normal and acceptable in society.

Indeed, studies performed in this widely accepted tradition in psychology found that following the viewing of a violent episode, children imitated televised violent behavior, performed newly acquired behavior even after a lapse of time, and were more prone to behave violently during a play session.[2]

Arousal theory offers a different interpretation for the effects mechanism. According to this approach, viewing violence on television generally arouses children and stimulates them to behave violently, though not necessarily through the imitation of the same specific behaviors. Arousal theory may also complement social learning theory, as arousal may prepare the ground for learning more specific behaviors.[3]

Here, too, it is important to note that caution is required, given the many ethical as well as methodological critiques posed with regard to studies that attempted to document direct causal effects of television violence. Is it moral to expose children in research settings to violent content, knowing that this exposure may be harmful to them? Is it ethical to create research circumstances that allow children to behave aggressively? Is it at all possible to isolate the many variables that may affect the relationship between viewing violence and the violent behavior (e.g., characteristics of the viewer, of the program, of the violent act, of the circumstances)? How similar are the television segments viewed in the experiments to those that children view at home on a daily basis? How similar are the viewing circumstances in the unnatural research setting in comparison to those at home? In summary, as in all studies examining human behavior in research settings, these conclusions are open to the central criticism leveled against studies that attempt to generalize from children's behaviors under artificial experimental circumstances to their everyday reality and behavior.

Cumulative effects of media violence

An even more complicated issue is the question of the nature of the relationship between long-term exposure to media violence and aggressive behavior. Put simply, do children who watch a lot of violent television and/or play violent video- and computer games tend to be more violent than those who have less exposure to violence, either because they watch less TV or because they have different viewing preferences? Or, perhaps, is it the other way around: children who watch more violence and play more violent digital games are much less violent because they have more opportunities to relieve their aggression through a process of catharsis activated through media consumption? And, a third possibility, perhaps there is no relationship between exposure to media violence and violent behavior? In statistical terms, such correlations will be termed positive when exposure to media violence is associated with violent behaviors; negative when heavy viewing and gaming is associated with lower violent behaviors; and zero when there is no clear relationship between the two. Researchers have applied two major strategies in their attempts to confront these questions: field experiments and correlational studies.

Field experiments are a form of a methodological compromise that attempts to study phenomena in more natural settings, while controlling for some variables (similar to attempts made in many experimental designs). Schools, daycare centers, and summer camps are the settings that are best suited to this kind of research, since it is possible to control to a large degree the kind of television programs children view there. A typical study assigns children to different viewing "diets" (i.e., research "treatments"). For example, one group (A) might view typical children's programs with violence on a daily basis (e.g., action-adventure cartoons); a second group (B) views programs that promote socially acceptable behaviors and non-violent resolution of inter-personal or social problems; and a third (C) views programs perceived to be "neutral" – they do not promote any kind of behavior (e.g., nature programs).[4]

Children's behaviors are rated in such studies on scales that cite the degree of aggressiveness, sociability (e.g., cooperation, mutual aid, verbal expression of feelings), and self-control (e.g., persistence, obedience, ability to handle frustration). Comparisons between these measures of behavior of children in the two periods before and after the exposure to the programs are expected to provide an indication of the cumulative effects of watching television: Would children in group A become more violent? Would children in group B become less violent and more involved in socially accepted behaviors? Would children in group C show any behavioral change?

Interestingly, studies that applied this design have not been able to arrive at nonequivocal conclusions. Some found that viewing violent programs made a significant difference for children who originally rated higher on measures of aggressive behavior. Others concluded that their findings do not allow them to indicate such an effect. Increasingly, researchers have been searching for alternative methods that will not involve the ethical problem of intentionally exposing children to violent programs and that will be less obtrusive in children's everyday lives.

The alternative approach, *correlational studies*, does not attempt to look for direct effects, but rather searches for long-term correlations between exposure to media violence and violent behavior. The amount of violent content a child is exposed to is calculated based on detailed reports of media use habits (for example, via questionnaires or weekly viewing diaries). The level of child aggressiveness is usually evaluated by others – reports of parents, teachers, or peers. These kinds of studies are characterized by the participation of very large numbers of a wide age range of children. Indeed, a few of these studies have been conducted over the span of a number of years and have even returned to the same children after extended periods to investigate changes that developed over time. One such study, conducted in Australia, Finland, Israel, Poland, and the USA, also attempted a cross-cultural comparison.[5] Overall, correlational studies have found that children who were rated as more violent by their friends were also those who were heavy viewers of violent television. Furthermore, the more a child watched violent television in a given year, the more likely it was that the child would be rated as aggressive in the following years.[6]

However, despite populist discussions of these effects, it is interesting to note that a more recent meta-analysis (i.e., an analysis of the results of a group of studies on the topic) has found that there is little evidence of effects of media on criminal violent behavior, and in these few cases, only on males.[7] One way to interpret such findings is to perceive them as a vicious circle: Viewing violent television stimulates aggression and this aggression stimulates more viewing of violent television, and vice versa. Several critiques of these studies have focused on the social context within which children involved in them reside. For example, would children growing up in a more violent society be more prone to accept television violence as justified and normative and thus be more prone to be affected by it? Would children raised in a peaceful environment where violent behavior is uncommon and is strongly sanctioned be more resilient to such an influence?

In summary, many academics conclude that despite the methodological diversity employed by researchers and the differences in specific findings produced, there does seem to be common agreement that is reinforced with each new study. Most studies conclude that there are positive correlations, although low, between violent behavior and exposure to television violence. That is, viewing television violence is related more to the aggressive behavior of an individual child.[8] Further, the more accurate the measure of television violence, the greater the potential for achieving results with positive correlation (for example, a calculation of the child's actual viewing with the level of violence in the specific programs viewed).[9]

These conclusions reinforce claims made by experimental researchers that there is a positive correlation between viewing violence and behaving violently. However, though this correlation has been found repeatedly within a relatively constant range, its level is not very high. Furthermore, it should be noted that a correlation does not necessarily indicate a causal relationship: that is, the positive correlation found does not offer a clear explanation regarding the nature of the relationships between the two measures. For example, is it possible for correlation studies to determine if viewing violent television is the cause of violent behavior or is it the case that violent children are more attracted to violence on television? Or, perhaps, both viewing violence and behaving violently are related to an external, unrelated variable (e.g., learning disabilities, attention deficits)?

Violent video games have also been a topic of much research. The added active ingredient of the game, in which players choose to inflict violence on others, in particular, has raised deep concern and stimulated a host of studies. Much in line with research on the effects of televised violence, these studies produced complicated findings, which seem to suggest that there is a positive but small effect (i.e., playing video games is correlated with aggressive behavior). The release year of the game – with ever more elaborated and realistic game designs year by year – seems to play a role in the relationship, in addition to all the other considerations such as time spent with play and the child's pre-disposition to violence. Several meta-analyses of such studies, cognizant of methodological challenges and shortcomings, have nevertheless concluded that playing violent video games does indeed contribute to aggressive behavior.[10]

One interesting explanation that is emerging and which seems reasonable is that the relationship between exposure to media violence and violent behavior is not uni-directional, but circular. Scholars developing this explanation argue that while there is very little doubt that children with aggressive tendencies tend to watch more violent television and play violent games more, at the same time, there is substantial evidence that viewing violent television and playing violent games encourages aggressive behavior even in children without such a previous record. Indeed, the existence of a "spiral" model of mutual reinforcement of exposure to violence and violent behavior was documented in a comprehensive study of young adolescents in the USA and their use of all types of violent media content, including television and films, computer and video games, as well as internet sites.[11] This conclusion can be viewed as complementing the conclusion from other studies presented earlier that children are not merely passive victims of television violence, but active initiators who search for content that appeals to their tastes and needs.[12]

Our discussion of this issue would not be complete without mentioning the popular *catharsis hypothesis*. Since the time of ancient Greece, drama in all its forms has been perceived as a means of emotional outlet for fears, tensions, and sorrow. Here, the underlying assumption is that physical and mental energies can be relieved in a variety of ways, including through fictitious violence. For example, frustration caused by failure or an insult may cause intensification of violent urges. Since this urge creates internal discomfort, the frustrated person searches for ways to rid themselves of it. Viewing television violence is perceived as one accessible and acceptable way of reducing violent urges and of creating a feeling of "purification" or "cleansing," otherwise known as *catharsis*. Following this line of argument, media violence may serve as a substitute for violent behavior in the real world.

While this hypothesis may appeal to many people, it has been often exploited by interested bodies (such as commercial companies) that cite it as "proof" of the social benefits of engaging with violent media content. Yet, researchers agree that, in general, there is no evidence to support such a process, certainly not among children. If catharsis was in operation, we should have found strong negative correlations: Children viewing violent programs would have had many more opportunities to relieve their aggressive urges and therefore to be less violent than those not watching such programs. From the general research evidence presented above it is quite clear that that this is not the case.[13]

Intervening variables

Who, then, among the children, are more prone to be affected by media violence? What are the intervening variables that differentiate between children and the process mediating these effects?

We have seen that many of the studies of effects repeatedly produce evidence to support claims of correlations between viewing violent programs, children's pre-disposition to violence, and their social and adjustment difficulties. One underlying assumption associated with these findings is that children with a variety of behavioral, social, cognitive, and emotional difficulties may turn to media as a substitute for the need to cope with real social situations and, thus, are much more prone to its nega-tive effects. An example of intensification of television's influence due to cognitive difficulties would be that children turn to viewing television as a substitute for other more cognitively challenging activities (e. g., schoolwork, reading, internet surfing). In addition, they may tend to accept more readily violent problem-solving behaviors viewed on television as relevant to their own reality when confronting difficulties in understanding television content.

The general level of the child's arousal during the viewing and gaming situation, too, may be related to the aforementioned personal characteristics. The more aroused the child (e.g., tense, frustrated, angry, hungry), the more likely the chance that his or her temper may flare. As a result, the same level of violence in a particular program or game may affect children, indeed even the same child, differently, given changing emotional states during the viewing or playing.

Research findings also provide evidence for quite consistent gender differences with regard to attraction to violent content as well as related behavior. For example, a UNESCO-sponsored global study of media violence of 5,000 12-year-old children in 23 countries, reflecting a representative range of human and technological variables, found that boys were fascinated by aggressive media heroes.[14] This and other studies suggest that, on the whole, girls enjoy violence much less than boys, are much more critical of it, and perceive it as less realistic. They also tend to react more emotionally to violence and to demonstrate signs of fear. Gender differences become more distinct from around the age of 10, perhaps due to growing consolidation of gender identity and socialization to social expectations of *masculine* and *feminine* appropriate behaviors.

Recent studies are finding evidence of a slight closing of the gender gap, as more girls are showing an interest in violent programs and characters traditionally perceived as masculine. Here we need to remember that while men still perform most of the violent acts on television (as in life) and women are presented much more often as victims than as aggressors (again, true to reality), there is a growing number of women, in both children's and adults' programs, appearing in active roles, in general, as characters in the powerful world of police, crime, and science fiction, as well as a new trend to present "sexy-tough" women as aggressors. Yet this trend does not seem to be working the other way around; that is, we have yet to see a trend of more boys distancing themselves from violent "masculine" role models or a growing interest in non-violent modes of "feminine" conflict resolution.[15]

Research studies on the role of the home in mediating the effects of exposure to mediated violence are few and far between and the findings are not clear-cut, leaving many parents concerned that the task of holding one's own in a world dominated by violent media is difficult. Yet, the following line of argument would seem to be a reasonable set of working assertions. First, the child's family background plays a major role in mediating the potential effects of media violence. The educational and value system guiding each family, in general, and attitudes toward violence, in particular, characterize the child's home environment. For example, we would expect that children raised by parents with an espoused ideology and practice of non-violence, in discipline or selection of media resources will watch less violent television and will be less affected by scenes of violence. In contrast, children who come from a home that employs physical punishments, where media are the sole source of leisure and where there is no parental control of the amount and content of media consumption, will be more prone to such effects.

We conclude this section by noting that caution is required with regard to the influence of cultural diversity. Most of the research about media violence reviewed here was undertaken in media-rich countries, primarily in Northern America and Europe. In contrast, research from other countries suggests cultural variance. For example, an argument has been put forth by a Japanese researcher that violence on Japanese television is represented quite differently from that portrayed in typical American television, and that it includes the after-effects of violence on victims and their suffering. Could this difference serve as a mediating variable that weakens the relationships between viewing violence by Japanese children in comparison to their American counterparts? Could the fact that Israeli children glorify wrestlers of the *World Wrestling Federation* as American heroes be due to their living with an omnipresent threat of violence and terrorism, and thus viewing the *WWF* intensifies their vulnerability to such portrayals of violence? Additional evidence comes from the UNESCO global study cited above in which it was found that 51 percent of the children from high-aggression environments (such as areas of recent-war zones and refugee camps in some African countries in the sample, as well as some crime-stricken, economically poor environments) wanted to be like their admired, aggressive, televised role model, in comparison to 37 percent of the children in low-aggression neighborhoods.[16]

By way of further reservation regarding the overall findings presented earlier, some researchers question charges that media have any contribution whatsoever to social violence these days. Their critique of specific studies suggests that it may be possible to ask serious questions about these findings and arguments. Others raise ideological arguments to refute the effect argument – both over the social assumptions underlying the studies as well as the search for causal explanations for human behavior. Media, it is argued, did not invent violence, but serve only as a means of presenting it. Further, it is important to remember that the majority of these studies were undertaken in the USA and thus contain an inherent cultural bias. Some would argue that both US society and television are more violent than in many places in the world. In any event, we cannot discuss media violence in a vacuum: it is necessary to contextualize it within the dominant forms of violence in each society, its consequences, and the societal norms associated with it.

Finally, it has been argued that coping with violence is part of childhood, just as it is in all periods of human existence. Exposure to media violence allows children to experiment with different feelings, such as fears and anxieties, to internalize definitions of good and bad, the permitted and the forbidden. Indeed, part of growing up includes the development of defense mechanisms against the unpleasant aspects of life, and these include, unfortunately, violence.[17]

In summary, it appears that a rebuttal can be made for each position on this issue. However, one claim that all can agree upon is that to date no one has been able to question the accumulative, general finding produced in hundreds of research projects, undertaken through a variety of research methods, by many different researchers in many countries all over the world, of the existence of at least some effect of media violence on children's behavior.

So, returning to answer our initial question: Does exposure to media violence influence aggressive behaviors among children? The answer seems to be yes, with reservations. Clearly, media are a factor, but certainly not the sole reason nor an isolated one in stimulating a-social behaviors. That is, the influence of media is confounded by a host of other factors and embedded in specific cultural contexts.

All research studies agree that this is a complicated issue with meaningful implications for both media policy related to children as well as for the undisputed need to develop critical media literacy skills in children, as discussed in Chapter 3. Finally, irrespective of whether or not there is an agreed-upon academic verdict on the effects of media violence, some families prefer to limit its presence in their home, as they find it unbefitting to the culture in which they wish to raise their children.

Media, Sex, and Sexuality

Sex is the "red flag" agitating public and educational debate about media's effects on children. However, while violence, as we have discussed, has been the focus of sustained research attention, the study of the contribution of media to the sexual behavior of children and youth is still relatively marginal. This is quite surprising, given the growing sexual permissiveness in some countries, as well as concerns over teen pregnancies and the spread of HIV-AIDS.

In contrast to the general consensus over the undesired nature of violence, attitudes toward human sexuality vary enormously: They are conflated, extensively, in mythologies, taboos, inhibitions, moral and religious beliefs, and cultural practices, which extend beyond intimate relationships.

Contrary to what many assume, sexuality is hardly limited to bodily functions – it involves many more aspects of our identities and lives, is socially constructed, and varies immensely within and across cultures and periods. Studying sex and sexuality, in particular in relation to minors, is a very sensitive issue in most societies that often raises a host of objections, involving in many cases an unthinkable taboo for public discussion.

Content analyses of mainstream media demonstrate that it is saturated with a wide range of sexual behaviors; from kissing and embracing, through love-making, and representations of scenes of full intercourse. Media also present a variety of verbal engagements with sex including courting behaviors, expression of fantasies and desires, exchange of experiences, and sexual provocations. The spread of HIV-AIDS since the 1980s brought into public discourse, as well as into families' private living rooms, the discussion of casual sex, unsafe sex and use of contraceptives, homosexual sex, and other topics that were taboo in the past (and remain so in many societies to date). Is there reason to believe that representations of sexual behavior in the media may affect viewers' behaviors, too?

As established previously, media have the potential for greater effect when real-life experiences with phenomena are minimal and there is limited involvement of other socializing agents. Sexuality is an excellent illustration of this line of argument: Most children are exposed to sexual behavior for the first time through the media, often on television or on the internet, years before they attain the physical, social, and emotional maturity needed to be sexually active. They also lack opportunities to examine media images in comparison to real life around them, as most sexual behaviors are conducted intimately, in the private sphere. In addition, the dominant socializing agents of family, school, or religious institutions generally repress activity or discussion of sex.

In contrast, sex and sexuality are central themes of the content of many media products, either explicitly (in many websites and films broadcast on movie channels, off prime time, or on rented videos rated in many societies as films for adults only) or implicitly in a wide variety of programs of all genres. The content addressed or alluded to includes not only erotic behavior, but also references to sex-roles, intimacy and care, marriage, and family life. Analyses of sex-oriented themes on television suggest that the content and images divert greatly from reality. For example, most televised sex takes place outside normal marital or otherwise committed relationships, or involves some kind of financial engagement. Often sexual behaviors are entangled with violence, and intimate relationships on the whole are not necessarily presented as part of a warm emotional relationship. Sex is often portrayed as something that happens "spontaneously," in the heat of the moment, without much planning. Attractive actors and actresses are depicted as being highly sexually active, but also highly sexually irresponsible. The potential negative implications of sexual relationships, such as undesired pregnancy, sexually transmitted diseases, or emotional distress, are hardly ever presented. However, more than anything else, the argument has been made that television in particular offers young viewers heavy exposure to conversations about sexual desires and practices. Indeed, many television programs seem to be preoccupied with discussion of sex, thus stimulating young people's naturally developing interest in it even more, and priming them to over-emphasize its centrality in human life.[18]

Children's media exposure to representations of sex has been blamed for a host of social ills, including the early onset of sexual activity and promiscuity, and the spread of teenage pregnancies and infectious diseases. More specifically, media productions are severely criticized on three counts: First, for cultivating a perspective that see children as sexual, and thereby putting them at risk of the ill-intentions of sexual predators;[19] second, for their effect on over-sexualizing young girls' emerging self-perception and their understanding of society's expectations of them and; third, for promoting self-objectification, particularly of girls. In short, media saturation with sexuality is accused of undermining children's healthy sexual development and wellbeing.[20]

A significant accumulation of evidence supports these claims. First, there is little doubt that children growing up in many societies around the world have access to a great deal of sexually oriented media content. The evidence of such exposure comes from a variety of sources, including commercial rating systems, as well as parents' and children's self-reports. Here, the same mechanisms explored in relation to media violence can be applied. In this regard, researchers have argued that media portrayals may affect behavior by inducing learning of new behaviors, reinforcing old ones, and/or converting existing behaviors to new ones. These kinds of changes can happen in various ways: a change in expectations regarding possible consequences of sexual behavior; identification with characters; removal of behavioral inhibitions; and assigning particular meaning to specific behavioral cues. As a result, it makes sense to assume that intensified exposure to sexual content may increase the chances of similar behavior, through imitation and/or sexual arousal and/or removal of inhibitions.

Second, several studies conducted in the USA that investigated possible correlations between viewing sexual programs and sexual practices found some evidence in support of effects. For example, the amount of viewing of sex on television and of adult-rated sexual content was related to the initial age of sexual activity (i.e., heavy viewers start being active sexually at a younger age); and intentional exposure to adult-rated violent sexual content by boys was correlated with a tendency to harass girls. Studies regarding exposure to sexual content and various risk behaviors (e.g., unprotected sex resulting in pregnancy or sexually transmitted diseases) conducted in the USA and Europe produced conflicting evidence.[21]

Here, too, the direction of the sexual behavior–media exposure relationship is not clear-cut. Are adolescents who are sexually active attracted more to sex in the media or are those watching more sex in the media more sexually active? As with violence, there is agreement that both directions are in operation: as youth mature physically, sexual content on television becomes more relevant – they seek out such content more actively, devote more time and attention to watching it, and thus become more influenced by it. Adolescents who were more sexually active seem to seek more sexually explicit media content, and in turn, media exposure seems to stimulate new sexual experiences.[22]

Gender and social expectations

Clearly, sexual behavior needs to be understood in the wider context of sexual development that includes attitudes, knowledge, and worldview. For example, the role that media play in children's evolving understanding of the place of sexuality in human relationships, its nature, and meanings produces differentiated expectations from the two genders, given the double standards applied to them. Not surprisingly, various studies do indeed suggest differences between boys and girls: In general, girls find fewer sexually active role models with which to identify and seem less affected by television sex than boys. This finding can be explained by the double standard that most societies still uphold regarding gender and sexuality: While sexually active adolescent males are commonly perceived as popular and "cool," sexually active adolescent girls are stereotyped as "slutty" and "troubled." Sexual activity is also still much more risky and costly for girls (e.g., losing virginity, chance of undesired pregnancy, lower self-image, social sanctions, even capital punishment in some societies). While these views may be gradually changing, young males in Anglo-European societies do associate sex more often with pleasure, fun, and physical gratification. In contrast, young females associate it more often with emotions, romantic love, and commitment. While young males' engagement in sex may be reinforced on television by gaining prestige and peer popularity, it is often negatively sanctioned when it is the young female's sexual exploits. These normative pressures on and off the television screen appear to be much stronger than any television portrayals in influencing actual behavior.

The scope and nature of media engagement with sex is of public concern in many societies. As with the discussion over violence, there are many opinions regarding the types of sexual relationships that are appropriate for children to watch and at what age. These views vary not only from one society to another, but also among sub-cultures within them. For example, in some European countries, particularly the Nordic ones, there is a much more relaxed and permissive approach regarding the inclusion of nudity, erotic behaviors, as well as free talk about sex in programs that are viewed regularly by young viewers. In contrast, media in the USA are, on the whole, much less permissive. Yet they, too, are perceived as overly revealing, indeed indecent, by many residents of the Middle East, Africa, Asia, and South America. Needless to say, when attempting to study this topic, one confronts considerable difficulties, given the many sensitivities involved regarding young people's own sexuality, questions of morals, values, and religion, as well as children's inhibitions.[23]

Several studies conducted in different countries applied various research methods and yet arrived at a similar conclusion: Exposure to television content that presents a variety of sexual behaviors may influence perceptions and value judgments related to intimacy and sexual relationships. Furthermore, children and youth who are active viewers raised in families with clearly defined values and who maintain open communication patterns seem to be least influenced by television values.[24] Such findings should not be too surprising, given discussions in previous chapters.

An examination of what children and young adults themselves have to say about sex on television reveals many additional complexities. A lot of what youngsters report attending to on television would not necessarily be described as sexual activity but rather as conversations about sexual experiences. These conversations offer rich content for fantasy and social learning, but also leave much to the imagination. Indeed, studies that involved listening to children and adolescents talk about their views of the world have found that they use television's portrayals of sex and sexuality as a basis for conversations about sex's relevance to their own lives. One such study conducted in the UK found that pre-adolescents and adolescents reported frequent encounters with sexual material in the media, valued the information received from it, and used it as a learning resource. Researchers noted, in particular, that interviewees demonstrated a range of critical skills in interpreting sexual content and evaluated such content through what they perceived to be sexual morality; that is, through views heavily influenced by their cultural backgrounds and gender.[25]

Clearly then, it is not only graphic depictions of sex that are of interest to young viewers, and their researchers. In addition, children value this source of information about sex in a social context that offers them little and mostly unsatisfactory alternatives. It also seems that they do not absorb it all uncritically, but bring to these encounters their existing worldviews and critical skills. Here, too, we find that the meaning made of sexual content on television is shaped by the context of its consumption. Viewing sexual content with peers, for example, allows for an experience that is quite different from that created in a family situation or in an intimate one.

There are many fascinating questions to which researchers have yet to find answers: How do young people relate sexual content to their own experiences? To what degree do they perceive television drama that dwells on intimacy as real, particularly in comparison to their own lives, especially if they consider the latter to be boring and void of romance? Do they compare themselves to the sexy television characters and feel that they have been unlucky in romance, or that they lack beauty or experience? What criteria do they use to compare themselves and their partners to television characters? Given that personal experiences of all kinds often leave much to be desired in comparison with television's glorified, romantic, and problem-free portrayals, does the degree to which youth perceive such portrayals to be realistic influence their assessment of and satisfaction with their own initial sexual experiences?

It is also important to consider the indirect – positive or negative – contributions media may be making to sexual development when such media serve as the dominant source of social scripts of possible attitudes and behaviors, language and forms of talking about sexual issues, as well as opportunities to bring such discussion into the open. Indeed, it is possible that sexual content "appearing" on the screen in the family's living room on a daily basis can provide an opportunity for social learning and, perhaps, open up discussion of topics that otherwise involve discomfort.

Finally, once again, we need to remind ourselves that young people's attitudes toward sex are most probably influenced by other variables, such as the scope and kind of previous sexual experience, and religious and moral perceptions. In addition, as with other areas of media impact, it is most likely that young people who are more sexually active are also more attracted to sexual media content and that their actual experiences, not their exposure to media, explain – or at least mediate – their perceptions. We also need to remember that the types of content to which most youth in the Anglo-European world are exposed, from a relatively young age, may be completely unavailable or even banned in other parts of the world, thus making the entire discussion above superfluous in those societies.

Pornography and teenage sexuality

A particular case of interest and concern related to the foregoing discussion is the study of pornography, a genre devoted entirely to the depiction of sexually explicit behavior intended to sexually arouse its audience. Pornography also differs from most sexual content on television because of its use of photographic conventions of genres dealing with the real world. In doing so, it creates the illusion that one is viewing a "documentary" of real people performing their regular sexual behaviors.

Stated succinctly, analyses of the content of pornography suggest the following characteristics:

- Pornography presents sexual relationships between people who have no intention to maintain a relationship following the sexual encounter.
- Pornography presents a high frequency of sexual acts with a variety of partners that emphasize the physical and technical aspects of sex, rather than the human and emotional.
- Pornography presents all types of sexual activities as providing ecstatic pleasures to the participants, including behaviors considered in many societies to be deviant, strange, and indeed violent.[26]

The prevailing feminist analysis of heterosexual pornography suggests that it presents a systematic portrayal of power relationships between men and women, in which women are presented to be whores by nature, who enjoy pain and humiliation, and who are always available for sex under any conditions.

Although the definition of pornography is the subject of intense ideological and methodological debate, there is agreement that a distinction may be made between "soft" pornography (depicting all kinds of sexual relationships perceived as consensual and non-harmful in a given culture) and "hardcore" pornography (depicting extraordinary and non-consensual sexual behaviors such as those involving violence, children, animals, and objects). Pornographic material of both kinds is now relatively easily accessible to children in many countries via special television channels, video stores, websites and downloads from the internet, as well as the traditional forms of pornography published in print format.

The nature of the debate over the effects of viewing pornography on children and youth is cast in terms very similar to those applied to the discussion of violence: Do youth imitate sexual behaviors depicted in pornographic materials? Do they learn to expect their sexual partners to perform acts that they perceive to be legitimate and enjoyable? Do they become less sensitive and caring with regard to their partners' sexual needs and expect them to enjoy pain and humiliation as depicted in the pornographic material? Do viewers of pornography become more sexually active and from a younger age? Or is it the other way around; do sexually active youngsters turn to pornography in search of relevant content, role models, and arousal? And what about intervening variables – are there particular adolescents that are more prone to viewing pornography and to being influenced by it?

In addition, researchers from several feminist schools of thought perceive pornography to be a form of racist content that is degrading women as sex objects and is aimed at maintaining women's subordinate status in all human societies. Pornography is assumed to feed the exploitation of women in the sex industry, including the enslavement and trafficking of girls and women around the world.

Does pornography in fact contribute to the sexual exploitation of women and to gender inequality in society?

Research conducted on the effects of pornography has been relatively limited and indeed restricted to young adults (imagine the methodological and ethical issues involved in attempting to study the effects of pornography on school-age children!). As a result, the questions listed above, which continue to cause great anxiety to many segments of society (e.g., sex education specialists, parents, religious groups, feminists), remain largely unanswered.[27] However, the existing body of research suggests that, indeed, pornography does shape and reinforce undesired attitudes toward women in sexual as well as non-sexual contexts. Both correlation and experimental studies of viewers of pornography, particularly of the more hardcore genres, revealed these viewers to have more negative attitudes toward women, to hold harsh and inconsiderate attitudes regarding the sexual needs of their partners, as well as to play down the severity of sexual crimes and their consequences for women and children. Several studies conducted in the USA, Taiwan, Japan, and the Netherlands, for example, found that exposure to pornography in the media was associated with more permissive and casual beliefs about sex. The studies also documented that heavy consumers of pornography tend to hold stronger perceptions that objectify women. However, here, too, the direction of the relationship may well be reciprocal: adolescents holding these views are more attracted to pornographic material and vice versa.[28] While many of these studies were criticized on methodological and ideological grounds, there is enough evidence gathered to raise concern over the potential influence that pornography may have on young people's sexual relationships.[29]

We have seen that the debate over the role of media in shaping human sexuality is embedded in many central ideological issues that are valued differently in different societies, for different age groups, and for different periods: sex-roles; the nature of male and female sexualities; the role of sexuality in human relationships; the inter-relationships between sex and violence, sex and emotions, sex and commitment, sex and family, sex and childbearing, sex and homosexuality; and the like. Furthermore, the role of media in shaping human sexuality also needs to be viewed in light of theories on the changing nature of childhood, including those that perceive all humans, including young children, to be sexual in nature.

Media and Advertising

Commercial media perceive children mainly as a market for advertising goods in the present, as well as an investment for the future. The growth of advertising has led to intensification in the increasing variety of its forms – commercials, sponsorships, covert and embedded advertising, social network marketing, *advergames* (online games sponsored by advertisers), pop-up advertising on websites, and program-related toys, foods, and merchandizing – as well as in the spread of such phenomena all over the world and in all media platforms. More specifically, advertising to children employs mostly affective appeals rather than informational ones, evoking emotions of fun, happiness, excitement, and feelings of affinity to celebrities and familiar media characters.

But this trend has also been growing in terms of defining the potential child-consumer: The targeted age of children has been lowered systematically – to the point that no age is now protected from commercial forces, not even baby-media consumers of just a few months old for whom early media experiences serve to entice parents to purchase goods for them. The child market has also witnessed a strong gender-related segregation as part of the drive for audience segmentation and specialization.[30]As a result, the effects of advertising on children are a very important area of concern in many places in the world and a topic of vivid scholarly theorizing and inquiry.

The trend in the growth of advertising is also affected by different interactions with various local cultural changes. For example, middle- and upper-class children in many high-resource societies have gradually become active consumers in their own right: They have their own money to spend (from gifts, allowances, work) and they influence many family purchase decisions, particularly in the areas of entertainment, leisure, and food. Furthermore, they are the present as well as the future's big spenders. As a result, advertisers highly value these *market segments* (as they are called). In lower-class societies, as well as developing countries, most children do not have funds available to them and their families live on a limited budget. Therefore, advertising raises a host of very different concerns: growing frustrations from unfulfilled expectations, family conflicts over purchasing decisions, and pressure to adopt a lifestyle that may be unattainable or socially and culturally inappropriate.

From a research perspective, the issue of advertising is of particular interest, as this is the content area of television where specific and more readily measured behavioral change is most clearly the goal, i.e., the purchase of a product or adoption of a particular lifestyle or habit. Many resources are invested in well-planned, detailed efforts to achieve this goal. Talented and creative professionals, enormous amounts of funds, and the most advanced forms of technology are recruited for this purpose. This is the media's ultimate "test": To what degree can media actually change our behavior?

As with studies of media violence, here, too, it is impossible to estimate the volume of exposure to commercials. Clearly, it is virtually impossible to offer accurate estimates of exposure of children to advertising worldwide.[31] However, a number often quoted in the USA estimated that the average child in the 1990s was watching about 130 commercials per day, 900 a week, or 45,000 a year. Added together, this amounts to about 7.5 hours of viewing commercials per week. While these numbers are constantly changing and should not be taken at face value, they can serve to impress upon us of the scope of the phenomenon. Given that these numbers refer to television exposure alone, and do not include exposure to advertising on the web and mobile media, the magnitude of the dominance of commercialized culture in children's lives is hard to even appreciate. The ubiquitous connectivity of children with media technologies allows the development of "360 degree" strategies – meaning full immersion in a branded entertainment environment,[32] be it online interactive games, social networking sites, or television program merchandizing.

The discussion of advertising and its effect on children's developing consumer culture is a fascinating illustration of the value-driven ambivalence involved in the discussion of media effects: Is advertising exploiting children's trust and naïveté as well as their limited cognitive capacities in order to sell products, at least some of which are superfluous, wasteful, and even harmful to their health? Is intensification of consumerism among children necessarily negative? From whose point of view? And what about advertising's contribution to the development of consumer skills and to the availability of relevant information? Is advertising entangled – and in what ways – with wider ideological issues, such as modernization, consumer society, and capitalism? Putting it more generally, we can ask: In what ways does advertising challenge children's wellbeing?[33]

Advertising for children

Obviously, companies must believe that advertising is effective or they could not justify investing so much money in it. Some argue that they cannot afford not to advertise, as it is not the effectiveness of the advertising sought, per se, but rather the desire to avoid a situation of non-visibility that will result from not advertising. Stated succinctly, one needs to advertise simply because everyone else does. So what does research tell us about advertising effectiveness?

In Chapter 2 we learned that as children grow older they gain the ability to distinguish between commercials and programs, to remember them for a longer period of time, and to recognize their persuasive intent, gradually.[34] As they mature, children also gain first-hand experience, both by "nagging" their parents to buy them advertised products, as well as with the products themselves. They learn from those interactions to restrain themselves, to repeat their requests in spite of parental refusal, and to become more realistic regarding those situations when there are greater chances of their requests being fulfilled. Experiences with the products enable children to be more critical of commercials, as they learn to compare the image with the actual product. Their developing cognitive abilities facilitate their understanding of advertising tactics and manipulations. In societies where children experience such advertising daily, signs of distrust of commercials have been found to be quite common from the age of 10. While initially children are more critical of the lack of realism of the product in comparison to its image on television, gradually they learn to focus on the persuasive nature of advertising and the tactics of manipulation when employed.[35]

Several studies suggest that beyond the first few exposures to a particular commercial, there is no increased intensification of the product's attractiveness. That is, the original impression of the product usually remains constant. Watching commercials over time does not seem to have the same cumulative effect as watching violent television. However, development of capabilities to be critical of commercials does not necessarily reduce the effectiveness of commercials in arousing desires in children for new products or in reinforcing existing purchasing habits. It seems that children's attitudes (perhaps like those of many adults) are not necessarily predictive of their actual purchasing behaviors.

Several specific advertising tactics have been proven to be particularly effective with children. Offering prizes and gifts (e.g., a toy within a cereal box) seems to be highly successful in enticing children to prefer one product over its competitors. Similarly, employing celebrities (such as actors, singers, athletes) in commercials positively affects children's evaluation of the product even when the celebrity's "expertise" is non-related to the product advertised. "Program-length" commercials, such as programs that present characters and accessories that are also offered for sale in the market for children (e.g., toys, clothing, accessories, school products, decorations, computer games, magazines, cards), seem to be particularly effective, as is evident from the market saturation with merchandise that accompanies the promotion of each new child-targeted television series or film release.[36]

Of the many products advertised in the media, special concern has been directed at those deemed inherently harmful to children, such as cigarettes and alcohol, and the role of advertising in promoting early onset of smoking and alcohol drinking among children and youth. Another, more recent, central concern is the contribution of advertising to the growing obesity of children worldwide. We will return to these topics below.

Social and emotional wellbeing, and advertising

The world of advertising is, as a whole, designed to make all of us – including children – feel dissatisfied with who we are and what we have obtained, materially and emotionally, in order to sustain the motivation to purchase new products that promise to improve our lives and lift us to a higher level of happiness. Thus, advertising results in making children feel "not good enough" and in need of constant improvement in at least three complementary ways: First, by presenting social, physical, materialistic or mental achievements that no one, including children, is capable of achieving (no matter how much money they might spend on products and services). Second, by presenting children who are similar to them, but who have been placed in subordinate roles (e.g., girls in comparison to boys, children in comparison to adults, members of a minority group in comparison to members of a majority group). Third, by presenting characters similar to the viewer who have a much better life, socially and economically.[37]

Thus, an indirect effect of advertising is the degree to which it contributes to the child's general sense of satisfaction or dissatisfaction with his or her life, in general, and materialistic conditions, in particular. This feeling can be stimulated by the ability or inability to purchase everything advertised that children have been lead to believe is "a must," as well as by the disappointments from products they have been motivated to purchase that do not fulfill their advertised promises (e.g., to make them happy, thrilled, popular, pretty, successful). In addition, children denied a product of their choice or disappointed with it may react by expressing strong feelings of disappointment, anger, frustration, and sadness.

A somewhat different concern regarding the harmful effects of advertising relates to indirect types of effects on parent–child relationships. For example, the role of advertising as a stimulant of conflict, and the effects on the general sense of parents' and children's wellbeing and happiness. The cycle that leads to such unpleasant feelings includes the fact that commercials can stimulate young children's requests of their parents to purchase a particular item. According to parents' and children's self-reports, frequent "buy me" demands (coined *nagging effect* or *pester power*) often lead to arguments, quarrels, and even temper tantrums. Researchers' observations of children's behaviors in supermarkets documented such exchanges. Thus, children exert direct influence over their parents' purchasing habits by requesting products, as well as indirect influence, as parents internalize their children's tastes and make purchases that will please them, even without children making explicit requests or even being present when purchases are made.

Clearly, commercials have become a central force in socializing children into consumer culture and different families respond to this force and handle this process in different ways; some, perhaps many, accede to children's requests to purchase an advertised product, while others help their children acquire skills, knowledge, and attitudes to evaluate commercials and the products advertised.

Is advertising working?

The direct influence of advertising on children's behavior is not as taken-for-granted as advertisers might have hoped or we might have thought. Once again, the overarching research finding seems to be related to developmental processes: As they grow older, children develop more awareness and more developed critical attitudes toward the world of advertising, even when such attitudes do not necessarily express themselves in their purchasing choices or habits. Younger children are more vulnerable to the prominence and attractiveness of commercials and less able, cognitively, to view them critically. They have more difficulty understanding the purpose of advertising and they watch it less discriminately in comparison to older children.

Overall, studying the direct effectiveness of commercials is complicated, as the actual behavior is grounded in dynamic interactions between different sets of intervening variables, including those related to personality, family background, society, and culture. Adults' reconstructions of the role advertising had in their past as children in the USA (through the employment of a method called "life history") reveals that it was a source of entertainment and family conversation and had a central role in the development of their consumer habits as well as critical skills. However, participants were aware of the fact that knowledge and understanding of the advertising world did not necessarily protect against the effects it had on them.[38] Furthermore, untangling commercials from non-commercial content has become much more complicated, if not impossible, as advertising has become so deeply embedded in every aspect of our daily lives and commodification of society such a central aspect of late modernity.

So, does exposure to advertising enhance materialistic attitudes and values? The overall conclusion from tens of studies is that it does (see also the discussion in Chapter 4).[39] And, does advertising for children sell goods? The answer, according to the research, seems to be affirmative, though under certain conditions. The views of companies seeking to sell their products as well as those of advertising agencies seem to be much more decisive, otherwise, how can we understand their costly and extensive efforts? Here, too, we can conclude that the search for causal effects of media on children has produced valuable, but limited, results of narrow scope. Furthermore, there is a need not only for more research, but for extending such investigations to a more holistic study of the complexity of children's behaviors.

This having been noted, we need to ask ourselves whether this is the only relevant research question to be pursued. For example, studies of the role of commercials in the everyday lives of children reiterate that, in addition to purchasing products, such commercials contribute to other realms of life: emotional responses such as enthusiasm and joy – demonstrated by children singing and dancing along with the ads – esthetic pleasure, dramatic imitation, or the impact on peer relationships. Other studies connect advertising to health-related concerns such as obesity, eating disorders, and body image, as will be discussed shortly. Critical theorists emphasize advertising's role in cultivating materialistic values and worldviews, as well as in shaping identities, self-image, and self-worth. We will revisit these issues in the following chapters.

Thus, commercials seem to have a wide variety of functions for children and their roles cannot be measured in terms of sales alone. Public debates about children as consumers, which often frame them in binary terms, as either vulnerable victims of manipulation or as sophisticated agents of their own desires, reflect broader discussions about the meaning of childhood and the nature of children. Alternatively, some scholars argue that we need to understand contemporary childhoods as commercial ones and thus analyze them in the broader cultural and historical contexts in which they exist.[40]

Media, Alcohol, and Smoking

There has been a growing concern over the effects of media on children and young people's developing habits of alcohol drinking and cigarette smoking. Young people's substance abuse has become a matter of great concern in societies all over the world due to the variety of health consequences resulting from addiction. In addition, alcohol and drug abuse are associated with car accidents, aggressive behavior, sexual crimes, and domestic violence. In contrast to unhealthy foods, promotion of alcohol and cigarettes in children's media spaces is restricted in many places, but is nevertheless pervasive in the general popular media consumed by children. Advertising messages are often associated with growing up and being "in," as well as with providing a wide range of physical and psychological pleasures, including within intimate relationships.

Studies that tackled the complexities of the many issues involved here present evidence that exposure to messages promoting alcohol and cigarettes can encourage non-drinkers and non-smokers to hold positive attitudes toward these behaviors and to express an interest in drinking and smoking when they grow up. Young media consumers seem to be impressed by the positive advertising message that associates alcohol and smoking with "the good life," adulthood, and independence. Higher exposure to advertising for alcohol drinking and cigarette smoking was also found to be associated with earlier initiation of these behaviors. Youth who are already drinking and smoking were influenced to change preferences to particular alcohol and cigarette brands. There is also an indication that advertising is particularly effective when other socializing agents and social pressures – such as parents, educators, religious authorities, peers – are non-committal, or even users themselves, and specifically at the beginning of the adolescent years. Here, too, gender plays a role, as males seem to be more prone to the influence of messages about drinking embedded in movies than females. Some scholars explain this finding by claiming that drinking is associated more with masculinity, and more specifically, getting drunk and losing control of one's behavior is specifically perceived as non-feminine and inappropriate for young women.[41]

In addition, as in earlier cases, we need to consider the socio-cultural context in which children are growing as well as their specific media ecology, as they learn to associate substance abuse with societal values and expectations. For example, awareness of the health hazards of smoking has gradually turned it into a much less glorified and popular behavior in certain societies, while it is still highly pervasive in others. Similarly, alcohol drinking is more popular among certain populations than others. In a related issue, prescription drugs are very aggressively promoted in the US media while being entirely absent in other societies. Thus, countries differ in expressing concerns related to media effects on unhealthy behaviors.

Media, Obesity, and Eating Disorders

Correlations found between media use and obesity is a relatively new and growing concern. This field of research has been supported by medical literature documenting the increased prevalence of childhood obesity worldwide, its many physical and emotional health risks, and the national costs involved in its treatment. Children's extraordinary weight gain is determined by a host of biological, social, and environmental factors. Media consumption, too, has been found to be among the contributing factors. For example, being overweight has been found to be associated with heavy television viewing (i.e., viewing more than 4–5 hours per day).

Numerous explanations have been offered for how media use can be a contributing factor to being overweight.[42] One commonsense explanation is that most media-related engagements involve little physical activity and thus lead to weight gain. Two related popular claims offered are, first, media consumption displaces other physical activities (e.g., involvement in sports and outdoor play); and, second, limited physical activity as well as extensive media use can disrupt healthy sleeping patterns (e.g., over-stimulation before bedtime; less sleep due to media-related activities late into the night; sleep interrupted by receiving phone calls and texts). While these findings may hold true for all kinds of children, in the USA they were found to be the case for generally less active children – particularly girls and several minority groups. Programs that succeeded in reducing children's viewing time, among other interventions, were successful in reducing body weight in children. While the accumulated evidence is quite convincing, it is also possible that a vicious circle is in operation here: overweight children prefer non-demanding physical activities, such as viewing television (and perhaps also eating during viewing), and thus television viewing reinforces their weight problems.

A different argument suggests that media and food consumption often go hand-in-hand – through habits of eating mindlessly while engaging in media activities.

Examples in support of this explanation include: familial and social habits of eating in front of the television, in the movie theaters, and in front of the computer. In addition, viewers may simply be encouraged to overeat given the excessive food-related stimulants in commercials and in general media content.

While research in support of these commonsense explanations is still too limited to establish clear relationships that strongly support the claims, evidence seems to be increasing in recent years. This evidence has inspired several policy directives, including the following two American Academy of Pediatrics recommendations (AAP, 2003): Media use for the youngest children should not begin before the age of two; and, parents should limit the screen time of children older than two years to no more than two hours per day.[43]

In addition to these two commonsense explanations and policy derivatives, the most studied hypothesis argues that it is advertising of unhealthy food that most impacts weight gain; particularly items containing high levels of sugar (e.g., sweets, cereals, soft drinks) and the unhealthy fats contained in many fast food meals. Advertising, and consuming, such unhealthy products constitutes a significant part of advertising directed at children in many countries around the world and has been a topic of much public debate and advocacy efforts in recent years.[44] The few studies that actually examined this issue indicated the effectiveness of such commercials on influencing children's food choices, particularly when they are reinforced by a variety of promotional strategies (including prizes, cross-selling in various media platforms, advergames) and when they are not presented with counter-messages (e.g., advertising for healthy fruit). Even brief exposures to televised food commercials were found to be effective, and many argue that the intensive efforts to market food to children and youth have had a detrimental effect on their overall eating habits. At the same time, this type of study has been criticized for remaining quite narrow in its conception of direct and immediate effects, as well as for being disassociated from other factors in children's lives and eating habits.

Assessing this hypothesis reminds us that, as in all other media-related issues, social and cultural contexts are extremely important considerations. For example, obesity rates have been documented as higher among low-income populations who are more dependent on cheap fast foods for their nutrition and who may be affected differently from other income groups by advertising. Given that racial differences are often entangled with social inequalities, it is no surprise that relationships between media consumption and obesity operate differentially for different races. For example, the obesity rate among Afro-American children is higher than for the majority Caucasian population in the USA, as is time spent with media, and with it exposure to unhealthy food commercials. Such a dynamic constellation of factors requires careful attention as we cannot generalize findings from one population of children to all children without taking into consideration racial and social-class differences.

In summary, then, researchers seem to agree that links between media use and obesity are somewhat elusive, and certainly cannot be reduced to a simple causal relationship. Furthermore, there are many limitations to existing research studies:[45]

For one, great difficulties are involved in measuring children's media use accurately. For example, how can researchers accurately measure the number of hours children are engaged with media? How can they accurately estimate the amount of exposure to advertisements? In addition, as we have argued above, many intervening variables need to be considered, such as family risk of obesity, race, class status, family nutrition awareness, and eating habits. The lack of longitudinal studies involved in examining these relationships over time, as well as the limited amount of research that considers all forms of media consumption beyond just television viewing, are also significant limitations.

Body image and eating disorders

Eating disorders constitutes a family of diseases that includes anorexia nervosa (i.e., starving oneself), bulimia (i.e., constant purging and induced vomiting), and compulsive eating. These are complicated diseases that have psychological, physiological, and social aspects, and whose treatment involves many medical professions. They are common in more wealthy societies, often among talented, ambitious, good-looking, and popular girls. However, they have been growing in other parts of contemporary societies as well. Generally, eating disorders seem to be a gendered phenomenon – most dominant among girls and young women.

The cultural aspects involved with eating disorders emerged as a matter of social concern in the 1990s. Here, the possible contribution of popular culture to the problem was the focus of much criticism due to familiar representations of women and girls of all ages via hyper-sexualization and unattainable portrayals of female beauty; glorification of especially thin models and actresses as "sexy" and "glamorous"; and presenting thinness as an expression of self-control and success. Recent attempts to construct thinness as feminine and beautiful have been claimed by many scholars to be a contemporary form of gender inequality and a significant impediment to girls' health and wellbeing.[46]

Studies of representations of girls in television programs distributed worldwide, with children as their target audience, have clearly documented and analyzed this trend.[47] The empirical finding is that the average female body in industrialized countries has been expanding gradually over the past half century, while its representation in the media has become thinner. By way of interpretation, the overall view expressed by scholars claims that the *beauty myth* enslaves girls and women of all ages to invest the best of their emotional, physical, and economic resources in a futile attempt to "fix" their appearance in a compulsory manner – via cosmetics, fashion, food, plastic surgery, beauty salons, fitness clubs, etc. – in order to attain a resemblance to the beauty ideal that serves consumer culture.[48] The cultural norms projected through media images are presumed to create inner contradictions: between a woman's internal definition of herself and the definition of the *ideal me*.

Researchers of what is referred to in this discourse as the general phenomenon of the *beauty myth* address such questions as: how do images of thin, boyish-looking female celebrities, actresses, and supermodels whose bodily signs of femininity (e.g., round hips and thighs) have been erased affect self-body image and the self-worth of girls as they are growing up? What value do they attach to the nearly impossible ideal of a very thin, tall figure with slim legs and disproportionately large breasts?

While the overall intent of a growing number of empirical studies is to unravel the tangled relationships between the *beauty myth* and girls' self-body image, an illustrative sub-set of studies deal with eating disorders, particularly in the USA where this has become a matter of serious concern. These studies employ both experimental designs for the study of short-term effects as well as correlation studies for the investigation of the longer-term accumulative effects. Overall they suggest that exposure to media images is one of a number of important variables that interact with and that are involved in the development of eating disorders.[49] For example, the more dissatisfied with their bodies the teenage girls were, the more they seemed to internalize the messages from the media. Accumulative exposure to stereotypical beauty models seems to contribute to a lower sense of body image, dissatisfaction with one's body, desire to lose weight, and attitudes that are indicative of eating disorders (e.g., obsessive concern with one's weight, strong guilt over eating, and depression over one's appearance). Such attitudes have been measured using scales developed from requests that respondents rank their degree of agreement with statements such as: "I think the ideal woman should be thin"; "I think of my body in comparison to the bodies of television characters"; or "I constantly think about wanting to be thin."[50]

Media images seem to have both direct and indirect effects on body image. They shape directly the way girls and young women process their own body image, but also indirectly encourage girls to internalize and believe in the thin body ideal. At the same time, there is evidence of many other intervening variables in these processes. For example, girls who perceive media content to be less realistic, who are more critical viewers, who dismiss television's influence on their worldviews, and those who are more critical of the *beauty myth* demonstrate resistance to such influence.

So far we have discussed this phenomenon only in reference to girls and women, as thinness is mostly associated with the female body and eating disorders have been almost exclusively a female issue. However, there are signs that this is gradually becoming a male issue, as well, due to developing changes in gender roles along with the economic and cultural pressures exerted on male audiences to become more aware of their bodies and to join in the consumption of related products and services. Indeed, exploratory studies suggest that the same emotional mechanisms that operate on girls may well be activated in some boys, too. For boys, however, the cultural pressure seems to be related to the development of an unnatural, "beefy," muscular body-building appearance that is assumed to communicate physical strength and power. Scholars studying what they claim is an emerging trend raise questions about the potential health-related issues for boys of over-exercising and weightlifting associated with such a popular masculine ideal.[51]

The discussion of media's contribution to body image and eating disorders is an excellent example of a culturally embedded concern that has been studied mainly from an ethnocentric, Euro-American perspective. Indeed, the ideal of the *beauty myth* is clearly Anglo-European in origin, and so pervasive that even the few non-Anglo-European celebrities, framed as "exotic," are mainly a colored version of the same ideal model (as are, for example, the colored Barbie dolls). Indeed, from a global perspective, these studies and phenomena may be completely irrelevant for societies where food is scarce or where women's bodies are mostly covered. Yet, global television does not offer girls around the world alternative models of beauty – a fully rounded body of an African or Latin beauty, or a small-boned Asian one. Excluding alternative forms of beauty of the fuller facial features and curly dark hair of the African woman or the slatted eyes and characteristic nose of the Asian woman, means that light skin and hair, as well as small facial features, are still the norm. To date there is no systematic research to provide us with a satisfying answer to the question of how this Anglo-European model is affecting girls and young women throughout the world. However, there is mounting evidence to point at processes in action: the growing industry of facial plastic surgery (e.g., "correcting" eyes and lips) of Asian women, dying hair and whitening skin by dark-skinned women, and the sucking of fat tissues from the hips and buttocks to give a narrower look for Latin women.[52]

Media and Pro-social Behavior

The focus in this chapter, so far, has been on potential *negative* consequences of media use, as these have primed public debates and academic research. Indeed, these are the topics that have received significant research funding. Therefore, we simply know a lot more about them than we do about positive impacts. However, the same principles and methods that characterize studies of media's effects on anti-social behaviors are also applicable to studying other types of behavior and health-related issues. If, indeed, it is possible to learn negative behaviors from media, and to be affected by their persuasive messages, would it not follow that is also possible to learn positive, pro-social behaviors and healthy lifestyle habits as well? This is an important question, as it reminds us that media are multifaceted and certainly cannot be cast in negative terms alone. More specifically, it calls our attention to the content offerings of the media as these are significant determinants of the direction that media effects on children might take.

Pro-social behaviors are those perceived to be desirable by society at large. For example, the following media contents have been evaluated as pro-social: contents that promote cooperation and mutual aid; expressions of regret for harm done; sympathy and empathy with another person's situation or emotions; resolving conflicts; learning to persist in a task and to delay gratification; seeing things from another person's point of view; controlling violent urges; expressing feelings; resisting temptations; and the like. In addition, contents that promote healthy nutrition and lifestyles and civic engagement would also be included in this concept.

Before proceeding further, we should raise a note of caution: What one group may define as "pro-social" may be perceived by another group or culture as anti-social or even illegal. Indeed, within pluralistic societies, there are many disagreements regarding what constitutes pro-social behavior. For example, is using contraceptives a pro-social behavior? Does volunteering for military service constitute pro-social behavior? Thus, since most countries are pluralistic in nature, we should not expect to find one unequivocal code of ethics regarding the kind of values and behaviors that television needs to promote, and thus producers often find themselves having to deal with a public debate over the issues and values they choose to present. Any binary division of "good" and "bad" behavior is bound to be value laden and specifically contextualized. In this chapter we focus on those behaviors that are more generally accepted as positive or negative.

In Anglo-European programming, for example, we find that educational programs and websites for young viewers often emphasize the value and uniqueness of each person, including the child-viewer, in order to encourage a positive self-image as well as respect for others. Such programs focus on learning to cope with problems, issues, and situations typical of children's lives (e.g., the first day of school, moving, arrival of a new baby, wearing glasses, going to the dentist, as well as having tolerance and accepting diversity for minorities, disabilities, foreigners). Yet, many of these situations and issues posed, while common to all societies, may be treated differently from one society to the other. For example, while in some Anglo-European societies we might well find a segment dedicated to divorce, another society in which the majority hold religious beliefs and values that do not recognize divorce might promote their own social concern of holding on to traditional family values in the face of assault by the dominant Anglo-European lifestyle. A few examples from around the world illustrate such differences: An educational program for preschool children in South Africa focuses on the emotions of a child orphaned by AIDS; a program in Israel teaches children how to wear a gas mask in preparation for war; in Thailand a program presents children with the value of helping parents work to harvest crops in the field; and in Brazil boys are encouraged to engage in traditional female household chores.[53] Programs for older children present topics appropriate to their stage of development: conflicts with parents, issues of self-identity, sexuality, professional career aspirations, peer pressure, rejection by friends, and many more.

Many media platforms and genres, not only educational and public ones, include pro-social role models among their many characters. A situation comedy, a sports program, a commercial, and indeed even a program with violent content often include a character who only demonstrates pro-social behaviors, or a more complex, and, some would argue, more realistic, figure might demonstrate both positive and negative social behaviors. Many of these behaviors are embedded in programs intentionally, as in the genres of *edutainment*, introduced in Chapter 3. Sometimes this is due to the producers' aims, but can occur as a result of social pressures exerted by advocacy groups who lobby for and even negotiate messages with commercial broadcasters that deal, for example, with such topics as non-smoking behaviors, wearing a seatbelt, eating nutritious food, saving money in the bank, learning to read and write, refraining from driving under the influence of alcohol, using various forms of birth control, or applying non-violent solutions to family conflicts. The logic of including such strategies is that incidental learning of behaviors while view-ing entertainment genres, surfing the web, and playing video games can be particu-larly effective as the child who chooses the media offering can be or become emotionally engaged with the content, identify with the characters, and perceive the message as a legitimate and natural form of behavior in the social setting depicted in the program, website, or game. Such encounters offer the possibility of learning via imitation of observed behavior, development of skills for managing emotions, and internalization of "scripts" of desirable ways of acting in various situations.

As with violence studies analyzed previously in this chapter, researchers have applied experimental as well as correlational and longitudinal methodologies in order to investigate the effectiveness of pro-social messages, mainly in relationship to television and young children. However, fewer studies have been devoted to such inquiry, as clearly the fear of violent effects of some television programs has been deemed to be much more central to the agenda of most societies than the explora-tion of the positive potential of media. However, there has been a growth of research in recent years, as well as an expansion to older ages and to media other than televi-sion. From the knowledge gained to date, it is clear that children are capable of learning positive behaviors from the media in the same manner as they are able to learn negative behaviors.

For example, studies conducted in the USA on educational preschool programs, including the iconic *Mr. Rogers' Neighborhood* and *Sesame Street*, as well as on the co-productions of the latter in countries around the world (e.g., Bangladesh, Ireland, South Africa, Turkey), found that viewing television can encourage generosity, cooperation, delay of gratification, social integration of minority children and those with disabilities, and many other pro-social behaviors. It can contribute to modi-fying many different kinds of specific behaviors, such as reducing young children's fears of dogs or dentists; wearing helmets while riding bikes; using sunscreen lotions; or wearing seatbelts. These findings were found not only with regard to segments designed specifically for research purposes and educational programs, but also as a result of viewing drama programs.[54]

Also evident from much of this research is that most of the documented behavioral learning is short term and that significant long-term changes require integration with educational and public campaigns that reinforce the televised message over a period of time. The question also remains as to whether children are able to apply these newly acquired behaviors in novel and unfamiliar situations.

Various health and emergency-management media interventions in low-resource countries attempt to teach children, and their families, important survival skills such as: good hygiene and nutrition practices; preparation for natural disasters; avoid-ance of mine-fields; safe sex; and gender equity. UNICEF (United Nations International Children's Educational Fund) continues to be a leading force in development and implementation of such initiatives. While anecdotal data suggests their usefulness, the vast majority of these efforts have not been systematically evaluated.[55]

More recently, there has been a budding interest in the role video games can play in teaching pro-social behaviors. The same arguments that perceive them to be potent socializers of aggressive behavior holds true for pro-social behaviors as well. Thus, children's role playing, persistence in practicing skills and problem-solving, and assuming responsibility for their actions are all effective ways to internalize a range of behaviors. Indeed, although scant, a series of studies pursuing such effects conducted in the USA, Japan, and Singapore by one research team and another group in the UK demonstrated that pro-social game play can effect desired behaviors in children.[56]

Concluding Remarks

In this chapter, we have seen how complicated it is to answer questions regarding media's effects on children and how difficult it is to achieve and to agree upon on clear-cut and accepted conclusions. Nevertheless, we can suggest with some confidence that media have an important role in children's everyday behavior. As in other areas of study in the social sciences, significant difficulties are encountered when seeking to discover or prove the existence of causal relationships between media use and specific behaviors. However, there is plenty of evidence that media consumption contributes to reinforcing existing behaviors and that it sometimes creates or converts behaviors.

Can we generalize from the accumulated body of research as to whether media's potential is greater for teaching negative or positive behaviors? One argument about this broad field of study suggests that the negative effects of media violence are significantly stronger than the pro-social effects. While pro-social behavior is highly regarded by adults, it is not necessarily perceived as valuable – or even understandable – by children. Furthermore, anti-social behaviors, such as violence, can seem much more attractive to children and often involve very simple, physical, and direct acts – both on the screen and in real life. This conclusion assumes that, as a general rule, it is much easier to imitate a specific violent act and to release aggressive urges than to control them and commit an act of generosity or patience. Others disagree with the above interpretation and suggest that children might model explicit behavior seen in the media – negative or positive to the same degree – provided they find it to be realistic and applicable to their own situation. The most recent comprehensive meta-analysis of existing research in this area concluded that pro-social content had an effect on children's behavior, but it was not a strong one.[57] However, with the growing interest in studies of pro-social learning from media, we may see this conclusion changing in the coming years.

Discussion of behavioral effects is deeply entangled in other areas of children's lives: it involves children's individual development, their viewing abilities, parental mediation, and the cultural context at large, as discussed throughout this book. It is also strongly related to the complex value systems involved in the processes of socialization and construction of reality, to which we turn in Chapter 5. Finally, it also has important implications for education for media literacy, a topic discussed in Chapter 7, as well as for the development of broadcasting policy for children, discussed in Chapter 8. Clearly though, similar mechanisms are at work in children's learning a repertoire of behaviors from the media: One cannot argue that children are easily persuaded by advertising to purchase products, but are immune to learning aggressive behaviors; or that they are becoming more violent as a result of exposure to violent media, but are incapable of learning pro-social behaviors from quality programming. What we can claim is that children are capable of learning from their media use, and that the content to which they are exposed makes a huge difference to what they will actually learn.

Notes

1. National Television Violence Study, 1996.
2. This line of research was originally associated with Bandura; see, for example, Bandura, 1965.
3. See, for example, Liebert & Sprafkin, 1988.
4. Based on the prototype offered by Stein & Freidrich, 1972.
5. Huesmann & Eron, 1986.
6. Lefkowitz, Eron, Walder, & Huesmann, 1977.
7. Savage & Yancery, 2008.
8. Paik & Comstock, 1994.
9. Comstock, 1991.
10. Anderson, Gentile, & Dill, 2012; Weber, Ritterfield, & Mathiak, 2006.
11. Slater, Henry, Swaim, & Anderson, 2003.
12. Jones, 2002; Tobin, 2000; Van der Voort, 1986.
13. For an extensive review see Bushman & Huesmann, 2001.
14. Groebel, 1998.
15. Lemish, 2010.
16. For discussion of these examples see a collection of essays in Carlsson & von Feilitzen, 1998.
17. Buckingham, 1993; Messenger Davies, 1989.
18. Greenberg, Brown, & Buerkel-Rothfuss, 1993; Gunter, 2002; Kunkel, Cope, & Biely, 1999.
19. Brown, 2008.
20. American Psychological Association, 2007; Levine & Kilbourne, 2008.
21. Peter, 2013.
22. Bleakley, Hennessy, Fishbein, & Jordan, 2008.
23. Lemish, 2010.
24. Gunter, 2002; Lee, 2004.
25. Buckingham & Bragg, 2004.
26. Zillman, 1994.
27. Cline, 1994; Gunter, 2002; Weaver, 1994.
28. Peter, 2013.
29. Lyons, Anderson, & Larson, 1994; Weaver, 1994.
30. Lemish, 2010.

31. Kunkel, 2001; Valkenburg, 2004; Van Evra, 2004.
32. Montgomery, 2012.
33. Naim, 2014.
34. See also integrated review in Buijzen, Rozendaal, & van Reijmersdal, 2013.
35. Valkenburg & Cantor, 2002.
36. Macklin & Carlson, 1999; Valkenburg, 2004; Van Evra, 2004.
37. Atkin, 1980; Comstock, 1991; Ward, Wackman, & Wartella, 1977.
38. Heintz, Shively, Wartella, & Oliverez, 1995.
39. Naim, 2014.
40. Buckingham, 2013.
41. For integrated reviews see Borzekowski, 2013; Strasburger, 2012.
42. Bond, Richards, & Calvert, 2013; Jordan, 2010.
43. American Academy of Pediatrics, 2003.
44. Horgen, Harris, & Brownell, 2012.
45. Vandewater & Cummings, 2008.
46. Durham, 2008; Lamb & Brown, 2006; Levine & Kilbourne, 2008.
47. Götz & Lemish, 2012.
48. Barky, 1988; Wolf, 1992.
49. Harrison, 2013.
50. Botta, 1999.
51. Brown, Lamb, & Tappen, 2009; Götz & Lemish, 2012.
52. Lemish, 2010.
53. Lemish, 2010.
54. For reviews of this literature see Fisch, 2004; Mares, Palmer, & Sullivan, 2008; Mares & Woodward, 2012.
55. Kolucki, 2013; Kolucki & Lemish, 2011.
56. Anderson, Gentile, & Dill, 2012.
57. Mares & Woodward, 2012.

References

American Academy of Pediatrics (AAP). (2003). Prevention of pediatric overweight and obesity. *Pediatrics, 112*, 424–430.

American Psychological Association. (2007). Report of the APA on the sexualization of girls. http://www.apa.org/pi/wpo/sexualization.html. Retrieved July 25, 2014.

Anderson, C.A., Gentile, D.A., & Dill, K.E. (2012). Prosocial, antisocial, and other effects of recreational video games. In D.G. Singer & J.L. Singer (Eds.), *Handbook of children and the media* (pp. 249–272). Thousand Oaks, CA: Sage Publications.

Atkin, C.K. (1980). Effects of television advertising on children. In E.L. Palmer & A. Dorr (Eds.), *Children and the faces of television: Teaching, violence, selling* (pp. 287–305). New York: Academic Press.

Bandura, A. (1965). Influence of models' reinforcement contingencies on the acquisition of imitative responses. *Journal of Personality and Social Psychology, 1*, 589–595.

Barky, S.L. (1988). Foucault, femininity, and the modernization of patriarchal power. In I. Diamond (Ed.), *Feminism and Foucault* (pp. 61–86). Boston, MA: Northeastern University Press.

Bleakley, A., Hennessy, M., Fishbein, M., & Jordan, A. (2008). It works both ways: The relationship between sexual content in the media and adolescent sexual behavior. *Media Psychology, 11*(4), 443–461.

Bond, B.J., Richards, M.N., & Calvert, S.L. (2013). Media and obesity. In D. Lemish (Ed.), *The Routledge international handbook of children, adolescents, and media* (pp. 232–239). New York: Routledge.

Borzekowski, D.L.G. (2013). Media and substance abuse: Alcohol, smoking and drugs. In D. Lemish (Ed.), *The Routledge international handbook of children, adolescents, and media* (pp. 240–246). New York: Routledge.

Botta, R.A. (1999). Television images and adolescent girls' body image disturbance. *Journal of Communication, 49*(2), 22–41.

Brown, J. (Ed.). (2008). Managing the media monster: The influence of media (from television to text messages) on teen sexual behavior and attitudes. Washington, DC: National Campaign to Prevent Teen and Unplanned Pregnancy.

Brown, L.M., Lamb, S., & Tappan, M.B. (2009). *Packaging boyhood: Saving our sons from superheroes, slackers, and other media stereotypes.* New York: St. Martin's Press.

Buckingham, D. (1993). *Children talking television.* London: Falmer.

Buckingham, D. (2013). Constructing children as consumers. In D. Lemish (Ed.), *The Routledge international handbook of children, adolescents, and media* (pp. 54–60). New York: Routledge.

Buckingham, D. & Bragg, S. (2004). *Young people, sex and the media: The facts of life?* New York: Palgrave Macmillan.

Buijzen, M., Rozendaal, E., & van Reijmersdal, E.A. (2013). Media, advertising, and consumerism: Children and adolescents in a commercialized media environment. In D. Lemish (Ed.), *The Routledge international handbook of children, adolescents, and media* (pp. 271–278). New York: Routledge.

Bushman, B.J. & Huesmann, L.R. (2001). Effects of televised violence on aggression. In D.G. Singer & J.L. Singer (Eds.), *Handbook of children and the media* (pp. 223–254). Thousand Oaks, CA: Sage.

Carlsson, U. & von Feilitzen, C. (Eds.). (1998). *Children and media violence.* Göteborg University: The UNESCO International Clearinghouse on Children and Violence on the Screen.

Cline, V.B. (1994). Pornography effects: Empirical and clinical evidence. In D. Zillman, J. Bryant, & A.C. Huston (Eds.), *Media, children and the family: Social scientific, psychodynamic and clinical perspectives* (pp. 229–247). Hillsdale, NJ: Lawrence Erlbaum.

Comstock, G. (1991). *Television and the American child.* New York: Academic Press.

Durham, G. (2008). *The Lolita effect: The media sexualization of young girls and what we can do about it.* Woodstock & New York: The Overlook Press.

Fisch, S. (2004). *Children's learning from educational television: Sesame Street and beyond.* Mahwah, NJ: Lawrence Erlbaum.

Götz, M. & Lemish, D. (2012). *Sexy girls, heroes and funny losers: Gender representations in children's TV around the world.* Frankfurt am Main: Peter Lang.

Greenberg, B.S., Brown, J.D., & Buerkel-Rothfuss, N.L. (1993). *Media, sex and the adolescent.* Cresskill, NJ: Hampton.

Groebel, J. (1998). The UNESCO global study on media violence: Report presented to the Director General of UNESCO. In U. Carlsson & C. von Feilitzen (Eds.), *Children and media violence* (pp. 181–199). Göteborg University: The UNESCO International Clearinghouse on Children and Violence on the Screen.

Gunter, B. (2002). *Media sex: What are the issues?* Mahwah, NJ: Lawrence Erlbaum.

Harrison, K. (2013). Media, body image, and eating disorders. In D. Lemish (Ed.), *The Routledge international handbook of children, adolescents, and media* (pp. 224–231). New York: Routledge.

Heintz, K.E., Shively, A., Wartella, E., & Oliverez, A. (1995). Television advertising and childhood: Form, function and future uses. Paper presented at the annual meeting of the International Communication Association, Albuquerque, NM.

Horgen, K.B., Harris, J.L., & Brownell, K.D. (2012). Food marketing: Targeting young people in a toxic environment. In D.G. Singer & J.L. Singer (Eds.), *Handbook of children and the media* (pp. 455–478). Thousand Oaks, CA: Sage Publications.

Huesmann, L.R. & Eron, L.D. (Eds.). (1986). *Television and the aggressive child: A cross-national comparison.* Hillsdale, NJ: Lawrence Erlbaum.

Jones, G. (2002). *Killing monsters: Why children need fantasy, super heroes, and make-believe violence.* New York: Basic Books.

Jordan, A.B. (2010). Children's television viewing and childhood obesity. *Pediatric Annals, 39*(9), 569.

Kolucki, B. (2013). UNICEF and communication for development: An integrated approach to developing capacity to produce communication for and with children. In D. Lemish (Ed.), *The Routledge international handbook of children, adolescents, and media* (pp. 433–441). New York: Routledge.

Kolucki, B. & Lemish, D. (2011). *Communicating with children: Principles and practices to nurture, inspire, excite, educate and heal.* New York: Communication for Development Unit, UNICEF. See http://www.unicef.org/cwc. Retrieved July 25, 2014.

Kunkel, D. (2001). Children and television advertising. In D.G. Singer & J.L. Singer (Eds.), *Handbook of children and the media* (pp. 375–393). Thousand Oaks, CA: Sage.

Kunkel, D., Cope, K.M., & Biely, E. (1999). Sexual messages on television: Comparing findings from three studies. *The Journal of Sex Research, 36*(3), 230–236.

Lamb, S., & Brown, L.M. (2006). *Packaging girlhood: Rescuing our daughters from marketers' schemes.* New York: St. Martin's Press.

Lee, A.Y.L. (2004). Critical appreciation of TV drama and reality shows: Hong Kong youth in need of media education. In C. von Feilitzen (Ed.), *Young people, soap operas and reality TV* (pp. 117–127). Göteborg University, Sweden: The International Clearinghouse on Children, Youth and Media.

Lefkowitz, N.M., Eron, L.D., Walder, L.O., & Huesmann, L.R. (1977). *Growing up to be violent: A longitudinal study of the development of aggression.* Elmsford, NY: Pergamon.

Lemish, D. (2010). *Screening gender on children's television: The views of producers around the world.* London: Routledge.

Levine, D.E. & Kilbourne, J. (2008). *So sexy so soon: The new sexualized childhood and what parents can do to protect their kids.* New York: Ballantine Books.

Liebert, R.M. & Sprafkin, J. (1988). *The early window.* New York: Pergamon.

Lyons, J.S., Anderson, R.L., & Larson, D.B. (1994). A systematic review of the effects of aggressive and nonaggressive pornography. In D. Zillman, J. Bryant, & A.C. Huston (Eds.), *Media, children and the family: Social scientific, psychodynamic and clinical perspectives* (pp. 271–310). Hillsdale, NJ: Lawrence Erlbaum.

Macklin, M.C. & Carlson, L. (Eds.). (1999). *Advertising to children: Concepts and controversies.* Thousand Oaks, CA: Sage.

Mares, M., Palmer, E., & Sullivan, T. (2008). Prosocial effects of media exposure. In S.L. Calvert & B.J. Wilson (Eds.), *The handbook of children, media, and development* (pp. 268–289). New York: Blackwell.

Mares, M.L. & Woodard, E.H. (2012). Effects of prosocial media content on children's social interactions. In D.G. Singer & J.L. Singer (Eds.), *Handbook of children and the media* (pp. 197–214). Thousand Oaks, CA: Sage Publications.

Messenger Davies, M. (1989). *Television is good for your kids*. London: Hilary Shipman.

Montgomery, K.C. (2012). Safeguards for youth in the digital marketing ecosystem. In D.G. Singer & J.L. Singer (Eds.), *Handbook of children and the media* (pp. 631–648). Thousand Oaks, CA: Sage Publications.

Naim, A. (2014). Advertising and child well-being In A. Ben-Aieh, F. Casas, I. Fornes, & J.E. Korbin (Eds.), *Handbook of child well-being: Theories, methods and policies in global perspective* (Vol. 4, pp. 2031–2055). Dordrecht, Netherlands: Springer.

National Television Violence Study (1996). *National television violence study, 1*. Thousand Oaks, CA: Sage.

Paik, H. & Comstock, G. (1994). The effects of television violence on antisocial behavior: A meta-analysis. *Communication Research, 21*(4), 516–546.

Peter, J. (2013). Media and sexual development. In D. Lemish (Ed.), *The Routledge international handbook of children, adolescents, and media* (pp. 217–223). New York: Routledge.

Savage, J. & Yancery, C. (2008). The effects of media violence exposure on criminal aggression: A meta-analysis. *Criminal Justice and Behavior, 35*(6), 772–791.

Slater, M.D., Henry, K.L., Swaim, R.C., & Anderson, L.L. (2003). Violent media content and aggressiveness in adolescents: A downward spiral model. *Communication Research, 30*(6), 713–736.

Stein, A.H. & Freidrich, L.K. (1972). Television content and young children's behavior. In J.P. Murray, E.A. Rubinstein, & G.A. Comstock (Eds.), *Television and social behavior vol. 2: Television and social learning (Surgeon General Report)*. (pp. 203–317). Washington, DC: US Government Printing Office.

Strasburger, V.C. (2012). Children, adolescents, drugs, and the media. In D.G. Singer & J.L. Singer (Eds.), *Handbook of children and the media* (pp. 419–454). Thousand Oaks, CA: Sage Publications.

Tobin, J. (2000). *"Good guys don't wear hats": Children's talk about the media*. New York: Columbia University, Teachers College Press.

Valkenburg, P.M. (2004). *Children's responses to the screen: A Media psychological approach*. Mahwah, NJ: Lawrence Erlbaum.

Valkenburg, P.M. & Cantor, J. (2002). The development of a child into a consumer. In S.L. Calvert, A.B. Jordan, & R.R. Cocking (Eds.), *Children in the digital age: Influences of electronic media on development* (pp. 201–214). Westport, CT: Praeger.

Van der Voort, T.H.A. (1986). *Television violence: A child's-eye view*. Amsterdam: North-Holland.

Van Evra, J. (2004). *Television and child development* (3rd ed.). Mahwah, NJ: Lawrence Erlbaum.

Vandewater, E.A. & Cummings, H.M. (2008). Media use and childhood obesity. In S. Calvert and B.J. Wilson (Eds.). *The handbook of children, media, and development* (pp. 355–380). New York: Blackwell.

Ward, S., Wackman, D.B., & Wartella, E. (1977). *How children learn to buy: The development of consumer information-processing skills*. Beverly Hills, CA: Sage.

Weaver, J.B. (1994). Pornography and sexual callousness: The perceptual and behavioral consequences of exposure to pornography. In D. Zillman, J. Bryant, & A.C. Huston (Eds.), *Media, children and the family: Social scientific, psychodynamic and clinical perspectives* (pp. 215–228). Hillsdale, NJ: Lawrence Erlbaum.

Weber, R., Ritterfield, U., & Mathiak, K. (2006). Does playing violent videogames induce aggression? Empirical evidence of a functional magnetic resonance imagery study. *Media Psychology, 8,* 39–60.

Wolf, N. (1992). *The beauty myth: How images of beauty are used against women.* New York: Doubleday.

Zillman, D. (1994). Erotica and family values. In D. Zillman, J. Bryant, & A.C. Huston (Eds.), *Media, children and the family: Social scientific, psychodynamic and clinical perspectives* (pp. 199–213). Hillsdale, NJ: Lawrence Erlbaum.

5

Media and Perceptions of Self and Society

Previous chapters referred, repeatedly, to media as a major socializing agent in children's lives, one that complements and often competes with other more traditional socializing agents, such as family, school, peer groups, community, and religious institutions. The popular view of successful socialization is that it enables children and youth to fit into the society in which they live because they have learned what is considered to be socially appropriate norms and behaviors for that society. Specifically, through socialization, the child learns about his or her culture and internalizes its values, belief systems, perceptions of self and of others.

Passive notions portray socialization as uni-directional – from socializing agent to the child – yet the process is much more complex and seems to include an important, activist process referred to as the *social construction of reality*. First learned in childhood but applied throughout life, this process involves using mental capacities to understand and to construct meaning as we interact with the world and society.

Making meaning of media experiences involves both approaches – passive socialization and the activist social construction of reality. On the one hand, media programs introduce us to the world outside our immediate "here" and "now." They expand, interpret, highlight, judge, legitimize, and exclude social phenomena that the child encounters in reality or in other media. Often media function as the first, sometimes the only, encounter young viewers have with varied and unfamiliar social situations. Some researchers go so far as to argue that media have replaced religious institutions: They constantly reinforce certain ideological, mythological, and factual patterns of thought and so function to define the world and to legitimize the existing social order.

Children and Media: A Global Perspective, First Edition. Dafna Lemish.
© 2015 John Wiley & Sons, Inc. Published 2015 by John Wiley & Sons, Inc.
Companion Website: www.wiley.com/go/lemish/childrenandmedia

Yet, on the other hand, children all over the world have been found to be active, selective young people who use media to learn about the world. Doing so helps them define their own place within it. Whether it be Latin American telenovelas, Japanese animated games, reality TV in Africa, or mobile media in the Middle East, children find that many platforms and genres are informative in addition to entertaining. Media consumption is also considered to be used by children in the process of identity formation – be it of gender, sexuality, or of a social, religious, or political nature.

Given these multiple processes, we can ask such general questions as: What are the media's contributions to children's emerging social definitions of good and bad, right and wrong, true and false? How do media share our collective identity definitions and exclude those deemed to be different and foreign? How do they shape gender perceptions, sexual expectations, social and professional knowledge?

These and other questions studied with regard to young audiences borrow the concept of *schema* from psychology (see Chapter 2). Again, a schema is a cognitive structure that organizes the knowledge of given phenomena. It functions to direct the way we perceive, remember, process, and relate to information. For example, a gender schema is a framework that organizes our knowledge and expectations regarding masculinity and femininity. In doing so, it frames a child's interpretation of encounters with male and female media characters. Similarly, schemas of minorities, professions, or places are enforced, even challenged, via the viewing of television, and so enrich our understanding and experiencing of the world.

Of particular interest are the two ways schemas are "used" when we encounter unfamiliar stimuli or information: According to Piaget, the original conceptualizer of the theoretical concept of schema, a child or adult might either attempt to assimilate it into existing cognitive schemas, or change the schema in a way that will enable it to accommodate the new information. Through the processes of *assimilation* and *accommodation*, schemas multiply, expand, and become more complex as the child matures, so adding to his or her accumulated experience, understandings, and skills.[1]

Schemas, therefore, are structures that assist in organizing social knowledge. They are formed through experience and include representations of the world gathered through first-hand encounters or mediated experiences with the media. Gender schemas, for example, develop in a dynamic process of interactions with men and women in real life, as well as those encountered in the media.

Now, from this slight theoretical diversion, let us return to the key research questions presented above. Exposing attitudes and social perspectives involves a complicated, if not problematic, research process. First, such a process is deeply value laden and therefore reflects to a large degree the ideological departure point of the researcher. For example, a researcher such as myself, who advocates the necessity of achieving full gender and racial equality, may study media's role in facilitating or preventing such a change in judgmental ways. Furthermore, the social views of researchers are not easily detected or measured. They, too, develop over time in complicated and salient ways. Most complex is the fact that media are as diverse in their forms and contents as the societies within which they are operating, and it is extremely difficult to isolate a particular source of influence or a homogenous message. Therefore, in order to study the relationships between exposure to particular media content and the construction of social reality, a sophisticated methodology must be applied that includes forthright reflexivity about the complexity of media exposure and the researcher's own values and processes of constructing reality. In addition, the findings must be grounded in deep understandings of specific socio-cultural contexts.

As a result of their development and experience in the world, children and adults use structures of comprehension that have been modified significantly. Therefore, social meanings, as children understand them, can be very different to those of adults. As we discussed in Chapter 2, the conventional approach taken by developmental psychology often assumes that children's understandings are "less" – as in less complete, accurate, or relevant – than those held by adults. On the other hand, researchers who study children from the perspective of cultural studies may define them not as "less" but as fundamentally different from adults. Furthermore, as explained in Chapters 1 and 6, we understand that children's media use is embedded in family life and social relationships, that is, it does not operate in a social void. Therefore, the media's role as a socializing agent is a function of its interaction with other agents. It is here, at the pivotal point of interaction, that the study of young media users' social perceptions and the role of media in their lives must focus. Further, to do so, researchers must listen as children express themselves in their own voices and present their own perspectives. With this proviso in mind, our discussion in this chapter examines several key domains of social science research by focusing on media's interaction with selected social phenomena – gender, violence, "otherness," politics, and social values.

Media and Gender

There is a growing recognition in the social sciences, due in large part to the intellectual contributions of feminist theories, that gender differences (in contrast to biological differences in the reproduction organs) are socially constructed, learned sets of behaviors and perceptions. For example, while it is a biological fact that women can give birth, it is a social construction that women should be expected to be the dominant caregiver of children, and therefore to be nurturing, compassionate, and more communicative. Thus, learning the characteristics and behaviors "accepted" as masculine and feminine in a given society is a process that starts at birth.

The role of media in such a construction of gender schemas and identities is particularly important, as much of media content presents characters that can be assigned to one of the two gender categories, be they humans, cartoon figures, animals, or science fiction characters. Such characters supply a varied pool of models for identification and imitation, as discussed in Chapter 2. They define for the young what is "normal" masculinity and femininity and accepted in their society, and therefore which behaviors receive positive reinforcement, as well as what is deemed exceptional, even deviant, and therefore negatively sanctioned, normatively.

The many studies that have examined media portrayals of females and males of all ages demonstrate that programs differentiate between the two quite systematically. On the whole, men are identified with "doing" in the public sphere and associated with such characteristics as activity, rationality, forcefulness, independence, ambitiousness, competitiveness, achievement, and higher social status. Women are associated with "being" in the private sphere and are characterized, generally, as passive, emotional, care-giving, childish, sexy, subordinate to men, and of lower social status. Popular media, as a general rule (but there are many exceptions, and these are growing gradually in number and scope), often define men by their action, and, in contrast, women by their appearance. Women's external appearance continues to be presented as the most central characteristic of her essence from birth on. This emphasis is most commonly expressed through glorification of a particular beauty model, referred to as the *beauty myth*,[2] that is highly Anglo-European in orientation and practically unattainable. External appearance is directly related to media's overemphasis on the portrayal of women as sexual beings whose central function is relegated to being objects of male sexual desire and pursuit. Thus, such dominant media messages continue to promote restrictive ideologies of femininity, glorify heterosexual romance as a central goal for girls, and encourage male domination in relationships. They stress the importance of beautification through consumption, while dismissing the validity of girls' own sexual feelings and desires apart from masculine desire; and say nothing about all the many other aspects of women's essence, capabilities, and potential contributions.[3]

Furthermore, children's popular television programs with global reach offer a significant under-representation of female main characters and under-development of female characters in general. Males – both young and old – are the main heroes of children's programs. They succeed in overcoming everyday problems, deal successfully with all sorts of dangers, and have lots of adventures. Even non-gendered imaginary characters – such as creatures and animals – are considered "naturally" to be male, unless they are specifically marked as female through processes of sexualizing their appearance (e.g., hair ribbons, long eyelashes, colored lips, short skirts).[4] In this way, female characters continue to symbolize a deviation from the dominant-male norms and remain the *second sex* in the classical, inferior sense criticized in feminist discourse.[5]

Most female characters in media texts aimed at children are there to be saved and protected by the males or provide the background for the adventure. Above all, their position is defined by their meaning for male heroes. Indeed, even educational programs were found to have an under-representation of females as well as to employ traditional stereotypes. Certain symbols, such as horses, dolphins jumping in front of a sunset, bunnies, and flowers appear in these programs as they are gendered in our societies, and reinforced by market forces as "girlish." Other areas, such as technology, action, or fighting, are almost always framed as male themes and pre-interpreted as masculine. Furthermore, advertising for children applies gendered clichés excessively in presenting goods for consumption by signaling gender intention via glittery or pink and pastel colors for girls, and action-packed dark hues for boys.[6]

Following this brief introduction, we turn now to consider whether such portrayals shape children's perceptions of femininity, masculinity, and gender roles, and whether they contribute to young people's emerging self-image and perceptions of sexual identity.

Construction of gender roles

Overall, research on media's role in developing gender stereotypes among children is not unequivocal. One possible explanation is the difficulty in separating the specific contribution a particular medium or genre makes from that of other socializing agents. Thus, at least traditional perceptions regarding gender roles are so deeply embedded in all societies and cultures that children have ample first-hand opportunities to internalize them regardless of the media they are using.

Consider, for example, stereotypical gender divisions in the workforce. Research studies found that preschool-age boys and girls already have different professional aspirations. Does television, the dominant medium in their lives at this stage, contribute to the development of these aspirations? First, according to school-age children who participated in several earlier studies, television does serve as an important resource for learning about the existence of a variety of professions, even when these children do not have first-hand acquaintance with certain jobs. Children tended to rate professions according to social expectations – assigning higher status to professions that were perceived as masculine (e.g., police officer, detective, surgeon, lawyer) and were wary of accepting breaks in stereotypes (e.g., female police officer or male nurse). Taken as a whole, this type of study, as well as others that experimented with alternative methods, suggests that there is a relationship between viewing television at a young age and holding stereotypical views regarding various roles occupied by men and women in our societies. Yet, we should note this relationship is complicated by many other variables:[7] First, most of these studies were conducted in the USA, and they are quite dated. In addition, most did not refer to the viewing of particular programs and their characteristics but rather to mere exposure to television in general terms. The logic behind such a general measure was that extended viewing of television by definition exposes children to a large quantity of stereotypical content.[8] However, many questions about this process remain unanswered. For example, is the quantity of viewing per se the best predictor of the influence television has on attitudes? Would there be a difference between children who watch a lot of educational or public television programs versus those who mainly watch commercial television? Does genre make a difference? And, a key methodological question: Is it possible that studies that measure only the amount of viewing are actually measuring different kinds of effects, some that may even cancel each other out?

Correlation studies that attempted to find a relationship between viewing habits and gender-related attitudes assume that stereotypical attitudes are absorbed from media *en masse*. Researchers have yet to consider the ways in which children comprehend and process content viewed. Furthermore, the social location of children in their families, peer groups, or schools, too, has great relevance in the examination of relationships. According to research findings that applied this methodology, media's influence is stronger when it provides consistent and complementary information to knowledge already obtained, while influences dim when media present a contradictory or deviant world from that with which the child is familiar. Since children do possess gender-related schemas, they apply them in processing mediated information. Therefore, rather than create new attitudes, correlation findings suggest that media may serve more to reinforce existing views toward gender roles learned in other social contexts. It is also important to emphasize that no necessary relationship has been found between attitudes, including those shaped by media, and actual behavior. For example, one study of children who were heavy viewers of television found that while they rated various types of housework as stereotypically something that "girls do" or "boys do," no necessary relationship was found to exist between viewing television and actually doing housework chores associated with the other gender (e.g., boys washing dishes, girls taking out the garbage).[9] It seems that in this matter, too, the behaviors of other family members and significant-others mediate exposure to media and actual behavior. Furthermore, we need to remind ourselves that stereotypical gender roles are in and of themselves controversial, with very deep cultural differences and motivations for and against change.

Interestingly, the same conclusions are upheld when we examine the few studies conducted on television programs that tried intentionally to rupture gender stereotypes. The rationale applied in such programs, as well as in the research studies, is that if television contributes, even to a small degree, to the construction of gender reality, then we could expect that exposure to socially challenging television content will contribute to the development of counter-stereotypical attitudes. Here, the assumption is that media can be a socializing agent that facilitates social change, and not just an agent that preserves and reinforces the existing social order. Accordingly, it is reasonable to assume that portrayals offering scenarios contradictory to normative expectations will arouse a variety of responses from children. On the one hand, their innovative and unpredictable nature makes them very conspicuous, but on the other, their rarity might make them difficult to remember amidst a sea of more traditional portrayals.

Not surprisingly, correlation studies reveal here, too, that adolescents who regularly view programs with counter-traditional gender roles hold more positive attitudes and aspirations about non-traditional occupations. The same was true for preschool children who were regular viewers of educational television in the USA (where more extensive efforts have been made to break gender stereotypes than with commercial programs).[10] Once again, we can pose the question relevant to all studies of this type: Is it the viewing of particular kinds of messages that shapes children's attitudes regarding gender roles or is it the case that the children attracted to these kinds of programs in the first place are more receptive to non-traditional gender roles due to family background, personality, and other contextual variables? What other sources of such openness might influence these children? For example, might the influence lie with parents who are more highly educated, hold liberal views regarding gender roles, and who encourage their children to view more educational or other programs that advance non-traditional gender roles? Overall, then, the direction of the primary effect remains an open, yet central, question to be clarified in future studies conducted in this research tradition.

Findings from several experimental studies investigated this phenomenon by means of controlled situations (e.g., children were presented with specific portrayals, and measurements were taken that revealed whether there were changes in their attitudes in comparison to control groups of children not exposed to such portrayals). The findings suggest that children can learn new gender roles from television characters, particularly those related to their own gender. With regard to gender identification with television characters, girls seem to be more open to accepting roles traditionally associated with men, in comparison to boys who are more reluctant to accept roles traditionally associated with women. However, here, too, there is no evidence that such changes are internalized, have a lasting effect, or are transferred from attitudes to actual behavior.[11] Clearly, deep social change requires ongoing presentation of non-stereotypical portrayals along with other environmental stimuli that reinforce and encourage such values. This is as true for gender portrayals as it is for any other type of portrayal, as we continue to reiterate: The media's roles in children's lives can only be understood in their social context.

Construction of gender identity

One central issue regarding gender socialization that has developed primarily through feminist theories and research is the role that popular culture, including media, plays in the processes of constructing personal gender identity. Here researchers have asked questions such as: What is the meaning of masculinity and femininity these days? Does media content reinforce hegemonic notions of patriarchy (i.e., the feminist claim that the overriding structure of society is controlled by men, masculine values, and worldviews) or serve to accelerate social change in gendered dimensions of social structures and power? How do young people negotiate meaning in their interactions with media content in general, and in relation to their personal gender identity in particular?

Research into such questions has been advanced via the communication tradition of Reception Studies that looks into the ways audiences receive media content (i.e., make meaning, interpret, relate it to their own lives). Such studies usually search for methodological ways of allowing people to express their inner worlds through in-depth interviews, individually or in focus groups, or through creative means, such as personal compositions, diaries, and artwork. Many of these studies have centered on women and girls in the context of media content traditionally associated with them (e.g., soap operas, women's magazines, romance novels, pop music, advertising) and uncovered the dynamics of how female viewers gain pleasure, sometimes even a sense of empowerment and control, from content that is seemingly oppressive to women.

Research on pre-adolescence and adolescence is particularly interesting as identity development and dealing with social pressures that dominate perceptions of femininity and masculinity are important tasks in this period. Researchers working through approaches such as feminism and/or cultural studies view media texts as *sites of struggle* between conflicting social forces, including: traditional patriarchal forces versus female resistance; capitalist value systems versus alternatives such as socialism, Marxism, or religious moralities; uncritical acceptance of the adults' way of life and worldviews versus the cynical, critical visions of the younger generation.[12] In-depth analysis of case studies is usually applied in this line of research. Such, for example, was the study of the role of the pop group the *Spice Girls* in the lives of pre-adolescent, middle-class Jewish girls in Israel in the 1990s, and their negotiation of multiple messages about friendship, sexuality, and the concept of *Girl Power* that the group introduced to popular culture.[13] Other scholars have explored how girls negotiate the concept of *Girl Power* as they try to consolidate expectations placed on them from principles of both Feminism as well as traditional femininity.[14] The evidence suggests that identification with the *Girl Power* culture of consumerism, independence, and defiance may facilitate individual empowerment, but does not necessarily encourage solidarity among girls and collective social action.

Recently, some girls studies scholars have been investigating the ways in which girls around the world use digital media to negotiate their many identities, including gender, ethnic, and national ones, as they experiment in presenting themselves to others via online social networks, the blogosphere, and in various forms of texting. Experimenting with a "self" created via writing, posting photos, linking to sites, "liking" others' postings, and via esthetic choices in designing their webpages are all creative ways through which girls express their inner worlds, their longings, and inner conflicts. In so doing they appropriate a technological arena traditionally dominated by males and turn it into a sphere of self-expression and community building as part of the coming of age process of girlhood.[15] For example, a study in Canada documented how girls experimented with girlhood practices online before implementing them offline; and a study on diasporic Korean girls in the USA revealed how their homepages served as sites for construction of a unique ethnic femininity through their postings and other forms of personal expression.[16]

Researchers speculate that these media texts and platforms offer girls opportunities to develop different aspects of their identity as maturing young women and to confront society's conflicting expectations that they be very sexy and pretty, but not yet act upon their own sexual desires; be independent and successful, and yet be submissive and well-behaved; do well in school, and yet prepare themselves for the grand moment of becoming a wife and mother.

Following development of studies in masculinities, a parallel interest in the role of media in the construction of male identity evolved recently as a separate field of scholarship. Researchers found that young males in many industrialized societies have low school achievement, growing involvement in violence, high levels of substance abuse, and a rising rate of suicide. By way of explanation, scholars suggest that boys feel unsafe and vulnerable trying to live up to expectations of traditional, stereotypical masculine behavior as projected in the *Boy Code* of toughness, emotional disconnection, and aggression. Researchers also posit that boys are pushed prematurely into harsh separation from an intense relationship with their mothers into proving their manhood. Further, in their struggle to become "ideal boys," they have a limited number of role models as their relationships with their fathers are often quite restricted due to the latter's limited presence in the private sphere. Also, interaction with other male role models is episodic and associated with specific functions (e.g., soccer trainer, guitar teacher, etc.). Finally, the traditional images of men and masculinity that still dominate the media offer a very limited range of alternative options.[17]

Within this complicated scenario, boys often receive ambivalent feedback and conflicting messages from their social environment – family members, teachers, peers, and media. Along with the traditional expectations, the new images of manhood prescribe expectations that they be more expressive emotionally and take upon themselves roles traditionally associated with women. Thus, according to this developing line of research, while being told in tough situations that they should "man-up," boys may well be growing up with constant fears of inadequacy and ask themselves "am I man enough?"[18]

These difficulties are reproduced in contrived research situations, which are themselves a form of social interaction. Here, too, boys are often reluctant to talk about their inner worlds, in general, or to expose the role media have in their lives and the many meanings media offer them, in particular. They adopt different strategies to avoid discussing their emotional reactions to media content or to share their viewing pleasures. For example, they adopt a mocking and condescending stance toward viewing of soap operas and serials perceived as "girly," although there is extensive research evidence to suggest that many are loyal viewers who apparently enjoy soaps. They disassociate themselves from programs dealing with interpersonal relationships, intimacy, and romance by relegating them to the "female" world. They report being more interested in traditional male programs, such as action-adventure, sports, and horror films. There is also research evidence that boys on the whole prefer closed narrative structures (i.e., storylines that pose a problem, solve it, and bring it to closure) over open narrative structures (i.e., storylines that remain open and unresolved, as in soap operas and serials).

Superheroes popular throughout the world – such as Superman, Batman, and Spiderman – have a particular role in boys' development of male identity. In many ways, they are the embodiment of the "perfect" traditional man: they are physically strong, brave, always on the lookout to defend the weak, undefeatable, active outdoors, full of adventure, and adored by women. As in the earlier discussion of girlhood, superheroes are not automatically reproduced in boys' quests for their male identities, as these heroes offer them opportunities to examine possibilities and expectations, and to challenge traditional views. Studies analyzing interviews, drawings, and fan letters written by boys reveal that they relate to media characters they admire on many emotional levels, and have deep concerns for idols' private lives, emotional worlds, aspirations, and behavioral motivations. Through these superheroes, they transpose their own desires and so create opportunities to discuss the characters' relevance to their own lives.[19]

At the same time, storylines involving dominance and aggression situated in the context of conflict and threats restrict boys' developing identity and limit their ability to experiment emotionally and experience other possible social scripts. So it seems that most stereotypical popular media fare constrains the inner worlds of both girls and boys, thereby reproducing a limited range of cultural expectations.

An interesting case in point is the restrictive role that media might be playing in constructing notions of *love* and *romance* for children and adolescents. One innovative study asked young people in the USA to choose, from a pool of typical advertising pictures, those that best depict "the couple most in love," the scene that is "the most romantic," and the "most romantic dinner." Analysis of the findings suggests that children framed romance in consumer terms. Hence, when these young people imagined ideal love stories, they incorporated in them elements of leisure and consumer culture. For example, eating in a restaurant and going out to the movies constitute a typical date. A more romantic relationship is expressed in a higher status restaurant atmosphere. Expressing romantic commitment involves purchasing luxury goods. And, when young participants in the research described courting relationships, they reconstructed typical television storylines.[20]

Studies of girls' interpretation of romantic messages in Disney movies, such as *Cinderella*[21] and *Pocahontas*,[22] reveal that while girls embraced the storylines and identified with the leading female character they also negotiated the text and developed their own narrative twists based on personal aspirations, knowledge, and experiences. For example, they added children into Cinderella's future or stated proudly that Pocahontas had a desire to stand by her people and not follow her lover to a typical "they lived happily after" ending. Thus, it is clear that the romantic stories serve not only as a source of learning and identification, but also as a site of multiple interpretations.

Another study documented the central role of a variety of media – television, movies, teenage books and magazines, and popular music – in constructing notions of romantic love among tween girls in Israel[23] and in shaping their "ideal love story" as variations of popular narratives and notions (e.g., "love at first sight," "love is all you need," "my other half," "the one and only," "without you I am nothing"[24]). The girls' love stories and focus group discussions were rich with *media traces*.[25] Such elements point to a variety of media messages, including: linguistic (e.g., *once upon a time; and they lived happily ever after*); specific texts (e.g., *High School Musical, Romeo and Juliet, Beauty and the Beast*); or incorporation of romantic media signifiers (e.g., sunsets, flowers, chocolate hearts, fireworks).

Given such findings, young people maturing today may be involved in reconciling the popular and exciting model of "love at first sight," embedded in consumer culture and stories of luxurious romance, with the much less exciting reality in which relationships are built up gradually through the routine of everyday life. Here we can only speculate, but it may be the case that mediated portrayals shape fantasies and expectations from partners that lead to possible disappointments.

Furthermore, we can ask if such media-based fantasies of romantic love are shared by children in non-Anglo-European societies. Is the cultural effect strong enough to become the fantasy of children growing up in poor countries? Do they, too, yearn for the capitalist model of romantic love? How do the forces of reality interact with the irrelevance of such media messages to their daily lives? These and related questions remain open for inquiry by scholars in these countries.

Gay identities

The identity development of homosexuals and lesbians is of particular interest in media studies due to difficulties they encounter in their lives and the interactions bet-ween media, gender construction, and human sexuality. Clearly, this is a phenomenon with many sensitive dimensions, some of which are discussed in some societies, and contested in others. In contrast to the other social phenomena discussed in this chapter, most gay adolescents do not stand out as a group but rather are involved in individual private processes often hidden within their own and family lives. Therefore, unlike other social and ethnic minorities, they may well lack the support and solidarity that comes with belonging to a social group, at least in the early stages of their gender identity development.

Despite the dramatic changes that have been taking place over the last few decades, it is still the case that many young gays continue to lack a range of adult role models for imitation and identification in their everyday social lives, in media fare, or in popular culture in general. Overall, there is an absence of both media offerings and research in this area. If both were to increase, we might find that media have the potential of presenting as well as connecting not only young gays but also their heterosexual peers and fellow citizens to a world not directly accessible to them. In that way, media may serve to bypass traditional socializing agents that could prove them-selves embarrassed, confused, non-supportive or even covertly, if not overtly, hostile.

As noted, portrayals of gays in popular media have been trickling gradually into our lives via television and movies, advertising and specialized magazines, as well as the less directly public online support groups and forums. In the past, most gay images were presented stereotypically and as a form of social, psychological, and/or physical deviation. One popular stereotype highlighted *hyper-feminization* of male homosexual behavior encountered in daily life. This type of behavior is easily detected, and often ridiculed, through tone of speech, body movement and hand gestures, professional preferences, and general mannerisms and lifestyle. While use of this stereotype is gradually changing, with media now offering more diverse portrayals, gay people are still presented quite differently from heterosexuals. For example, gay youth are mostly portrayed as confused about their sexual identity, while heterosexu-ality is mostly presented as a natural, unchallenged state of affairs. Inter-gay relations are often reduced to sexual activities devoid of any emotional relationship. Subtle messages reinforce the notion that homosexuality is a deviation that can be "cured" by a strong-willed person and/or with the help of the ideal partner of the opposite sex.

The absence of diverse, constantly present, alternative models and perspectives in mainstream media is an example of the mass communication *spiral of silence* theoretical construct that can be applied to portrayals of gays. Namely, de-legitimization can be achieved when a message is perceived to be in conflict with dominant social norms, and therefore is not represented in the media. In turn, this absence reinforces the misperception of the dominant view. While gay youth can increasingly find media texts in some Anglo-European societies that reinforce their identity or interpret them in oppositional ways, for the most part they are not offered a means through mainstream media of connecting to the rich and productive gay culture emerging in many societies, and with which they have the potential to be integrated and to find fulfillment.[26]

On the other hand, the internet is proving to be a source of unique opportunities for gay youth to explore, connect, and build a community. A study that analyzed the discourse of gay youth on the Israeli "young pride" website found that active participation in such a support forum was essential to their gradual process of "coming out of the closet." This was achieved through refuting homosexual stereotypes, learning to accept one's sexual preferences, social support and encouragement to come out, and a sense of belonging to a larger community with which one can identify and from whom one can seek support.[27] The possibility of experimenting with one's homosexual tendencies in the virtual world (e.g., in identity play or sites like *Second Life*) is of particular value for youth whose life circumstances do not allow the presence of LGBTQ (Lesbian-Gay-Bisexual-Transgender-Queer) groups or individuals, such as might be the case in isolated rural environments.[28] At the same time, digital and mobile media have also become an outlet for bullying of young gay people by publicly outing and ridiculing them.

The studies and social phenomena reviewed here remind us of the importance of considering the general socio-cultural context in which children and youth consume media when attempting to understand the influence such media might have on their identity development. They also substantiate a strong theme promoted in this book – that media in themselves are not inherently "good" or "bad," but rather have the potential to be used by us in positive as well as negative ways.

The Social Construction of Reality

The discussion of media's contribution to gender construction can facilitate our understanding of other social issues in terms of the kinds of questions asked, methodologies applied, and findings revealed. Here, our general question is: How does the social reality presented regularly in the media shape the way young media consumers come to view the social world in which they live, the power relationships in it, the dominant values that underlie it, as well as their own place in it compared to members of other social groups?

Violence and the *mean world* hypothesis

Violence in the media is among the primary phenomena discussed, and debated, in relation to the possible roles of media in cultivating a particular worldview. Before we begin this discussion, we note the following working assumptions: First, violence is a way to present the social order and division of power within it. For example, most popular television programs, movies, and video games that are successful in the global market legitimate and reinforce white-male domination. Second, media representations of violence and its consequences (and/or the lack of attention to them) provide children with a series of "lessons," such as: some criminals can escape a crime without punishment; and, there are dangerous and safe places and people. Proponents of the *mean world* hypothesis argue that what viewers learn from media violence is fear, threat, distrustfulness, and a strong sense of vulnerability.[29]

Over the years, this tradition of research that has focused on television and more recently extended to include video games as well has arrived at the overall conclusion that heavier consumers of television see the world as much more cruel and dangerous and hold stronger attitudes expressing distrust, alienation, and depression than those who view less television. These researchers argue that we should be concerned about this conclusion because historical analyses of societies in distress suggest that people who feel insecure are much more dependent, easier to manipulate and to control, are more easily swayed by hardline political and religious attitudes, and are more open to accepting forceful solutions to social problems. For example, some commentators pondered over the possible contribution of the heavy violence in the US popular media to the strong lobby in support of private ownership of weapons which remains a strongly contested issue in that society. Based on what we have learned so far, we can also pose the opposite question: Could it be that the strongly entrenched support of private ownership of weapons in the USA (with very strong historical, cultural, and constitutional roots dating back to the period prior to the establishment of the country) feeds into the prevalence of violence in media produced in this country? The answer is probably favorable to both interpretations, as well as to many other contextual variables.

A related consequence of the *mean world* hypothesis is the possibility that constant exposure to screen violence desensitizes viewers to the pain and suffering of fellow humans. Over time, researchers argue, viewers become accustomed to violence, less anxious while watching it, and gradually come to see violent actions as less extreme. This may lead young viewers to treat violent acts more lightly, as well as to diminish their willingness to help victims of violence. This line of argument assumes that desensitization is a longitudinal process that affects all viewers over time.[30]

In general, evidence-based arguments are still inconclusive in that we have few empirically sound conclusions regarding the complicated relationships between viewing violence and cultivation of worldviews. For example, a study of Japanese high-school students who were observed as they completed a questionnaire survey while viewing television found evidence of desensitization (e.g., laughter during violent sequences) and argued, from inference, that a correlation exists between such behavior and the extensive viewing of violent programs reported by respondents.[31]

An interesting Australian study of preschool and elementary school children found that they distinguished between fictional and realistic violence. For example, they were more critical of realistic violence in sports programs than of its appearance in a fictional family series. Similarly, they claimed to be disinterested in news, because it is "boring" and also presents realistic and scary violence.[32]

Findings from a cross-national report on media violence prepared during 1996–1997 for UNESCO investigated the role of media violence, television included, in the lives of 5,000 12-year-olds in 23 countries in a variety of regions and cultures across the world.[33] The survey results suggest, among other things, that despite the many cultural differences, the media in all countries perpetuate the perception that violent behavior is normal and that it functioned as a form of positive reinforcement. A major contribution of the UNESCO study is the evidence that the consequences of media violence are related to the social reality in which children are growing up. For example, violent media messages reinforce the life experiences of children in the study who were living at the time in more violent environments (war zones or urban areas with high crime rates). These children were also more attracted to famous violent characters. Children who were living in non-violent environments demonstrated a similar perception but to a lesser degree.

From the limited research efforts undertaken to date, we can conclude that there seem to be many intervening variables in the relationship between viewing screen violence and internalizing a particular worldview. Among these variables are the degree of realism of the violence portrayed, the real-life circumstances of the children, and the type of gratifications children derive from consuming media.

Materialism

The role of media in cultivating a worldview oriented to consumer culture is another major research topic. Moving beyond studies of children's developing abilities to understand the persuasive power of advertising (discussed in Chapter 2), as well as their capabilities to discern use of media for manipulation and exploitation (discussed in Chapters 4 and 7), we can ask: How are the media contributing to children's development of a capitalistic understanding of the world and the values associated with it? For example, might children internalize a worldview in which ownership of materialistic goods is perceived as evidence of personal self-worth and happiness, and in which this becomes a cure for social or psychological problems? Research has found that consumption of commercial media, particularly advertising, is associated with attitudes of materialism and can even strengthen them.[34] A study of adolescents in Singapore found that exposure to advertising was associated with materialistic values: Advertising in all its forms demonstrates to adolescents that material possessions not only help realize their life goals, but are actually life goals themselves.[35] Other research findings regarding the glorification of celebrities, glamor, and hedonistic lifestyles in the media have led scholars and critics to claim that children learn to emphasize appearance and beautification over character and achievements.

Discussions of children's consumer culture challenge the concept of childhood altogether,[36] as they problematize the notion of child vulnerability, morality, and value judgments embedded in commercialization of children's culture. The debates between conflicting positions that celebrate the empowered and skilled child-consumer on the one hand, and the exploited and manipulated one on the other, have not necessarily contributed to our understanding of much larger questions related to children's developing understanding of the social world. Such, for example, is the question of whether the omnipresence of consumerism as a way of life contributes to children's *false consciousness*, to use a Marxist term, which allows for the naturalization of capitalist ideology as preferred and unchallenged. According to this view, such acceptance continues to acculturate future generations to preserve a social status quo that is not necessarily in their interest. Given that there is very little research that actually studies these processes with a child audience, many of these claims remain on the level of ideological propositions advocated by competing social groups.

Since capitalism is highly associated with the US economic system and way of life, these discussions are deeply integrated within criticism of *Americanization*, a phenomenon that has many names, including the *McDonaldization* of society.[37] We will return to the discussion of *Americanization* below, toward the end of this chapter.

Perceptions of "us" in comparison to "others"

Content analyses of popular commercial television programs, advertisements, and video games traded around the world suggest dominance of the lifestyles and culture of the white Anglo-European middle class. Accordingly, we find that other ethnic groups are presented as minorities, assigned minor or negative roles, devaluated, and stereotyped in ways characteristic of the Anglo-European point of view. Thus, while American television has become gradually more inclusive of multiculturalism, it still mainly divides the social world racially, as whites and non-whites. For example, large minority groups of color in the USA, particularly African-Americans, receive their own "ghettoes" on television (e.g., an all-black situation comedy or rap-music program) with limited interaction with the white world. Other large minority groups, such as the Latino and Asian populations, appear rarely in Northern American commercial media. Neither is the diversity within these groups recognized (e.g., Mexicans, Argentineans, Peruvians, and the like within Latino ethnicity; and Chinese, Japanese, Korean, and the like within Asian ethnicity). Pressure from advocacy groups for more inclusive programming has resulted in some significant changes over the last decade. For example, we find use of a strategy of creating racial ambiguity by presenting "brown" characters that allows for an open interpretation as to their racial identity. However, the appearance of non-white persons on the screen has been often criticized as a form of "tokenism," or as a means of blurring differences rather than celebrating them.[38]

Locally produced, *quality* media productions are a different matter, as they represent local populations and cultures. Indeed, it is important to note that audiences all over the world express great affinity for such programs and, consequentially, their ratings are usually high. However, the expense required in the local production of just one episode, including the human and technological resources, is usually much greater than the cost to the station of purchasing a year's worth of old re-runs of an American series. As a result, television all over the world, particularly in low-resource countries, is heavily dominated by American programs. In addition, there are indications that even young viewers notice the often lower production quality and esthetics of their own country's productions in comparison with those made in the USA (for example, less sophisticated use of photographic techniques, sparser settings, lower professional quality of actors and actresses), thus reinforcing the supremacy of American television and the social world it represents.[39]

Again, what is the contribution of largely Anglo-European portrayals in the social construction of reality by children all over the world? Do white, middle-class European-American children perceive their own dominance on the screen over other social classes and ethnic groups? What influence do the media have in the emerging self-identity of the non-white minority child in the USA, France, Peru or Uganda, or for an Asian child growing up among a majority within his/her society, yet who is a minority within the global media fare? What are the consequences of the absence of images that are similar to a child's self-definition or the stereotypical presentation of that self-definition for the child's emerging self-image?

The type of content viewed, too, is of importance. For example, on the one hand, heavy viewing of television fiction that portrays African-American people in the USA was associated with over-estimating the social, economic, and educational status of African-American people in reality; but, on the other hand, heavy viewing of television news was related to perceiving the status of black people to be much inferior to that of the white population. In addition, viewing educational television aimed at boosting African-American children's self-esteem has been found to have particularly strong appeal and attracted identification with black characters. As in other areas, this research reveals that television has both reinforced existing attitudes as well as added new information when no prior knowledge existed, thus playing an important role in the formation of racial knowledge and attitudes.[40] Thus, studies found that viewing television was associated with attributing positive characteristics to white characters and negative to minority ones.[41]

Clearly, children are much more critical and realistic in their evaluation of a program when the reality portrayed on the screen is similar to their real-life experiences. And, conversely, when it presents a reality that is removed from them, they lack the skills and experience to evaluate it critically. For example, African-American youth were found to believe that television's social world is realistic, except when it referred to their own ethnic group. Similarly, African-American children expressed a desire to identify with white characters, to whom they assigned positive personality traits and a much higher social status than their own group. Studies of Japanese students soon after their arrival in the USA, and who had not had any previous first-hand contact with African-Americans, were much more "vulnerable" to the latter's portrayals on television in comparison to local white Americans who had first-hand experience with African-American peers.[42]

Unfortunately, we do not have enough research-based knowledge to assess the contributions of new images of a variety of ethnicities that have begun to appear more frequently in recent movies and television programs. Research studies that could be advanced include the following questions: How do portrayals of actors and actresses of African, Asian, Latin, or indigenous origin on television and movies in typical high-status roles (such as medical doctors, lawyers, journalists, detectives, politicians) contribute to the development of a positive self-image and future aspirations among children? Does the presentation of a multicultural world (i.e., where in the same emergency room, law firm, or police station there are professionals of all ethnicities, ages, and disabilities working side by side, making friends, having fun together, falling in love, and having sexual relationships) contribute to the social integration and reduction of prejudices among viewers? Do African-American girls take pride in an African-American female judge who appears on television, and does such a role encourage them to believe in such professional possibilities for their own career aspirations? How does a boy in Japan perceive a Japanese surgeon in an American television program? All of these examples are attempts to involve such popular characters in recent productions for children, with a view to cultivating more tolerance of diversity and stronger self-worth among minority children (e.g., Dora, the Latin American girl character from the very successful preschool program *Dora the Explorer*; or the variety of multi-racial Disney princesses catering to global demands – Persian Jasmine, Native American Pocahontas, Chinese Mulan, African-American Tiana).

While these newer images may be inspiring and appealing to those who seek a more diverse viewing fare, there is no substantial body of empirical evidence that would enable us to speak about the influence of these changes in media portrayals on young viewers. As we have seen, most of what we know from research relates to ethnic minorities in the USA, and in particular to African-Americans. However, the same questions need to be pursued regarding different social minorities that are also victims of discrimination on the basis of age as well as physical or mental disabilities, in the USA and in many other countries. This having been noted, existing theories can help us make intelligent predictions: The "cultivation hypothesis" suggests that viewing such images on a regular basis is likely to contribute to the cultivation of a multicultural worldview tolerant of difference. According to the *uses and gratifications* theory, we can assume that the reasons for watching the specific programs or movies and the gratifications provided by viewing will mediate between the child and the perception of the realism of the content consumed. Cultural studies will help us understand the active role the child plays in making meanings of these images. However, as noted, these and other theories await continuing exploration in future studies.

Nevertheless, in a multicultural world experiencing new waves of immigration, it is clear that media can have an important role in shaping children's worldviews as well as cultivating tolerance, understanding, and openness to difference.[43]

Cultural integration of immigrant children

A particular case of relevance with regard to the social construction of reality is the emerging research interest in the roles media serve for immigrant children, given the large migration movements taking place worldwide today. Initial conclusions suggest that media roles are not unequivocal and often have conflicting influences. Media in the host country can assist children to adjust to and integrate into a new society, yet in doing so they can work counter to the desire, particularly of migrant adults, to preserve the homeland's cultural identity and social segregation. Similarly, research on adult immigrants suggests that exposure to the host media plays an important role in how they learn about the new society and their opportunities to take part in it. Yet, the host media are also powerful tools that shape and nurture negative stereotypes of new immigrants, thus causing the latter's sense of alienation and social isolation.

An interesting current innovation is the production of media in the immigrants' native language, via, for example, special broadcast and cable channels, internet sites, print culture, and broadcasts delivered through satellites from the original country. Yet, here, too, such media can play a double role: On the one hand, media produced for immigrant communities or by them serve as tools for learning about the new society and ways of accommodation to it. On the other hand, they also preserve the immigrants' cultural heritage; strengthen their inter-group solidarity; and, in this era of globalization, enable immigrant communities of the same origin, dispersed over different countries, to retain ties with the "motherland" as well as with their fellow ethnics in other countries. That is to say, the global media are one of the main forces that shape and nurture transnational diaspora communities.

From the research perspective, several initial studies explored the various roles the media actually play in the lives of immigrant children who, undoubtedly, face unique personal and social challenges, as well as inter-generational tensions. More than their parents, these children are "in between" two worlds and are expected to handle two cultural identities, to speak two languages, and to be able to negotiate between the two worlds. Empirical evidence from studies conducted in the USA suggests that, in comparison to children born in the country, immigrant children at the end of the 20th century spend more time watching television and express a more positive attitude toward educational and information-oriented programs. Moreover, at the time these studies were conducted, foreign-born children appeared to use television more for learning about others and themselves, exhibited significantly greater identification with television characters, and expressed stronger beliefs in the televised reality of people and events.[44] Thus, television seemed to be an important source of education and information about their new society for immigrant children, particularly during the first few years following immigration, when their lives tended to be characterized by isolation and lack of close relationships with local children. In fact, television characters were probably among the first Americans to whom they were introduced and with whom they could easily "interact."

Initial evidence from a European study suggests that young children involved in immigration to various communities (e.g., from North Africa into the south of France; from Turkey and Somalia into Denmark; from the former Soviet Union into Israel) often resist parents' efforts to interest them in media content from their countries of origin. The researchers concluded that what serves as a tool for immigrant parents' retention of their original cultural identity may be perceived by their children as an obstacle to their own full integration into the new homeland. Nevertheless, the children do become part of "Sunday culture" when they join their parents to watch television programs and movies from their former homeland for the sake of family togetherness.[45]

One product of these studies is documentation of a variety of roles and strategies employed by parents and children in using media to both facilitate integration into the host country and to maintain affiliation with the culture of origin.[46] For example, an ethnographic study conducted among young Indians in London focused on the interplay of different media content and its crucial role in the construction of their cultural identity. Here, researchers found that exposure to Indian movies and dramas ensured a degree of preservation of traditional norms and values, while exposure to British and transnational television content enabled these teenagers to challenge the traditional values and norms of their parents and develop a new cultural identity that supported their efforts to integrate into British society.[47] Another in-depth case study of first-generation Indian female adolescents in the USA provided evidence of the multi-roles that both American as well as Indian television play in the construction of ethnic identities, and how ethnic identity is intertwined with gender and sexuality.[48] The roles media play for immigrant children in the formation of a multicultural sense of belonging, too, was documented in studies of Latino immigrants in the USA, and found to assist in connecting them to their families and the larger ethnic community as well as in negotiating their evolving identities.[49]

Similar processes have been identified in a comparative study of immigrant children from the former Soviet Union to Germany and Israel. The study, based on in-depth interviews, revealed that media play a significant role for immigrant families in both countries. In this context, cable and satellite channels originating in the former Soviet Union were of special interest. Parents wishing to preserve their children's affinity with the Russian language and culture encouraged joint viewing of programs broadcast from Russia. Although the children themselves were not too eager to watch television in Russian, they usually acceded to their parents' request in order to maintain smooth communication with them. A similar pattern was found in some of the families with regard to viewing programs on local channels, as watching the programs in the host language seemed to assist in bridging the cultural gap between immigrant children and their parents, since parents' integration into the host culture was much slower. At the same time, television was found to have a central role in immigrant children's sense of fitting into the local and global culture and in constructing their new identities.[50]

More recent studies have found that the internet is playing a very significant role in the lives of immigrant children as they grow up, since it allows them to overcome language and geographical barriers, to connect to children similar to them, and to facilitate experimentation with local peers with minimal risk of social sanctions. Immigrant youth use it as a source of information and cultural knowledge about both their new host country and the home they have left behind. They cultivate personal relationships with both fellow ethnics as well as native-born peers that facilitate the development of their language skills in both the native as well as the host languages.[51] Studies have also found that the internet is perceived by many immigrant youth to be a "lifeline" during their challenging years of adjustment.[52] We will return to this topic in Chapter 6.

Our discussion of the roles served by media in the lives of immigrant children therefore highlights, once again, the interplay between media, identity issues, and cultural context - a constant theme throughout this book.

The Construction of Political Reality

The political world is an instructive example of a part of reality that most children are detached from, yet are directly influenced by (as well as expected to influence in due course, as they gradually become active, involved citizens). With the aid of media, very young children learn to identify their own as well as other countries' political leaders; listen as these leaders give political speeches or argue before their governing bodies; follow demonstrations; and recognize major issues on their national political agenda. Aside from these general claims, what roles do media and other socializing agents play in the process of children's emerging understanding of political reality?

A series of studies conducted on this topic in the 1970s in the USA set the ground for the research area.[53] They found that media serve as the primary source of political information for young audiences, and that most political learning by children was assisted at the time by newspapers and television. Younger children were more dependent on television and, as they matured, newspapers were added as a source of information about news and current events on television. Television remained the central source of political information for young viewers from lower socio-economic classes. More recent studies document the centrality of online news and social media in providing such information.[54]

Adolescents, in the earlier studies, identified the media as a significant influence in shaping their political perceptions, in addition to their role as a central source of information. According to adolescents' self-reporting, the media influence their attitudes in specific areas and in some cases even more than their parents, peers, and teachers. Adolescents with more interest in news and current affairs obtained in part via the media tended also to discuss it more within their family. As a result, in their case, the socializing agents reinforce one another. However, adolescents did not necessarily adopt their parents' habits of consuming political content via the media, nor their parents' political attitudes. One of the conclusions of these earlier research studies was that the main contribution of news reporting was to attitudes and knowledge, and not to actual political activism, with several suggesting that there was no clear relationship between the shaping of knowledge and attitudes following exposure to the media and their practical application in various forms of political activities. This finding may need re-visiting given the advent of the internet and social networks which have opened up ample opportunities for more civic engagement. We will tackle this aspect of participation in Chapter 6.

Not surprisingly, one of the foci in this research area is the direction of the influence. In this regard, studies have found that youth who have a greater interest in political issues approach the media more selectively in their search for relevant information. Furthermore, youth who report heavy consumption of news are also those who have more political knowledge. This leads to the question – is heavier consumption of political content in the media dependent on other variables (such as political interest, family background, education, gender) or is it an independent variable on which other variables depend (e.g., knowledge, attitudes, political involvement)? The general conclusion seems to be that there are longitudinal inter-relationships between all of these variables: parents and peers interact with the consumption of media, and this is accompanied by maturing political values and attitudes. Youth who are more involved socially and, therefore, more exposed to the attitudes and interpretations of their peers, may also use media more as sources for information and attitude formation.

It is interesting to note that children learn about the political world from a variety of sources, not only traditional news coverage. For example, entertainment pro-grams such as political satire, talk shows, and comedies are often reported as valuable sources, as well as a variety of online forums and social networking sites that, for example, post personal opinions, viral YouTube videos, political advertising, carica-tures, and other bits and pieces of information and commentaries. According to some research, satire and entertainment media increase cynicism and apathy toward the political world that discourages actual willingness to participate in political life. Other studies found such non-traditional sources of public affairs information served various educational roles, particularly when combined with the development of media literacy critical skills of examining the information presented by them.[55]

There are many additional questions that require investigation in this area, such as: Can media encourage development of a particular kind of political society? How can parents and educators take advantage of the potential contributions of media for political socialization? What is the nature of the relationship between political information transferred in the media and emotional aspects of affiliation with a particular political movement or identification with a particular ideology? How does the selective and fragmented nature of information distributed on social networks contribute to children's political socialization? While many of these and other questions involve aspects that are discussed by some media and political commentators as controversial and value laden, they refer to a very important dilemma that lies at the heart of how the media are involved in the construction of political reality: If youth are not exposed to political issues in the media, their knowledge, critical skills, and involvement in these areas will be deficient. This is undoubtedly an undesirable situation for a society seeking, even committed, to developing an active citizenship in the public sphere. Yet if children are indeed informed by self-selective media content, they may be exposed only to particular frames of reference to reality, to particular political ideologies, to a limited social agenda, and therefore excluded from specific social and ideological peripheries. When other socializing agents do not fulfill their duties in such an active manner, media reports can serve as the primary political reality for young people, especially in the absence of alternative sources of information.

Interesting insights into this issue emerged in a study of the role of news among US and UK teens. The study employed a qualitative methodology in interviewing adolescents and in analyzing news programs designed for them.[56] Interviewees expressed the desire to be more informed about the world and to be treated respectfully, but at the same time they expected to be entertained and stimulated. The researcher concluded, among other things, that there is a need for innovation in traditional forms of news presentations in order to stimulate young people's engagement and to penetrate the wall of apathy and cynicism they often exhibit.

Finally, by way of introduction, this research area also involves the study of the role of media in the political involvement of young, maturing future citizens. Here, some researchers point to the formal exclusion of reporting on youth activity in the public sphere, and the absence of discussion of their capabilities to realize their political rights. Here, too, we find strong traces of the debate over children as *being* versus *becoming*; that is, the assertion that young people should be treated as actual citizens (being), rather than as "citizens-in-the-making" (becoming). If they are to "be," they need access to the mediated public domain of media news and current events – both as an audience whose needs, skills, and interests are taken into consideration and as participants whose opinions and concerns are being voiced. Indeed, various societies have been experimenting with special news programs aimed at children of various ages.[57]

The construction of conflicts

Of special interest is research regarding political socialization conducted in conflict-driven societies, and particularly during times of war and armed struggle. If in the past attempts were made in some societies to shield the young from war and other forms of political violence, today, as we have already argued, children worldwide cannot escape being exposed through media to traumatizing events such as natural and human-made disasters as well as the many violent conflicts that have taken and are taking place around the globe. Researchers found that children learn about such events from the media, react to them emotionally, and construct their worldview of politics through them. Clearly, here, too, their media experiences are mediated through the political environment in which they live. Not surprisingly, then, a comparative case study of children's reactions to the war in Iraq, conducted at its outset in the spring of 2003, revealed that the American children who participated in the study wholeheartedly supported the attack, while German children who were exposed to the strong European opposition to the war expressed views similar to those of the adults in their environment. Israeli children, who were being prepared at the time for the possibility of their country being a target for Iraqi missiles (as was the case in the 1991 Gulf War), interpreted the war as entangled within the complexities of the enduring Israeli–Arab conflict. These and other studies of children's reactions to the war in Iraq underline how interested and involved they wish to be, as well as how hard children endeavor to assimilate the fragments of information they receive, but yet how limited is the availability of appropriate resources with which they can undertake this complex process.[58]

More specific is the role of media for children growing up in societies divided by deep, enduring conflict. A series of studies on the political socialization of Israeli youth, who are growing up in a society divided by the Israeli–Arab conflict, provides us with interesting insights. One study correlated the attitudes of Jewish-Israeli youth with the news coverage of the conflict and found that television had a central role in shaping the subjective perceptions of adolescents regarding the political agenda in Israel, the dimensions of the conflict, and the stereotypes associated with the Arabs as an enemy. Such processes were related to the amount of time the adolescents devoted to viewing television news and their attitudes toward the medium, such as the willingness to learn from television, dependency on television as a source of political information, and the perception youth had about the degree of influence television had upon them.[59]

A variety of studies in the USA documented the role of family communication patterns in political socialization[60] (see also the discussion in Chapter 1). Another study in Israel suggested that, as a general rule, teenagers held more extreme political views than their parents. Peer pressure as well as adolescence, being a period in which ideas, values, and options are being tested, may partially account for these findings. However, a complementary explanation offered was that the extreme nature of the coverage of the conflict (e.g., dwelling on violence and on negative aspects rather than on possible solutions and cooperation) reinforced negative attitudes toward Arabs, in general, and their role in the conflict, more specifically. The results also indicated that teenagers raised in families that do not conduct critical discussions about television coverage of the conflict may be more influenced by its content in the shaping of their worldview.[61]

Whether research studies have focused on the role of media or the role of the family, all agree that media do not operate in a social vacuum, but as part of complicated social contexts that work sometimes cooperatively, sometimes in conflict, but always within a process of negotiation of meaning.

This conclusion, too, sheds light on methodological and conceptual concerns involved in the study of children and youth. Analysis of transcripts of conversations conducted with families involved in watching television news in Israel suggested that opinions and attitudes are formed and contested during the viewing itself, and political opinions, which are often full of contradiction, constantly undergo a dynamic process of reconsideration and consolidation.[62] Accordingly, the role of media in the political socialization process uncovered in such conversations is not linear – from media to young people – but involves dynamic, dialectical, and reciprocal processes as well as conservative and subversive undercurrents. Studies such as this, conducted through participant observation, stand in contrast to research involving completion of questionnaires, which requires participants to take a stance with regard to each question (e.g., fully agree with the position, somewhat agree with the position, disagree with the position) and thus portray themselves as having clear-cut opinions. The implications of these methodological differences have import not only for understanding the roles of the media in political socialization but also for questioning what are the most fruitful and appropriate ways to study such processes.

Peacebuilding interventions

The complementary side of the same issue is the employment of media for peace-building interventions. One of the most notable efforts has been experimental work initiated by *Sesame Workshop* with co-productions in the Middle East. An early initiative in the 1990s, which coincided with what seemed at the time to be the beginning of a peace process in the region, was aimed at preschool children in Israel and the occupied territories of Palestine. While the basic production model followed the classic *Sesame Street* format (see Chapter 3), it deviated in developing storylines in two separate *Sesame Streets* (*Rechov Sumsum* and *Shara'a Simsim*), representing the two-states solution of nations destined to live as neighbors and with two sets of characters speaking in two languages (Hebrew and Arabic). The curriculum that accompanied the program included a focus on mutual respect between and within Israeli and Palestinian societies, modeling pro-social interactions, visits to each other's street, presentation of conflict resolution by positive and non-stereotypical characters, and highlighting similarities and differences between the two nations.

The study found that children's attention was generally high, that they were able to follow and describe the plotline, and that they had a high level of recall. These findings were perceived as evidence for the potential of educational television to present authentic and positive portrayals of both the Palestinian and Israeli cultures to children of both groups. The fact that many children related the different segments to their personal experiences and were very involved in the viewing was an encouraging indication that producers were achieving their educational goals. Thus, the study provided support for the claim that television does have the potential to challenge negative stereotypes by exposing children to the everyday life of peers on the other side of a conflict. The mere presentation of peaceful, normalized relationships between groups constantly portrayed on the news as violent enemies offered momentary relief from reality and a vision of an alternative future.[63] An evaluation of an updated co-production coordinated between Israeli, Palestinian, and Jordanian television stations provided additional support for the potential of such media interventions to help foster values such as mutual respect and cultural understanding, while reducing prejudice, stereotypes, and negative attitudes.[64]

Inspired by the Middle Eastern co-productions of *Sesame Street*, another initiative designed to encourage mutual respect and understanding among ethnic Albanians, Macedonians, Romas, and Turkish children was developed in Macedonia. *Nash Maalo* ("our neighborhood") featured a multi-ethnic case of four children-friends and employed dialogue in their various languages. A study of knowledge and attitudes of children who viewed the series over the course of several months revealed many gains: Children's negative stereotyped perceptions and attitudes toward the various ethnic groups were reduced; they were better able to identify the three minority languages; and were more willing to invite children from other ethnic groups to their homes.[65]

These encouraging results led to additional efforts by *Sesame Workshop* including *Gimme6* in Cyprus, designed to provide positive images of the Greek and Turkish Cypriot communities, and *Sesame Tree* in Northern Ireland, between Catholic and Protestant communities, to highlight their similarities and differences, and to disperse negative stereotypes. Earlier attempts to address the Northern Ireland "troubles" (i.e., the common term used to describe the conflict) included media interventions such as *Off the Walls*, aimed at youth, and *Respecting Difference*, for preschoolers.[66]

Of special note is the work of Media Initiatives for Children who created a series of short animated episodes aimed at preschoolers that convey simple messages about the inclusion of others in the everyday life of young children growing up in a society of deep historical conflict. The series was broadcast regularly on television and integrated within the preschool curriculum in Northern Ireland and the Republic of Ireland, and was found to be effective in teaching young children to recognize exclusion, to know how an excluded child feels, and to be willing to play with a previously excluded child.[67]

Many other initiatives for using media to promote conflict resolution and peacebuilding have been implemented worldwide.[68] While few research efforts are associated with these pioneering efforts, the results available do indicate that there is a need and desire to involve media in a much more proactive way in facilitating peacebuilding, mutual understanding, prejudice reduction, and conflict-resolution efforts.

Media have also had a role as conduits for dialogue in such peacebuilding efforts, mainly via digital technologies, including video-conferencing, chats, social media, game-simulations, and forums. Studies of such experiments have been conducted in Israel, where online chats between Israeli and Palestinian youth took place in an effort to bring about attitudinal change in their mutual perspectives of each other as well as to facilitate the various forms of interaction themselves. Virtual space, once again, has been found to be helpful in creating a safe space to experiment with relationship building with adversaries, to discover commonalities shared by youth of all backgrounds, and to put aside stereotypes and labels associated with nationality, ethnicity, and religion.[69] Similar uses of digital technologies in educational settings for "dissolving boundaries" and building bridges between different groups have been successfully experimented with, for example, in Northern Ireland and the Republic of Ireland. Collaborative virtual projects between students from these two societies attempted to improve inter-cultural understanding while developing a host of skills such as problem solving, development of creativity, and improved communication.[70]

Edutainment genres

The potential of television, specifically, in children's construction of social reality has been attended to quite differently in different parts of the world. In sharp contrast to many of the dramatic and reality programs produced in Anglo-European countries, a trend has developed in other parts of the world – including Africa, Asia, and Latin America – to deliberately incorporate social issues in the entertainment program-ming (such as soaps and telenovelas, cartoons, reality-TV genres, as well as recently with some websites) viewed regularly by children and youth. The variety of issues addressed includes health, literacy, and social dangers.

This approach of using popular screen texts to advance awareness of social issues, even social change, aims to contribute to the empowerment of young viewers by providing them not only with information and knowledge, but also with role models, reasons, values, and the motivation to be involved in shaping attitudes and actions that can be incorporated into their everyday lives. In South Africa, for example, entertainment television was recruited as part of the *Soul City* project for health training regarding contraception against the backdrop of the HIV-AIDS epidemic. Also, the *Yizo Yizo* (*This is How Things Are*) series tackled complex problems that are the reality of life in South African schools in the black townships including violence, sexual harassment and rape, drug abuse, and HIV-AIDS. This series set off a heated public debate about the program's blunt treatment of these problems. A research project that evaluated how young viewers engaged with the program found it was a source of both redemption from the hardships of their everyday lives and an inspiration to seek ways to find a better future for themselves. This series demonstrates the complex issues involved in television's efforts to present reality to children and youth via dramatic formats. For example, could it be claimed that the presentation of violence, drug abuse, and sexual crimes serves to normalize these behaviors and perpetuate them as legitimate, particularly in the South African con-text in which they are raised?[71]

Of special interest is a UNICEF gender-related initiative with the creation of *Meena*, a popular cartoon figure of a South Asian girl. Originating in Bangladesh in 1991, it has since spread to India, Pakistan, Nepal, Sri Lanka, the Maldives, and Bhutan, among other countries. This is an example of television intervention, as the series was created with the intention of fostering social change by specifically addressing issues of gender discrimination (e.g., in food, education, and domestic workloads) without threatening the audience with too radical a set of changes.[72] An additional

UNICEF-originated gender initiative is the animated series *Sara*, which aims to serve as a role model for girls in Africa facing HIV-AIDS.

Many other creative, well-intentioned and produced, quality edutainment programs for children and families in the area of social change are being developed worldwide.[73] A selection of exemplary programs is presented every two years in Germany during the *Prix Jeunesse* International Festival for quality media for children. Entries to more recent meetings of this festival are illustrative of the breadth and depth of quality media for children as well as their authentic cultural nature. For example, programs from African countries focused on helping young children who had lost their parents to AIDS deal with their loss, while other programs impressed upon viewers the importance of being more tolerant of peers who have HIV. Programs from Scandinavian countries were concerned with allowing boys to express their inner worlds during puberty, discuss their sexual development, and their yearning for intimacy. Several Asian programs brought up the issue of equal schooling and literacy for both boys and girls. A Palestinian-Jordanian co-production dealt with the life of one family under the Israeli military occupation, while one from Israel presented the life of an immigrant family whose daughter was killed in a suicide terrorist attack. Some Latin American producers struggled with infusing anti-"macho" values in their programs as part of a campaign against domestic violence.[74]

Overall, we can say that there is a very long list of social goals that many producers of media for children all over the world have set, and continue to set, for themselves. The effectiveness of most of these programs has yet to be studied in a systematic, comprehensive manner, although the knowledge we already have at our disposal from the previous chapters should suggest to us that such an approach does have great potential to contribute to the wellbeing of children.[75]

Americanization and Globalization

As we have seen in the discussion above, a significant issue in the field of children and media involves arguments that juxtapose locally produced with globally distributed media content. A key claim in this discussion, to date, asserts that American values and interests are perpetuated around the world through popular culture originating in the USA and deeply embedded in that society's culture, economic interests, and political power. Proponents of this claim draw upon arguments made in the general academic debate on globalization. More specifically, the particular argument that globalization is a form of Anglo-European, ethnocentric, patronizing cultural imperialism which invades local cultures and lifestyles, deepens the insecurities of indigenous identities, and contributes to the erosion of national cultures and historical traditions. This definition of globalization focuses on processes that lead to countries losing their independence, perhaps informally, through transnational powers in various dimensions of life: economics, culture, information, production, and ecology. Media are blamed or praised, depending on perspective, for being the central mobilizers of these globalization processes, since they serve as a channel for transmitting Anglo-European worldviews, including values, cultural tastes, and economic and political interests. A sub-set of this scholarship presents evidence that amidst this more general form of cultural imperialism, there is a complementary push-back involving strong resistance to the perceived takeover by a superpower Western culture. This resistance advances efforts that advocate pride in, and the need to strengthen self-awareness of, local sub-cultures, which are striving for recognition and opportunities to flourish. *Glocalization* is the term coined by scholars to refer to this tension involving global and local processes. Here, consumption of global cultural products by local audiences is embedded in specific cultural contexts and results in the creation of meanings that serve their needs. Thus, rather than focusing solely on a critique of Western cultural domination, an alternative research and educational approach explores multiculturalism and the multiplicity of forms of hybridity created worldwide.

Returning to our domain, what, then, are the expressions and implications of these processes on young viewers around the world? How do these viewers struggle with cultural tension and what roles do they assign themselves in this world? While there is a very rich and multifaceted literature on this topic, there is little research that actually pursues to what degree, and how, this ideology is internalized, resisted, and molded by young consumers of media around the world.[76]

A comprehensive examination of these questions was undertaken in an extensive cross-cultural study called the *Global Disney Audiences Project*. In order to assess the place of *Disney* culture in societies around the world, this study employed standardized questionnaires, interviews, and participant observations in 17 countries outside the USA and at five locations within it.[77] Findings derived from the primary question – "Is Disney uniquely American" – varied greatly from country to country and the variation was most marked in young adults. Overall, approximately 50 percent related to Disney as uniquely American, thinking that it was prototypically American, as in the "American dream" and/or perceived it to be culturally imperialist. Interestingly, others who expressed the opinion that *Disney* was not uniquely American argued that it was "Western," "universal," or even "mine." This alternative interpretation suggests that the viewers' perception of American is interchangeable with terms such as "Western" or even "universal," and as such represents interviewees' own existential experience. If indeed non-American children understand new experiences, among other things, through an American worldview presented in American media, then it may be an argument in favor of the "Americanization" of popular culture thesis.

A related illustration comes from China, where VCDs with Disney characters, songs, and stories are used in order to teach children the highly valued English language. While it is unclear how much English is being retained through this method, it is clear that Disney products are growing in popularity in China as are many other popular texts originating in the West. This study contributes what may be come to be viewed, with further research, as a rival interpretation to the Americanization thesis and one which challenges notions of the development of a cosmopolitan perspective: Namely, though they derive great pleasure from these texts, Chinese children relate to and interpret them through a domestic lens that includes strong political allegiance to their own local culture.[78] For example, children cited the educational quality of their national television programs as opposed to the solely entertainment markers of foreign programming.

Another cross-cultural study that examined the leisure culture of children and youth in 12 European countries in the mid-1990s found that children used a variety of criteria to distinguish between local and imported programs.[79] For example, in Denmark and Israel the use of subtitles marked programs as foreign, but children used other markers too: Israeli children noticed the blond hair of the actors and actresses, which contrasted with their own mostly darkish colored hair; Danish children pointed out the quick editing style and special effects that characterize an American program; and French children noticed the different skin color and eating habits of the Japanese animation series. Interestingly, in this European study, children's identification of programs as foreign did not necessarily mean they derived less viewing pleasure from them compared to locally produced programs; indeed, this was quite the opposite in some cases. Foreign programs, particularly those imported from the USA, were often identified as of higher quality, more original, "cooler." In comparison, local programs were perceived as less professional, with bad acting, and even as less realistic. For example, local soap operas were criticized for being non-realistic, while the popular American ones at the time (e.g., *Beverly Hills*; *Baywatch*) were evaluated as more realistic. One possible explanation, already suggested, is that the perception of "realism" is, among others, a result of a critical view that emerges from the degree of familiarity with the world presented in the program. When this world is more familiar to viewers (e.g., their own local soap opera), they are more capable of comparing it to their own reality and, therefore, of identifying more easily the constructed and unreal nature of the program. However, when this world is more distant (e.g., imported soap operas), familiarity with it is almost solely based on previous screen encounters, so children are less able to look at it critically.

The creation of a hybrid glocalized culture that emerges from the struggle between local and global forces and results in a culture that is a combination of different characteristics has produced a number of interesting studies. For example, popular music, such as that offered on MTV and other music channels, is an illustration of this process. Many children worldwide seem to prefer foreign music, particularly American and UK pop and rock music, that symbolizes for them innovation and style, even if the lyrics in English are incomprehensible (as is often the case for the younger audiences). Thus, the words are of secondary significance in comparison to the "English sound" of the songs. Popular local bands are often an imitation of that style. However, at the same time, children also express a strong attraction to their local ethnic music. In short, children demonstrate a preference for a variety of musical styles simultaneously without any sign of uneasiness or internal contradiction.

Interestingly, the older children are the more they seem to be attracted to global culture, as shown by the popularity of programs originating in the USA. Globalization also seems to be associated with socio-economic status, with mastery of the English language, and preference for American content characteristic of the higher social classes. An additional aspect that surfaced in the European study related to the feeling of a "utopian common world" created as a result of this global Anglo-European culture. Popular screen content, for example, is that which centers on universal interests such as interpersonal relationships, feelings, conflicts, and struggles. These children were not concerned with where the program originated, but rather with the fact that it dealt with humanity. The researchers' impression was that television culture offered children a symbolic sphere of a common world populated by people and relationships disconnected from defined contexts and cultural borders. It seemed to connect children to an illusion of a social universal "center," similar to the interest of children and young adolescents in science fiction and magic programs that relate to a "different" world to which all belong. For example, studies in Israel and Europe found that children and youth perceive North American texts as connecting them to some global "entity."[80]

More broadly, some scholars argue that integrating post-colonial theories opens up a more complicated and nuanced way of understanding how identities are mediated in developing nations in an era of transnational media. Such, for example, was the case with a field study of Indian youth and their negotiation of their unique identity under pressures of cultural globalization and neoliberalism.[81] Other studies on children, media, and culture in countries such as Brazil, China, and in the Arab world are few and far between.[82] Unfortunately, there is still too little research available from marginalized societies to more fully inform us on how globalization is actually experienced in former colonized countries in the current era of changing power relationships.

What is "America"?

The dominance of American media culture all over the world raises a related question: What do the media contribute to the construction of the concept of "America" by children who have never been there? This question provides a unique opportunity to inquire into the role of media in the construction of social reality when there is a void in real-life experience.

A series of studies conducted during the 1990s and devoted to this very question presented revealing conclusions.[83] For example, a small study based on focus groups with adolescents in Germany found that television viewers were aware that the programs were produced in the USA, but were not terribly preoccupied with this fact.[84] When discussing the inter-personal relationships presented in the programs, they did not refer at all to the culture in which these relationships took place. The fact that the characters were American did not prevent the interviewees from identifying with them and feeling emotionally close to them. Many of these youth related the social issues addressed in the programs to similar ones in their own social environment: The desire for equality within a couple in a situation comedy; inter-relationships among family members; or friendship in a soap opera. These were interpreted and related to through the background of their own contextualized experiences and values. The American identity of the programs, so it seems, was not a significant element in their analysis of the social world presented to them.

The findings of the German study are not unexpected, given the European–Christian nature of the culture and therefore its similarity to that of the USA, as well as the selection of programs that center on universal themes of relationships in the family, between friends, and couples. In contrast, it is interesting to examine these issues in a culture that differs significantly from the USA. A study conducted in India, for example, included a survey of 450 youth in three large Indian cities that focused on their acquaintance with American characters and their perceptions of American society and culture.[85] The study found that the most salient aspect of American culture for the youth were brand names of American products (e.g., Coca Cola and Levi jeans), as well as names of celebrities in the film and pop music industries. The specific choices made by the interviewees reflected the particular timing of the study (in late 1990s), when the most popular American programs were soap operas and Disney movies. Above all, what viewing these programs appeared to achieve was to reinforce the popularity of American cultural products in the non-Western world.

In addition, 80 percent of the interviewees in the Indian study claimed that television was their central source of information about the USA. They recognized mainly the names of famous American white males, and believed that Americans enjoyed a very high standard of living, had powerful media, and advanced technology. They perceived the USA's scientific progress as the most important contribution to the world, with building nuclear weapons among its chief achievements. A majority of respondents agreed with the claim that "America is a racist country"; about half agreed that "America symbolizes equality of opportunity"; and about 40 percent that "American involvement in international politics is justified" (which means that most respondents did not agree with this statement, well before the many international crises involving the USA at the beginning of the third millennium, in particular the wars in Iraq and Afghanistan); and only 20 percent agreed with the statement that "America is a male-dominated society."

In Greece, two-thirds of over 500 youth who completed questionnaires reported that American programs constituted most of their viewing diet, second only to Greek programs.[86] They perceived people in the USA to be living a comfortable life, but over-estimated the ability of an average American family to take an annual vacation in Europe or to purchase a luxury car. At the same time, about half thought that Americans led boring lives. They also believed that Americans were happy with their lot, friendly, and trustworthy, and that youth their age in the USA enjoyed more personal freedom. The more those surveyed viewed American programs, the more they believed these programs to be realistic; the more they liked them; the more they described American society and American characters in positive terms and rated their wealth to be at a high level. Age was an important variable in these correlations: younger viewers (who obviously had less experience and fewer alternative sources of information) had less accurate evaluations of both the crime rate and levels of wealth in the USA.

Given these and other findings, the Greek study concluded, in a manner similar to other studies of social perceptions, that the quantity of television viewing in and of itself does not predict attitudes. Viewing American programs does not directly produce an effect of a particular perception of American society, but rather there are additional variables that intervene in this process, such as program appeal, perception of its realism, the particular programs watched, viewer age, gender, and social status. According to this study, the most salient variable was the strength of the adolescents' Greek identity. Thus, adolescents who watched a lot of Greek television felt a strong sense of personal safety in Greece, and expressed positive attitudes toward the culture and values of Greece. They viewed American society as less rich, more violent, with a less comfortable standard of living, greater boredom among Americans, and with less personal freedom enjoyed by American youth.

A study conducted in Israel of 900 elementary schoolchildren's viewing of wrestling programs produced by the World Wrestling Federation (WWF) revealed that some of the stereotypes of the USA prevalent throughout the world seemed to be reinforced by viewing these programs.[87] For example, researchers learned in the personal interviews that the children used a variety of reasons to explain that the program was American, such as statements about it being the richest and most developed country in the world, as well as the homeland of most celebrities. The USA was also admired for its innovativeness and seen as the country with the greatest potential to fulfill the *American dream*. At the same time, they perceived the USA to be the most violent and dangerous country, and Americans to be the most violent of all people. Furthermore, Israeli respondents thought Americans lacked self-control and lived according to behavioral norms that are unacceptable in other parts of the world. Interviewees specifically named movies and programs, and cited them as the sources of their information and "proof" of their claims.

In summary, popular television programs and films viewed all over the world do seem to contribute to cultivation of a worldview which in turn shapes expectations and perceptions regarding American society and within which new information – from additional media sources as well as from first-hand experiences – is absorbed. We have discussed this topic in some detail, as from it we can learn about the role that screen culture may be playing in terms of how children and youth grow to understand the world around them, as well as the world that is beyond their physical reach. Globalization, it seems, is not a matter of oppositions for young viewers: it is not globalization in contrast with localization, internalization in contrast with nationality, universalism in contrast with particularism. Rather, globalization is integrated within the specific location of the child in the world at large. We may conclude that these are integrative processes: adoption of a global perception of social life alongside the existence of multiculturalism, even hybrid cultures, in the lives of children. The meeting between the global and local is a meeting of integration and co-existence, and not a choice between two contradictory options. It is a dialectic process of "push and pull" between the two poles.

Concluding Remarks

In summarizing the role of media in the development of perception of self and society and in the construction of social reality, we return once again to the conclusion that media consumers, even young ones, located as they are within social and ideological contexts, are selective consumers of media content and active and creative in their interpretations of it. They gain pleasure from their use of various texts, be they comedies, cartoons, sports coverage, movies, video games, or Facebook pages. They learn and accept advice offered to them in a variety of ways; they recognize themselves and feel self-affirmed, and complete (or conceal) what is missing in their own life-worlds. Media consumption, too, serves as an outlet for the expression of their feelings and fantasies and functions as an important activity that enables them to reconstruct the meaning of everyday life.[88]

However, if we are too hasty in our celebration of the symbolic creativity and critical thinking of young people we risk underestimating the potential political and social implications of media for these audiences in contemporary societies. The interaction of children with mediated texts is complicated, taking place in conjunction with and incorporating many other socializing forces.

Academic discussion of this area of research shifts between the over-emphasis on the power of media to construct the social world of "captive" young audiences, on the one hand, and dismissal of the power of media, on the other. This may be due to over-glorification of young people as critical consumers who debate the content and struggle with the many interpretations embedded in the text. Such views emphasize the role of cognitive processes in their estimation of the attention devoted to media, to the analysis of the texts themselves, their content and power to construct reality, or focus on the audience as an ideological product of the text.

We should remember that it is impossible to treat separately discussion of media roles in the construction of reality, as they all deal with the same realms of life and reinforce each other by creating an incorporated worldview. All such media-related research reveals that the relationship between exposure to popular media and the construction of reality is complicated and multifaceted.

Study of most of the issues raised throughout this chapter is far too underdeveloped to allow us to arrive at the overarching conclusions sought by many parents, educators, and politicians, as well as media producers. Yet society cannot be relieved of its responsibility for the content offered to children by many media outlets, and it cannot leave that content unchallenged. The reinforcement of similar messages in many programs, advertisements, games and websites (such as gender and racial messages, consumer ideology or political views) makes it very hard for children to resist them, or to undertake an oppositional process of negotiation with them. Media, we have seen, are much, much more than wasteful entertainment, as is popularly claimed. Indeed, among their many roles, media may well serve as an alternative form of "schooling." This conclusion reinforces the need for all media stakeholders to realize and to manifest social responsibility when producing content for children. The implications of these issues for media policy and advocacy will be discussed in Chapter 7.

Notes

1. Van Evra, 2004.
2. Wolf, 1992.
3. Based on an integrated review in Lemish, 2010, excerpts reprinted with permission.
4. Götz & Lemish, 2012.
5. De Beauvoir, 1989[1952].
6. Based on an integrated review in Lemish, 2010, excerpts reprinted with permission.
7. Signorielli, 2012.
8. See Gunter, 1995, for an integrative summary.
9. Morgan, 1987; Signorielli & Lears, 1992.
10. See Durkin, 1985.
11. See, for example, Drabman, Robertson, Patterson, Jarvie, & Hammer, *et al.*, 1981; Pingree, 1978.
12. See such discussions in Currie, 1997; Douglas, 1994; Frazer, 1987; Mazzarella & Pecora, 1999; and Peterson, 1987.
13. Lemish, 1998.
14. Hains, 2012; Zaslow, 2011.
15. See, for example, Mazzarella, 2010.
16. Mazzarella, 2013.
17. Brown, Lamb, & Tappen, 2009; Pollack, 1998.
18. Pollack, 1998; Seidler, 1997.
19. Götz, Lemish, Aidman, & Moon, 2005; Lemish, Liebes, & Seidmann, 2001; Neubauer & Winter, 2008.
20. Bachen & Illouz, 1996.
21. Baker-Sperry, 2007.
22. Aidman, 1999.
23. Reznik, 2014; Reznik & Lemish, 2011.
24. Galician, 2004.
25. Götz, Lemish, Aidman, & Moon, 2005.
26. Lemish, 2010.
27. Marciano, 2009.
28. Gray, 2009.
29. Based on Gerbner and Gross, 1976, later summarized by Signorielli, 1990, and Weimann, 2000.
30. Donnerstein, Slaby, & Eron, 1994; Wilson, Kunkel, Kintz, Potter, & Donnerstein, *et al.*, 1996.
31. Kodaira, 1998.
32. Durkin & Low, 1998.
33. Groebel, 1998.
34. Opree, Buijzen, van Reijmersdal, & Valkenburg, 2013.
35. Chia, 2010.
36. Buckingham & Tingstad, 2010; Sparrman, Sandin, & Sjöberg, 2012.
37. Ritzer, 2013.
38. Lemish, 2010; Valdivia, 2008.
39. Lemish, Drotner, Liebes, Maigret, & Stald, 1998; Reznik & Lemish, 2011.
40. Asamen & Berry, 2012.
41. See, for example, Graves, 2008.

42. Fujioka, 1999.
43. Asamen & Berry, 2012.
44. Zohoori, 1988.
45. Lemish, Drotner, Liebes, Maigret, & Stald, 1998.
46. Christopoulou & de Leeuw, 2004; de Block & Buckingham, 2007.
47. Gillespie, 1995.
48. Durham, 2004.
49. Katz, 2010; Moran, 2011.
50. Elias & Lemish, 2011.
51. Elias, 2013.
52. Elias & Lemish, 2009.
53. Chaffee & Yang, 1990.
54. Austin Weintraub, 2013.
55. Austin Weintraub, 2013.
56. Buckingham, 2000.
57. Carter, 2013.
58. Lemish & Götz, 2007.
59. First, 1997.
60. Austin Weintraub, 2013.
61. Liebes & Ribak, 1992.
62. Ribak, 1997.
63. Cole, Arafat, Tidhar, Zidan, Fox, *et al.*, 2003; Cole, Richman, & McCann Brown, 2001; Killen & Fox, 2003; Killen, Fox, & Leavitt, 2004.
64. Brenick, Lee-Kim, Killen, Fox, Raviv, *et al.*, 2007.
65. Shochat, 2003.
66. Lemish & Götz, 2014.
67. Connolly, 2009; Connolly, Fitzpatrick, Gallagher, & Harris, 2006.
68. P. Lemish, 2008; P. Lemish & Schlote, 2009.
69. Kampf, 2011.
70. Austin & Anderson, 2008.
71. Gultig, 2004; Sherry, 1997; Smith, 2004; Tufte, 2003.
72. McKee, Aghi, & Shahzadi, 2004.
73. Singhal, Cody, Rogers, & Sabido, 2004.
74. Lemish, 2010.
75. Kolucki & Lemish, 2011.
76. Parameswaran, 2013.
77. Wasko, Phillips, & Meehan, 2001.
78. Hemelryk, 2005.
79. Lemish, Drotner, Liebes, Maigret, & Stald, 1998.
80. Elias & Lemish, 2011; Lemish, 2002.
81. McMillin, 2009.
82. See, for example, the collection of articles by Drotner and Livingstone, 2008.
83. See, for example, Kamalipour, 1999.
84. Palmer & Hafen, 1999.
85. Das, 1999.
86. Zaharoponlous, 1999.
87. Lemish, 1999.
88. Götz, Lemish, Aidman, & Moon, 2005.

References

Aidman, A. (1999). Disney's Pocahontas: Conversations with Native American and Euro-American girls. In: S.R. Mazzarella & N.O. Pecora (Eds.), *Growing up girls: Popular culture and the construction of identity* (pp.133–159). New York: Peter Lang.

Asamen, J.K. & Berry, G.L. (2012). Television, children, and multicultural awareness: Comprehending the medium in a complex multimedia society. In D.G. Singer & J.L. Singer (Eds.), *Handbook of children and the media* (pp. 363–378). Thousand Oaks, CA: Sage Publications.

Austin, Weintraub E. (2013). Processes and impacts of political socialization. In D. Lemish (Ed.), *The Routledge international handbook of children, adolescents, and media* (pp. 263–270). New York: Routledge.

Austin, R. & Anderson, J. (2008). Building bridges online: Issues of pedagogy and learning outcomes in intercultural education through citizenship. *International Journal of Information and Communication Technology Education 4*(1), 86–94.

Bachen, C.M. & Illouz, E. (1996). Imagining romance: Young people's cultural models of romance and love. *Critical Studies in Mass Communication, 13*(4), 279–308.

Baker-Sperry, L. (2007). The Production of meaning through peer interaction: Children and Walt Disney's Cinderella. *Sex Roles, 56,* 717–727.

Brenick, A., Lee-Kim, J., Killen, M., Fox, N., Raviv, A. *et al.* (2007). Social judgments in Israeli and Arabic children: Findings from media-based intervention projects. In D. Lemish & M. Götz (Eds.), *Children and media at times of war and conflict.* (pp. 287–308). Cresskill, NJ: Hampton.

Brown, L.M., Lamb, S., & Tappan, M.B. (2009). *Packaging boyhood: Saving our sons from superheroes, slackers, and other media stereotypes.* New York: St. Martin's Press.

Buckingham, D. (2000). *The making of citizens: Young people, news and politics.* London: Routledge.

Buckingham, D. & Tingstad, V. (Eds.). (2010). *Childhood and consumer culture.* London: Palgrave Macmillan.

Carter, C. (2013). Children and the news: Rethinking citizenship in the twenty-first century. In D. Lemish (Ed.), *The Routledge international handbook of children, adolescents, and media* (pp. 255–262). New York: Routledge.

Chaffee, S.H. & Yang, S-M. (1990). Communication and political socialization. In O. Ichilov (Ed.), *Political socialization, citizenship education and democracy* (pp. 37–157). New York: Teachers College Press.

Chia, S.C. (2010). How social influence mediates media effects on adolescents' materialism. *Communication Research, 37*(3), 400–419.

Christopoulou, N. & de Leeuw, S. (2004). *Home is where the heart is: Family relations of migrant children in media clubs in six European countries.* Institute of Education, University of London.

Cole, C., Arafat, C., Tidhar, C., Zidan, W.T., Fox, N., *et al.* (2003). "So they will be friends": The educational Impact of Rechov Sumsum/Shara'a Simsim, A Sesame Street television series to promote respect and understanding among children living in Israel, the West Bank, and Gaza. *International Journal of Behavioral Development, 27*(5), 409–22.

Cole, C.F., Richman, B.A., & McCann Brown, S.K. (2001). The world of *Sesame Street* research. In S.M. Fisch & R.T. Truglio (Eds.) *"G" is for growing: Thirty years of research on children and Sesame Street* (pp. 147–179). Mahwah, NJ: Lawrence Erlbaum.

Connolly, P. (2009). *Developing programmes to promote ethnic diversity in early childhood: Lessons from Northern Ireland.* Working paper no. 52, Bernard van Leer Foundation, The Hague/The Netherlands.

Connolly, P., Fitzpatrick, S., Gallagher, T., & Harris, P. (2006). Addressing diversity and inclusion in the early years in conflict-affected societies: A case study of the Media Initiative for children - Northern Ireland. *International Journal of Early Years Education, 14*(3), 263–278.

Currie, D. H. (1997). Decoding femininity: Advertisements and their teenage readers. *Gender and Society, 11*(4), 453–477.

Das, U. (1999). What does America symbolize to the urban, educated youth in India? In Y.R. Kamalipour (Ed.), *Images of the U.S. around the world: A multicultural perspective* (pp. 209–220). New York: State University of New York Press.

De Beauvoir, S. (1989[1952]). *The second sex.* New York: Vintage Books.

de Block, L. & Buckingham, D. (2007). *Global children, global media: Migration, media and childhood.* Basingstoke: Palgrave Macmillan.

Donnerstein, E., Slaby, R., & Eron, L. (1994). The mass media and youth violence. In J. Murray, E. Rubinstein, & G. Comstock (Eds.), *Violence and youth: Psychology's response 2* (pp. 219–250). Washington, DC: American Psychological Association.

Douglas, S. (1994). *Where the girls are: Growing up female with the mass media.* New York: Penguin Books.

Drabman, R., Robertson, S., Patterson, J., Jarvie, G., Hammer, D., *et al.* (1981). Children's perceptions of media-portrayed sex-roles. *Sex Roles, 7,* 379–389.

Drotner, K. & Livingstone, S. (2008). *The international handbook of children, media, and culture.* Los Angeles, CA: Sage.

Durham, M.G. (2004). Constructing the "New ethnicities": Media, sexuality and diaspora identity in the lives of South Asian immigrant girls. *Critical Studies in Media Communication, 21*(2), 140–161.

Durkin, K. (1985). *Television, sex roles and children: A developmental social psychological account.* Philadelphia, PA: Open University Press.

Durkin, K. & Low, J. (1998). Children, media and aggression. In U. Carlsson & C. von Feilitzen (Eds.), *Children and media violence* (pp. 107–124). Göteborg University, Sweden: The International Clearinghouse on Children, Youth and Media.

Elias, N. (2013). Immigrant children and media. In D. Lemish (Ed.), *The Routledge international handbook of children, adolescents, and media* (pp. 336–343). New York: Routledge.

Elias, N. & Lemish, D. (2009). Spinning the web of identity: Internet's roles in immigrant adolescents' search of identity. *New Media & Society, 11*(4), 1–19.

Elias, N. & Lemish, D. (2011). Between three worlds: Host, homeland, and global media in the lives of Russian immigrant families in Israel and Germany. *Journal of Family Issues, 32*(9), 1245–1274.

First, A. (1997). Television and the construction of social reality: An Israeli case study. In M.E. McCombs, D.L. Shaw, & D. Weaver (Eds.), *Communication and democracy* (pp. 41–50). Hillsdale, NJ: Lawrence Erlbaum.

Frazer, E. (1987). Teenage girls reading *Jackie. Media, Culture, and Society, 9,* 407–425.

Fujioka, Y. (1999). Television portrayals and African American stereotypes: Examination of television effects when direct contact is lacking. *Journal of Mass Communication Quarterly, 76*(1), 52–75.

Galician, M. (2004). *Sex, love, & romance in the mass media.* New Jersey and London: Lawrence Erlbaum Associates, Publishers.

Gerbner, G. & Gross, L. (1976). Living with television: The violence profile. *Journal of Communication, 26*(2), 172–199.

Gillespie, M. (1995). *Television, ethnicity and cultural change.* London: Routledge.

Götz, M. & Lemish, D. (2012). *Sexy girls, heroes and funny losers: Gender representations in children's TV around the world.* Frankfurt am Main: Peter Lang.

Götz, M., Lemish, D., Aidman, A., & Moon, H. (2005). *Media and the make believe worlds of children: When Harry Potter met Pokémon in Disneyland.* Mahwah, NJ: Lawrence Erlbaum.

Graves, S.B. (2008). Children's television programming and the development of multicultural attitudes. In J.K. Asamen, M.K. Ellis, & G.L. Berry (Eds.) *Child development, multiculturalism, and media* (pp. 213–232), Thousand Oaks, CA: Sage.

Gray, M. (2009). Negotiating identities/queering desires: Coming out online and the remediation of the coming-out story. *Journal of Computer-Mediated Communication, 14,* 1162–1189.

Groebel, J. (1998). The UNESCO global study on media violence: Report presented to the Director General of UNESCO. In U. Carlsson & C. von Feilitzen (Eds.), *Children and media violence* (pp. 181–199). Göteborg University, Sweden: The UNESCO International Clearinghouse on Children and Violence on the Screen.

Gultig, J. (2004). "This is it" – South African youth's reading of Yizo Yizo 2. In C. von Feilitzen (Ed.), *Young people, soap operas and reality TV* (pp. 227–241). Göteborg University, Sweden: The International Clearinghouse on Children, Youth and Media.

Gunter, B. (1995). *Television and gender representation.* London: John Libbey and Company.

Hains, R.C. (2012*). Growing up with girl power: Girlhood on screen and in everyday life.* New York: Peter Lang.

Hemelryk, D.S. (2005). *Little friends: Children's film and media culture in China.* Oxford, UK: Rowman and Littlefield Publishers.

Kamalipour, Y.R. (Ed.). (1999). *Images of the U.S. around the world: A multicultural perspective.* New York: State University of New York Press.

Kampf, R. (2011). Dialogue between rival groups in the net. In A. Cohen & A. Lev-On (Eds.), *Technology, society and politics in Israel* (pp. 277–302). Tel-Aviv: The Israeli Political Science Association (in Hebrew).

Katz, V.S. (2010). How children of immigrants use media to connect their families to the community: The case of Latinos in South Los Angeles. *Journal of Children and Media, 4*(3), 298–315.

Killen, M. & Fox, N. (2003). Evaluations of children's reactions to Israeli–Palestinian Sesame Street. *Maryland International, 2,* 12.

Killen, M., Fox, N.A., & Leavitt, L. (2004). Stereotypes and conflict resolution in the Mid-East: Young children's social concepts as a function of exposure to a media intervention. Paper presented at the Annual Meeting of the Jean Piaget Society: Society for the Study of Knowledge and Development. Toronto, Canada.

Kodaira, S.I. (1998). A review of research on media violence in Japan. In U. Carlsson & C. von Feilitzen (Eds.), *Children and media violence* (pp. 81–106). Göteborg University, Sweden: The International Clearinghouse on Children, Youth and Media.

Kolucki, B. & Lemish, D. (2011). *Communicating with children: Principles and practices to nurture, inspire, excite, educate and heal.* New York: Communication for Development Unit, UNICEF. See http://www.unicef.org/cwc.

Lemish, D. (1998). Spice Girls' talk: A case study in the development of gendered identity. In S.A. Inness (Ed.), *Millennium girls: Today's girls around the world* (pp. 145–167). New York: Rowman and Littlefield.

Lemish, D. (2002). Between here and there: Israeli children living cultural globalization. In C. von Feilitzen & U. Carlsson (Eds.), *Children, young people and media globalization* (pp. 125–134). Sweden: Göteborg University Press, The UNESCO International Clearinghouse on Children Youth and Media.

Lemish, D. (2010). *Screening gender on children's television: The views of producers around the world*. London: Routledge.

Lemish, D., Drotner, K. Liebes, T., Maigret, E., & Stald, G. (1998). Global culture in practice: A look at children and adolescents in Denmark, France and Israel. *European Journal of Communication, 13,* 539–556.

Lemish, D. & Götz, M. (Eds.). (2007). *Children and media at times of war and conflict.* Cresskill, NJ: Hampton.

Lemish, D. & Götz, M. (2014). Conflict, media and child well-being. In A. Ben-Aryeh, I. Frønes, F. Casas, & J.E. Korbin (Eds.), *Handbook of child well-being: Theories, methods and policies in global perspective.* (Vol. 4, pp. 2013–2029). Dordrecht: Springer.

Lemish, D., Liebes, T., & Seidmann, V. (2001). Gendered media meanings and uses. In S. Livingstone & M. Bovill (Eds.), *Children and their changing media environment: A European comparative study* (pp. 263–282). Mahwah, NJ: Lawrence Erlbaum.

Lemish, P. (2008). Peacebuilding contributions of Northern Ireland producers of children and youth-oriented media. *Journal of Children and Media, 2*(3), 282–299.

Lemish, P. & Schlote, E. (2009). Media portrayals of youth involvement in social change: The roles of agency, praxis, and conflict resolution processes in TV programs. In T. Tufte & F. Enghel (Eds.), *Youth engaging with the world.* (pp. 193–214). Göteborg: Nordicom, Göteborgs universitet. (Yearbook/The International Clearinghouse on Children, Youth and Media; No. 2009).

Liebes, T. & Ribak, R. (1992). The contribution of family culture to political participation, political outlook, and its reproduction. *Communication Research, 19*(5), 618–641.

Marciano, A. (2009). The role of newspapers in coping with the coming-out process of gay male youth. *Media Frames, 4,* 1–28. (in Hebrew).

Mazzarella, S. (2010). (Ed.). *Girl Wide Web2.0: Revisiting girls, the internet, and the negotiation of identity.* New York: Peter Lang.

Mazzarella, S.R. & Pecora, N. (Eds.). (1999). *Growing up girls: Popular culture and the construction of identity.* New York: Peter Lang.

Mazzarella, S.R. (2013). Media and gender identities: Learning and performing femininity and masculinity. In D. Lemish (Ed.), *The Routledge international handbook of children, adolescents, and media* (pp. 279–286). New York: Routledge.

McKee, N., Aghi, M., & Shahzadi, N. (2004). Cartoons and comic books for changing social norms: *Meena*, the South Asian girl. In A. Singhal, M.J. Cody, E.M. Rogers, & M. Sabido (Eds.), *Entertainment-education and social change: History, research, and practice* (pp. 331–349). Mahwah, NJ: Lawrence Erlbaum.

McMillin, D.C. (2009*). Mediated identities: Television, youth, and globalization.* New York: Peter Lang.

Moran, Kristin C. (2011). *Listening to Latina/o youth television consumption within families.* New York: Peter Lang.

Morgan, M. (1987). Television, sex-role attitudes and sex-role behavior. *Journal of Early Adolescence, 7*(3), 269–282.

Neubauer, G. & Winter, R. (2008). Cool heroes or funny freaks? *TelevIZIon, 21E*.

Opree, S.J., Buijzen, M., van Reijmersdal, E.A., & Valkenburg, P.M. (2013). Children's advertising exposure and materialistic orientations: A longitudinal study into direct and mediated effects. *Communication Research, 41*(5), 717–735.

Palmer, A.W. & Hafen, T. (1999). American TV through the eyes of German teenagers. In Y.R. Kamalipour (Ed.), *Images of the U.S. around the world: A multicultural perspective* (pp. 135–146). New York: State University of New York Press.

Parameswaran, R. (2013). Media culture and childhood in the age of globalization. In D. Lemish (Ed.), *The Routledge international handbook of children, adolescents, and media* (pp. 75–82). New York: Routledge.

Peterson, E.E. (1987). Media consumption and girls who want to have fun. *Critical Studies in Mass Communication, 4*(1), 37–50.

Pingree, S. (1978). The effects of nonsexist commercials and perceptions of reality on children's attitudes about women. *Psychology of Women Quarterly, 2*, 262–277.

Pollack, W. (1998). *Real boys: Rescuing our sons from the myths of boyhood*. New York: Henry Holt and Co.

Reznik, S. (2014). All you need is love. *TelevIZIon, 26E*.

Reznik, S. & Lemish, D. (2011). Falling in love with "High School Musical": Girls' talk about romantic perceptions. In M.C. Kearney (Ed.), *Mediated Girlhoods* (pp. 151–170). New York: Peter Lang.

Ribak, R. (1997). Socialization as and through conversation: Political discourse in Israeli families. *Comparative Education Review, 41*(1), 71–96.

Ritzer, G. (2013). *The McDonaldization of society: 20th anniversary edition*. Los Angeles: Sage.

Seidler, V.J. (1997). *Man enough: Embodying masculinities*. London: Sage.

Sherry, J.L. (1997). Pro-social soap operas for development: A review of research and theory. *The Journal of International Communication, 4*(2), 75–102.

Shochat, L. (2003). Our neighborhood: Using entertaining children's television to promote interethnic understanding in Macedonia. *Conflict Resolution Quarterly, 21*(1), 79–93.

Signorielli, N. (1990). Television's mean and dangerous world: A continuation of the cultural indicators perspective. In N. Signorielli & M. Morgan (Eds.), *Cultivation analysis: New directions in media effects research* (pp. 85–106). Newbury Park, CA: Sage.

Signorielli, N. (2012). Television's gender role images and contribution to stereotyping: Past, present, future. In D.G. Singer & J.L. Singer (Eds.), *Handbook of children and the media* (pp. 321–340). Thousand Oaks, CA: Sage Publications.

Signorielli, N. & Lears, M. (1992). Children, television and conceptions about chores: Attitudes and behaviors. *Sex Roles, 27*(3/4), 157–170.

Singhal, A., Cody, C.J., Rogers. E.M., & Sabido, M. (Eds.). (2004). *Entertainment-education and social change: History, research and practice*. Mahwah, NJ: Lawrence Erlbaum.

Smith, R. (2004). Yizo Yizo: This is it? A critical analysis of reality-based drama series. In C. von Feilitzen (Ed.), *Young people, soap operas and reality TV* (pp. 241–251). Göteborg University, Sweden: The International Clearinghouse on Children, Youth and Media.

Sparrman, A., Sandin, B., & Sjöberg, J. (2012). *Situating child consumption: Rethinking values and notions of children, childhood and consumption*. Lund: Nordic Academic Press

Tufte, T. (2003). Entertainment-education in HIV-AIDS communication. Beyond marketing, towards empowerment. In C. von Feilitzen & U. Carlsson (Eds.), *Promote or protect? Perspectives on media literacy and media regulations* (pp. 85–97). Göteborg University, Sweden: The International Clearinghouse on Children, Youth and Media.

Valdivia, A.N. (2008). Mixed race on Disney Channel: From *Johnnie Tsunami* through *Lizzie McGuire* and ending with the *Cheetah Girls*. In M. Beltran & C. Fojas (Eds.), *Mixed race Hollywood: Multiraciality in film and media culture* (pp. 269–289). New York: New York University Press.

Van Evra, J. (2004). *Television and child development* (3rd ed.). Mahwah, NJ: Lawrence Erlbaum.

Wasko, J., Phillips, M., & Meehan, E.R. (Eds.). (2001). *Dazzled by Disney?: A global Disney audiences project*. London: Leicester University Press.

Weimann, G. (2000). *Communicating unreality: Modern media and the construction of reality* (pp. 79–121). Thousand Oaks, CA: Sage.

Wilson, B., Kunkel, D., Kintz, D., Potter, J., Donnerstein, E., *et al.* (1996). *National television violence study*. Thousand Oaks, CA: Sage.

Wolf, N. (1992). *The beauty myth: How images of beauty are used against women*. New York: Doubleday.

Zaharoponlous, T. (1999). Television viewing and the perception of the United States by Greek teenagers. In Y.R. Kamalipour (Ed.), *Images of the U.S. around the world: A multicultural perspective* (pp. 279–294). New York: State University of New York Press.

Zaslow, E. (2011). *Feminism, Inc: Coming of age in girl power media culture*. New York: Palgrave Macmillan.

Zohoori, A.R. (1988). A cross-cultural analysis of children's television use. *Journal of Broadcasting and Electronic Media, 32*(1), 105–113.

6

Media, Sociality, and Participation

One of the most dramatic changes introduced by the digital media environment in which children and young people are immersed today is the social nature of a large part of their activities. If in the past viewing television, listening to music, and playing video games was often blamed in public discourse for promoting self-absorption, alienation, and anti-social behavior, as children mostly engaged in these activities on their own, the vibrant social life facilitated via their use of the internet and mobile media poses very different challenges and opportunities, including in the social domain. Some consider a large portion of social networking posting to be narcissistic in nature, overwhelming focused on "me" – where I am, what I am doing, how I am feeling – and documenting mundane everyday experiences in words and in *selfies* (digital self-portraits). Others consider these postings to be performative and expressive, shaping an individual identity and a desire to leave a unique trace behind to be shared with a collective. Accordingly, this chapter is devoted to discussing what we know and need to investigate regarding the unique social nature of the current media environment and its place in children's lives.

We start by recalling various types of activities that children and youth are engaged in on the web. These have been categorized in the current literature in a variety of ways. Some approaches focus on content. For example, we can distinguish between information-seeking and entertainment-related activities (e.g., surfing websites; downloading content; gaming), as well as those commercial in nature, with or without parental involvement (e.g., purchase and sale of products and services). In addition, a large portion of children's activities are communicative and social, including the use of social networks, email, instant messaging (IM) programs, forums, and blogs, as well as many varieties of civil engagement activities, such as

Children and Media: A Global Perspective, First Edition. Dafna Lemish.
© 2015 John Wiley & Sons, Inc. Published 2015 by John Wiley & Sons, Inc.
Companion Website: www.wiley.com/go/lemish/childrenandmedia

organizing for participation in protests, signing petitions and bans, and mobilizing others to participate in events.

Another way of categorizing these activities is by conceptualizing them as *incoming* and *outgoing* content. Incoming content refers to content created by others that children seek on the web, are exposed to, or download. Outgoing content, on the other hand, refers to the activities that children themselves create and/or in which they participate.[1]

A third way to conceptualize online activities is to divide them into three categories: *content* activities, in which the child is the recipient of content; *contact* activities, with the child as a participant in the relationship; and *conduct* activities, with the child as an active actor.[2] Thus, the category of content can be seen as the equivalent of the incoming category above, while the categories of contact and conduct are two forms of outgoing activities.

A different, yet complementary, way of conceptualizing these many activities is by making a distinction between three types of participation of young people on the internet: *Hanging Out* is a form of social behavior typical of social networking through which participants develop social and communication skills; *Messing Around* is a form of participation by "trial and error" while deliberating upon various options for participation; and *Geeking Out* refers to a very goal-oriented or topic-specific social behavior shared by the participants.[3]

The variety of ways in which scholars talk about these activities suggests to us how complicated and rich young people's engagement with the media world is today.

In addition to contents, we can also seek to understand children's new media usage through a developmental perspective. For example, a composite, comparative analysis of over 400 studies from 21 European countries found that as children grow older they move from heavier engagement with *incoming* activities to more *outgoing* social ones. In addition, only a small portion of teenagers actually engage in more advanced social activities; such as co-gaming, file-sharing, participation in virtual worlds (e.g., *Second Life*), and blogging. Even fewer engage in civic activities and protests.[4] It is interesting to note that studies, such as one completed in the UK, found that young people show a strong preference in their online activities for the major sites developed by leading corporate entities, such as (at the time of the study) Google, MSN, YouTube, and Facebook.[5]

The variety of mobile devices that allow children to remain connected at all times, and across all physical spaces, means that virtual-social world is ever present, and is just as dominant and central to children's lives as the concrete reality within which they live. As discussed in Chapter 3, these many forms of personal and social engagements, along with active participation in the virtual world, characterize the *participatory culture* of online life. Even the most routine activities that children engage in on social networks – such as information sharing, personal comments, posting of photos, celebrating birthdays and events – are indicative of the blurring of active and passive consumption of media content, or what has been termed "prosumption" (i.e., production + consumption).

Social Networking

As they grow up, children's technological skills, social needs, and dependency on peer groups grow steadily, as does the amount of time they spend on the internet, with the latter gradually becoming a central social space in their lives. The freedom that children acquire on the net to "move about" and explore the world, with its endless social possibilities, offers them alternatives and substitutes for the restrictions and limitations they experience in reality; whether imposed by geographical borders and distances, or by constraints on their leisure activities, such as time and freedom of movement. Even before reaching adolescence, children worldwide are experiencing significant peer pressure to create a profile and use social networking sites. The data accumulating from several studies in the USA, Europe, Brazil, and several Asian countries suggest that they are mostly connected through Facebook and Twitter, networks that do not specifically cater to children's needs.

Social media take many forms and serve such functions as: expression (e.g., blogging, participating in forums and chats); sharing (e.g., video and music, recommending platforms); networking (via a variety of online and mobile tools); gaming; as well as participating in platforms (e.g., Facebook, MySpace). Children and youth text on their mobile phones, network on various platforms, and play social games online. Some of the hardware, such as mobile smartphones, gives them access to the entire range of social functions.[6]

In general, engaging in these social functions contributes to children's social and emotional development in multiple ways as they can express themselves, explore different identities, build relationships, and develop their self-concept. Similar to any social relationship offline, social media opportunities can also be misused or abused, and can damage self-esteem and social relationships.[7] All these qualities and concerns have implications for aspects of digital literacy, discussed in Chapter 3.

Online and mobile communication requires complicated social skills, including: interpreting abbreviated language and iconic messages often used in texting (e.g., LOL – laughing out loud; XOXO – hugs and kisses); using symbols and emoticons to express emotions such as ☹, ☺, and then interpreting nuances without voice intonations and facial expressions; internalizing a special etiquette appropriate for different means of communication while shifting back and forth between them (e.g., how quickly one expects a response from phone texting versus email versus a Facebook posting). As with many social cues learned in the real world, these skills and expectations evolve collaboratively within communities of users, and are learned by doing.

One particular sphere that requires specific social as well as technical skills is that of gaming sub-cultures. In contrast to earlier computer and video games, internet games offer unique social opportunities.[8] For example, *MMORPG* (Massively Multiplayer Online Role-Playing Games) create social youth communities that have clear formal and informal social expectations and use specific social rules of behavior, embedded in other social practices among players on- and offline.[9]

Similarly, *MUVE* (Multi-User Virtual Environment) is an immersive social space in which collaborative projects are created as each participant builds upon the creative work of other participants while sharing *DIY* (Do-It-Yourself) tools.[10]

Being active on social media affords a similar experience, as most participants leverage content created by others, for example when they post it, re-contextualize and reinterpret it, add and delete, or mold it in innovative ways. In all of these examples, and many others not presented, the meaning-making process is social by definition.

Comparing offline and online relationships

Initially, questions were raised about the possibility of a displacement effect occurring with the introduction of the internet into children's lives. Similar to the process analyzed in Chapter 1 with regard to the introduction of television, here, too, we will discuss whether online social relationships are displacing those in children's everyday lives, so vital for healthy development of social skills as well as self-identity.[11] The initial body of research suggests that most of the online social relationships reinforce those already existing offline[12] (e.g., such was the case for 87% of the children in the 2011 multi-country European study mentioned above[13]).

If so, a corollary line of investigation seeks to identify the types of online and everyday life relationships, as well as the similarities and differences between them. Interestingly, researchers found that different communication modes are better suited to different types of relationships, as children are adapting to the unique characteristics and advantages of different forms of communication. For example, a study in Belgium found that while all platforms support ties between very close friends (e.g., texting, phoning, IM), IM was also frequently used for contacts with less close friends. Another study in the USA found that while IM practices did indeed have a positive correlation with close friendships and romantic relationships, chat rooms and gaming were related to a decline of the relationship. With all these preliminary studies, there is clear evidence that close friends use all available means of communication: face to face, texting, phone calls, email, chats, or social media.[14] The sense of constant contact and co-presence would seem to be attractive for children whose mobility and ability to explore public spaces is restricted, and whose time is controlled by adults. If so, online social networks may be an outstanding example of McLuhan's conceptualization of media as "an extension of man."[15]

A related domain of inquiry investigates the nature of these relationships – what does online contact do that is different from or even better than face-to face relationships? What makes online relationships so attractive to children and youth that they would prefer to stay online to walking over to a friend's house to hang out in her house or yard?

Interesting answers to these questions are provided by ethnographic studies and direct investigations of young people's social relationships. We learn from these studies that social networks are characterized by three key opportunities: the chance to learn about participants from their personal profiles; to have a network of "friends" to follow and with whom to be in contact, that is, "connected"; and the means to respond to what others are doing on the network quickly and efficiently. Furthermore, social networking embodies two seemingly opposing features: On the one hand, online allows for more boldness, self-disclosure, and intimacy in relationships that is easier for some people than in face-to-face situations. On the other, online one can easily ignore, as well as hide, aspects of a relationship that may hinder the development of a thriving friendship, such as a lack of self-confidence (e.g., due to disability, physical appearance, marginalized ethnicity). Researchers who interviewed children about their interactions online heard variations on the following statement: "On the internet I can be my real self." In this way, children seemed to be referring to a sense of a core self that exists independent of external "packaging" of physical appearance and social demographics.[16] Indeed, a study conducted in Canada suggested that socially anxious adolescents seemed to rely more heavily on online communication in their social relationships.[17] Referring to this phenomenon as the "internet attribute hypothesis," researchers argued that developing intimacy in relationships can be advanced more readily via the internet for some people who are reticent about self-exposure and have a need to overcome inhibitions. For example, feedback that friends give each other on social networking sites can contribute in meaningful ways to participants' self-esteem and sense of wellbeing. Studies of teenagers in the Netherlands support this line of argument.[18] Thus, evidence suggests that, irrespective of the means of communication, deepening relational closeness is dependent on the positive nature of the communication as well as the level of the individual's self-disclosure in an ongoing relationship.[19]

A study of North American youth on the social network MySpace found that the nature of the public space in the social network differs from non-mediated reality in four ways.[20] The first difference is the possibility of *persistence* of communication between participants over time, given the fact that all interaction is permanently documented. Second, *searchability* of others online is a-temporal, as their identity and traces of character remain active when the person in question is physically offline. Third, there is *replicability* of verbal as well as audio-visual utterances via continuous citing and distributing. Finally, *invisibility* of audiences attending to one's activities and messages online is a given and may be less threatening to participants. Together, these characteristics contribute to a continuous blurring of the private and the public in participants' lives, as the private is exposed to a large and heterogeneous audience we now call "friends" (on social sites), while the public is incorporated into individual and private posts, timelines, and personal pages.

Creating and maintaining a lively self-profile, including posting visuals and texts, sorting friends, creating collages of messages that represent the self, etc., all constitute activities of identity shaping and display that we know to be a central part of social processes during adolescence.[21] Indeed, this discussion enables us to understand that mediated social networks may provide many opportunities for self-expression that differ, and may even divert, from everyday life offline.

Marginalized identities

The unique characteristics of online relationships has also been found to play an important role for marginalized minority and immigrant groups. As discussed in Chapter 5, members of these groups face complicated challenges and need special efforts in the transition to living in their host society (e.g., learning the language, culture, holidays) as well as maintaining their home country and ethnic identity (e.g., cultural transmission, maintaining the mother tongue or dialect, keeping strong family ties).[22] For example, studies of youth who emigrated from the former USSR to Israel and Germany documented how internet use enabled them to maintain contact with friends in their home country as well as to connect with immigrants in other places experiencing similar challenges. At the same time, they perceived the internet as a relatively safe and positive arena for experimenting with host country youth. Interestingly, they claimed a number of positive aspects of communicating via the internet, including the fact that they could have time to compose their thoughts and use a dictionary when expressing themselves, that their foreignness was not visible on the net, and that they had no accent when writing online.[23]

Similarly, minority groups, such as Arab youth in Israel, are able to connect seamlessly with other youth in the Arab world, as the internet enables them to cross geographical, cultural, and political borders.[24] And, a study of Korean youth in the USA documented the central role of diasporic media practices in their lives, such as downloading and consuming ethnic applications on their smartphones. Thus, in addition to consuming media in ways similar to US-born peers, they knew media were instrumental in exploring and formulating their Korean ethnic identity.[25]

Another illustration of this process comes from researchers studying youth in Accra, Ghana's capital. Here, marginalized, low-resource youth visiting internet cafes discussed how the web provided them with endless opportunities in the global world, in contrast to the frustrating condition of *involuntary immobility* that characterized their daily lives. This is but one example of a common practice in many countries in which it seems that internet cafes serve as the only public places where patrons are free from the control, norms, and tight disciplining of their lives by traditionalist adults, and where they have some degree of control over their own space. They meet other youth within and beyond their borders, share online activities – including trickery – such as joining "frequent flyer" programs (which allow users to accumulate travel points to be applied to receive discounts on future travel – both of which are entirely imaginary for these youth, as none have ever been on a plane or have the prospect of going abroad in the near future), and connect through email to other worlds of possibilities. The fact that these behaviors are perceived by adults to be frivolous and even harmful provides them with an even stronger sense of empowerment and liberation.[26]

For some youth who may be "on the fringe" and feeling marginalized (e.g., those identifying themselves with sub-cultures such as LGBTQ (i.e., sexual identity groups), pro-mia/ana (i.e., groups promoting binging and/or anorexia), or punks), online social networking may provide them with solace and support (see also discussion in Chapter 5). For at-risk youth, on the other hand, peer interaction online can also become a platform through which to be drawn into crime and, for those in post-rehabilitation, a road back into recidivism, as a study of juvenile delinquents in Singapore demonstrates.[27]

In summarizing the research available to us to date, it seems that online relationships neither compete with nor damage offline relations, as was feared. On the contrary, online communication seems to open up a host of new opportunities for enriching the social life of children and youth. It allows them to overcome physical, psychological, and social barriers as well as to strengthen existing ties and expand circles of potential new ones. Furthermore, evidence demonstrates that a significant overlap exists between the online and offline contacts, and young people use integrated, multiple forms of interaction to maintain their social lives.[28] That being so, we can say that the dichotomous division between online and offline social worlds has lost its relevance today as for the most part young people's relationships exist in both worlds and feed into each other.

Yet, let us also be minded of matters of social equity: Who benefits socially most from online potentiality? Is the "rich get richer" hypothesis also in operation here? One might argue that those who already have good social skills and strong networking can make much better use of the opportunities afforded to them by social networks online. However, a competing hypothesis suggests that there might also be a *social compensation* process in place, according to which the online world is particularly beneficial for marginalized and isolated children who are enabled to experiment with social relationships, remain anonymous, overcome inhibitions, and be selective as to which parts of themselves they wish to expose through communication conducted through new media.

Risk and Harm

The various online activities available provide children with a myriad of opportunities for growth, development, and empowerment. At the same time, as in the real world, each poses many risks to children's wellbeing which can lead to actual harm.[29] Accordingly, risks embody the potential for both opportunity as well as harm. In general, leaving home to enter the public world – be it concrete or virtual – can provide opportunities for personal growth, widening horizons, development of resilience and independence. Yet, one can also encounter danger, temptation, loss of way and purpose. Thus, children can engage in social encounters on the net with others who are different and removed from them, culturally and/or geographically. Doing so enables them to explore humanity in new ways, to learn to bridge differences, overcome stereotypes, and contribute to developing capacities for tolerance and collaboration. It can also put them in touch with others who share their interests and hobbies, sexual orientation, cultural background, physical and/or mental disability – and allow them to feel a sense of community and belonging. However, at the same time, social encounters on the net can also expose children to people with ill intentions, impostors, and even criminals. This can create a situation in which risks can become actually harmful to children – harmful physically, psychologically, socially, financially, or a combination of these.

Given that risk does not necessarily imply harm, one basic question studied is: How often do children actually encounter threats to their wellbeing via internet use? One set of evidence was produced by the large European project cited above, as well as by other countries that have used the same survey instrument, such as Australia, Russia, and Brazil. Researchers found that about a third of the participants claimed they were exposed to undesired content (e.g., pornography, violence, hate speech), a fifth were harassed or bullied, and about one tenth had personal encounters with strangers met via the net.[30] A study in Israel found that around a third of pre-adolescents and adolescents provided personal information to strangers on the internet, including personal photos.[31]

Since the range of activities and degree of risk vary, as do definitions of threat, findings that shed light on when and how children encounter actual threats are dependent on the research method used to collect information from children, cultural context, period during which data was collected, and children's age. There are also a host of ethical issues involved in inquiring into behaviors. For example, the definition of privacy and the need to protect it are quite fluid and contested. Thus, it could well be that what adults take as an invasion of their privacy is quite acceptable to the younger generation that has been raised with digital media. It also seems that definitions change as children grow up and explore risk-taking as their way to check boundaries and develop their independent identity and perception of "self." Risk behaviors are strongly age related, and as children mature their web of social relationships expands, as does the centrality of peer groups in their lives. In parallel, as children become more skilled with use of online media, they expand their repertoire of activities and the amount of time they spend there. As we have said, many young people are attracted to online life as a means to explore boundaries and experiment with freedoms that are restricted in their concrete society, which are often fraught with risk in of themselves.[32] All these processes and experiences contribute to internet use moving into the center of their social life, and their identity formation.

Cyberbullying

Cyber (or online) bullying has attracted much public attention, following some highly publicized and troubling suicidal cases of bullied youth. Bullying by means of communication technologies, like other forms of bullying, is meant to hurt others, usually those perceived as weak and vulnerable, via persistent and premeditated hostile and aggressive behavior. Bullying can have devastating consequences for victims' physical and mental health. The aggressors, on the other hand, are often associated with other forms of anti-social behavior in their everyday life.[33]

Cyberbullying is facilitated by the unique characteristics of media technology. Online anonymity frees the aggressor of inhibitions, as well as possible social sanctions and retaliation. At the same time, abuse is spread well beyond other, more familiar, sites of bullying in the playground or school gym. Online, the victim has no place to escape as bullying reaches the child in the privacy of his bedroom, or via her mobile phone screen. Thus, the web creates a situation in which the victim is never safe or protected, and the bullying reaches the child everywhere, at all times, without the awareness and support of parents and close friends, and without the supervision and intervention of school authorities. Some young people who have been bullied for their "otherness" (e.g., sexual orientation, appearance) or their behavior (e.g., sending naked photos of themselves to a romantic partner, a phenomenon coined "sexting"[34]), have been driven through one or a combination of these elements to desperation and even suicide.

Despite extensive media coverage of these phenomena and tragic events, there is very little systematic evidence gathered to date about the scope of cyberbullying due, among other reasons, to the methodological difficulties of collecting evidence and measuring such behaviors. Different studies report a range from 6 percent to 72 percent of the children studied who claim to have been bullied at least once online or via text messaging. More commonly, reports range from 20–40 percent of children studied. According to some studies, frequency of being bullied seems to grow with age and development of digital skills, and reaches a peak around the ages of 12 to 14.[35] Interestingly, there are significant gaps between what children report about their involvement in bullying – both as victims as well as perpetuators – and their parents' lower estimates of these activities.[36]

Another interesting group of research projects studied the relationship between offline and online activities of children in order to explore whether young people engaged in bullying do so in both worlds. That is, to discover whether bullying online is just another setting and opportunity for bullies and whether it encourages and/or intensifies other forms of bullying. There are no clear results yet about this question. What we do now is that online settings allow bullying without any physical contact between the aggressor and the victim, do not require much planning, and minimize the risk of being caught while engaged in the activity. Indeed, several studies present evidence suggesting that cyberbullies spend twice as much time on the internet in general as other users and four times more on internet-related risk behaviors. Other initial evidence found that victims might, too, be heavier internet users and risk-takers.[37] Yet further studies found that children who are victims of bullying offline are also more likely to be the target of bullying online.[38]

The gender of bullies is also an important consideration. Given that physical aggression has been traditionally associated with males and social aggression with females, it is no surprise that cyberbullying, which relies on interpersonal communication strategies, caters to girls' strengths and preferences. Indeed, there is well-substantiated evidence that gender differences associated with bullying offline seem to be somewhat canceled out when it comes to online bullying, since girls are more active in that sphere than they are in face-to-face bullying.[39]

As a tentative summary we can say that at this point in time cyberbullying, like other risk activities online, requires a much better understanding of the personal, social, and contextual circumstances of both the aggressors as well as the victims, something that future research will no doubt need to contend with.[40]

Organized Production and Participation

Youth, around the world, are engaged in producing their own media. Juxtaposed with commercial or institutional productions, youth media production can be divided into individual and group activities. Individual production is advanced via a teen's social network, conducted, for example, by posting, web-designing, blogging, or gaming. In contrast, a more structured and organized approach is often initiated, mediated, and/or guided by adults in schools, organizations, social and political movements, or communities, with the goal of engaging youth in what is often referred to as "participatory culture."

Grouped under the title "youth-produced media," these diverse activities have been sorted into the following nine major categories, many of which are often inter-related:[41]

1. Social justice: Projects addressing issues of social justice and economic, political, and social inequalities.
2. Political action: Projects involved in formal political action and promoting specific agendas.
3. Arts: Projects promoting involvement in the arts and artistic expression on all levels, personal and social.
4. Communication: Projects encouraging interactions with peers and adults that focus on the communication process itself.
5. Workforce: Projects preparing participants for employment in the workforce of the media and information industries.
6. Academic support: Projects providing academic support, particularly to struggling students.
7. Overall development: Projects invested in overall development including health, wellbeing, and safety.
8. Recreation: Projects providing joyful and entertaining engagement.
9. Community development: Projects that facilitate social change in communities and encourage positive development.

Youth production projects involve all forms of media: a video on warzone graffiti; photos of a family history of immigration; digital graphic art; or sound recordings of birds. Examples of youth-produced media come from all over the world. Youth in Palestine and in Israel express the complexity of their life experiences; Christian youth groups in Brazil explore their interests and identities in integrating religious beliefs within the context of contemporary popular culture; projects by Singaporean youth promote high-tech skills in young people; in South Africa, a community radio station offering professional training for youth explores alternatives to mainstream post-apartheid content. At my own university, our summer video-camps facilitate girls' empowerment.[42] Many more examples abound.[43]

While the numerous benefits for the individual as well as for society of youth media engagement, as opposed to mere consumption, have been celebrated, notes of caution have also been raised. First and foremost is an awareness of the tendency – noted throughout the book – to assume technological determinism; that is, technology will set the creative spirit of youth free and empower them to become engaged and productive participants in their communities. The reality is that the technology – whether this means oral storytelling or a production that employs the most advanced digital software – is not inherently positive or negative; rather it is a tool in our hands to use creatively. Thus, it does not in and of itself liberate young people from passivity, disengagement, or a non-productive life.

There is still a great lack of research that systematically evaluates the short- and long-term benefits of global initiatives to engage youth in media production. Many involved in such research often warn of the danger that youth devoid of proper guidance and education will imitate existing commercial formulas, re-create racial and gender stereotypes, and reinforce violence, materialism, and intolerance. Simply providing children and youth with a camera or computer software is not going to change such tendencies. It requires in-depth educational processes to promote awareness, capabilities to problematize reality, apply moral judgment, and turn knowledge into action.[44] Additionally, criticism of some youth-produced media pro- jects also points to the fact that adults have often taken over these projects, so that they are framed from an adult perspective, with adults' interests in mind; and that the activities and products are advanced by adults to serve their needs, rather than facilitating independent expression of young voices. Child-focused research sug- gests the importance of participatory work that is determined by the youth partici- pants themselves as presented by an example coming out of South Africa, employing photovoice, video and digital storytelling, blogging, and children's radio.[45]

The increasing accessibility of production tools via digital technologies as well as, interestingly, debates over the disengagement of young people from the public sphere, have contributed to a growing interest in this area. Nevertheless, the creation of organized youth-produced media is still marginal to most educational endeavors, suffering as it does from a lack of resources and recognition.

Civic engagement and activism

When it comes to production of media and participation through media, one specific area of interest has been receiving more attention than others: the potential of the especially rich new media environment and technological innovations to lead to different outcomes in terms of engagement. This interest, or perhaps hope, seems to be driven partly by the anticipation of youth resistance to *adultism*[46] (i.e., adults' systematic discrimination of young people) and their sense of exclusion from the public sphere (as discussed in Chapter 2). However, the research evidence gathered to date suggests that, among all the activities of children and youth online, civic engagement and activism accounts for very little. What does seem to be taking place includes: seeking out relevant civic information; producing content that deals with issues pertaining to politics and the public sphere; participating in dialogues on such topics; and initiating and organizing online activities that will take place offline.

One multicultural project aimed at studying the potential contribution of the internet to promoting young people's civic engagement and participation examined a host of online sites, as well as the way they are put into use, by youth in seven diverse European countries (Hungary, the Netherlands, Slovenia, Spain, Sweden, Turkey, and the UK).[47] The results reinforced the claim that most young people are disconnected, bored, and even feel alienated from the public sphere. It also found that online resources are not necessarily the most effective means of engaging young people or disseminating information to them. Such resources tend to be underused as they are often dated (for lack of resources), and often do not take advantage of the various technologies available today (e.g., they do not allow for interactivity). Furthermore, this study found that despite the popular claim that new media platforms offer a "safe haven" for the expression of opinions, this is not always the case, as youth reported being harassed for their sexual orientation, immigrant status, or racial identity. Many sites fail to contextualize themselves within a contemporary issue of concern, and to interlink with offline activities, which, as we have seen, is a dominant requirement of youth culture today. Indeed, the absence of opportunities for peer-to-peer conversations, as well as interaction with adults in authoritative positions, are all central to the lack of interest and involvement with these resources.

However, this project did demonstrate that the internet is particularly useful for those young people who are already interested in public issues and wish to be more engaged. Thus, based on this study, new technologies are seen as an additional avenue through which youth can engage in social change; that is, they are not in and of themselves sufficient to bring about a major change in youth-society relations.

This conclusion seems to cut across many of the issues that we have discussed throughout the book: Children and youth actively seek, in all forms of media, the content and activities that contribute to their interests, as well as their personal tastes and life circumstances. Therefore, we cannot analyze youth civic engagement and use of media independently of each other. The evidence documented in the research literature suggests that those young people who are already interested in civics and politics offline will seek out those interests online as well, but also that online use may lead to more offline activities.[48]

With regard to online activities such as visiting as well as creating one's own website, it is possible to point to three general clusters of youth:[49] Some youth are *interactors*: they are active on the web in a variety of ways, but do not necessarily demonstrate an interest in the civic sphere; *civic-minded* youth are more goal oriented in their use of the internet to pursue civic interests; *disengaged* youth are the least active online in terms of visiting or creating sites. Clearly, children and youth of the three types require different approaches to facilitate or to produce active engagement. Again, we should remember that online lives are tightly related to offline lives and cannot be studied in isolation.

Many cite the great potential of digital media literacy education in advancing civic and political engagement, as discussed in Chapter 7. Such an approach challenges our conceptions of literacy itself as it perceives it to be political in nature. A study in California,[50] for example, demonstrated that digital media literacy educational activities were related to greater levels of political participation online, as well as greater exposure for youth to diverse viewpoints on a variety of topics.

It is of particular interest to explore the role of digital media in the civic engagement of youth in the light of disparate reports from scholars in countries experiencing significant social and political transformations. A case study in Egypt, for example, demonstrated a high level of integration of online–offline relationships. The researchers argued that being active on Facebook meant that the Egyptian children felt they were part of a regional community and this contributed to increasing their exposure to the public sphere and civic engagement.[51] In Belarus, a digital underground magazine served as a forum for youth to debate, critique, and become involved in various forms of activism, thus challenging notions of freedom of expression in a non-democratic political environment.[52] In the borderland of Argentina, a group of young disadvantaged people took part in a guided online workshop that led to their creating video productions about their lives, identities, and the active role they were playing in their communities.[53]

Despite the advent of digital media, reports state that traditional media have the potential to play a central role in activism and social change, particularly through the use of community media, in the form of radio, newspapers, and video. For example, as pointed out in Chapter 5, many initiatives involving youth and media in Africa deal specifically with the HIV-AIDS epidemic and related health matters,[54] such as when involvement in anti-AIDS campaigns served as a stimuli for social change for a youth club in Malawi.[55] In a small town in Turkey, bordering on Iran, young people's use of radio and mobile phones contributed to a process of social change by facilitating self-expression and networking, and also challenged the traditional generational and gendered power structure.[56] Many other examples of media activism of children and youth from countries around the world exist, often integrated within a framework of empowerment via media education.[57]

Several scholars have claimed, recently, that understanding the role of young people in civic engagement requires expanding the definition of the political world beyond traditional acts of voting, membership of a political party, or signing a petition to a much broader notion of engagement in the public sphere.[58] They argue that the incorporation of digital technologies is changing the forms and practices of citizenship in the context of globalization, as well as the nature and character of the public sphere. For example, Web 2.0 technologies should stimulate us to re-conceptualize the very notion of civic engagement in ways that reflect how participation is actually incorporated in the everyday life of young people, in which there is a blurring of former boundaries separating civic life and leisure. Participating in various online communities, out of interest or as a form of leisure, can foster responsibility, commitment to a collective, voluntarism, and other qualities that are central to any social and political form of life.

Some would go as far as to argue, more radically, that children's participation in social networking is of itself a form of democratic participation by a group usually excluded from the public sphere.[59] Young people's casual writing online expresses their anxieties, their alienation from civic life and democratic processes, and their hopes for the future. These activities can be interpreted as an appeal to the adult world for attention, empathy, and understanding, as well as for guidance and mentoring. Efforts to increase participation from this perspective require, among others, consideration of the mismatch between adult and youth expectations and an understanding of their place in society.[60]

More generally, and viewed through concrete reality, we need to keep in mind that while youth may be encouraged to have a voice, it is unclear whether adults are actually listening when they speak. Furthermore, it seems that many producers of online opportunities for youth tend to approach them through a "top-down" model of delivering information, rather than seeking to open up avenues that allow for dialogue; and are not transparent about their own involvement in the process.

Therefore we need to ask: Assuming there is a new public sphere, what kind of presence do young people today have in it and are they producing new forms of citizenship? A review of the research literature reporting on projects in Latin America, India, Europe, and the US identified four perspectives through which these processes are studied: First, how youth use media to communicate about and to argue for their identity and rights; second, how youth express their own views about the social world, report coping mechanisms, criticize it, and search for social change; third, how youth, as subjects, are represented in various media contents as well as in discussions of policy and regulations of these contents; and fourth, how youth are involved in processes of change through communication for development.[61]

Concluding Remarks

We close this chapter with two notes of caution. First, while the research and scholarship in this area is relatively young, most of it is based on the later teen years and even young adults in their 20s. Therefore, we should be wary of applying the findings about questions of sociality and civic engagement to children and the younger teen age group. Second, we tend to forget that not all participation and collective engagement is constructive and positive. There are, unfortunately, many online communities that support and foster racism, violence, and exclusivity. This reminds us, once again, that technologies are only tools in our hands without a life of their own. It is up to us to use them responsibility for the better good. It remains true that the dynamic relationships between risks, opportunities, and harm in the virtual world are yet to be fully explored.

Notes

1. Lemish, Ribak, & Alony, 2009.
2. Livingstone, 2009.
3. Ito *et al.*, 2009.
4. Livingstone, Haddon, Görzig, & Ólafsson, 2011.

5. Livingstone, 2013.
6. Ling & Bertel, 2013.
7. Zhao, Qiu, & Xie, 2012.
8. Axelsson & Regan, 2006; Chan & Vorderer, 2006.
9. Aarsand, 2013.
10. Peppler, 2013.
11. Valkenburg & Peter, 2009.
12. Mesch & Talmud, 2010.
13. Livingstone, Haddon, Görzig, & Ólafsson, 2011.
14. Mesch, 2013.
15. McLuhan, 1964.
16. Elias & Lemish, 2009.
17. Desjarlais & Willoughby, 2010.
18. Valkenburg & Peter, 2007, 2009.
19. Mesch, 2013.
20. boyd, 2008.
21. Livingstone, 2008.
22. Elias & Lemish, 2011.
23. Elias & Lemish, 2009.
24. Mesch & Talmud, 2007.
25. Park, forthcoming.
26. Burrell, 2012.
27. Lim, Basnyat, Vadrevu, & Chan, 2013.
28. Mesch, 2013.
29. Livingstone, 2013.
30. Livingstone, 2009.
31. Lemish, Ribak, & Alony, 2009.
32. Livingstone, 2009.
33. Görzig & Ólafsson, 2013.
34. Durham, 2013.
35. Tokunaga, 2010.
36. Livingstone & Bober, 2006; Lemish, Ribak, & Alony, 2009.
37. Görzig & Ólafsson, 2013.
38. Tokunaga, 2010.
39. Görzig & Ólafsson, 2013.
40. Livingstone, 2009.
41. Fisherkeller, 2013.
42. "Girls Making Movies" camp in the College of Mass Communication and Media Arts at Southern Illinois University, Carbondale.
43. Fisherkeller, 2011; Tufte & Enghel, 2009.
44. P. Lemish, 2011.
45. Stuart & Mitchell, 2013.
46. Goldman, Booker, & McDermott, 2008.
47. Banaji & Buckingham, 2013.
48. Kahne, Lee, & Feezell, 2012.
49. Livingstone, 2009.
50. Kahne, Lee, & Feezell, 2012.

51. El Baghdady, 2008.
52. Vidanava, 2011.
53. Zanotti, 2009.
54. Pecora, Osei-Hwere, & Carlsson, 2008.
55. Jensen & Hansen, 2011.
56. Algan, 2011.
57. Carlsson, Tayie, Jacquinot-Delaunay, & Tornero, 2008.
58. Banaji & Buckingham, 2013; Papaioannou, 2013.
59. Agger, 2013.
60. Livingstone, 2009.
61. Tufte & Enghel, 2009.

References

Aarsand, P. (2013). Children's digital gaming cultures. In D. Lemish (Ed.), *The Routledge international handbook of children, adolescents, and media* (pp. 120–126). New York: Routledge.

Agger, B. (2013). *Texting toward utopia: Kids, writing, and resistance.* Boulder & London: Paradigm Publishers.

Algan, E. (2011). Being read by a DJ: Youth interaction via radio and cell phones in Southeast Turkey. In C. von Feilitzen, U. Carlsson, & C. Bucht (Eds.), *New questions, new insights, new approaches: Contributions to the research forum at the World Summit on Media for Children and Youth 2010* (pp. 251–260). Göteborg University, Sweden: The International Clearinghouse on Children, Youth and Media.

Axelsson, A-S. & Regan, T. (2006). Playing online. In P. Vorderer, & J. Bryant (Eds.), *Playing video games: Motives, responses, and consequences* (pp. 291–306). Mahwah, NJ: Lawrence Erlbaum.

Banaji, S. & Buckingham, D. (2013). *The civic web: Young people, the internet, and civic participation.* Cambridge, MA: MIT Press.

boyd, d. (2008). Why youth love social network sites: The role of networked publics in teenage social life. In D. Buckingham (Ed.), *Youth, identity, and digital media* (pp. 119–142). Cambridge, MA: MIT Press.

Burrell, J. (2012). *Invisible users: Youth in internet cafes of urban Ghana*, Ch. 2: Youth and the indeterminate space of the internet café (pp. 29–53). Cambridge, MA: MIT Press.

Carlsson, U., Tayie, S., Jacquinot-Delaunay, F., & Tornero, J.N.P. (2008). *Empowerment through media education: An intercultural dialogue.* Göteborg University, Sweden: The International Clearinghouse on Children, Youth and Media.

Chan, E. & Vorderer, P. (2006). Massively multiplayer online games. In P. Vorderer & J. Bryant (Eds.), *Playing video games: Motives, responses, and consequences* (pp. 77–88). Mahwah, NJ: Lawrence Erlbaum.

Desjarlais, M., & Willoughby, T. (2010). A longitudinal study of the relation between adolescent boys' and girls' computer use with friends and friendship quality: Support for the social compensation or the rich-get-richer hypothesis? *Computers in Human Behavior, 26*(5), 896–905.

Durham, M.G. (2013). Children's technologized bodies: Mapping mixed reality. In D. Lemish (Ed.), *The Routledge international handbook of children, adolescents, and media* (pp. 156–163). New York: Routledge.

El Baghdady, L. (2008). Playing at cyber space: Perspectives of Egyptian children's digital socialization. In N. Pecora, E. Osei-Hwere, & U. Carlsson (Eds.), *African media, African children* (pp. 165–173). Göteborg University, Sweden: The International Clearinghouse on Children, Youth and Media.

Elias, N. & Lemish, D. (2009). Spinning the web of identity: Internet's roles in immigrant adolescents' search of identity. *New Media & Society, 11*(4), 1–19.

Elias, N. & Lemish, D. (2011). Between three worlds: Host, homeland, and global media in the lives of Russian immigrant families in Israel and Germany. *Journal of Family Issues, 32*(9), 1245–1274.

Fisherkeller, J. (Ed.). (2011). *International perspectives on youth media: Cultures of production and education*. New York: Peter Lang.

Fisherkeller, J. (2013). Young people producing media: Spontaneous and project-sponsored media creation around the world. In D. Lemish (Ed.), *The Routledge international handbook of children, adolescents, and media* (pp. 344–350). New York: Routledge.

Girls Make Movies. (2012). A residential filmmaking experience. College of mass Communication and Media Arts at Southern Illinois University, Carbondale.

Goldman, S., Booker, A., & McDermott, M. (2008). Mixing the digital, social, and cultural: Learning, identity and agency in youth participation. In D. Buckingham (Ed.), *Youth, identity, and digital media* (pp. 185–206). Cambridge, MA: MIT Press.

Görzig, A. & Ólafsson, K. (2013). What makes a bully a cyberbully? Unraveling the characteristics of cyberbullies across twenty-five European countries. *Journal of Children and Media, 7*(1), 9–27.

Ito, M., Baumer, S., Bittani, M., boyd, d., Cody, R. *et al.* (2009). *Hanging out, messing around, and geeking out: Kids living and learning with new media*. Cambridge, MA: MIT Press.

Jensen, L.G. & Hansen, M.G. (2011). Strengthening civil society: A communication for social change agenda? In C. von Feilitzen, U. Carlsson, & C. Bucht (Eds.), *New questions, new insights, new approaches: Contributions to the research forum at the World Summit on Media for Children and Youth 2010* (pp. 241–250). Göteborg University, Sweden: The International Clearinghouse on Children, Youth and Media.

Kahne, J., Lee, N-J., & Feezell, J.T. (2012). Digital media literacy education and online civic and political participation. *International Journal of Communication, 6*, 1–24.

Lemish, D., Ribak, R., & Alony, R. (2009). Israeli children online: From moral panic to responsible parenthood. *Megamot, 46*(1–2), 137–163. (in Hebrew).

Lemish, P. (2011). Facilitating the social reality challenge with youth filmmakers. In J. Fisherkeller (Ed.), *International perspectives on youth media: Cultures of production and education* (pp. 283–300). New York: Peter Lang.

Lim, S.S., Basnyat, I., Vadrevu, S., & Chan, Y.H. (2013). Critical literacy, self-protection and delinquency: The challenges of participatory media for youths at-risk. *Leaning, Media and Technology, 38*(2), 145–160.

Ling, R. & Bertel, T. (2013). Mobile communication culture among children and adolescents. In D. Lemish (Ed.), *The Routledge international handbook of children, adolescents, and media* (pp. 127–133). New York: Routledge.

Livingstone, S. (2008). Taking risky opportunities in youthful content creating: Teenagers' use of social networking sites for intimacy, privacy and self-expression. *New Media & Society, 10*(3), 393–411.

Livingstone, S. (2009). *Children and the internet*. Cambridge, UK: Polity.

Livingstone, S. (2013). Children's internet culture: Power, change and vulnerability in twenty-first century childhood. In D. Lemish (Ed.), *The Routledge international handbook of children, adolescents, and media* (pp. 111–119). New York: Routledge.

Livingstone, S. & Bober, M. (2006). Regulating the internet at home: Contrasting the perspectives of children and parents. In D. Buckingham & R. Willett (Eds.), *Digital generations* (pp. 93–113). Mahwah, NJ: Lawrence Erlbaum Associates.

Livingstone, S., Haddon, L., Görzig, A., & Ólafsson, K. (2011). *EU Kids Online II: Final report.* LSE, London: EU Kids Online. www.eukidsonline.net. Retrieved July 25, 2014.

McLuhan, M. (1964). *Understanding media: The extensions of man.* New York: Singet Books.

Mesch, G.S. (2013). Internet media and peer sociability. In D. Lemish (Ed.), *The Routledge international handbook of children, adolescents, and media* (pp. 287–294). New York: Routledge.

Mesch, G.S. & Talmud, I. (2007). Privacy and networking: Ethnic differences in the use of cell phones and IM in Israel. In James Katz (Ed.), *Mobile communication and social change in a global context* (pp. 313–335). Boston: MIT Press.

Mesch, G.S. & Talmud, I. (2010). *Wired youth: The social world of adolescence in the information age.* London & New York: Routledge.

Papaioannou, T. (2013). Media and civic engagement: The role of Web 2.0 technologies in fostering youth participation. In D. Lemish (Ed.), *The Routledge international handbook of children, adolescents, and media* (pp. 351–358). New York: Routledge.

Park, J. (forthcoming). (Re)Constructing ethnic identities: New media as an important platform among Korean American adolescents in the United States. PhD dissertation. Carbondale, IL: Southern Illinois University.

Pecora, N. (2013). Media policies for children: Issues and histories in the U.S. In D. Lemish (Ed.), *The Routledge international handbook of children, adolescents, and media* (pp. 371–377). New York: Routledge.

Pecora, N. Osei-Hwere, E., & Carlsson, U. (Eds.). (2008). *African media, African children.* Göteborg University, Sweden: The International Clearinghouse on Children, Youth and Media.

Peppler, K. (2013). Social media and creativity. In D. Lemish (Ed.), *The Routledge international handbook of children, adolescents, and media* (pp. 193–200). New York: Routledge.

Stuart, J. & Mitchell, C. (2013). Media, participation, and social change: Working within a 'youth as knowledge producers' framework. In D. Lemish (Ed.), *The Routledge international handbook of children, adolescents, and media* (pp. 359–365). New York: Routledge.

Tokunaga, R.S. (2010). Following you home from school: A critical review and synthesis of research on cyberbullying victimization. *Computers in Human Behavior, 26*(3), 277–287.

Tufte, T. & Enghel, F. (2009). *Youth engaging with the world: Media, communication and social change.* University of Göteborg, Sweden: Nordicom, The International Clearinghouse on Children, Youth and Media.

Valkenburg, P.M. & Peter, J. (2007). Preadolescents' and adolescents' online communication and their closeness to friends. *Developmental Psychology, 43*(2), 267–277.

Valkenburg, P.M. & Peter, J. (2009). Social consequences of the internet for adolescents: A decade of research. *Current Directions in Psychological Science, 18*, 1–5.

Vidanava, I. (2011). On disc and online: Expanding digital activism in Belarus. In C. von Feilitzen, U. Carlsson, & C. Bucht (Eds.), *New questions, new insights, new approaches: Contributions to the research forum at the World Summit on Media for Children and Youth*

2010 (pp. 227–240). Göteborg University, Sweden: The International Clearinghouse on Children, Youth and Media.

Zanotti, A. (2009). Views in progress, views in process. A participatory video experience with young people in a space of borderlands. In T. Tufte & F. Enghel (Eds.), *Youth engaging with the world: Media, communication and social change* (pp. 283–300). Göteborg University, Sweden: The International Clearinghouse on Children, Youth and Media.

Zhao, Y., Qiu, W., & Xie, N. (2012). Social networking, social gaming, texting. In D.G. Singer & J.L. Singer (Eds.), *Handbook of children and the media* (pp. 97–112). Los Angeles: Sage.

7

Media Literacy Education

The term *media education* has been alternatively referred to as *media literacy*, *critical viewing skills*, and *media competencies*. These terms have been used interchangeably and, generally, with little conceptual distinction when referring to the capacities needed to engage in analyses of media texts, audiences, and viewing contexts and cultures. The terms have also been used in discussion of issues of public policy, in domains of cultural criticism, as a set of pedagogical tools for teachers, in production skills, as educational guidelines for parents, as hypotheses in the spirit of technological determinism, or as topics for research on cognitive processing of information. More recently, we find scholars using the term *media literacy education*; that is, education for media literacy.

Thus, media literacy, in general terms, is commonly understood to refer to the ability to access, analyze, evaluate, and communicate messages in a variety of ways. It is perceived to be a form of literacy necessary for participation in civic and cultural life that requires an informed, critical, and creative citizenry. The goals of educational programs around the world that advance media literacy education, as stated in the extensive extant literature, are diverse and not necessarily complementary. For some advocates and program developers, media literacy is a way to develop creativity in children by providing them with another domain within which they can be creative and have opportunities for self-expression. Creativity, in this sense, is defined not in comparison to some external formal criteria defined by experts, but in terms of the ability to create something that is novel for the child, as is often the case on social networking sites.[1]

Other analysts stress media literacy education's potential to empower children by allowing them to present their own voices, pursue social and political goals, and advance particularly those who are socially disadvantaged and marginalized.

Children and Media: A Global Perspective, First Edition. Dafna Lemish.
© 2015 John Wiley & Sons, Inc. Published 2015 by John Wiley & Sons, Inc.
Companion Website: www.wiley.com/go/lemish/childrenandmedia

Yet others believe that the central feature of media literacy education is that it enables media consumers to have a critical perspective, to challenge mainstream media and the existing social order, to advance democratization and civic participation, and to return some power to popular citizenry. Media literacy education has also been employed as vocational training for future employment in the growing media-saturated workplace. Sometimes media literacy education has been employed to tackle specific social ills – such as bullying, obesity, or racism. Finally, for some educators, media literacy is an opportunity to challenge traditional educational institutions by experimenting with alternative pedagogies.

This variety of educational goals has led to the development of a host of curricula that employ different pedagogies, different assessment practices of children's achievements, and different approaches to the institutionalization of media literacy programs in formal and non-formal settings. Though there are many differences, writers agree that media literacy skills incorporate at least an understanding of the following five elements:

- Media messages are constructed and not merely a reflection of reality.
- Messages are created in specific contexts that represent interests that are economic, social, political, historical, cultural, and esthetic in nature.
- The process of interpreting media messages is a product of an interaction between the interpreter, the text, and the cultural context.
- Different media use various languages that are expressed in a variety of symbol systems, forms, and genres.
- Different representations in the media play a part in the way we understand our social reality.

Notice that all five characteristics refer to central issues in the study of media, as discussed in the previous chapters. Developing the ability to explain and apply these understandings in the process of interpretation, analysis, critique, and creation of media messages is a lifelong process.

Let us consider, by way of illustration, one of the most popular models of media literacy that has served as a basis for many curricula around the world to date. Developed by the British Film Institute (BFI) in London in the 1980s, this curriculum advances central concepts, rather than educational goals or skills. The BFI model defined the following of areas of knowledge and understanding in media education:[2]

Media Agencies: Who is communicating, and why?
Who produces a text; roles in the production process; media institutions; economics and ideology; intentions and results.
Media Categories: What type of text is this?
Different media (e.g., television, radio, cinema, internet); forms (e.g., documentary, advertising); genres (e.g., science fiction, soap opera); other ways for categorizing texts; how categorization relates to understanding.

Media Technologies: How is it produced?
  What kinds of technologies are available to whom; how to use them; the differences they make to the production processes as well as the final product.
Media Languages: How do we know what it means?
  How do the media produce meanings; codes and conventions; narrative structures.
Media Audiences: Who receives it, and what sense do they make of it?
  How audiences are identified, constructed, addressed, and reached; how audiences find, choose, consume, and respond to texts.
Media Representations: How does it present its subject?
  The relation between media texts and the actual places, people, events, ideas featured; stereotyping and its consequences.

The components of the model are not a "grocery list" required of each media literacy program, nor are they hierarchical or mutually exclusive. On the contrary, they are understood to be interdependent – each presents an alternative means of entry into the study of media, and at the same time requires that the other issues be addressed. Note that while these areas were formalized during the period that preceded the advent of digital media, they are nevertheless just as relevant today, with one very major exception – the absence of reference to the realm of participation and production, which is so central to the current screen culture. Nevertheless, each of these topics also has an additional value for applied production work.

Many consider the advantage of this model to be that it does not present facts to be memorized or point to a list of canonical texts to be studied. On the contrary, it allows media literacy to be adapted to different cultures and to changes in the experiences and interests of children. The model offers a theoretical framework that can be applied to a variety of media, old and new, in order to understand the inter-relationships between them, and to transfer knowledge and understanding between them. For example, it is expected that children will apply the knowledge acquired in their studies of the construction of stereotypes in a television situation comedy to the analysis of a literary work; or they might apply their skills for critical analysis of persuasive messages in television advertising to their engagement with pop-up commercials that appear on favorite internet sites, or to *advergames* that embed advertisements in a gaming environment.

Since the BFI developed this model, media literacy education has expanded to incorporate the many challenges created by digital media and participatory culture, and addressed the urgency to incorporate them into basic literacy requirements at the turn of the third millennium. Following the discussion in Chapter 3, it is clear that the goals of such education are comprehensive and complicated. One framework proposes the following life skills:[3]

- Make responsible choices and access information by locating and sharing materials and
- comprehending information and ideas;

- Analyze messages in a variety of forms by identifying the author, purpose, and point of view, and evaluating the quality and credibility of the content;
- Create content in a variety of forms, making use of language, images, sound, and new digital tools and technologies;
- Reflect on one's own conduct and communication behavior by applying social responsibility and ethical principles;
- Take social action by working individually and collaboratively to share knowledge and solve problems in the family, workplace, and community, and by participating as a member of a community.

Note that incorporating digital media into discussions of literacy shifted the emphasis from cognitive skills to more action-oriented participation, as well as the collaborative and social dimensions not addressed in the BFI model.

The Central Debates in Media Literacy Education

A historical review of the early days of media literacy education allows us to understand the changes in this field and the principles underlying present efforts. In the UK, the cradle of media literacy in the school system, media literacy was strongly influenced by the development of cultural studies in the 1950s and 1960s. Cultural studies redefined the approach to culture so that it was perceived not only as a canon of preferred works of art, but as a way of life that includes a host of forms of expressions, including those that are part of everyday life, such as television. Applied to media literacy education, the cultural studies approach perceived media to be part of a more general trend of democratization in which children's leisure was treated to be a relevant contributing factor to their education and a legitimate topic for study in school. At the same time, the early work of media literacy education in the UK did develop the still dominant (in other places in the world) *protective* approaches whereby teachers are expected to develop in pupils skills that immunize them against the negative effects of television, such as: protecting the elitist culture with its valued qualities (since television was seen as populist, low culture); protecting moral values regarding such phenomena as violence, sex, consumerism; and developing political protection from false beliefs and discriminatory ideologies of enslavement expressed in the media with regard to ethnicity, class, and gender issues.

In all of these realms, media literacy was expected to struggle with vast and complicated social issues. The media were perceived to be the cause of both society's and children's troubles, with education for media literacy as the solution. Teachers were expected to be able to place themselves outside of these processes of media influence and so be able to provide pupils with skills for critical viewing that empowered them, too.[4]

Since media literacy education first emerged in the 1980s, the demand for its incorporation in school systems in many countries has been fed by studies on children and media, television in particular, as discussed throughout this book. An alternative to the *immunization* approach, advanced particularly with the advent of new media, suggests that media literacy programs build on an understanding of children's preferences, knowledge, and experiences with media as a pre-requisite to discussing them critically. Children's needs, interpretations, pleasures, self-expression, empowerment, and social contexts are at the center of this educational process.

Clearly, these two approaches – the protectionist versus the empowerment – are based upon different assumptions about pupils, pursue different goals, employ different pedagogies, and are grounded in different scholarly literatures. Recently, some scholars have argued against such a dichotomy and encouraged a view that encompasses the multiplicity of approaches to media literacy education[5] and focuses on the development of critical thinking in approaching media.[6]

Media literacy education today is, for the most part, no longer defined in the narrow sense of opposition to children's media consumption pleasures, neither is it a process of education that distinguishes between good and bad uses, involves a demystification of the medium, or seeks to immunize against its negative effects. The studies presented in previous chapters assumed that children are active, conscious media consumers, rather than passive and naive. This is also the case for media literacy education today. Similarly, children are no longer viewed as a homogenous group but, like any other social category, are distinguished by their personality characteristics, gender, age group, race, life experience, and social and cultural background. Nor are teachers perceived to be the omniscient holders of the magic key to the one and only "true" interpretation of media messages. Rather, teachers and pupils are assumed to be involved in a complicated process of negotiation that takes place, continuously, between audiences and texts, a process characterized by the possibility that multiple readings and interpretations exist for each and every text and that actively producing media messages can serve a variety of purposes.

Media Literacy Education Around the World

The differentiated development of media literacy throughout the world is due to the specific academic environment of media studies in each country, as well as to national goals, educational systems, and media environments. A 2001 survey of 38 countries worldwide conducted on behalf of UNESCO revealed uneven diffusion of media education.[7] Countries appear to be going through different phases of development, from initiation of activities, some quite innovative, to well-established implementation of curricula. In addition, while a few countries are developing a budding interest in media literacy education, some countries who led initial efforts are showing signs of weariness.

When examining the development in the USA, for example, we find that while it is the largest producer and exporter of entertainment, it lags far behind many other countries in developing media literacy programs in its school systems. This is surprising given the vibrant civil society in the USA, including the many informal education and non-profit organizations engaged in media activism. How can we explain these limited educational efforts and what can we learn from them about the consequences of political, economic, and cultural variables on trends in the development of media literacy? Several of the complementary explanations offered[8] include: the large size of the country; its decentralized educational system; the absence of concern for *Americanization*, which has driven many other initiatives worldwide; and capitalist forces that discourage educational initiatives in order to maintain economic interests. Thus, the US case illustrates how multiple variables, including economic interests and political ideologies, geography, demography, and culture, are interlinked in influencing educational policy.

The development of media literacy education in South Africa presents a very different history. Media literacy education was assigned a central role in the advancement of a political agenda that sought to promote significant social changes in South Africa in the late 1980s and during the 1990s with regard to issues related to the abolishment of the apartheid regime, the process of reconciliation between the races, and human rights. The experience of South Africa is of value not only in its own right, but also as an instructive role model for other societies undergoing political revolutions and national reformation.[9] Media literacy education was conceived to be a means to incorporate children's real-life experiences within the formal knowledge acquired in schools, allowing them to develop as citizens critical of their environment. In South Africa media activists encouraged teachers to adopt the various educational activities proposed, to attend teacher training workshops, and to use learning materials as subversive strategies. Often, these activists themselves became teachers of media literacy, thus blurring the boundaries between critical action and critical teaching. The development of *civic courage* – the courage to express an opinion, to resist, to offer alternatives, to act – was defined as a central goal for media literacy. Through this process, the curricula involved media literacy, and encouraged discussion of social and moral issues, while promoting freedom of speech and critical thinking skills. Empowering children became a key concept in the goals of media literacy within this perspective. The South African case is an example of how media literacy has the potential to develop a citizenry critical of a political regime and which encourages and, indeed, guides children to become active citizens in their changing world.

A third example comes from Israel, where media literacy education gained the status of a "much debated consensus" in the 1990s.[10] On the one hand, there seemed to be agreement about the importance of media literacy in children's education, yet, on the other, there was deep disagreement about almost every aspect of it. Understanding this peculiar situation requires familiarity with the nature of Israeli society as one deeply divided over many issues, including such difficult matters as the nature of Israel as a Jewish and democratic state as well as the future of the occupation of the Palestinian people and their land. Four particular issues influenced the development of media literacy in Israel and these can be illuminating to other societies as well:

Media literacy as an issue of ethnic identity: The concern over the potential Americanization of Israeli society, with its capitalist values of commercialization, privatization, and individualization, has been central to the history of the introduction and development of television in Israel. The demand for media literacy was an ancillary argument that emerged in the process of introducing television as a means of resisting Americanization and the primal threat it represents to the development of an authentic Israeli society and culture.

Media literacy as a political issue: The media in Israel have to function in a society deeply divided over central issues, and they are attacked by opponents on all sides of the political map. Each side blames the media for leaning toward the other side, and each side calls for media literacy to demystify the news media for young people and to educate them in developing a critical understanding of the sociology of news production as well the content, structural, and political constraints of the major sources of information.

Media literacy as an ethical issue: On occasion, various coalitions of interests have formed around ethical issues concerning media content; such as, representations of minorities and women, pornography and sexual promiscuity, violence, glorification of drug and alcohol abuse, and other locally defined social ills. Educators, non-governmental activists concerned with human rights, child welfare, social justice, and religious leaders – while differing in ideological motivation – share the belief that the media function as socializing agents and that a literate audience can and should resist the value systems and behaviors that undermine proponents' ideological dispositions.

Media literacy as a current affairs issue: Educators feel that there is a desperate need for curricula, learning materials, and pedagogical tools that will enable classroom teachers to deal in an academic, non-political way with the often highly charged events that are affecting their pupils' everyday life. Many teachers believe that focusing attention and analysis on media functioning and roles may be a mechanism to avoid the need to take sides and an easy solution to the difficulty of dealing with highly volatile topics in the classroom.

In summary, media literacy policies in Israel developed out of pressure from the public, the educational establishment, academia, and politicians. Within this broad consensus, alliances developed among people whose political and ideological views differed on almost every other issue.

Similar to the Israeli case, many other countries are concerned with the tension between the more global issues of media literacy advocates and their own unique local needs. Thus, from a global perspective, it seems that media literacy education is being advanced through a vision that aims to develop civic engagement. This vision is driven, in part, by a desire to resist Americanization of local culture. For example, while media literacy in India and Australia seeks to engage pupils in examination of local issues related to class, gender, and ethnic differences, in South Korea it is perceived to be a facilitator of technological education and social mobility. In Japan, it is related to the discourse of the rights of children as individuals, while in Spain, development of democratic citizenship is emphasized. In Sweden, the concern is for children's opportunities for self-expression, while in South Africa, in addition to media literacy being advanced to develop critical citizenship, it has been recruited in the struggle for HIV-AIDS education. Countries such as Italy, Denmark, India, Scotland, and South Africa emphasize media literacy's potential contribution to civic education, originally formulated in the British Film Institute-inspired tradition in the field. There they relate media literacy efforts to the burning ideological-political issues of their respective societies. Thus, in general, we can say that media literacy education is involved in developing in young people an awareness of issues such as: Whose voice is being heard and whose is not, and why? More specifically, which classes and ethnic groups in society are excluded from the public sphere? And, how can young people have a voice in the media themselves? We can say in summary that recent discussions of media education around the world focus heavily on the concept of *empowerment*, as media-literate young people are perceived as key to the democratization and development of society.[11] In this sense, media literacy can be perceived as a social movement, in addition to being an interdisciplinary academic field.[12]

Practical Aspects of Media Literacy Education

How do these theoretical and ideological issues translate into the practicality of work in formal educational institutions, in terms of curriculum, teaching, and assessment?

The curriculum

This area deals with such basic educational issues and questions as: What are the goals of the media literacy curriculum? How do we incorporate media literacy into the school program? What knowledge, skills, attitudes, and values should be taught? Responses differ depending on the approach taken to media literacy, as well as the stance adopted with regard to more general educational tensions between the desire to educate children to be literate citizens in today's complex societies and the desire to equip them with practical production skills. Rather than see these two approaches as extremes, many societies develop educational policies in a complementary fashion, particularly in the light of the recent proliferation of digital media and the participatory culture referred to previously. For example, children and youth's rich experience of producing media messages can be used to assist them in understanding communication processes and to sharpen their critical skills in examining the relationships between media and reality. Here, it is important to note that involvement in production does not automatically elicit an analytical or critical perspective, as children may be tempted to uncritically imitate the genres and contents familiar to them or to post personal messages and *selfies* on social networks (see also Chapter 6) rather than to challenge them or use them critically for civic engagement.

A second issue relates to the placement of media literacy education within the general school curriculum. Here, educational systems have adopted one of four approaches: (1) media literacy education as an independent discipline; (2) media literacy education as a component of another discipline (e.g., civic education, art); (3) media literacy education integrated across the entire spectrum of the school curriculum (i.e., each discipline integrates aspects of media literacy education deemed relevant); and (4) media literacy education as part of an integrative inter-disciplinary curriculum (e.g., contemporary society, liberal arts education).

Teaching

Teaching media literacy involves questions that relate to the traditional roles played by teachers in the educational process. In general, media literacy poses considerable challenges and opportunities for teachers: integration of many subjects; open-ended teaching that encourages tolerance, interpretation, and creativity over the transmission of knowledge; and a need to relate media literacy studies to children's life experiences. Indeed, some developers of media literacy education claim that it requires an innovative teaching style, one that is more democratic and egalitarian, since the teacher does not own knowledge and is a partner in the dialogic process. According to this view, the mere engagement with media can assist in democratization of relationships between pupils and teachers, one characterized by reflection and critique.

The re-examination of the nature of pupil–teacher relationships required by media literacy education brings to the forefront not only the variety of teaching styles, but also the variety of learning styles that children bring to the study of media, as well as a host of personal interests, needs, goals, experiences, prior knowledge, skills, and motivations. For example, sometimes children expect to be entertained in class, while at other times they may feel that their personal tastes and self-worth are being threatened, or that they are expected to become television producers or bloggers against their will.

Assessment

How can the educational effectiveness of the various media literacy curricula be evaluated? What do children need to do or express in order for us to define them as media literate? Should we test their knowledge? Production skills? Media consumption behaviors? Attitudes? Emotions? Values? Creative abilities? Critical evaluation of texts? Protection of their privacy and identity? Indeed, those involved in media literacy education wrestle with the problem of whether to require knowledge tests, critical analyses of texts, production of a text, or a combination of all of the above. Some models of evaluation base their concepts on literary and artistic forms of critique, others on the capability for self-reflection. Clearly, there are thorny issues involved in assessing the success of media literacy curricula as well as of pupils' achievements.

Evaluating Media Literacy Education

With such high expectations for media literacy education around the world, it is appropriate that we summarize some of the key findings from evaluation studies of media literacy education. These studies focus on the following five domains and deal with the central questions embedded within them.[13]

Suitability of educational goals. This area seeks to identify the nature and effectiveness of learning processes for specific child-audiences of different ages. Here, conventional pre-post studies have proven to be effective; that is, studies that compare the achievements of children before the introduction of the curriculum with their achievements after it has been implemented over a period of time. By using control groups of pupils who do not study media literacy we can sharpen our understanding of how children spontaneously apply skills in analyzing and creating media messages in comparison to those groups of pupils who have acquired these skills through formal learning.

Studies of teachers' experiences and attitudes. Through such studies we can ask such questions as: Are teachers resistant or raise objections to teaching media literacy? What motivates those teachers that are enthusiastic about teaching media literacy? How do they apply the curricula? What is the nature of such applications?

Studies of children's experiences and attitudes. This allows us to ask questions such as: What do children think they gain from media literacy education? Do they feel it "spoils" their media-related pleasures or adds to it? What are their attitudes toward such studies – do they feel enthusiasm, resentment, or boredom? What would they like to study in their media literacy classes?

Evaluation of the inter-relationships between media literacy studies and other disciplines. This area focuses on the question: Does media literacy advance skills in other areas, such as civic studies, art, science, literature, technology?

Evaluation of curriculum goals addressing specific issues. Here we can ask: Does the curriculum reduce racist stereotypes? Does it promote healthy nutrition or safe sex practices? Can it reduce online bullying?

Overall, evaluation studies have found that well-designed and implemented media literacy interventions do have the potential to help even young children gain knowledge about and develop better understandings of the media and society.[14] However, whether these achievements are carried over to everyday experiences to be implemented and applied in children's media engagements and in their own production of media texts as *prosumers* has yet to be determined. Several studies conducted in this area suggest that while educational interventions may be effective in transmitting knowledge, the ability to develop critical skills in relation to the world of media and apply these to real-world situations outside of the classroom or particular experiment requires a much more complex educational process. For example, positive results were found in a variety of educational interventions in the USA designed to develop media literacy skills to enhance children's ability to be critical about media messages related to violence, smoking, and unhealthy food,[15] gender and bullying,[16] the implications of media violence,[17] sexual behavior,[18] and body image.[19] In contrast, an experiment in the Netherlands demonstrated that children exposed to an educational intervention improved their understanding of the process of news production, but not their ability to critique the reliability of news reports.[20] In the younger age group, following an intervention in Israel, preschool children were better able to identify fiction elements in television programs, to understand time and logic gaps in the narrative, as well as to identify specific camera shots as they related to specific meanings.[21]

Evaluation studies of the achievements of media education are very complex endeavors given the variance in defining the goals of media literacy as well as the lack of consensus over what constitutes the "media-literate child." As a result, media education seems to be caught up in a vicious circle: only the development of a systematic and cumulative body of research regarding the teaching and learning of media literacy can help clarify goals, define clear policies, identify effective teaching practices and teacher education, and explain the educational process that pupils undergo when they study media, yet to create such a body of research requires a sophisticated media education program. All forms of research methodologies can contribute to such an effort. Furthermore, there is an acute need for longitudinal studies that document, perhaps through ethnographic methods, educational processes taking place in classrooms from the points of view of both pupils and teachers. There is also a need for large-scale surveys, measuring changes in achievements, attitudes, perspectives, media consumption, and production habits, in schools that go through media education interventions in comparison to those that do not. Finally, tightly planned small-scale experiments are needed to study the effectiveness of specific teaching methods or teaching aids.

In summary, we have seen that media literacy education is a dynamic, developing, and complicated field. It is highly embedded in cultural contexts and educational structures and often involves politicized agendas. Recent reviews of the state of media literacy in the world suggest that the field is maturing, with its own journals, conferences, and networks of scholars who share similar understandings of the theoretical framework and goals.[22] There is also a growing sense of the urgency to develop media literacy skills in young people in order to support an engaged citizenry. Those who promote such a process expect that it to have far-reaching influences on the definition of schooling, democracy, and even on our understanding of knowledge all together. Whether it will live up to these ambitious promises has yet to be seen. Finally, we need to remember that media literacy is a lifelong process that is not confined to the school system: parents, caregivers, siblings, peers – all have the potential to contribute to the development of media literacy, as indicated in our discussion in Chapter 1.

Notes

1. Peppler, 2013.
2. Based on Bazalgette, 1998, p. 8; and Bowker, 1991, p. 17.
3. Hobbs, 2010.
4. Based on Buckingham, 1998.
5. Hobbs, 2011.
6. Scharrer, 2007.
7. Buckingham & Domaille, 2003.
8. Based on Kubey, 1998.
9. Criticos, 1997; Prinsloo & Criticos, 1991.
10. Lemish & Lemish, 1997.
11. See, for example, the collection of articles in Carlsson, Tayie, Jacquinot-Delaunay, & Tornero, 2008.
12. Hobbs, 2013.
13. Adopted and updated from Bazalgette, 1989.
14. See, for example, a meta-analysis conducted by Jeong, Cho, & Huang, 2012.
15. Bickham & Slaby, 2012.
16. Walsh, Sekarasih, & Scharrer, 2014.
17. Webb & Martin, 2012.
18. Pinkleton *et al.*, 2008.
19. Wilksch & Wade, 2009.
20. Vooijs, van der Voort, & Hoogeweij, 1995.
21. Tidhar, 1996.
22. Cappello, Felini, & Hobbs, 2011.

References

Bazalgette, C. (Ed.). (1989). *Primary media education: A curriculum statement*. London: British Film Institute.

Bazalgette, C. (1998). Still only 1898. *Media Education Journal, 24*, 2–9.

Bickham, D.S. & Slaby, R.G. (2012). Effects of a media literacy program in the US on children's critical evaluation of unhealthy media messages about violence, smoking, and food. *Journal of Children and Media, 6*(2), 255–271.

Bowker, J. (Ed.). (1991). *Secondary media education: A curriculum statement*. London: The British Film Institute.

Buckingham, D. (1998). Media education in the UK: Moving beyond protectionism. *Journal of Communication, 21*, 6.

Buckingham, D. & Domaille, K. (2003). Where are we going and how can we get there? General findings from the UNESCO Youth Media Education Survey 2001. In C. von Feilitzen & U. Carlsson (Eds.), *Promote or protect? Perspectives on media literacy and media regulations* (pp. 41–54). Göteborg University, Sweden: The International Clearinghouse on Children, Youth and Media.

Cappello, G., Felini, D., & Hobbs, R. (2011). Reflections on global developments in media literacy education: Bridging theory and practice. *Journal of Media Literacy Education, 3*(2), 66–73.

Carlsson, U., Tayie, S., Jacquinot-Delaunay, F., & Tornero, J.N.P. (2008). *Empowerment through media education: An intercultural dialogue*. Göteborg University, Sweden: The International Clearinghouse on Children, Youth and Media.

Criticos, C. (1997). Media education for a critical citizenry in South Africa. In R. Kubey (Ed.), *Media literacy in the information age* (pp. 229–240). New Brunswick, NJ: Transaction.

Hobbs, R. (2010). *Digital and media literacy: A plan of action*. A white paper on the digital and media literacy recommendations of the Knight Commission on the information needs of communities in a democracy. Washington, DC: The Aspen Institute, pp. vii–viii.

Hobbs, R. (2011). The state of media literacy: A response to Potter. *Journal of Broadcasting & Electronic Media, 55*(3), 419–430.

Hobbs, R. (2013). Media literacy. In D. Lemish (Ed.), *The Routledge international handbook of children, adolescents, and media* (pp. 417–424). New York: Routledge.

Jeong, S.H., Cho, H., & Huang, Y. (2012). Media literacy interventions: A meta-analysis review. *Journal of Communication, 62*, 454–472.

Kubey, R. (1998). Obstacles to the development of media education in the US. *Journal of Communication, 48*(1), 58–69.

Lemish, D. & Lemish, P. (1997). A much debated consensus: Media literacy in Israel. In R. Kubey (Ed.), *Media literacy in the information age* (pp. 213–228). New Brunswick, NJ: Transaction.

Peppler, K. (2013). Social media and creativity. In D. Lemish (Ed.), *The Routledge international handbook of children, adolescents, and media* (pp. 193–200). New York: Routledge.

Pinkleton, B.E., Weintraub, E., Cohen, M., Chen, Y-C, & Fitzgerald, E. (2008). Effects of peer-led media literacy curriculum on adolescents' knowledge and attitudes toward sexual behavior and media portrayals of sex. *Health Communication, 23*, 462–472.

Prinsloo, J. & Criticos, C. (Eds.). (1991). *Media matters in South Africa*. Durban, South Africa: University of Natal.

Scharrer, E. (2007). Closer than you think: Bridging the gap between media effects and cultural studies in media education theory and practice. In A. Nowak, S. Abel, & K. Ross (Eds.), *Rethinking media education: Critical pedagogy and identity politics* (pp. 17–35). Cresskill, NJ: Hampton Press.

Tidhar, C.E. (1996). Enhancing television literacy skills among preschool children through an intervention program in the kindergarten. *Journal of Educational Media, 22*(2), 97–110.

Vooijs, M.W., van der Voort, T.H.A., & Hoogeweij, J. (1995). Critical viewing of television news: The impact of a Dutch schools television project. *Journal of Educational Television, 21*, 23–36.

Walsh, K., Sekarasih, L., & Scharrer, E. (2014). Mean girls and tough boys: Children's meaning making and media literacy lessons on gender and bullying in the US. *Journal of Children and Media, 8*(3), 223–239.

Webb, T. & Martin, K. (2012). Evaluation of a US school-based media literacy violence prevention curriculum on changes in knowledge and critical thinking among adolescents. *Journal of Children and Media, 6*(4), 430–449.

Wilksch, S.M. & Wade, T.D. (2009). Reduction of shape and weight concern in young adolescents: A 30-month controlled evaluation of a media literacy program. *Journal of American Academy of Child and Adolescent Psychiatry, 48*(6), 652–661.

8

Policy and Advocacy

I hope that the discussion throughout this book has made it clear why there is a growing demand for broadcasters, internet suppliers, game designers, and other producers of media to control the content they provide for children. We find this demand throughout the world, and thus advocating for such an expectation constitutes an important route of intervention on behalf of children and their wellbeing.

For a host of reasons, advocacy groups, politicians, legislators, and scholars have called for both external (enforced by legislation) as well as internal (voluntary) regulation over programming for children. As we discussed with regard to the development of media literacy education in Chapter 7, there is a strong protectionist tradition driving such pressure which often competes with traditions of freedom of speech and free market capitalism, as is the case in the USA.[1] As a result, many countries eventually develop media-related policies, including regulations and agreements that benefit children but which also compromise the needs and constraints imposed on the industry. Interestingly, several European countries as well as Australia are experimenting with a model of co-regulation that involves voluntary collaboration between regulatory authorities and the broadcast industry.[2]

By way of overview, we can organize considerations that influence the development of media policies for children into four groups. First, *structural* considerations relate to the nature of the country's broadcast systems (e.g., private or public) and the responsibility each has for a variety of national populations. Second, *ideological* considerations manifest themselves in relation to the centrality of national or religious identity, cultural self-definitions, traditions of freedom of speech, and the economic system, as tested by society's willingness to impose restrictions on its media industry. Third, the degree of *economic* influence that corporations and industries have through their inter-relationships with government play an important role in terms of determining the degree of each sides' independence or dependence (e.g., taxes paid by corporations, licensing fees, and/or consumer / "listener" fees) as well as the extent of corporate influence on policy decisions; for example, in imposing or freeing up advertising regulations. Finally, we can point to the Gordian knot of *political* considerations, with political stakeholders dependent on the media to advance themselves and their political programs, while at the same time having to submit to the demands of the media in order to maintain their power.

These four groups of considerations are, naturally, interdependent, and require deeper investigation. However, investigating them is crucial if we want to gain a comparative understanding of how various countries develop media policies, what they share in common, and how they differ.[3]

Criteria for Quality Media

Perhaps the primary difficulty in developing media-related regulations is the vagueness of the concept of *quality media* as a production aim best able to serve children. As we have noted, "quality" is often a matter of what is important *in the eye of the beholder*. According to children, for example, a quality television program, internet site, or mobile application is one that attracts and interests them. For parents and public organizations, quality may be determined by educational value; for industry production professionals, it may be measured by production values (such as use of famous actors, advanced camerawork and audio-visual effects, music, humor, and the like); for corporate or public executives a program's sales or audience ratings are probably the most important in determining quality. Broadcasters in the USA often include popular cartoons and popular prime time series in their definition of "quality" television. In appealing for license renewal, they justify such programs in a variety of creative, yet some might say cynical, ways. An action-adventure cartoon is perceived as having positive value, because the protagonists defend their universe from others who want to destroy it thereby demonstrating concern for others and a distinction between good and bad; and a stereotypical situation comedy is presented as educational since it deals with everyday conflict within families.[4]

The debate over the definition of "quality" in children's media is dependent, to a large degree, on the conflict of interests of the various stakeholders. For example, for public or private educational broadcasters the question of broadcasting policy for children is very different since their view of educationally oriented television is usually influenced by the realities of functioning under severe financial constraints in an aggressively competitive market.

Overall, there does seem to be some agreement among these various perspectives that quality media for children should be expected to abide by the following principles:[5]

- Provide children with media content prepared especially for them without taking advantage of them; content that entertains but at the same time tries to advance children physically, mentally, and socially.

- Allow children to hear, see and express themselves, their culture, their language and their life experiences through their media in ways that affirm their personal identity, community, and place.
- Encourage awareness and appreciation of other cultures as well as the child's own.
- Offer a variety of genres and content and not just reproduce texts according to a successful formula.
- Deliver media content to children at times and through technologies that are accessible to them.
- Recognize differences between children that are a result of their cognitive and emotional development, talents, interests, personality characteristics, interpersonal relationships, and social environment.
- Take steps to protect and encourage content that reflects local and marginalized cultures and those with minority languages and needs.
- Avoid unnecessary presentation of violence, sex, and racism.

A UNICEF initiative to define quality media for children, with a specific emphasis on children being raised in low-resource societies and marginalized communities, established four overarching principles for quality media:[6] (1) Communication for children should be age-appropriate and child friendly; (2) it should address the child holistically; (3) it should be positive and strengths based; and (4) it should address the needs of all, including those who are most disadvantaged.

More specifically, various criteria are often applied in assessing specific educational content, as in the following examples:

- Does the content invite children to see things they have not seen in the past, hear things they have not heard, and, most importantly, think or imagine things that they would not have thought or imagined before?
- Does the content tell a good story? Does it rely on the familiar in order to bridge the new and unfamiliar for young children? Are the verbal and visual components compatible?
- Does the content offer characters that children really care about? Is there a struggle between good and bad that is not too extreme? Are the children in the text capable of overcoming difficulties in a reasonable manner? Is the end of the story dependent on the generosity, fairness, honesty, caring, and responsibility of the main characters?
- Does the content avoid preaching to children or talking to them in a condescending manner?
- Does it avoid presenting adults as behaving in an unfair, irrational or foolish manner that undermines children's trust in the adult world?
- Does the content expand the children's world of experiences in an esthetically attractive way?
- Does the content include a degree of wit and humor that is not exploitive of others?

When a specific lesson is being promoted in the media text, there may be additional criteria used to examine its educational value:[7]

- Is the educational lesson clear enough for the audience to understand?
- Is the educational lesson prominent, presented systematically, or as an integral part of the program?
- Is the educational lesson engaging and challenging for the audience?
- Is the educational lesson presented in a way that is deemed applicable by the audience?

Additional attempts to determine quality can be based on external criteria, such as awards given to various media products, or rating systems that determine the suitability of content (e.g., of television programs, movies, and video games) for different age groups.

Clearly, then, there are many ways to define quality media content, and these include the use of many overlapping and inter-related criteria. Furthermore, these lists are neither exhaustive nor are they agreed by all stakeholders. Complicating such discussions is the fact that children access various content through multiple media options which provide them with a variety of opportunities and benefits that raise additional challenges. Seemingly, each medium requires that caregivers and educators develop different mastery skills in monitoring children's use, whether in a private or social context, to sort through the available content and make informed decisions about choices.[8] We can conclude that the required framework for discussing quality in children's media considers "the nature of children's development, including the interplay of social, emotional, and intellectual development, children's social and cultural contexts, and the importance of human relationships for supporting learning and development."[9]

Broadcasting Policy for Children

Since television programs are distributed around the globe and viewed through broadcast television, cable, satellites, videotapes, CDs, computers, and mobile devices, their broadcasting policies are of local, national, and global concern and must relate to multi-media platforms. A case in point is the action-adventure animation television series (and later movie series) *The Power Rangers*, which was very popular worldwide in the 1990s. Due to the program's violent nature, attempts were undertaken to limit its broadcast in many countries, including Australia, Canada, Denmark, and New Zealand. In turn, this forced the producers in the USA to re-examine its content as forced broadcasters to consider their broadcasting policies. Advocacy groups concerned about the excessive presence of violence in children's programming argue that the fact that children around the world often view the same programs creates an urgent need to develop international broadcasting policies that employ internationally supported criteria to be applied in different national contexts.

A comparative analysis of broadcast policies for children's media usage worldwide can be divided into three domains: content-related issues, including more specifically discussion of locally produced programs and sponsorship; violence and sex; and advertising for children and during children's viewing hours.

Content-related policy issues

Many countries and international organizations (e.g., UNESCO and the European Union) have attempted to monitor television content that targets children. Most of these efforts are aimed at limiting children's exposure to content deemed inappropriate for their age, emotional and cognitive abilities, as well as content that presents a social world based on a-social values and behaviors that might have negative impacts on children. Policies in this realm are directed at limiting broadcast hours of such content to parts of the day when children are presumably not around television (e.g., late-night hours). For example, many European countries that regulate their children's programs adopted the "watershed" guideline that specifies broadcast hours before and during which broadcasters need to adapt their content to an audience that includes children. Some countries refer specifically to the need to protect young viewers from exposure to inappropriate content such as pornography, racism, and violence.[10] Complementary content-related policies are directed toward the encouragement of broadcasting quality programs for children that have an added educational and social value.

The struggle over the regulation of children's television in the USA is a particularly interesting case, due to the fact that, first, many programs for children are produced there and exported globally; and, second, the USA is a point of reference for other regulatory systems, as well as being a model of a broadcast system that is mostly commercial and privately owned. Without going into detail about the evolution of the regulatory system in the USA, we can pinpoint many of the central issues by examining the Children's Television Act (CTA) legislated by the American Congress in 1990. Following years of public debate and many attempts at legislation, this act restricted the amount of advertising time allowed during children's programs, required broadcasters to televise programs of educational and informative value for children, and allocated a budget for production of children's programs. Fulfilling these requirements became a prerequisite for the renewal of the broadcast license (at the time, every five years, and since 1996 every eight years). The Federal Communication Commission (FCC), the supervising body of the broadcast system in the USA, was charged with enforcing these requirements. However, review of the impact of the Children's Television Act over the years suggests that it has not been able to dramatically change the landscape of television for children in the USA,[11] and therefore, for the rest of the world.

Interviews with broadcasters for children in the USA revealed that the clear-cut opinions they have about their target audience dictates their policies.[12] The opinions and policies share the following assumptions: children lose interest in quality educational programs when they enter the school system around age six; the only way to bypass children's resentment of instructional content is to focus on social aspects of the programs; it is more expensive to produce educational programs. In addition, broadcasters argue that it is better to target programs to boys rather than to girls or to a mixed audience, for several reasons: boys are in charge of the remote control at home and dictate the viewing habits of the family; girls watch boys' programs but not vice versa; boys are more easily persuaded to purchase program-related merchandise. The result of these findings is that broadcasters do not believe in producing educational programs for children over preschool age and prioritize action and adventure genres with male protagonists that appeal traditionally to boys.

When we move away from the USA to other countries, we find that an additional policy concern is prominent – the requirement that broadcasters offer children locally produced, "home-grown" programs that take into consideration the cultural context in which they are raised.[13] Countries apply a number of mechanisms to support this policy, including the application of programming quotas, a ban on imported programs, support for locally produced content, and funding for local and regional channels. In Australia, for example, broadcasters are required to offer a minimum of 25 hours of locally produced programs out of the 390 hours of children's programs per year, and are only allowed to broadcast Australian programs for preschoolers.

Concerns over the infiltration of programs originating in the USA into other societies and cultures, as well as a desire to protect local production, are strongly evident in many other countries as well. In Canada, for example, the requirement was set at 60 percent local programming on public channels and 50 percent on commercial ones. The Canadian Association of Broadcasters developed a self-regulatory mechanism that included a request that programs for children should reflect the social and ethical standards of Canadian society. In addition, Canadian broadcasters are required to deal specifically with issues of morals, violence, and stereotypes, including reference to gender portrayals.[14]

In the 1980s, Australia was among the first countries to recognize the importance of governmental support for educational broadcasting, and several countries since then have followed suit. The frameworks offered for such sponsorship vary: establishment of independent funds for production of quality programs for children; requiring advertisers and commercial broadcasters to allocate a certain percentage of their income to quality productions; government sponsorship; and private philanthropic funds. Additional examples of funding of local programing include government subsidies in Denmark for children's programming and the Qatari funding of local production of children's programs in partnership with the Al Jazeera Network which, at the time of this writing, has reached 22 Arab countries via satellite.[15]

The most extreme regulatory strategy of actually banning non-local programs has been mainly practiced in non-democratic countries – with various levels of effectiveness. China, which has employed some level of banning, probably for both ideological as well as economic reasons, has set a maximum of 30 percent of transmission time for imported programs. It also bans foreign programming for children during prime time, in order to encourage the local animation industry.[16]

Violence and sexually explicit content policy

Not surprisingly, the issue of television's harmful content, and particularly scenes of violence and sex, is central to debates over broadcasting policy worldwide, though emphases differ from country to country. For example, on the whole Western and Northern European countries are less preoccupied with children's exposure to sex and nudity in the media than they are with violence. Yet the opposite is true in the USA, where there seems to be much less of a consensus on the need to limit violent content, and much more of a preoccupation with issues related to sex and nudity.

Cultural differences are clearly present in public discourse and on the pressures exerted on regulatory bodies, resulting in the often differing policies around the world. The fierce debate over this issue in the USA is particularly illuminating given the deeply engrained tradition of freedom of speech, as stated in the First Amendment to the American constitution: "Congress shall make no law … abridging the freedom of speech, or the press … ." The American Congress can only regulate forms of expression, including television broadcasts, when there is a "compelling interest" to do so. With regard to television violence, therefore, judicial authorities have set the criterion that clear evidence of a causal relationship between viewing television violence and violent behavior must be presented in order to determine the existence of a compelling interest that justifies formal intervention. As we have seen in Chapter 4, presenting such evidence is quite problematic. More specifically, judicial precedent regarding this issue distinguishes between "immediate and clear danger," when there is a certainty that watching violence has harmful effects, and research evidence that suggests such possible relationships, but cannot prove "immediate and clear danger."[17]

Decades of transferring the responsibility for this issue back and forth between the broadcasting industry and the American Congress has resulted in the development of several strategies for the supervision of violence on television. Many countries around the world have adopted and adapted some of these strategies to meet their own needs. While none of these have been proven to offer a fully satisfactory solution, they nevertheless deserve our attention:[18]

- *Banning and zoning*: Limiting the broadcast of violent and sexual content to particular hours of broadcasting.
- *Balancing*: A requirement to balance each violent program with the broadcast of a non-violent one. This proposal assumes that it is possible to "counteract" harmful content by broadcasting "corrective" programs.
- *Labeling*: Broadcasting a warning announcement before each program deemed problematic ("parental and viewer discretion is advised") or rating programs, movies, and games according to a scale (for example: G – suitable for a general audience; PG – Parental guidance is advised; PG13 – Parental guidance for children under 13; R – a rated program that is unsuitable for children).
- *User block*: Using various technological means to block reception of programs at the individual home. This can be achieved through blocking a particular channel

(Lockbox), blocking particular hours, or using a violence chip (the V-chip) that is inserted into the television set and allows for selective blocking of programs.

Each of these strategies presents different challenges to freedom of speech, and at the same time fails to offer a comprehensive solution to the complexity of the issues involved. These complexities include the following: children view television at all hours of the day and on many devices; labeling programs as age inappropriate has been inconsistent and may have the opposite effect of even attracting more children; rating and blocking programs is dependent on predetermined criteria enforced by others and not by viewers themselves; ratings that appear on printed television-program guides are not always comprehensible or inclusive of content important to parents. Despite the availability of technological blocking devices, the evidence to date suggests that parents are not particularly receptive to their adoption.

Television advertising policy

Advertising is a third central concern of policymaking for broadcasting to children. Most policies regarding advertising for children focus on the amount of advertising, the clear distinction between advertising and other content, and on the nature of the product being advertised. Here, too, the US example stands out, as it relates to a highly commercialized television environment and a strong tradition of free speech rights that serve as an example to other countries.

The Children's Television Act of 1990 in the USA limits the amount of time dedicated to commercials during children's hours: no more than 10.5 minutes per hour during the weekend and not more than 12 minutes per hour during week-days. Programs that constitute a commercial in and of themselves are prohibited (such as when program hosts promoting products during the show). Other requirements include banning of advertising by celebrities presented during their own programs (*host selling*); clear separation of commercials from programs (*bumpers*); and a requirement that advertisements must include disclaimers (such as: "assembly required"; "parts sold separately"; "batteries required").

Some countries, such as Brazil and Israel, have general policy statements prohib-iting offensive or manipulative advertising. Others, such as Nigeria, Thailand, and the UK, restrict food advertising. Sweden, Norway, Denmark, Finland, and Austria prohibit any advertising during children's programming and Sweden and Norway also prohibit any advertising directed at children under 12 altogether. Australia does not allow advertising during programs directed at preschoolers, and Greece does not allow toy advertisements on prime time television.[19]

All these regulations are directed at restricting the exploitive nature of advertising for young children who may find it difficult to understand the persuasive intent of advertising and thereby assign it high credibility, as we discussed in Chapters 2 and 4. In addition, regulations are also designed to address specific concerns over the advertising of unhealthy and dangerous products to children, such as unhealthy food, tobacco, and alcohol; medication, including for age-inappropriate content such as erectile dysfunction and depression (prevalent in the USA, for example); as well as trailers promoting programs, movies, and games with violent and sexual content.

In an attempt to prevent legislative intervention, the Association of National Advertisers, Inc. (ANA) in the USA offered a substantive list of guidelines for advertisers for children as long ago as 1972, in an attempt to advance self-regulation. These guidelines are of interest to us because they acquaint us with what advertisers themselves define as problematic issues in advertising for children. The guidelines can be divided into several areas.[20] The first area is concerned with values contained in advertising. The ANA recommended, for example, that commercials should not present unacceptable behaviors from the point of view of social, legal, religious, institutional, or family values; should not show disrespect for parents and/or other authorities responsible for children; should not present bad habits; and should avoid suggesting that ownership of a product will improve the child's social position, or that without it the child will be a target of ridicule or contempt.

The second area of guidelines is concerned with protecting children from exploitation and includes such demands as the following: avoid all attempts to take advantage of the fact that children experience difficulties in distinguishing between reality and fantasy; strive to direct children's imagination toward healthy and productive growth; guarantee that each component of the commercial – verbal, audio, and visual – as well as the commercial in its entirety do not deceive the children with regard to the functioning of the product (e.g., speed, size, color, durability, nutrition value, noise) or with regard to the perceived benefits (e.g., gaining power, popularity, growth, expertise, intelligence); guarantee that the commercial clearly explains what is included in the original purchase price, including statements regarding items sold separately and products that require assembly of parts; present products clearly; and ensure that demonstrations of how to use the product or the prize are done in a way that the average target child could model it.

The third area covers guidelines concerning the difficulties young children may have in distinguishing between commercials and programs. These guidelines demand that no actors or characters from children's programs (real or animated) be employed in commercials in order to encourage the selling of products, prizes, or services during, right before, or after a program in which that character appears; that actors and characters – such as those cited above – identified with a product will be employed only under the condition that they are not committing any misleading acts intended for imitation by children with regard to the product or service's characteristics; and that national celebrities will only be employed when they are identified as having the authority to talk about the topic involved in the commercial, and provided they are considered credible.

The fourth area covers guidelines concerning pressures that may be exerted on parents through advertising. The guidelines prescribe that commercials should: encourage children to consult their parents about purchasing the product rather than exerting pressure on them; refrain from approaching children with regard to products that are not intended for them, and refrain from encouraging children to purchase them; present the products' prices clearly and without any pressure, and avoid using terminology that suggests a discounted price (e.g., the price is only x dollars, etc.).

Finally, guidelines concerning the safety of children state that with the exception of public announcement broadcasts, it is forbidden to present adults or children in commercials involved in unsafe activities, situations, or conditions of any kind; and that commercials should avoid demonstration or presentation of any product in a way that encourages inappropriate use or use that exceeds accepted safety regulations.

Studies of these and many other guidelines not cited here found that there is a wide range of concerns regarding advertising for children. In practice, however, these guidelines have no legal force, are hardly ever applied, and cannot be enforced. Indeed, there is a huge gap between the official discourse stating the good intentions of advertisers and their everyday practices – which regularly divert from these guidelines, particularly with the common practice of embedding (i.e., employing, and so displaying, a specific manufacturer's product in a media production).

A related concern is for the rapidly growing practice of allowing advertising within school environments by way of installing snacks and soft drink machines, as well as via sponsorship of events and activities, often in exchange for donations made to the school for purchase of athletic equipment and technologies. Here, too, policy recommendations have been heavily contested.

Convention on television broadcasting for children and youth

By way of summary of broadcast-related issues, we present an example of a convention on television broadcasting for children and youth that is a result of a combined effort by academics and broadcasters in Israel – both public and private – concerned with the wellbeing of children. Framed as the "Ten Commandments of Broadcasting" the convention specifies five principles of "thou shalt do" and five principles of "thou shalt not do."[21] There are several other examples of similar initiatives, such as the Brazilian best practices[22] and policy on content classification by age.[23]

Internet-related Policy Issues

The proliferation of internet and mobile media use among children and adolescents, along with related concerns for the risks and potential harms involved, presents policymakers with new and complicated challenges. Various attempts in the USA to impose legislation that restricts access by minors have not proven to be particularly successful. The European approach to facilitate collaborative agreements between stakeholders resulted in forms of self- and co-regulation that serve as evidence that no one solution can be accepted by all concerned in attempts to ensure a safe environment for children on the internet. Clearly though, there is interest around the world in restricting children's access to inappropriate, not to mention illegal, content

Convention on television broadcasting for children and youth

We are committed to the happiness and welfare of all the children from all social classes and sectors without distinction in regard to gender, ethnicity, or religion, as delineated in the UN Convention Regarding the Rights of Children and Youth ratified by the state of Israel.

In view of our understanding of the important role that the medium of television plays in shaping the spiritual, emotional, and behavioral lives of children and youth; and

In accordance with the basic laws, legislation, regulations, as well as ethical codes that apply to the different broadcasting authorities; and

In view of our strong sense of responsibility for our roles as creators, producers, and broadcasters of television programs;

We have committed ourselves, collectively, as the representatives of those involved in the production and broadcast of programs for children and youth, in consultation with relevant members of the academic and educational communities, and in recognition of our right to preserve the distinctive uniqueness of each constituent organization, to this convention regarding television broadcasting.

In the spirit of this joint agreement, we proclaim that we shall act:

1. *To promote the presentation of a social world based upon humanitarian principles of human rights, tolerance toward difference, social justice, freedom of religion, conscience, and belief, the dignity and freedom of mankind, the authority of the law and the status of the court of justice, in the spirit of the basic values and laws of the State of Israel.*

   We shall act to promote the production of TV programs and the acquisition of foreign programs that profess this worldview and present it as desirable, conceivable, and a positive embodiment of ideas.

   We shall act to promote, actively, programs that seek to develop social awareness in the fields of social justice, as well as those that encourage social involvement and responsibility. Programs that deviate from the spirit of this commitment will be presented in a context that conveys a clearly critical message regarding negative projections broadcast to young viewers and society, in general.

2. *To promote presentation of a multicultural world in which the distinctive characteristics of local culture are valued along with trends in the creation of a global culture, while observing openness toward diversity and the expression of different opinions.*

   We shall act to promote the production of TV programs and the acquisition of foreign programs that represent a variety of cultural worlds that characterize the different ethnic, cultural, linguistic, and religious backgrounds that are present in Israeli society and beyond. We shall act to promote the production of original programs reflective of the society and contemporary affairs of Israel, as well as to advance understanding of the heritage of the Jewish people over the generations and in all countries of the Diaspora.

We shall provide for appropriate expressions of all facets of the Israeli society and the diverse groups that compose it as well as their culture, language, and heritage. We shall enable children and youth with the opportunity to become acquainted with the diversity of human life in regard to physical properties (such as color of the skin, pronunciation) and cultural attributes (such as clothing, cultural and religious ceremonies, philosophy and art, etc.).

3. *To advance addressing the specific needs of children and youth of different ages living under different circumstances.*

    We shall act to promote the production of TV programs and the purchase of foreign programs that appropriately address the needs, abilities, and life experiences of children of different age groups and genders living under different cultural and social circumstances. We will relate to the mental and emotional needs that arise due to contemporary events. We shall devote special attention to populations whose alternatives for leisure activities are the most limited. We shall endeavor to help children and youth who suffer from psychological, cognitive, and physical handicaps.

4. *To assist children and youth to offer their own views and to enable them to present their views of the world on television.*

    We shall act to promote the production of TV programs that provide children and youth from all sectors of the population with opportunities to express themselves, their worldviews, and relate to issues of concern to them, in the production process as well as during the broadcast. We shall listen to their voices respectfully and shall take note of their wishes, keeping in mind that at every stage of their development they are persons in their own right with their own views.

5. *To promote quality productions for children and youth characterized by investment, audio-visual richness, and by a high level of content that will enrich their aesthetic and creative world.*

    We shall act to promote the production of television programs and acquisition of foreign programs that are rich in quality in every domain of production and genre: in their linguistic richness; presentation of appropriate and well-developed humor; high standards of acting or moderation; quality of musical performances, photography, and editing; as well as the profundity of ideas. We will take into account that, in spite of their young age, all audiences acquire their own cultural tastes and should be honored with programs of high production quality.

    And, based upon such agreements, we shall act in order to:

6. *Refrain from presenting the world as a place of violence, cruelty, and inhumanity, as well as one where violence is presented positively and as the only way to solve problems.*

    We shall act to promote the production of TV programs and acquisition of foreign programs that lack violence, of any kind – physical, emotional and verbal, that is directed against people, other living creatures, nature, and property. In the event that acts of violence are present, as an integral part of the description of reality or an essential component in a plot that is deemed to be of value, we shall refrain from glorifying and presenting it humorously, as enjoyable, and inconsequential. We shall avoid the presentation of content that encourages destructive behavior and unnecessary physical risks.

7. *Refrain from overemphasizing or presenting sex and sexuality as a means of titillation or as an expression of a power relationship that involves the domination of others.*

    We shall act to promote the production of TV programs and acquisition of foreign programs that contribute to the equality of the genders and presentation of human sexuality as a natural and worthy aspect of human relations, and not as a means for achieving objectives, domination, exploitation, and oppression. We shall avoid using sexuality as a means of titillating children and youth and attracting their attention. We shall refrain from presenting content that combines violence and sexuality as well as common stereotypes of femininity and masculinity.

8. *Refrain from a stereotypical presentation of groups according to their religious background, ethnicity, gender, as well as physical attributes of age, disability, or appearance.*

    We shall act to promote the production of TV programs and acquisition of foreign programs that present humanity with all its diversity, without use of stereotypes regarding difference and otherness of any kind whatsoever. We shall be particularly aware of stereotypes that portray central divisions within Israeli society. We shall refrain from presenting contents that may encourage physical and mental self-affliction.

9. *Refrain from presenting consumption and materialism as an ultimate value, as a means of self-satisfaction, or solving human problems.*

    We shall act to promote the production of TV programs and acquisition of foreign programs that abstain from presenting materialism and persistent consumerism as a way to cope with individual and social hardships, as a means of competition applied to advance personal aims, and as a manifestation for self-esteem. We shall abstain from making a connection between the possession of property and individual self-worth. We shall present the diversity of other resources that exist for use by the individual, such as education, family, friends, positive activity, and so forth.

10. *Refrain from exploitation of children and youth in the process of production and in TV programs proper.*

We shall relate to children and youth who participate in the production of programs or who appear in them in a variety of roles as we relate to mature adults – as persons with rights, their own will, and value. We shall ensure appropriate working conditions, rest, food, and beverage. We shall honor the aspirations of employees and not exploit them. We shall not present them in programs in a way that might impair them or their reputation, even if their consent has been obtained. It is our duty to encourage them to consult with persons who fulfill a meaningful role in their lives and not to take advantage of their feelings in situations of weakness.

on the internet, as well as to minimize their vulnerability as either victims or perpetuators of negative behaviors. However, while there is general agreement that children lack the maturity to be critical consumers of harmful content such as pornography, and content dealing with racism, terrorism, and suicide, it is also clear that we cannot generalize about all children, and especially all age groups. In addition, public discussion and policymaking are grounded in different value systems, and different religious and cultural systems. This was demonstrated, for example, in a study that reviewed different regulatory initiatives in China, Japan, and Korea. The protective parenting style, emphasis on academic performance, authoritarian approach, and discipline characteristic of these nations have led to the development of codes of proper conduct online and rules of obedience.[24]

As noted, different countries are experimenting with adaptations of various forms of regulation, and/or they have laid responsibility more in the laps of parents, offering them various technological tools for monitoring and restricting accessibility to harmful content. In addition to what researchers argue is the limited effectiveness of such solutions, some also point to the economical motivation of large corporations to cultivate *web-anxiety* among consumers, in order to be able to sell them technological promises for an unattainable safe internet environment.[25] In recent years, however, we have witnessed a move in European academic discourse from a safer to a *better* internet for children. This discourse stresses positive contents, and makes the connections between safety concerns and opportunities, development of skills, and empowerment.

Classification of internet content and labeling in Europe has followed precedents created in previous attempts to restrict use by children of earlier media platforms (such as self-labeling of video games) but has had very limited success, due to the complexities involved in such self-regulation. Web developers who were expected to self-label content-related issues such as the presence of nudity, sexual content, violence, inappropriate language, and other harmful content (e.g., gambling, drugs, alcohol), as well as to report the presence of user-generated content, were not particularly supportive of the system.[26]

Access to illegal content and behavior, including grooming and sexual abuse of children, as well as offenses by children toward themselves, and against others (such as cyberbullying and sexting), has also been a concern for legislators, given the ability of digital media to facilitate such contact risks. Many countries have extended existing legislative measures to include cyber-offenses. For example, sexting has been used in recent cases in North America to convict adolescents of distributing child pornography. Of specific interest is the issue of illegal downloading of copyright content and file sharing by children, particularly of music and games. Furthermore, various attempts at legislation and implementation have been deeply contested to date, and much of the issue discussed here remains unresolved.

A related contact-risk posed to children by the digital world is the opportunity to take advantage of their trust and naiveté and to collect valuable personal information from them. In this regard, the Federal Trade Commission in the USA issued the Children's Online Privacy Protection Act (COPPA) in 1998, which forbids the collection of personal information from children under the age of 13 without parental consent. This provision also forbids children under the age of 13 from registering on social network sites, such as Facebook, and is intended to protect children from giving away information that might be used against them in a variety of ways.[27] This requirement is, however, easily bypassed by millions of children worldwide, often with parental blessing. Furthermore, legislators did not establish how to monitor or determine whether an internet company is abusing or abiding by the law. Many parents believe that issuing a sweeping ban on young children's participation in social network sites deprives them of opportunities to take advantage of the internet and does not prepare them properly for literate and responsible conduct in the virtual world.[28] They argue that instead of trying to enforce unreasonable (and unworkable) regulations, children and parents should have access to an age-appropriate social network site that facilitates inter-generational communication and develops internet literacy. The updated ANA Guidelines on Advertising addressed this issue specifically and urged advertisers not to link their websites to sites that do not abide by this requirement.

As we have seen, here, too, advertising to children on the web is a particularly complicated matter, given the new digital marketing paradigm and proliferation of attractive sponsored websites that blur the traditional distinction between advertising and content. Games designed around products (i.e., advergames), immersive virtual and interactive environments that are heavily branded and networked, and pop-up ads are just few of these innovative tactics employed by advertisers to keep children engaged with brands and products. These marketing strategies for children are characterized by the following features, among others.[29] First, they build upon the sense of ubiquitous connectivity, according to which children are always "on" and connected to their social networks and virtual world. Second, they take advantage of the mobility of these experiences via all the media devices available to children today. Such technologies allow marketers to collect data in order to target specific consumer groups and individuals via very personalized marketing that caters to their unique profiles. Third, they integrate advertising and content to create an environment of branded entertainment which is strongly amplified and distributed via social media marketing. Employing short videos that go "viral" via social network sites, as well as children's generated advertising through creating and distributing supportive material, magnifies the potential of such marketing to become widespread. Finally, via the common practice of in-game advertising integrated into interactive games, marketing strategies offer powerful engagement vehicles for children.

To date, observers claim that no effective governmental restrictions on such internet practices nor any fair marketing policies have been enacted in the USA, and few other efforts have been documented in other places in the world. Given the complexities involved in any attempt to regulate the internet and its ever-changing dynamic nature, much of the responsibility has been placed in the hand of caregivers and educators, with the hope that they will implement expectations and standards deemed appropriate in their particular environment. Here, too, a variety of technical solutions to assist parents in restricting their children's activities online have been developed, with varying degrees of effectiveness.

In summary, we can say that, to date, countries around the world have not been able to keep up with technological innovations, nor develop clear, binding policies to regulate media for children. While the vast majority of past interventions have dealt with broadcasting regulation, it is clear that current and future challenges must contend with the technological developments of the internet and its accessibility via multi-platforms. It is also becoming clear that since there is hardly any possibility to control and/or regulate the multiplicity of platforms via which children access media, policy efforts would perhaps do better to concentrate on content and children's interaction with it, across all media.[30] It seems that only a combination of strategies that includes regulation, as well as co-regulation and self-regulation, media literacy education, and parental mediation, can best serve, collectively, the needs of children for a safe and quality media ecology that will contribute to their wellbeing and healthy development. Finally, in many policy discussions, as well as in the documents produced from them, we also find a call to involve children themselves, as social actors whose voices matter and should be taken into account.

Interventions on Behalf of Children

Interventions on behalf of children's media experiences have been an important part of the debates about media use around the world. There is a wide array of organizations advocating their particular goals with regard to media in the lives of children, each with their own motivations: research and teaching bodies in academic institutions; protectionist groups with religious or moral agendas; political and social groups with a specific ideology; parental and educational groups seeking more control on the media environment of the children under their care; or professionals with particular interests in children's wellbeing, such as pediatricians and psychologists. Many of these groups have well-developed websites that provide users with access to valuable resources. Some are primarily research and evidence based, others are more ideological in nature and present a clear point of view. Some advocate for a particular solution or specific regulation, others are educational, while yet others engage in various forms of awareness raising. There are way too many groups involved to name individually, so we can only selectively highlight, in this final section of the chapter, a few aggregate organizations that gather professionals who share concern for quality media for children.

The World Summit on Media for Children. Every three years, this organization brings together representatives of the media industry, public organizations, educators, activists, and scholars to discuss, among other issues, policy recommendations that encourage quality programming and cultural diversity. It also puts forward initiatives and policies that advance opportunities for children's voices to be heard.[31]

UNICEF (The United Nations Children's Fund), discussed above, is another key international organization that promotes communication for development of marginalized and vulnerable children. Applying an integrated approach, *Communicating with Children* is a recent example of UNICEF's efforts. This resource package is intended for use by those interested in promoting communication for and with children, including producers, educators, caregivers, health professionals, and policymakers.[32] This initiative is but the most recent in a long tradition of field involvement in training interventions in many low-resource countries with a view to communicating effectively and positively with children via many forms of media – from traditional to digital – in the name of advancing children's wellbeing. UNICEF also led an initiative to create a resource guide for journalists on the protection of children's rights to be used when, for example, they are given an opportunity to speak in news coverage in the media.[33] A final example is the UNICEF-led attempt to advance a global agenda for children's rights in the digital age.[34]

The International Clearinghouse on Children, Youth, and Media. This was established by UNESCO in 1997 to advance the UN convention on the rights of children. The Clearinghouse, housed at the University of Gothenburg in Sweden,[35] serves as a network for collecting and sharing knowledge about issues related to media and children, via regular newsletters and thematic yearbooks that are distributed worldwide. Several regional networking initiatives with similar missions are also in place.

The *Prix Jeunesse* is an international festival and gathering, sponsored by Germany's Bavarian Broadcasting Corporation, that holds competitive screenings of the work by professionals from a wide variety of countries. Aside from these biennial meetings convened in Munich, Germany since 1964, the *Prix Jeunesse*[36] also conducts many training sessions around the world for producers of quality media for children, develops guidelines for the treatment of special topics (e.g., conflict and war; gender and diversity equality; use of humor and emotions) and distributes a professional magazine in English on a variety of relevant topics. All these initiatives are part of their efforts to provide ongoing training for producers around the world to ensure quality in children's media.

The *Japan Prize*[37] for educational television in Tokyo is sponsored by the Japan Broadcasting Corporation NHK and has been a showcase for quality television programs since its establishment in 1965. Its aim is to improve the quality of programs around the world and to contribute to the development and fostering of international understanding and cooperation. Participants meet annually in Tokyo to compete for awards and to learn from each other.

The Center on Media and Child Health[38] (CMCH) is affiliated with Boston Children's Hospital and Harvard University Medical School and focuses on media's effects on children's health and wellbeing. It provides accessible information on current and past research in the field, distributes newsletters, responds to parental queries and concerns, and promotes awareness of these issues in a variety of public forums. It also supports original research on media and health.

Other organizations include a variety of health associations in the USA, such as the American Academy of Pediatrics (AAP) and the American Psychological Association (APA). They have passed resolutions, written reports, and issued statements that recommend practices regarding children's media use, parental practices, as well as declarations about the media's potential negative implications for children's health. Examples include the proposal by the American Academy of Pediatrics to restrict early age exposure to screens and the warning issued by the American Psychological Association (APA) about the sexualization of girls in the media. These and similar statements regarding violence, pornography, advertising, and social networking have fueled a great deal of controversy and public discourse. Overall, their recommendations (1) endorse media education programs for children, parents, and health providers of children; (2) call for a limit on the time children spend with media and the type of content they consume; (3) propose that caregivers play a more active role in mediating children's media experiences; (4) recommend use of technology to monitor and intervene in media use; (5) suggest keeping children's bedrooms free of electronic media so they cannot be used unsupervised; and (6) strongly recommend avoidance of screen media for children under the age of two years.[39] The most common critique of these recommendations, offered generally by researchers, is that they are often not evidence based and are too quick to offer sweeping judgments without adequate research support. Such, for example, is the critique of their introduction of the term *Facebook depression* that triggered significant public interest but which was not accompanied by research evidence.[40]

Again, these are just a few examples of the wide range of organizations active throughout the world and dedicated to promoting their point of view with regard to the relationship between children and media. Overall, these efforts can be summarized as follows: First, while some base their claims and/or recommendations on solid research, others are more ideological in nature. Second, they operate on a variety of financial models, each with its own strength and emphases. Indeed, maintaining their momentum is not an easy task, as they are often driven by the energy and dedication of a main leader, and suffer from shortage of funding and lack of stability and continuity. Third, their activities include lobbying efforts to effect policy change, mobilization of public opinion, awareness raising and informational sessions with industry professionals, educating children, parents and educational systems, organizing campaigns and boycotts, as well as providing consulting services.[41]

Examples of the increasing number and range of initiatives advanced by activist organizations and policymakers include, on the one hand, campaigns to restrict media use by individuals and families and, on the other, a broad array of online resources to manage media in everyday life as well as to provide tools for accomplishing this goal. In this light, a very different type of campaign was launched in March 2013: The National Day of Unplugging sought to raise awareness, globally, of individual and social choices for media avoidance practices. Such forms of resistance to new technologies indicate the ambivalence with which many families deal with the role media have in their lives.[42] While the resistance phenomenon is limited in scope, it nevertheless sheds an important light on concerns shared by numerous families around the world regarding media and their quest to have better control over children's media use.

Finally, growing numbers of academic researchers around the world dedicate their professional work to the field of children and media relations. One major development has been the creation of sub-groups of research in the field. For example, the Children, Adolescents and Media (CAM) Division of The International Communication Association (ICA) meets annually, to share new research, as well as to discuss issues related to pedagogy and policy.[43] A similar interest group has been established within the European Communication Research and Education Association (ECREA). New research as well as reviews and commentary on related topics are published quarterly in the *Journal of Children and Media*.[44] The USA-based National Association for Media Literacy Education (NAMLE) convenes conferences and publishes an academic journal.[45] More broadly, several institutions around the world have established research centers, support scholarly study, and offer taught courses at both the undergraduate and graduate level on various topics related to children and media. Furthermore, scholars are often called to provide expert testimony before legislators and governmental committees worldwide, and often receive requests to be interviewed in media outlets in order to provide advice to parents and educators. Public, academic, and home libraries are accumulating more and more publications in this area. Indeed, increasingly, scholars, myself included, see ourselves as *engaged academics*, meaning that we believe that translating academic knowledge into tools for social change is one of our chief roles as scholars. We contribute to the development of media literacy initiatives, train professionals, educate new generations of students and researchers, and advocate for evidence-based policy change.

Some scholars make it a point to have their voice heard in the media, often to counter the tendency of journalistic coverage to look for causal relationships between media and effects, to over-emphasize negative effects, to sensationalize isolated extreme cases, and to feed one-sided *moral panic* claims, referred to in Chapter 4. Indeed, the need to train academics to talk to the media in accessible ways, and to educate journalists in responsible and evidence-based reporting, has been echoed in many academic circles in recent years. This need goes hand in hand with a call for a dialogic approach to public engagement with science, which recognizes the role public opinion has on setting agendas for policy and research.[46] Clearly, the dissemination of research created by the scientific communities needs to be a high priority.

There are many challenges facing academics eager to build bridges in order to achieve such goals. Different stakeholders – be they state related (e.g., governments, policymakers, regulatory bodies); market related (e.g., media industries and companies); civil society (e.g., non-governmental and non-profit organizations); or the public-at-large (e.g., families, educators, caregivers) – occupy different professional *habitats*, each with different agendas, priorities, professional norms, work-styles and jargon. For example, relationships between academics and media industry professionals have been described as the work of "turtles and peacocks."[47] Academics (as well as non-profit organizations) are perceived by the media industry to be slow and heavy like turtles. First, they take too much time to make decisions, to plan and execute research, not to mention the time taken to write up, publish, and distribute their studies. They do not understand the financial constraints of the media industry, and all too often their opposition is seen as a threat to creative freedom. Media professionals, for their part, are often perceived by academics to be arrogant, highly competitive and profit-driven peacocks, uncaring about the implications of their work. Such perceptions often contribute to an atmosphere of distrust and miscommunication which some of the organizations cited above try to dissipate by convening meetings with a wide range of people involved in the field of media and children.

At the same time, a number of collaborations of various forms do exist between interested parties. Collaborations between academics and various stakeholders develop in different ways. Sometimes research is initiated and sponsored by the stakeholder to address a specific question or need (e.g., a company studying the effectiveness of baby videos they produce on language acquisition). At other times research initiated in academic institutions is presented to the stakeholders (e.g., presenting to advertisers research findings about the relationship between images of women and poor body image of girls). And, in some unique cases, stakeholders and academics create a true partnership and collaborate in all aspects of the research project, from inception to application of results.[48] The UNICEF resource package described above is one such example.[49]

Thus, by all measures and criteria, the area of children and media is now a maturing field with work being undertaken in academia, advocacy, and interventions. While much is yet to be discovered, and certainly we are far from being able to prevent some of the non-desired implications of media use by children, there is a significant and growing body of scholarship to allow us to pose the right questions and to offer some meaningful answers. This accumulating body of knowledge needs to continue to feed into, if not guide, intervention efforts on behalf of children and youth, assist in evidence-based policy and advocacy initiatives, and inform the media industry on ways to maintain their business while keeping children's wellbeing in mind. Certainly, public discourse, too, fuels these efforts, often stimulated by concerns for harmful media effects, and a culture of anxiety over the changing nature of childhood. These debates often neglect to consider children's rights, including their communication rights as delineated in the UN Convention on the Rights of Children.[50] The Convention specifically refers to the need to advance children's rights, as well as to allow children and youth the opportunity to voice their concerns and to be taken seriously; to protect free speech and distribution of information; to maintain privacy; to develop cultural identity; and to be proud of one's heritage and beliefs. The convention, according to the UNICEF report mentioned above, offers a framework that can facilitate a discussion on the progress necessary for maximizing opportunities and minimizing harms associated with children's media use.[51]

Concluding Remarks

Many individuals and organizations are involved in advocacy for better media for children, as well as in attempts to develop policy and regulatory environments that best serve children's needs. However, as this chapter demonstrates, what is "best" for children is not an objective or agreed-upon set of rules and expectations. Such discussions are value driven, intellectually diverse, and culturally grounded. The many stakeholders in this field – media organizations, parents, educators, policymakers, NGOs, and the children themselves – are pulling and pushing the policy "blanket" in many different directions and often putting the responsibility for media use by children in the lap of each other. Corporate capital structures and interests around the globe are extremely hard to resist and overcome. Technology, itself, is a constantly moving target posing new challenges at an ever-increasing rate. Only strong collaborations among civically responsible stakeholders as well as major investment in the education of the consumers themselves – children and young people – can bring us closer to securing a better media environment for them.

Notes

1. Pecora, 2013.
2. Von Feilitzen & Bucht, 2001; Lustyik, 2013; Von Feilitzen & Carlsson, 2003.
3. Lisosky, 1997.
4. Alexander, Hoerrner, & Duke, 1998; Kunkel, 1998.
5. The discussion is based with modifications on Lesser, 1996; Kolucki & Lemish, 2011; Lauricella, Robb, & Wartella, 2013; Livingstone, forthcoming.
6. Kolucki & Lemish, 2011.
7. Jordan & Woodward, 1997; Kunkel, 1998.
8. Fred Rogers Center, 2011.
9. Lauricella, Robb, & Wartella, 2013, p. 429.
10. Aroldi, 2003; Blumler, 1992.
11. Kunkel & Wilcox, 2012.
12. Bryant, 2007; Jordan & Woodward, 1997; Lemish, 2010.
13. Lustyik, 2013.
14. Lisosky, 1997; Shipard, 2003.
15. Lustyik & Zanker, 2013.
16. Lustyik, 2013.

17. Ballard, 1995.
18. Edwards & Berman, 1995; Price, 1998; Price & Verhulst, 2002; Simpson, 2004.
19. Jordan & Gilmore, 2013.
20. Original guidelines have been re-ordered and slightly reworded.
21. The Convention on Television Broadcasting for Children and Youth was signed in July 2002 by representatives of all Israeli broadcasters for children and youth, in the Israeli Knesset (Parliament). It was initiated by the Israel Educational Television and written by Lemish, D., Damari, A., Limor, Y., and Segal, Z. It was reaffirmed in 2011.
22. Mendel & Salomon, 2011.
23. ANDI, 2012.
24. Lim, 2012.
25. Fuchs, 2011.
26. O'Neill, 2013.
27. Jordan & Gilmore, 2013.
28. boyd, Hargittai, Schultz, & Palfrey, 2011.
29. Montgomery, 2012.
30. Kunkel & Wilcox, 2012.
31. http://www.wsmcf.com/
32. Kolucki, 2013; Kolucki & Lemish, 2011 http://www.unicef.org/cwc/
33. UNICEF, 2005.
34. Livingstone & Bulger, 2013.
35. http://www.nordicom.gu.se/en/clearinghouse
36. http://www.prixjeunesse.de/
37. http://www.nhk.or.jp/jp-prize/english/
38. http://www.cmch.tv/
39. Evans, Schmidt, Bickham, Branner, & Rich, 2008.
40. Guernsey, 2014.
41. Trotta, 2012.
42. Rosenthal & Ribak, in progress.
43. http://community.icahdq.org/ohana/groups/details.cfm?id=3
44. http://www.tandfonline.com/toc/rchm20/current#.UiOo6z_OCSo
45. http://namle.net/
46. Buckingham, 2013.
47. Bouman, 2002.
48. Lemish, 2014.
49. Kolucki & Lemish, 2011.
50. United Nations, 1989.
51. Livingstone & Bulger, 2013, p. 5.

References

Alexander, A., Hoerrner, K., & Duke, L. (1998). What is quality children's television? *The Annals*, *557*(May), 70–82.

ANDI (2012). *The rights of children and the right to media: Strengthening convergences in legal frameworks and public policies*. Braśilia, Brazil: ANDI – Communication and Rights; Latin America Network. See http://www.andi.org.br/sites/default/files/I%26C_Ingles_SITE.pdf

Aroldi, P. (2003). Television and protection of minors in some European countries: A comparative study. In C. von Feilitzen & U. Carlsson (Eds.), *Promote or protect? Perspectives on media literacy and media regulations* (pp. 179–195). Göteborg University, Sweden: The International Clearinghouse on Children, Youth and Media.

Ballard, I.M. (1995). See no evil, hear no evil: Television violence and the first amendment. *Virginia Law Review, 81*, 175–185.

Blumler, J.G. (1992). *Television and the public interest: Vulnerable values in West European broadcasting.* London: Sage.

Bouman, M. (2002). Turtles and Peacocks: Collaboration in Entertainment—Education Television. *Communication Theory, 12*(2), 225–244.

boyd, d., Hargittai, E., Schultz, J., & Palfrey, J. (2011). Why parents help their children lie to Facebook about age: Unintended consequences of the "Children's Online Privacy Protection Act." *First Monday, 16*, 11.

Bryant, J.A. (Ed.). (2007). *The children's television community.* Ahwah, NJ: Lawrence Erlbaum Associates.

Buckingham, D. (2013). Representing audiences: Audience research, public knowledge and policy. *Communication Review, 16*(1–2), 51–60.

Center on Media and Child Health. (2013). See http://www.cmch.tv/. Retrieved July 25, 2014.

Edwards, H.T. & Berman, M.N. (1995). Regulating violence on television. *Northwestern University Law Review, 89*(4), 1487–1566.

Evans Schmidt, M., Bickham, D.S., Branner, A., & Rich, M. (2008).Media-related policies of professional health organizations. In S.L. Calvert & B.J. Wilson (Eds.), *The handbook of children, media, and development.* (pp. 503–526). Blackwell.

Fred Rogers Center for Early Learning and Children's Media (2011). *A statement on the development of a framework for quality digital media for young children.* Latrobe, PA: Saint Vincent College.

Fuchs, C. (2011). An alternative view of privacy on Facebook. *Information, 2*, 140–165.

Guernsey, L. (2014). Garbled in translation: Getting media research to the press and public. *Journal of Children and Media, 8*(1), 87–94.

Jordan, A.B. & Gilmore, J.S. (2013). Children and advertising policies in the US and beyond. In D. Lemish (Ed.), *The Routledge international handbook of children, adolescents, and media* (pp. 386–394). New York: Routledge.

Jordan, A.B. & Woodward, E.H. (1997). *The 1997 state of children's television report: Programming for children over broadcast and cable television.* University of Pennsylvania: The Annenberg Public Policy Center.

Kolucki, B. (2013). UNICEF and communication for development: An integrated approach to developing capacity to produce communication for and with children. In D. Lemish (Ed.), *The Routledge international handbook of children, adolescents, and media* (pp. 433–441). New York: Routledge.

Kolucki, B. & Lemish, D. (2011). *Communicating with children: Principles and practices to nurture, inspire, excite, educate and heal.* New York: Communication for Development Unit, UNICEF. See http://www.unicef.org/cwc.

Kunkel, D. (1998). Policy battles over defining children's educational television. *The Annals of the American Academy of Political and Social Science Special Issue: Children and Television, 557*, 39–53.

Kunkel, D. & Wilcox, B. (2012). Children and media policy: Historical perspectives and current practices. In D.G. Singer & J.L. Singer (Eds.), *Handbook of children and the media* (pp. 569–594). Thousand Oaks, CA: Sage Publications.

Lauricella, A.R., Robb, M.B., & Wartella, E. (2013). Challenges and suggestions for deter-mining quality in children's media. In D. Lemish (Ed.), *The Routledge international handbook of children, adolescents, and media* (pp. 425–432). New York: Routledge.

Lemish, D. (2010). *Screening gender on children's television: The views of producers around the world.* London: Routledge.

Lemish, D. (2014). Audience transformations and social integration: Building bridges and making a real difference in the world – Report of the WG4 dialogue with stakeholders. In G. Patriarche, H. Bilandzic, N. Carpentier, C. Ponte, K.C. Schrøder *et al.* (Eds.), *Building bridges: Pathways to a greater societal significance for audience research* (pp. 131–136). EU: COST. http://www.cost.eu

Lemish, D., Damari, A., Limor, Y., and Segal, Z. (2009). Convention on television broad-casting for children and youth: A case study of academic-professional collaboration in Israel. *Communication Research Trends, 28*(3), 31–32.

Lesser, G.S. (1996). Programmes for young children. Paper presented at the EBU workshop, Montreal.

Lim, S.S. (2012). Regulatory initiatives for managing online risks and opportunities for youths – the East Asian experience. In M. Wakrave (Ed.), *e-Youth: Balancing between opportunities and risks?* (pp. 271–290). Brussels: Peter Lang.

Lisosky, J.M. (1997). Controlling children's channels: Comparing children's television policies in Australia, Canada, and the United States. PhD dissertation, University of Washington.

Livingstone, S. (forthcomingh). What does good look like? Developing great online content for kids. *Children's media yearbook 2014.*

Livingstone, S. & Bulger, M. (2013). *A global agenda for children's rights in the digital age: Recommendations for developing UNICEF's research strategy.* New York: UNICEF.

Lustyik, K. (2013). Media regulation: The protection and promotion of home-grown chil-dren's television. In D. Lemish (Ed.), *The Routledge international handbook of children, adolescents, and media* (pp. 378–385). New York: Routledge.

Lustyik, K. & Zanker, R. (2013). Is there local content on television for children today? In A.N. Valdivia & S.R. Mazzarella (Eds.), *The international encyclopedia of media studies. Vol. 3: Content and representation* (pp. 179–202). Oxford, UK: Blackwell.

Mendel, T. & Salomon, E. (2011). *The regulatory environment for broadcasting: An interna-tional best practice survey for Brazilian stakeholders.* Braśilia, Brazil: UNESCO & Ford Foundation. http://unesdoc.unesco.org/images/0019/001916/191622e.pdf. Retrieved July 25, 2014.

Montgomery, K.C. (2012). Safeguards for youth in the digital marketing ecosystem. In D.G. Singer & J.L. Singer (Eds.), *Handbook of children and the media* (pp. 631–648). Thousand Oaks, CA: Sage Publications.

O'Neill, B. (2013). Internet policies: Online child protection and empowerment in a global context. In D. Lemish (Ed.), *The Routledge international handbook of children, adoles-cents, and media* (pp. 395–402). New York: Routledge.

Pecora, N. (2013). Media policies for children: Issues and histories in the US. In D. Lemish (Ed.), *The Routledge international handbook of children, adolescents, and media* (pp. 371–377). New York: Routledge.

Price, M.E. (Ed.). (1998). *The V-Chip debate: Content filtering from television to the Internet.* Mahwah, NJ: Lawrence Erlbaum.

Price, M.E. & Verhulst, S.G. (Eds.). (2002). *Parental control of television broadcasting.* Mahwah, NJ: Lawrence Erlbaum.

Rosenthal, M. & Ribak, R. (in progress). *Media ambivalence in everyday life.* Boston: MIT (under contract).

Simpson, B. (2004). *Children and television.* New York: Continuum.

Shipard, S. (2003). A brief look at the regulation in Australia: A co-regulatory approach. In C. von Feilitzen & U. Carlsson (Eds.), *Promote or protect? Perspectives on media literacy and media regulations* (pp. 237–241). Göteborg University: The International Clearinghouse on Children, Youth and Media.

Trotta, L. (2012). Children's advocacy groups: A history and analysis. In D.G. Singer & J.L. Singer (Eds.), *Handbook of children and the media* (pp. 697–714). Thousand Oaks, CA: Sage Publications.

UNICEF (2005). The media and children's rights. http://www.unicef.org/ceecis/The_Media_ and_Children_Rights_2005.pdf. Retrieved September 1, 2013.

United Nations (1989). Text of the UN Convention on the Rights of the Child. http://www. un.org/documents/ga/res/44/a44r025.htm. Retrieved July 25, 2014.

Von Feilitzen, C. & Bucht, C. (2001). *Outlooks on children and media.* Göteborg University, Sweden: The International Clearinghouse on Children, Youth and Media.

Von Feilitzen, C. & Carlsson, U. (Eds.). (2003). *Promote or protect? Perspectives on media literacy and media regulations.* Göteborg University: The International Clearinghouse on Children, Youth and Media.

Conclusions
Growing Up with Media

Throughout this book we have seen how media are integrated into children's everyday lives and the many roles they play in their family, social, and leisure activities. We reviewed media's interaction with children's growth and wellbeing, and the implications of that interaction for cognitive development, learning, behavior, health, perceptions of self and social reality, and social relationships. We noted that children seem to be navigating their "on" and "off" lives smoothly, and that almost all aspects of virtual experiences are just as concrete and real for them as the non-mediated ones. We noted the exponential growth in the consumption of mobile media and the formidable challenges that this shift poses to the nature of childhood, scholarship, media content, and parental mediation. With the proliferation of personal portable devices, owned and used by children and young people, and the flourishing market that provides their contents – apps, games, social media platforms – children and media are constantly on the move. All this led us to ask complicated questions regarding the consequences of this accumulated knowledge for education for media literacy, as well as for media policy and advocacy for children. We pointed out, consistently, that many questions still remain open for further intellectual engagement, academic research, and civic activism. This is an intriguing field that challenges what we know about children and stimulates our imagination as to what childhoods might look like in the not too distant future.

Furthermore, we have demonstrated how in many countries around the world media activists and educators have sought to confront the consequences of children's media use in two central ways: first, attempts to educate children, teachers, parents, and others to be literate, selective, and critical media users; and, second, attempts to supervise, regulate, and control the media. Media education curricula, as well as

Children and Media: A Global Perspective, First Edition. Dafna Lemish.
© 2015 John Wiley & Sons, Inc. Published 2015 by John Wiley & Sons, Inc.
Companion Website: www.wiley.com/go/lemish/childrenandmedia

specific media policies and regulations, are the result of the variety of unique characteristics particular to each society. However, all efforts and social struggles are anchored in the recognition that young people have complex relationships with media, just as adults do, and it is our duty to pay attention to media just as we should pay attention to all of the other central socializing agents in children's lives. At the same time, many inherent conflicts are involved in intervention attempts, including: the conflict with such basic rights as freedom of speech and protecting children's rights; the tension between paternalistic and liberal approaches to child rearing; the tension between high and popular culture in the education of the young; and the lack of agreement on the appropriate balance between "knowledge" and "pleasure" involved in media experiences and between "opportunities" and "harm." There is also a tendency by different stakeholders to divert responsibility for children's media education and behavior: the school system places it on parents and the media industry; parents claim that schools and the media industry are responsible; and the media industry argues that they are only responsible for providing opportunities, and that schools and parents need to assist children to make the most of them.

In the yet to be foreseen future, academic, educational, policy, and advocacy efforts may become engaged with new concerns given emerging trends, such as: *open skies* (an international policy concept that calls for the liberalization of the rules and regulations of the international broadcast and satellite industry); growth of global commercial corporations and the expansion of the number and variety of media alternatives available to children; convergence of communication technologies; growth of interactive media; and improvement of reception and production qualities. Furthermore, as the ability to control content available to children becomes more limited, so may there be increased demands that stakeholders develop ways to empower young people themselves as critical media prosumers. There may also be a more urgent and significant rise in public demand for self-regulation by producers of media content and delivery systems.

The Changing Nature of Childhood

One of the central aspects of the discussion of the processes of globalization with regard to the construction of reality and youth culture focuses on the claim encapsulated in the concept of the *disappearance of childhood*, inspired by technological determinists.[1] The disappearance of childhood, or as more critical writers would say, the changing of its nature, was understood originally as a process stimulated by television's central role in children's lives. According to this perspective, childhood, as a social construction, is a by-product of the print era and the gradual need to separate children from the world of adults in order to prepare them to function in a print-culture world in which reading and writing skills are central. Prior to the invention of print in the fifteenth century, followed by the gradual development of modern Western enlightenment, children were not perceived as a unique group of people deserving special attention. They were regarded as physically small people who had no specific needs or rights of their own. The development of print culture brought with it, among other things, the institution of the school as well as growing interest in children, the need to legally protect them (e.g., by setting laws in many – but not all – countries that protect them from labor and sexual exploitation, as well as establishing mandatory education for certain age groups), and the formation of professional fields of expertise related to the education of children, their health, their mental and cognitive development, culture, fashion, and leisure. According to this view, the twentieth century represents the golden age of the recognition and protection of childhood.

However, also according to this approach (which is highly Anglo-Euro-centric, as it focuses on North American, European, and colonialist history), media, and television in particular, gradually eroded this protection. Through television, as we have already discussed, children are exposed to the world of adults; a world that was largely concealed from them in earlier modern times for the purpose of protecting them from sensitive domains of life, for which they were perceived to be too immature to handle, such as: death and disasters, physical and mental sicknesses, sexual intimacy, and the evil nature of some of human life. The argument goes that all these realities have been revealed to them via the television screen: sexual acts, exploding bodies, atrocities, and hunger – all at the push of a button. Thus, rather than their discovering the realities of the world in a gradual manner as they grow up, such developments mean that children share a world without protective walls. In other words, this approach claims that the medium of television and its content deprive children of a naive childhood and of the gradual process necessary for healthy mental development. Furthermore, the television world that exposes adults at their weaknesses – meanness, intrigues, crime, injustices, dangers, insecurities – undermines parental authority and the basic trust in adults as knowledgeable and responsible people who can guard children from harm. As a result, so goes the argument, children grow up with distrust, hopelessness, and an absence of boundaries. The social knowledge that children acquire from hours of watching television, as well as the values and perspectives they internalize, are frequently in contradiction with the ideals and myths that traditional socializing systems seek to cultivate. The disappearance of childhood is, therefore, a threat not only to children and the construction of childhood as a period of life, but also to human society as a whole.

The blurring of traditional social constructions of childhood and adulthood has been attributed, to a large extent, to the technological changes and virtual worlds that have freed children from constraints of mobility, parental control, and lack of economic independence. Indeed, it appears that the advent of the internet and mobile media have breathed new life into the *disappearance of childhood* thesis. The glorification of youth culture that media advance, proponents of the thesis argue, also encourages children to rush into adolescence, and make adults strive to preserve their youth. Both groups try to belong to that seemingly "ideal" age of youth: an age of attractiveness and adventure; sexual blossoming and romance; when interesting life stories supposedly happen; and when the media open up for youth seemingly endless possibilities. This is not necessarily an age defined by specific years, but more an abstract concept. Attempts to blur different periods of life can be observed through fashion, musical tastes, forms of leisure, speech styles, as well as preferences for television programs, personalized social network pages, and choice of mobile phone applications. The focus on this period in life – at the expense of the period of adulthood characterized by maturity, life experience, accumulated knowledge, and wisdom – is also typical of much of the culture around technological innovations, and the idolizing of brilliant young computer wizards who become famous multimillionaires, seemingly overnight.

The disappearance of childhood hypothesis and its various off-shoots have received a great amount of public and academic exposure, accompanied by lively debates. Many are attracted by what appears to be a commonsense approach, and find that it resonates with their own experiences. Others argue, in contrast, that external attempts to join adulthood through accessories and makeup, mining Wikipedia, or online flirtatious exchanges are not necessarily an indication of serious psychological changes and maturing mindsets. At the same time, the fact that adults wear T-shirts with favorite cartoon figures and post jokes on Facebook is no proof that they are childish or that they do not apply their many years of experience in handling their own life affairs. Furthermore, there is no evidence that heavy exposure to screen content fundamentally transforms processes such as childish egocentrism or the ability to distinguish between reality and fantasy. Nor is there evidence that children with heavy online presence are more emotionally mature than those who are lighter users due to their accumulated exposure to the adults' world. If anything, some critics of this thesis argue, it seems that childhoods in the Anglo-European world seem to be dragging on longer than before, especially as increasing numbers of young people live with their parents during their college years and beyond, and remain financially and emotionally dependent on them well into their mid-twenties, if not beyond. Such trends have stimulated academic discussion of what constitutes "adolescence" and whether there is a need to construct a new life-stage of "later-adolescence" or "early-adulthood" that relates to this period of life as distinctively different from adolescence and adulthood.

Children in all societies and throughout history were always smaller, weaker, less developed, and less experienced than adults, regardless of whether they lived with or without television, the internet, or a tablet. Furthermore, children have always required care and supervision, with or without these devices. A different line of critique suggests that even before the new media era children found ways to "peek" into adults' worlds of secrets, through eavesdropping on conversations, following older siblings, reading adult books, and just being physically present in tight living arrangements. In addition, the assumption that children are better off staying ignorant about the physical, social, and emotional world of adults, too, is debatable. Perhaps it is better for children's wellbeing and healthy development to challenge adults' monopoly of knowledge, to have an opportunity to have a say about the world in which they exist, and to take an active part in making it a better place for themselves and others.

Despite the growing number of researchers who devise, employ, and advocate ways that allow young people to express their own voices – that is, to listen closely to the views of the "subjects" they study – we still do not know much about how children and youth feel about this, or, for that matter, how they feel about many other media-related debates. This observation has theoretical and methodological implications, and, as some argue, moral dimensions. The fundamental claim is that children have their own experiences and perspectives, and we need to hear their point of view, stated in their own words, without necessarily assuming a judgmental stance. In doing so, we need not only examine children's perceptions and analyze them in comparison with our adult values and assumptions, but also to refrain from employing criteria that judge their behaviors in terms of right or wrong.

Thus, the dynamic discussion of the meaning of "childhood" continues with the growing concern for children's rights and the claim that each child should be perceived as a creative and autonomous person in their own right, one entitled to voice their own perspective – whatever their stage of development. Concomitantly, media are expected to bolster the process of children and youth's empowerment in the third millennium by providing them with access, interactive technologies, and creative production skills. Accordingly, the expectation is that children throughout the world will become more active creators, as well as, consumers of culture.

Research Involvement in the Debate

Research, too, is embracing both the changing technologies and the public agenda that follows from such changes. Also, intrigued by the forces of globalization, some researchers at the turn of the millennium engaged in multinational projects examining children's culture around the world. Studies of the unprecedented commercial success of the *Pokémon* phenomenon in various countries (with its television series, movies, computer games, cards, toys, and ancillary products) are one such example.[2] Studies of the global audiences of the *Disney* culture phenomenon that has dominated children's culture for many decades (with its movies, theme parks, and thriving industry of related products) represent another impressive effort at examining the similarities and differences in the reception of media products worldwide.[3] These groundbreaking projects have been followed by other multinational projects including the leading *EU Kids Online* network of researchers,[4] and the UNICEF resource package of *Communicating with Children*.[5]

What these and other studies demonstrate, among other things, is that side by side with globalization forces, we are also witness to the opposite axis of fragmentation of media use, tailored by individual needs and tastes. This has stimulated a complementary line of research, investigating individual children's everyday life experiences through small-case, ethnographic studies. Examples of such studies include that of a researcher who gathered together a handful of adolescents in the urban east coast of the USA to share their everyday learning experiences while growing up with television[6]; or the in-depth case study of youth in four global cities - Johannesburg (South Africa), Bangalore (India), Munich (Germany), and New York (United States) - who discussed how they negotiated their identities around experiences with both transnational as well as local media.[7]

Between these two ends of a research continuum that spans large multinational studies to in-depth, ethnographic case studies sit the majority of research projects. These employ a variety of methodologies – experiments, surveys, focus groups, interviews, observations, employment of art work, life-histories, and occasionally a combination of several methods in deductive as well as inductive approaches. As a result, we can say that research in the field of media and children has expanded its reach from laboratories and classrooms to bedrooms, playgrounds, cybercafés, and shopping malls. All of these studies are conducted in the hope of enriching our understanding of what it means to grow up today in a technologically saturated environment, one which some researchers prefer to call the *mediascape*.[8]

But as media continue to evolve and change, so should our research questions and methods of studying them. For example, *transmedia* content organized across multi-platforms of media, toys, games, accessories, cloths, and bedroom furnishings challenges us to explore how each element is making a unique and valuable contribution to the whole experience of the child,[9] be it the *Harry Potter, Star Wars*, or *Disney Princesses* cultural phenomena. New interactive modes of consuming traditional and new media require that researchers expand and combine their use of a variety of methods of inquiry. These new research demands are pushing scholars to reflect on potential challenges to their assumptions and on the theoretical underpinnings of both empirical research and the discourses in which children and media relations are discussed.

Furthermore, as some of my colleagues working with the most vulnerable and marginalized children constantly remind me, we should not ignore the continuing, deep inequalities in children's lives and opportunities worldwide. Millions of children have never owned a book of their own, not to mention a tablet or a games console. Even within the most resource-rich countries, we constantly have to ask ourselves who is excluded from the vivid participatory culture and who is marginalized within it? In most neoliberal societies, as the rich of this world get richer and the poor get poorer, studying the role of Facebook on identity formation or the effects of gaming on problem-solving skills are questions of the very privileged. The use of media to promote education, hygiene, or comfort for traumatized children is a more burning and relevant question. Thus, we should remind ourselves that even our research questions or, perhaps better stated, especially our research questions, should be culturally situated and context sensitive.

Neither Good nor Bad

We have repeatedly emphasized throughout this book that in examining media experiences we have to consider the interactions among the three big "Cs:" the Child, the Content of the media, and the Context in which media are integrated.

- *Child*: Age is a significant indicator of children's possible relationships with media, as it points to many of the changes that may take place in children's lives as they mature. More specifically, development of cognitive, emotional, social, and behavioral skills, as well as the accumulated everyday experience with both mediated and unmediated reality, all interact as the child grows, develops, and matures. Gender, understood to be a socially constructed set of identities and expectations, is also a central predictor of the nature of many of the child's relationships with media and is strongly entangled with the nature of those experiences. However, it is a child's unique personality, characteristics, and needs that matter most.

- The *Content* of media experiences is, as we have seen, as diverse and rich with possibilities as part of life itself. It is not the amount of time spent with media alone that needs to be considered in attempting to evaluate the centrality of media in children's lives, but rather the diverse forms, contents, and opportunities offered by media worldwide and the nature of the interaction they elicit.
- The *Context* within which childhood is constructed and the individual child is situated is crucial to our understanding of the diversity and complexity of the roles media play in children's lives: family and peers, culture and social structures, religion and political systems – neither media nor children exist outside of their particular contexts.

Thus, we can never talk about the fourth C – the potential for *Consequences* of media experiences – independently of the *Child*, the *Content*, or the *Context*.

So is it good or bad that children are constantly "on"? Is it fostering an inability to relax, to handle boredom, to look inward, to suspend gratification, or is it keeping them constantly stimulated, restless, eager, and unsatisfied with the moment? Is it empowering, encouraging creativity, widening horizons, expanding social participation? Probably both, in different proportions, for different children, in different circumstances, and at different times. This conclusion brings to mind a heavily quoted maxim from early communication research in 1948: "Some kinds of communication on some kinds of issues, brought to the attention of some kinds of people under some kinds of conditions, have some kinds of effects."[10] I was in graduate school when I was introduced to this article, and chose to quote it in my comprehensive general PhD examinations as one of the ten articles that most influenced my thinking at that early stage of my scholarship. We have come a long way since then in understanding that our experiences with media are not linear but multi-dimensional, and that "effects" do not flow from the media to the audiences but are interactive and negotiated. Some scholars, including myself, shy away from using the term "effects" and instead talk about "roles," "consequences," or "influences." However, the basic truth remains: We cannot generalize about the place of media in children's lives universally; rather, we need to consider "some kinds" of communication, "some kinds" of content, "some kinds" of children, "some kinds" of conditions, in order to say anything meaningful and reliable about the consequences of these experiences beyond the individual child. This is, indeed, a complicated story.

In the fall of 2013 the American Academy of Pediatrics published an updated policy statement entitled "Children, Adolescents, and the Media"[11] that attracted media attention worldwide and stirred public and scholarly debate, including among academics specializing in this disciplinary area. There was not much new in this statement – except perhaps the urgency with which it was framed, given evidence on the exponential growth of media use in the early years. The policy mainly reiterates the concern for causal negative effects, distinguishes between "good" and "bad" media content, treats media exposure as an indication of potential problems, and calls for pediatricians to take an active role in recommending a healthy use of media, just as they would for a healthy diet, immunization, or exercise. The health-oriented framing of the discussion is in and of itself an interesting illustration of the complex and multifaceted nature of the phenomena under discussion, and how different frames of reference can bring to light different aspects of children's relationship with media. This *medicalization frame*, for example, does not ask children for their views or opinions as, clearly, they are presumed to lack the knowledge of what's best for them and the maturity to act responsibly. Another favorite frame is that of the *media diet*, according to which there are good and bad mental "foods" and it is adults' role to ingrain in their children the lifelong adoption of a healthy media diet that will promote their wellbeing. I use this frame often in my own encounters with the media and the public, as it seems to be an easy way to convey a very simple message: adults have a responsibility to offer children a healthy cultural environment, just as they do a nutritious one. Yet culture is a lot more complicated than food, argue many, and framing media interaction in this way is too limiting and simplistic in scope.

Regardless of the frame of discussion chosen, the question of whether media are "good or bad" for children seems to be an entirely irrelevant and even misdirected question. There is no doubt that media are a constantly evolving and wonderful part of children's lives. Do media also have some potentially negative influences on children? Of course they do, as all life experiences might. Are children today more creative and active, more social and engaged, more informed and entertained than they were ever before? Or are they over-stimulated, excitement driven, disconnected from those around them, unable to look inward and handle boredom and personal reflection? Blaming the media for society's ills has proven to be a too narrow-minded and over-simplistic understanding of the complexity of our relationships with technologies. At the same time, blindly celebrating their empowering and liberating character is just as misguided. Thus, many will argue that it is not an "either/or" question, but probably a mixture of both, depending on the Child, the Content, the Context…

Edward R. Murrow, a famous American broadcast journalist gave a speech in Chicago on October 15, 1958. He was referring to television at the time when he said: "This instrument can teach, it can illuminate; yes, and it can even inspire. But it can do so only to the extent that humans are determined to use it to those ends. Otherwise it is merely wires and lights in a box."[12] In recalling Murrow's famous statement, we are reminded that we are responsible for the wise use of media in order to maximize their potential for children's wellbeing and fulfillment and to minimize their potential for harmful consequences.

This book is being written at a time of dynamic transition in the scholarly world of children and media, as we move from a dominant television-focused body of work to the much younger but booming field of media convergence, mobility, and virtuality. This is a time of significant transformations to an unknown future. Over half a decade of studying media and children has taught us that emerging and new media quickly become the mainstream media and new technologies become older technologies. They bring with them unpredictable and unintended consequences, unexpected forms of commercialization and exploitation, but also a wealth of opportunities and possibilities. We can conclude, therefore, that the many current changes taking place in screen culture, combined with the changing construction of childhood, present us with a series of challenges in a variety of areas, including academic, moral, educational, cultural, and political. We will continue to face them not only as students and researchers of media but also as parents and citizens concerned with the wellbeing of our children worldwide.

An age-old *Bird in the Hand* fable tells the story of a young adolescent who challenged a wise man in his village. Facing him with a bird held firmly in his closed hands, the youth asked the wise man: "Is it alive or dead?" To this the wise man, appreciating the challenge, responded: "The answer lies in your hands."

Can media be good and/or bad for children? The answer lies in our hands.

Notes

1. Meyrowitz, 1996; Postman, 1979.
2. Tobin, 2004.
3. Wasko, Phillips, & Meehan, 2001.
4. Livingstone, Haddon, Görzig, & Ólafsson, 2011.
5. Kolucki & Lemish, 2011.
6. Fisherkeller, 2002.
7. McMillin & Fisherkeller, 2009.
8. Appadurai, 1996.
9. Jenkins, 2006.
10. Berelson, 1948, p. 172.
11. American Academy of Pediatrics, 2013.
12. Murrow, 1958.

References

American Academy of Pediatrics (2013). Policy statement: Children, adolescents, and the media. *Pediatrics, 132*(5), 958–961.

Appadurai, A. (1996). *Modernity at large: Cultural dimensions of globalization.* Minneapolis: University of Minnesota Press.

Berelson, B. (1948). Communication and public opinion. In W. Schramm (Ed.), *Communications in modern society: Fifteen studies of the mass media* (pp. 167–185). Urbana: University of Illinois Press.

Fisherkeller, J. (2002). *Growing up with television: Everyday learning among young adolescents.* Philadelphia, PA: Temple University Press.

Jenkins, H. (2006). *Convergence culture: Where old and new media collide*. New York: New York University Press.

Kolucki, B. & Lemish, D. (2011). *Communicating with children: Principles and practices to nurture, inspire, excite, educate and heal*. New York: Communication for Development Unit, UNICEF. See http://www.unicef.org/cwc.

Livingstone, S., Haddon, L., Görzig, A., & Ólafsson, K. (2011). *EU Kids Online II: Final report*. LSE, London: EU Kids Online. www.eukidsonline.net. Retrieved July 25, 2014.

McMillin, D. & Fisherkeller, J. (2009). Local identities in globalized regions: Teens, everyday life, and television. *Popular Communication: The International Journal of Media and Culture, 7*(4), 231–251.

Meyrowitz, J. (1996). Taking McLuhan and "medium theory" seriously: Technological change and the evolution of education. In S.T. Kerr (Ed.), *Technology and the future of schooling* (pp. 73–110). Chicago, IL: The University of Chicago Press.

Murrow, E. (15 October, 1958). http://www.pbs.org/wnet/americanmasters/education/lesson39_organizer1.html. Retrieved July 25, 2014.

Postman, N. (1979). The first curriculum: Comparing school and television. *Phi Delta Kappan, November*, 163–168.

Tobin J. (Ed.). (2004). *Pikachu's global adventure: Making sense of the rise and fall of Pokémon* (pp. 165–186). Durham, NC: Duke University Press.

Wasko, J., Phillips, M., & Meehan, E.R. (Eds.). (2001). *Dazzled by Disney?: A global Disney audiences project*. London: Leicester University Press.

References

Aarsand, P. (2013). Children's digital gaming cultures. In D. Lemish (Ed.), *The Routledge international handbook of children, adolescents, and media* (pp. 120–126). New York: Routledge.

Agger, B. (2013). *Texting toward utopia: Kids, writing, and resistance*. Boulder & London: Paradigm Publishers.

Aidman, A. (1999). Disney's Pocahontas: Conversations with Native American and Euro-American girls. In S.R. Mazzarella & N.O. Pecora (Eds.), *Growing up girls: Popular culture and the construction of identity* (pp.133–159). New York: Peter Lang.

Al Qurashy, F. (2008). Role of the family in forming the rational interaction with mass media: A case study of a Saudi Family. In U. Carlsson, S. Tayle, G. Jacquinot-Delaunay, & J.M. Perez Tornero (Eds.), Empowerment through media education: An intercultural dialogue, (pp. 225–234). Göteborg University, Sweden: The International Clearinghouse on Children, Youth and Media.

Alexander, A., Hoerrner, K., & Duke, L. (1998). What is quality children's television? *The Annals, 557*(May), 70–82.

Alexander, A., Sallayanne Rayan, M., & Munoz, P. (1984). Creating a learning context: Investigations on the interaction of siblings during television viewing. *Critical Studies in Mass Communication, 1*(4), 358, 446–453.

Algan, E. (2011). Being read by a DJL Youth interaction via radio and cell phones in Southeast Turkey. In C. von Feilitizen, U. Carlsson, & C. Bucht (Eds.), *New questions, new insights, new approaches: Contributions to the research forum at the World Summit on Media for Children and Youth 2010* (pp. 251–260). Göteborg University, Sweden: The International Clearinghouse on Children, Youth and Media.

Alper, M. (2013). Children and convergence culture: New perspectives on youth participation with media. In D. Lemish (Ed.), *The Routledge international handbook of children, adolescents, and media* (pp. 148–155). New York: Routledge.

Children and Media: A Global Perspective, First Edition. Dafna Lemish.
© 2015 John Wiley & Sons, Inc. Published 2015 by John Wiley & Sons, Inc.
Companion Website: www.wiley.com/go/lemish/childrenandmedia

American Academy of Pediatrics (2003). Prevention of pediatric overweight and obesity. *Pediatrics, 112*, 424–30.

American Academy of Pediatrics (2013). Policy statement: Children, adolescents, and the media. *Pediatrics, 132*(5), 958–961.

American Psychological Association. (2007). Report of the APA on the sexualization of girls. http://www.apa.org/pi/wpo/sexualization.html. Retrieved July 25, 2014.

Anderson, C.A., Gentile, D.A., & Dill, K.E. (2012). Prosocial, antisocial, and other effects of recreational video games. In D.G. Singer & J.L. Singer (Eds.), *Handbook of children and the media* (pp. 249–272). Thousand Oaks, CA: Sage Publications.

Anderson, C.A., Shibuya, A., Ihori, N., Swing, E.L., Bushman, B.J. *et al.* (2010). Violent video game effects on aggression, empathy, and prosocial behavior in Eastern and Western countries: A meta-analytic review. *Psychological Bulletin, 136*(2), 151–173.

Anderson, D. & Lorch, E.P. (1983). Looking at television: Action or reaction? In J. Bryant & D.R. Anderson (Eds.), *Children's understanding of television: Research on attention and comprehension* (pp. 1–33). New York: Academic Press.

Anderson, D.R. & Field, D.E. (1986). Children's attention to television: Implications for production. In M. Meyer (Ed.), *Children and the formal features of television* (pp. 56–96). Munich: K.G. Saur.

Anderson, D.R. & Pempek, T.A. (2005). Television and very young children. *The American Behavioral Scientist, 48*(5), 505–522.

ANDI (2012). *The rights of children and the right to media: Strengthening convergences in legal frameworks and public policies.* Brasília, Brazil: ANDI – Communication and Rights; Latin America Network http://www.andi.org.br/sites/default/files/I%26C_Ingles_SITE.pdf. Retrieved July 25, 2014.

Andreason, M.S. (2001). Evaluation in the family's use of television: An overview. In J. Bryant & J.A. Bryant (Eds.), *Television and the American family second edition* (pp. 3–30). Hillsdale, NJ: Lawrence Erlbaum.

Appadurai, A. (1996). *Modernity at large: Cultural dimensions of globalization.* Minneapolis: University of Minnesota Press.

Aroldi, P. (2003). Television and protection of minors in some European countries: A comparative study. In C. von Feilitzen & U. Carlsson (Eds.), *Promote or protect? Perspectives on media literacy and media regulations* (pp. 179–95). Göteborg University, Sweden: The International Clearinghouse on Children, Youth and Media.

Asamen, J.K. & Berry, G.L. (2012). Television, children, and multicultural awareness: Comprehending the medium in a complex multimedia society. In D.G. Singer & J.L. Singer (Eds.), *Handbook of children and the media* (pp. 363–378). Thousand Oaks, CA: Sage Publications.

Association of National Advertisers, Inc. (2000). *The Children's Advertising Review Unit.* Self -Regulatory Guidelines for Children's Advertising http://www.ftc.gov/privacy/safeharbor/caruselfreg.pdf. Retrieved August 31, 2013.

Atkin, C.K. (1980). Effects of television advertising on children. In E.L. Palmer & A. Dorr (Eds.), *Children and the faces of television: Teaching, violence, selling* (pp. 287–305). New York: Academic Press.

Austin, E.W. (2013). Processes and impacts of political socialization. In D. Lemish (Ed.), *The Routledge international handbook of children, adolescents, and media* (pp. 263–270). New York: Routledge.

Austin, R. & Anderson, J. (2008). Building bridges online: Issues of pedagogy and learning outcomes in intercultural education through citizenship. *International Journal of Information and Communication Technology Education* 4(1), 86–94.

Axelsson, A-S. & Regan, T. (2006). Playing online. In P. Vorderer & J. Bryant (Eds.), *Playing video games: Motives, responses, and consequences* (pp. 291–306). Mahwah, NJ: Lawrence Erlbaum.

Bachen, C.M. & Illouz, E. (1996). Imagining romance: Young people's cultural models of romance and love. *Critical Studies in Mass Communication, 13*(4), 279–308.

Baker-Sperry, L. (2007). The production of meaning through peer interaction: Children and Walt Disney's Cinderella. *Sex Roles, 56,* 717–727.

Ballard, I.M. (1995). See no evil, hear no evil: Television violence and the first amendment. *Virginia Law Review, 81,* 175–185.

Banaji, S. & Buckingham, D. (2013). *The civic web: Young people, the internet, and civic participation.* Cambridge, MA: MIT Press.

Bandura, A. (1965). Influence of models' reinforcement contingencies on the acquisition of imitative responses. *Journal of Personality and Social Psychology, 1,* 589–595.

Barak Brandes, S. & Levin, D. (2014). "Like my status": Israeli teenage girls constructing their social connections on the Facebook social network. *Feminist Media Studies, 14*(5), 743–758.

Barky, S.L. (1988). Foucault, femininity, and the modernization of patriarchal power. In I. Diamond (Ed.), *Feminism and Foucault* (pp. 61–86). Boston, MA: Northeastern University Press.

Bazalgette, C. (Ed.). (1989). *Primary media education: A curriculum statement.* London: British Film Institute.

Bazalgette, C. (1998). Still only 1898. *Media Education Journal, 24,* 2–9.

Berelson, B. (1948). Communication and public opinion. In W. Schramm (Ed.), *Communications in modern society: Fifteen studies of the mass media* (pp. 167–185). Urbana: University of Illinois Press.

Bickham, D.S. & Slaby, R.G. (2012). Effects of a media literacy program in the US on children's critical evaluation of unhealthy media messages about violence, smoking, and food. *Journal of Children and Media, 6,* 2, 255–271.

Bickham, D.S., Wright, J., & Huston, A.C. (2001). Attention, comprehension, and the educational influences of television. In D.G. Singer & J.L. Singer (Eds.), *Handbook of children and the media* (pp. 101–119). Thousand Oaks, CA: Sage.

Bleakley, A., Hennessy, M., Fishbein, M., & Jordan A. (2008). It works both ways: The relationship between sexual content in the media and adolescent sexual behavior. *Media Psychology, 11*(4), 443–461.

Bloch, L.R. & Lemish, D. (2003). The Megaphone Effect: International culture via the US of A. *Communication Yearbook, 27,* 159–190. Mahwah, NJ: Lawrence Erlbaum Associates.

Blosser, B. (1988). Television, reading, and oral language development: The case of the Hispanic child. *Bilingual Research Journal: The Journal of the National Association for Bilingual Education,* 21–42.

Blumler, J.G. (1992). *Television and the public interest: Vulnerable values in West European broadcasting.* London: Sage.

Bobkowski, P.S., Brown, J.D., & Neffa, D.R. (2012). "Hit me up and we can get down:" US youths' risk behaviors and sexual self-disclosure in MySpace profiles. *Journal of Children and Media, 6,* 119–134.

Bond, B.J., Richards, M.N., & Calvert, S.L. (2013). Media and obesity. In D. Lemish (Ed.), *The Routledge international handbook of children, adolescents, and media* (pp. 232–239). New York: Routledge.

Borzekowski, D.L.G. (2013). Media and substance abuse: Alcohol, smoking and drugs. In D. Lemish (Ed.), *The Routledge international handbook of children, adolescents, and media* (pp. 240–246). New York: Routledge.

Botta, R.A. (1999). Television images and adolescent girls' body image disturbance. *Journal of Communication, 49*(2), 22–41.

Bouman, M. (2002). Turtles and peacocks: Collaboration in entertainment–education television. *Communication Theory, 12*(2), 225–244.

Bowker, J. (Ed.). (1991). *Secondary media education: A curriculum statement*. London: The British Film Institute.

boyd, d. (2008). Why youth love social network sites: The role of networked publics in teenage social life. In D. Buckingham (Ed.), *Youth, identity, and digital media* (pp. 119–142). Cambridge, MA: MIT Press.

boyd, d., Hargittai, E., Schultz, J., & Palfrey, J. (2011). Why parents help their children lie to Facebook about age: Unintended consequences of the 'Children's Online Privacy Protection Act'. *First Monday: Peer Reviewed Journal on the Internet, 16*(11). http://firstmonday.org/ojs/index.php/fm/article/view/3086/2589. Retrieved July 25, 2014.

Brenick, A., Lee-Kim, J., Killen, M., Fox, N., Raviv, A. *et al.* (2007). Social judgments in Israeli and Arabic children: Findings from media-based intervention projects. In D. Lemish & M. Götz (Eds.), *Children and media at times of war and conflict*, pp. 287–308. Cresskill, NJ: Hampton.

Brown, J. (Ed.). (2008). Managing the media monster: The influence of media (from television to text messages) on teen sexual behavior and attitudes. Washington, DC: National Campaign to Prevent Teen and Unplanned Pregnancy.

Brown, J.D. & L'Engle, K.L. (2009). X-rated: Sexual attitudes and behaviors associated with US early adolescents' exposure to sexually explicit media. *Communication Research, 36*(1), 129–151.

Brown, L.M., Lamb, S., & Tappan, M.B. (2009). *Packaging boyhood: Saving our sons from superheroes, slackers, and other media stereotypes*. New York: St. Martin's Press.

Bryant, J.A. (Ed.). (2007). *The children's television community*. Mahwah, NJ: Lawrence Erlbaum Associates.

Buckingham, D. (1993). *Children talking television*. London: Falmer.

Buckingham, D. (1998). Media education in the UK: moving beyond protectionism. *Journal of Communication, 21*, 6.

Buckingham, D. (2000). *The making of citizens: Young people, news and politics*. London: Routledge.

Buckingham, D. (2006). Is there a digital generation? In D. Buckingham & R. Willett (Eds.) *Digital generations* (pp. 1–13). Mahwah, NJ: Lawrence Erlbaum.

Buckingham, D. (2013a). Constructing children as consumers. In D. Lemish (Ed.), *The Routledge international handbook of children, adolescents, and media* (pp. 54–60). New York: Routledge.

Buckingham, D. (2013b). Representing audiences: Audience research, public knowledge and policy. *Communication Review, 16*(1–2), 51–60.

Buckingham, D. & Bragg, S. (2004). *Young people, sex and the media: The facts of life?* New York: Palgrave Macmillan.

Buckingham, D. & Domaille, K. (2003). Where are we going and how can we get there? General findings from the UNESCO Youth Media Education Survey 2001. In C. von

Feilitzen & U. Carlsson (Eds.), *Promote or protect? Perspectives on media literacy and media regulations* (pp. 41–54). Göteborg University: The International Clearinghouse on Children, Youth and Media.

Buckingham, D. & Tingstad, V. (Eds.). (2010). *Childhood and consumer culture.* London: Palgrave Macmillan.

Buerkel-Rothfuss & Buerkel (2001). Family mediation. In J. Bryant & J.A. Bryant (Eds.), *Television and the American family* (2nd ed.) (pp. 355–376). Hillsdale, NJ: Lawrence Erlbaum.

Buijzen, M., Rozendaal, E., & van Reijmersdal, E.A. (2013). Media, advertising, and consumerism: Children and adolescents in a commercialized media environment. In D. Lemish (Ed.), *The Routledge international handbook of children, adolescents, and media* (pp. 271–278). New York: Routledge.

Bulgar, M. & Livingstone, S. (2013). *A global agenda for children's rights in the digital age: Recommendations for developing UNICEF's research strategy.* New York: UNICEF.

Burrell, J. (2012). *Invisible users: Youth in internet cafes of urban Ghana*, Ch. 2: Youth and the indeterminate space of the internet café (pp. 29–53). Cambridge, MA: MIT Press.

Bushman, B.J. & Huesmann, L.R. (2001). Effects of televised violence on aggression. In D.G. Singer & J.L. Singer (Eds.), *Handbook of children and the media* (pp. 223–254). Thousand Oaks, CA: Sage.

Cantor, J. (1994). Confronting children's fright responses to mass media. In D. Zillman, J. Bryant, & A.C. Huston (Eds.), *Media, children and the family: Social scientific, psychodynamic and clinical perspectives* (pp. 87–116). Thousand Oaks, CA: Sage.

Cantor, J. (1996). Television and children's fear. In T. MacBeth (Ed.), *Tuning in to young viewers: Social science perspectives on television* (pp. 87–115). Thousand Oaks, CA: Sage.

Cantor, J. (2001). The media and children's fears, anxieties, and perceptions of danger. In D.G. Singer & J.L. Singer (Eds.), *Handbook of children and the media* (pp. 207–221). Thousand Oaks, CA: Sage.

Cantor, J. (2002). Fright reactions to mass media. In J. Bryant & D. Zillmann (Eds.), *Media effects: Advances in theory and research* (pp. 287–306). Mahwah, NJ: Lawrence Erlbaum.

Cantor, J., Mares, M.L., & Oliver, M.B. (1993). Parents and children's emotional reactions to TV coverage of the Gulf War. In B.S. Greenberg & W. Gantz (Eds.), *Desert Storm and the mass media* (pp. 325–340). Cresskill, NJ: Hampton.

Cappello, G., Felini, D., & Hobbs, R. (2011). Reflections on global developments in media literacy education: Bridging theory and practice. *Journal of Media Literacy Education, 3*(2), 66–73.

Carlsson, U. & von Feilitzen C. (Eds.). (1998). *Children and media violence.* Göteborg University, Sweden: The International Clearinghouse on Children and Violence on the Screen.

Carlsson, U., Tayie, S., Jacquinot-Delaunay, F., & Tornero, J.N.P. (2008). *Empowerment through media education: A intercultural dialogue.* Göteborg University, Sweden: The International Clearinghouse on Children, Youth and Media.

Carter, C. (2013). Children and the news: Rethinking citizenship in the twenty-first century. In D. Lemish (Ed.), *The Routledge international handbook of children, adolescents, and media* (pp. 255–262). New York: Routledge.

Casper, V. & Theilheimer, R. (2009). *Early childhood education: Learning together.* New York: McGraw-Hill.

Center for Media and Child Health. (2013). http://www.cmch.tv/. Retrieved July 25, 2014.

Chaffee, S.H. & McLeod, J.N. (1972). Adolescent television use in the family context. In G.A. Comstock & E.A. Rubenstein (Eds.), *Television and social behavior* (vol. 13, pp. 149–172). Washington, DC: US Government Printing Office.

Chaffee, S.H., McLeod, J.N., & Wackman, D. (1973). Family communication patterns and adolescent political participation. In J. Dennis (Ed.), *Socialization to politics: A reader* (pp. 349–363). New York: Wiley.

Chaffee, S.H. & Yang, S-M. (1990). Communication and political socialization. In O. Ichilov (Ed.), *Political socialization, citizenship education and democracy* (pp. 37–157). New York: Teachers College Press.

Chan, E. & Vorderer, P. (2006). Massively multiplayer online games. In P. Vorderer & J. Bryant (Eds.), *Playing video games: Motives, responses, and consequences* (pp. 77–88). Mahwah, NJ: Lawrence Erlbaum.

Chandler, D. (1997). Children's understanding of what is 'real' on television: A review of the literature. *Journal of Educational Media, 22*(1), 65–80.

Chia, S.C. (2010). How social influence mediates media effects on adolescents' materialism. *Communication Research, 37*(3), 400–419.

Chia, S.C. & Poo, L.Y. (2009). Media, celebrities, and fans: An examination of adolescents' media usage and involvement with entertainment celebrities. *Journalism & Mass Communication Quarterly, 86*(1), 23–44.

Christakis, D.A. (2010). Infant media viewing: First, do no harm. *Pediatric Annals, 399*, 578–582.

Christopoulou, N. & Leeuw, S. (2004). *Home is where the heart is: Family relations of migrant children in media clubs in six European countries*. Institute of Education, University of London.

Cline, V.B. (1994). Pornography effects: Empirical and clinical evidence. In D. Zillman, J. Bryant, & A.C. Huston (Eds.), *Media, children and the family: Social scientific, psychodynamic and clinical perspectives* (pp. 229–247). Hillsdale, NJ: Lawrence Erlbaum.

Cohen, A.A. & Salomon, G. (1979). Children's literate television viewing: Surprises and possible explanations. *Journal of Communication, 29*(3), 156–163.

Cole, C., Arafat, C., Tidhar, C., Zidan, W.T., Fox, N. *et al.* (2003). "So they will be friends": The educational impact of Rechov Sumsum/Shara'a Simsim, a *Sesame Street* television series to promote respect and understanding among children living in Israel, the West Bank, and Gaza. *International Journal of Behavioral Development, 27*(5), 409–422.

Cole, C.F., Richman, B.A., & McCann Brown, S.K. (2001). The world of *Sesame Street* research. In S.M. Fisch & R.T. Truglio (Eds.), *"G"is for growing: Thirty years of research on children and Sesame Street* (pp. 147–179). Mahwah, NJ: Lawrence Erlbaum.

Collins, W.A. (1983). Interpretation and inference in children's television viewing. In J. Bryant & D.R. Anderson (Eds.), *Children's understanding of television: Research on attention and comprehension* (pp. 125–150). New York: Academic Press.

Common Sense Media (2013). Zero to eight: Children's media use in America 2013. US: Common Sense Media. http://www.commonsensemedia.org/research/zero-eight-childrens-media-use-america. Retrieved December 23, 2013.

Comstock, G. (1991). *Television and the American child*. New York: Academic Press.

Connolly, P. (2009). *Developing programmes to promote ethnic diversity in early childhood: Lessons from Northern Ireland*. Working paper no. 52, Bernard van Leer Foundation, The Hague/The Netherlands.

Connolly, P., Fitzpatrick, S., Gallagher, T., & Harris, P. (2006). Addressing diversity and inclusion in the early years in conflict-affected societies: A case study of the Media Initiative for Children - Northern Ireland. *International Journal of Early Years Education, 14*(3), 263–278.

Council of Better Business Bureaus. (1991). *Self-regulatory guidelines for children's advertising*. New York: The Council of Better Business Bureaus.

Criticos, C. (1997). Media education for a critical citizenry in South Africa. In R. Kubey (Ed.), *Media literacy in the information age* (pp. 229–240). New Brunswick, NJ: Transaction.

Currie, D.H. (1997). Decoding femininity: Advertisements and their teenage readers. *Gender and Society, 11*(4), 453–477.

Das, U. (1999). What does America symbolize to the urban, educated youth in India? In Y.R. Kamalipour (Ed.), *Images of the U.S. around the world: A multicultural perspective* (pp. 209–220). New York: State University of New York Press.

De Beauvoir, S. (1989[1952]). *The second sex*. New York: Vintage Books.

de Block, L. & Buckingham, D. (2007). *Global children, global media: Migration, media and childhood*. Basingstoke: Palgrave Macmillan.

Desjarlais, M. & Willoughby, T. (2010). A longitudinal study of the relation between adolescent boys and girls' computer use with friends and friendship quality: Support for the social compensation or the rich-get-richer hypothesis?. *Computers in Human Behavior, 26*(5), 896–905.

Donnerstein, E., Slaby, R., & Eron, L. (1994). The mass media and youth violence. In J. Murray, E. Rubinstein, & G. Comstock (Eds.), *Violence and youth: Psychology's response 2* (pp. 219–250). Washington, DC: American Psychological Association.

Dorr, A. (1983). No shortcuts to judging reality. In J. Bryant & D.R. Anderson (Eds.), *Children's understanding of television: Research on attention and comprehension* (pp. 190–220). New York: Academic Press.

Douglas, S. (1994). *Where the girls are: Growing up female with the mass media*. New York: Penguin Books.

Drabman, R., Robertson, S., Patterson, J., Jarvie, G., Hammer, D. *et al.* (1981). Children's perceptions of media-portrayed sex-roles. *Sex Roles, 7*, 379–389.

Drotner, K. (1992). Modernity and media panics. In M. Skovmand & K.C. Schrøder (Eds.), *Media cultures: Reappraising transnational media* (pp. 42–62). London: Routledge.

Drotner, K. (2013). The co-construction of media and childhood. In D. Lemish (Ed.), *The Routledge international handbook of children, adolescents, and media* (pp. 15–22). New York: Routledge.

Drotner, K. & Livingstone, S. (2008). *The international handbook of children, media, and culture*. Los Angeles, CA: Sage.

Durham, G. (2008). *The Lolita effect: The media sexualization of young girls and what we can do about it*. Woodstock & New York: The Overlook Press.

Durham, M.G. (2004). Constructing the "New ethnicities": Media, sexuality and diaspora identity in the lives of South Asian immigrant girls. *Critical Studies in Media Communication, 21* (2), 140–161.

Durham, M.G. (2013). Children's technologized bodies: Mapping mixed reality. In D. Lemish (Ed.), *The Routledge international handbook of children, adolescents, and media* (pp. 156–163). New York: Routledge.

Durkin, K. (1985). *Television, sex roles and children: A developmental social psychological account*. Philadelphia, PA: Open University Press.

Durkin, K. & Low, J. (1998). Children, media and aggression. In U. Carlsson & C. von Feilitzen (Eds.), *Children and media violence* (pp. 107–124). Göteborg University, Sweden: The International Clearinghouse on Children, Youth and Media.

Edwards, H.T. & Berman, M.N. (1995). Regulating violence on television. *Northwestern University Law Review, 89*(4), 1487–1566.

El Baghdady, L. (2008). Playing at cyber space: Perspectives of Egyptian children's digital socialization. In N. Pecora, E. Osei-Hwere, & U. Carlsson (Eds.), *African media, African children* (pp. 165–173). Göteborg University, Sweden: The International Clearinghouse on Children, Youth and Media.

Elias, N. (2013). Immigrant children and media. In D. Lemish (Ed.), *The Routledge international handbook of children, adolescents, and media* (pp. 336–343). New York: Routledge.

Elias, N. & Lemish, D. (2009). Spinning the web of identity: Internet's roles in immigrant adolescents' search of identity. *New Media & Society, 11*(4), 1–19.

Elias, N. & Lemish, D. (2011). Between three worlds: Host, homeland, and global media in the lives of Russian immigrant families in Israel and Germany. *Journal of Family Issues, 32*(9), 1245–1274.

Enghel, F. & Tufte, T. (2011). Citizenship practices among youth: Exploring the role of communication and media. In C. von Feilitizen, U. Carlsson, & C. Bucht (Eds.), *New questions, new insights, new approaches: Contributions to the research forum at the World Summit on Media for Children and Youth 2010* (pp. 261–270). Göteborg University, Sweden: The International Clearinghouse on Children, Youth and Media.

Evans Schmidt, M., Bickham, D.S., Branner, A., & Rich, M. (2008). Media-related policies of professional health organizations. In S.L. Calvert & B.J. Wilson (Eds.), *The handbook of children, media and development* (pp. 503–526). Oxford: Blackwell.

First, A. (1997). Television and the construction of social reality: An Israeli case study. In M.E. McCombs, D.L. Shaw, & D. Weaver (Eds.), *Communication and democracy* (pp. 41–50). Hillsdale, NJ: Lawrence Erlbaum.

Fisch, S. (2004). *Children's learning from educational television: Sesame Street and beyond.* Mahwah, NJ: Lawrence Erlbaum.

Fisch, S.M. (February 01, 2007). Educational media in the twenty-first century. *Journal of Children and Media, 1*(1), 55–59.

Fisch, S.M. & Truglio, R.T. (Eds.). (2001). *"G" is for growing: Thirty years of research on children and Sesame Street.* Mahwah, NJ: Lawrence Erlbaum.

Fisherkeller, J. (2002). *Growing up with television: Everyday learning among young adolescents.* Philadelphia, PA: Temple University Press.

Fisherkeller, J. (Ed.). (2011). *International perspectives on youth media: Cultures of production and education.* New York: Peter Lang.

Fisherkeller, J. (2013). Young people producing media: Spontaneous and project-sponsored media creation around the world. In D. Lemish (Ed.), *The Routledge international handbook of children, adolescents, and media* (pp. 344–350). New York: Routledge.

Fitch, M., Huston, A.C., & Wright, J.C. (1993). From television forms to genre schemata: Children's perceptions of television reality. In G.L. Berry & J.K Asamen (Eds.), *Children and television in a changing socio-cultural world* (pp. 38–52). Newbury Park, CA: Sage.

Frazer, E. (1987). Teenage girls reading *Jackie. Media, Culture, and Society, 9,* 407–425.

Fred Rogers Center for Early Learning and Children's Media (2011). *A statement on the development of a framework for quality digital media for young children.* Latrobe, PA: Saint Vincent College.

Fuchs, C. (2011). An alternative view of privacy on Facebook. *Information, 2,* 140–165.

Fujioka, Y. (1999). Television portrayals and African American stereotypes: Examination of television effects when direct contact is lacking. *Journal of Mass Communication Quarterly, 76*(1), 52–75.

Galician, M. (2004). *Sex, love, & romance in the mass media.* New Jersey and London: Lawrence Erlbaum Associates.

Gerbner, G. & Gross, L. (1976). Living with television: The violence profile. *Journal of Communication, 26*(2), 172–199.

Gillespie, M. (1995). *Television, ethnicity and cultural change.* London: Routledge.

Gilligan, C. (1982). *In a different voice: Psychological theory and women's development.* Cambridge, MA: Harvard University Press.

Girls Make Movies. (2012). A residential filmmaking experience. College of Mass Communication and Media Arts at Southern Illinois University, Carbondale.

Goldman, S., Booker, A., & McDermott, M. (2008). Mixing the digital, social, and cultural: Learning, identity and agency in youth participation. In D. Buckingham (Ed.), *Youth, identity, and digital media* (pp. 185–206). Cambridge, MA: MIT Press.

Görzig, A. & Ólfasson, K. (2013). What makes a bully a cyberbully? Unraveling the characteristics of cyberbullies across twenty-five European countries. *Journal of Children and Media, 7*(1), 9–27.

Götz, M. (2013). Media, imagination and fantasy. In D. Lemish (Ed.), *The Routledge international handbook of children, adolescents, and media* (pp. 186–192). New York: Routledge.

Götz, M., & Lemish, D. (2012). *Sexy girls, heroes and funny losers: Gender representations in children's TV around the world.* Frankfurt am Main: Peter Lang.

Götz, M., Lemish, D., Aidman, A., & Moon, H. (2005). *Media and the make believe worlds of children: When Harry Potter met Pokémon in Disneyland.* Mahwah, NJ: Lawrence Erlbaum.

Graves, S.B. (2008). Children's television programming and the development of multicultural attitudes. In J.K. Asamen, M.K. Ellis, & G.L. Berry (Eds.), *Child development, multiculturalism, and media* (pp. 213–232). Thousand Oaks, CA: Sage.

Gray, A. (1987). Behind closed doors: Video recorders in the home. In H. Baehr & G. Dyer (Eds.), *Boxed-in: Women and television* (pp. 38–54). London: Pandora Press.

Gray, M. (2009). Negotiating identities/queering desires: Coming out online and the remediation of the coming-out story. *Journal of Computer-Mediated Communication, 14*, 1162–1189.

Greenberg, B.S., Brown, J.D., & Buerkel-Rothfuss, N.L. (1993). *Media, sex and the adolescent.* Cresskill, NJ: Hampton.

Greenfield, P. & Beagles-Roos, J. (1988). Radio vs. television: Their cognitive impact on children of different socio-economic and ethnic groups. *Journal of Communication, 38*(2), 71–72.

Greenfield, P., Farrer, D., & Beagles-Roos, J. (1986). Is the medium the message? An experimental comparison of the effects of radio and television on imagination. *Journal of Applied Developmental Psychology, 7*(4), 237–255.

Groebel, J. (1998). The UNESCO global study on media violence: Report presented to the Director General of UNESCO. In U. Carlsson & C. von Feilitzen (Eds.), *Children and media violence* (pp. 181–199). Göteborg University, Sweden: The UNESCO International Clearinghouse on Children and Violence on the Screen.

Gultig, J. (2004). "This is it" – South African youth's reading of Yizo Yizo 2. In C. von Feilitzen (Ed.), *Young people, soap operas and reality TV* (pp. 227–241). Göteborg University, Sweden: The International Clearinghouse on Children, Youth and Media.

Gunter, B. (1995). *Television and gender representation.* London: John Libbey and Company.

Gunter, B. (2002). *Media sex: What are the issues?* Mahwah, NJ: Lawrence Erlbaum.

Guernsey, L. (2014). Garbled in translation: Getting media research to the press and public. *Journal of Children and Media, 8*(1), 87–94.

Haeffner, M.J. & Wartella, E.A. (1987). Effects of sibling coviewing on children's interpretations of television programs. *Journal of Broadcasting and Electronic Media, 31*(2), 153–168.

Hains, R.C. (2012). *Growing up with girl power: Girlhood on screen and in everyday life.* New York: Peter Lang.

Hansen, F., Rasmussen, J., Martensen, A., & Tufte, B. (Eds.). (2002). *Children – Consumption, advertising and media.* Copenhagen: Copenhagen Business School Press.

Harrison, K. (2013). Media, body image, and eating disorders. In D. Lemish (Ed.), *The Routledge international handbook of children, adolescents, and media* (pp. 224–231). New York: Routledge.

Hawkins, R. (1977). The dimensional structure of children's perceptions of TV reality. *Communication Research, 4*(3), 299–320.

Heintz, K.E., Shively, A., Wartella, E., & Oliverez, A. (1995). Television advertising and childhood: Form, function and future uses. Paper presented at the annual meeting of the International Communication Association, Albuquerque, NM.

Hemelryk Donald, S. (2005). *Little friends: Children's film and media culture in China.* Oxford, UK: Rowman and Littlefield Publishers.

Hemelryk Donald, S. (2008). Children, media and regional modernity in the Asia Pacific. In K. Drotner & S. Livingstone (Eds.), *The international handbook of children, media, and culture* (pp. 299–313). Los Angeles, CA: Sage.

Hemelryk Donald, S. (2010). Introduction: Why mobility matters: Young people and media competency in the Asia-Pacific. In S. Hemelryk Donald, T. Anderson, & D. Spry (Eds.), *Youth, society and mobile media in Asia* (pp. 3–12). London: Routledge.

Herr Stephenson, B. (2013). New media and learning. In D. Lemish (Ed.), *The Routledge international handbook of children, adolescents, and media* (pp. 410–416). New York: Routledge.

Hijazi-Omari, H. & Ribak, R. (2008). Playing with fire: On the domestication of the mobile pohone among Palestinian teenage girls in Israel. *Information, Communication & Society, 11*(2), 149–166.

Himmelweit, H.T., Oppenheim, A.N., & Vince, P. (1958). *Television and the child.* London: Oxford University Press.

Hobbs, R. (2010). *Digital and media literacy: A plan of action.* A white paper on the digital and media literacy recommendations of the Knight Commission on the information needs of communities in a democracy. Washington, DC: The Aspen Institute, pp. vii–viii.

Hobbs, R. (2011). The state of media literacy: A response to Potter. *Journal of Broadcasting & Electronic Media, 55*(3), 419–430.

Hobbs, R. (2013). Media literacy. In D. Lemish (Ed.), *The Routledge international handbook of children, adolescents, and media* (pp. 417–424). New York: Routledge.

Hoffner, C. (1996). Children's wishful identification and para-social interaction with favorite television characters. *Journal of Broadcasting and Electronic Media, 40,* 289–402.

Hoffner, C. & Cantor, J. (1991). Perceiving and responding to mass media characters. In J. Bryant & D. Zillman (Eds.), *Responding to the screen: Reception and reaction processes* (pp. 63–101). Hillsdale, NJ: Lawrence Erlbaum.

Hoffner, C. & Haeffner, M. (1993). Children's affective responses to news coverage of the war. In B.S. Greenberg & W. Gantz (Eds.), *Desert Storm and the mass media* (pp. 364–380). Cresskill, NJ: Hampton.

Horgen, K.B., Harris, J.L., & Brownell, K.D. (2012). Food marketing: Targeting young people in a toxic environment. In D.G. Singer & J.L. Singer (Eds.), *Handbook of children and the media* (pp. 455–478). Thousand Oaks, CA: Sage Publications.

Huesmann, L.R. & Eron, L.D. (Eds.). (1986). *Television and the aggressive child: A cross-national comparison.* Hillsdale, NJ: Lawrence Erlbaum.

Huizinga, M., Nikkelen, S.W.C., & Valkenburg, P.M. (2013). Children's media use and its relation to attention, hyperactivity, and impulsivity. In D. Lemish (Ed.), *The Routledge international handbook of children, adolescents, and media* (pp. 179–185). New York: Routledge.

Ito, M., Baumer, S., Bittani, M., boyd, d., Cody, R. *et al.* (2009). *Hanging out, messing around, and geeking out: Kids living and learning with new media.* Cambridge, MA: MIT Press.

IZI (2004). *Children watching war: A few reminders about potential contribution of the media to children in times of conflict & war.* Munich, Germany: International Central Institute for Youth and Educational Television (IZI). http://www.br-online.de/jugend/izi/guidelines/reminders.htm. Retrieved July 25, 2014.

Jenkins, H. (1990). "Going Bonkers!:" Children, play and *Pee-wee.* In J. Jenkins (Ed.), *Camera Obscura* (pp. 169–193). New York: Johns Hopkins University Press.

Jenkins, H. (2006). *Convergence culture: Where old and new media collide.* New York: New York University Press.

Jenkins, H., Purushotma, R., Weigel, M., Clinton, K., & Robinson, A. (2006). Confronting the challenges of participator culture: Media education for the 21st century (part two). *Digital Kompetanse, 2,* 97–113.

Jensen, L.G. & Hansen, M.G. (2011). Strengthening civil society: A communication for social change agenda? In C. von Feilitzen, U. Carlsson, & C. Bucht (Eds.), *New questions, new insights, new approaches: Contributions to the research forum at the World Summit on Media for Children and Youth 2010* (pp. 241–250). Göteborg University, Sweden: The International Clearinghouse on Children, Youth and Media.

Jeong, S.H., Cho, H., & Huang, Y. (2012). Media literacy interventions: A meta analysis review. *Journal of Communication, 62,* 454–472.

Jones, G. (2002). *Killing monsters: Why children need fantasy, super heroes, and make-believe violence.* New York: Basic Books.

Jordan, A. (1992). Social class, temporal orientation, and mass media use within the family system. *Critical Studies in Mass Communication, 9,* 374–386.

Jordan, A., Bleakley, A., Manganello, J., Hennessy, M., Steven, R. *et al.* (2010). The role of television access in the viewing time of US adolescents. *Journal of Children and Media, 4*(4), 355–370.

Jordan, A.B. (2010). Children's television viewing and childhood obesity. *Pediatric Annals, 39*(9), 569.

Jordan, A.B. & Gilmore, J.S. (2013). Children and advertising policies in the US and beyond. In D. Lemish (Ed.), *The Routledge international handbook of children, adolescents, and media* (pp. 386–394). New York: Routledge.

Jordan, A.B. & Woodward, E.H. (1997). *The 1997 state of children's television report: Programming for children over broadcast and cable television.* University of Pennsylvania: The Annenberg Public Policy Center.

Jung, J-Y., Lin, W-Y., & Kim, Y-C. (2012). The dynamic relationship between East Asian adolescents' use of the internet and their use of other media. *New Media & Society, 14*(6), 969–986.

Kahne, J., Lee, N-J & Feezell, J.T. (2012). Digital media literacy education and online civic and political participation. *International Journal of Communication, 6,* 1–24.

Kamalipour, Y.R. (Ed.). (1999). *Images of the U.S. around the world: A multicultural perspective.* New York: State University of New York Press.

Kampf, R. (2011). Dialogue between rival groups in the net. In A. Cohen & A. Lev-On (Eds.), *Technology, society and politics in Israel* (pp. 277–302). Tel Aviv: The Israeli Political Science Association (in Hebrew).

Katz, V.S. (2010). How children of immigrants use media to connect their families to the community: The case of Latinos in South Los Angeles. *Journal of Children and Media, 4*(3), 298–315.

Killen, M. & Fox, N. (2003). Evaluations of children's reactions to Israeli–Palestinian Sesame Street. *Maryland International, 2*, 12.

Killen, M., Fox, N.A., & Leavitt, L. (2004). Stereotypes and conflict resolution in the Mid-East: Young children's social concepts as a function of exposure to a media intervention. Paper presented at the Annual Meeting of the Jean Piaget Society: Society for the Study of Knowledge and Development. Toronto, Canada.

Kodaira, S.I. (1998). A review of research on media violence in Japan. In U. Carlsson & C. von Feilitzen (Eds.), *Children and media violence* (pp. 81–106). Göteborg University, Sweden: The International Clearinghouse on Children, Youth and Media.

Kohlberg, L. (Ed.). (1984). *The psychology of moral development: The nature of validity of moral stages*. Cambridge, MA: Harper and Row.

Kolucki, B. (2013). UNICEF and communication for development: an integrated approach to developing capacity to produce communication for and with children. In D. Lemish (Ed.), *The Routledge international handbook of children, adolescents, and media* (pp. 433–441). New York: Routledge.

Kolucki, B. & Lemish, D. (2011). *Communicating with children: Principles and practices to nurture, inspire, excite, educate and heal*. New York: Communication for Development Unit, UNICEF. http://www.unicef.org/cwc. Retrieved July 25, 2014.

Koolstra, C.M. & Beentjes, J.W.J. (1999). Children's vocabulary acquisition in a foreign language through watching subtitled TV programs at home. *Educational Technology Research and Development, 47*, 51–60.

Krcmar, M., Grela, B., & Lin, K. (2007). Can toddlers learn vocabulary from television? An experimental approach. *Media Psychology, 10*(1), 41–63.

Krotz, F. (2007). The meta-process of "mediatization" as a conceptual frame. *Global Media and Communication, 3*(3), 256–260.

Kubey, R. (1998). Obstacles to the development of media education in the US. *Journal of Communication, 48*(1), 58–69.

Kunkel, D. (1998). Policy battles over defining children's educational television. *The Annals of the American Academy of Political and Social Science Special Issue: Children and Television, 557*, 39–53.

Kunkel, D. (2001). Children and television advertising. In D.G. Singer & J.L. Singer (Eds.), *Handbook of children and the media* (pp. 375–393). Thousand Oaks, CA: Sage.

Kunkel, D. & Wilcox, B. (2012). Children and media policy: Historical perspectives and current practices. In D.G. Singer & J.L. Singer (Eds.), *Handbook of children and the media* (pp. 569–594). Thousand Oaks, CA: Sage Publications.

Kunkel, D., Cope, K.M., & Biely, E. (1999). Sexual messages on television: Comparing findings from three studies. *The Journal of Sex Research, 36*(3), 230–236.

Lachover, E. & Vaisman, C. (2014). Jewish-Israeli girls online discourse about International Women's Day: Post-feminism or "feminist insensibility"? *Journal of Children and Media, 8*(2), 110-126.

Lamb, S. & Brown, L.M. (2006). *Packaging girlhood: Rescuing our daughters from marketers' schemes*. New York: St. Martin's Press.

Lauricella, A.R., Robb, M.B., & Wartella, E. (2013). Challenges and suggestions for determining quality in children's media. In D. Lemish (Ed.), *The Routledge international handbook of children, adolescents, and media* (pp. 425–432). New York: Routledge.

Lee, A.Y.L. (2004). Critical appreciation of TV drama and reality shows: Hong Kong youth in need of media education. In C. von Feilitzen (Ed.), *Young people, soap operas and reality TV* (pp. 117–127). Göteborg University, Sweden: The International Clearinghouse on Children, Youth and Media.

Lefkowitz, N.M., Eron, L.D., Walder, L.O., & Huesmann, L.R. (1977). *Growing up to be violent: A longitudinal study of the development of aggression.* Elmsford, NY: Pergamon.

Lemish, D. (1987). Viewers in diapers: The early development of television viewing. In Lindlof, T. (Ed.), *Natural audiences: Qualitative research of media uses and effects* (pp. 33–57). Norwood, NJ: Ablex.

Lemish, D. (1997). Kindergartners' understandings of television: A cross-cultural comparison. *Communication Studies, 48*(2), 109–126.

Lemish, D. (1998a). What is news? A cross-cultural examination of kindergartners' understanding of news. *Communications: European Journal of Communication Research, 23,* 491–504.

Lemish, D. (1998b). Spice Girls' talk: A case study in the development of gendered identity. In S.A. Inness (Ed.), *Millennium girls: Today's girls around the world* (pp. 145–167). New York: Rowman and Littlefield.

Lemish, D. (1999). "America the beautiful": Israeli children's perception of the US through a wrestling television series. In Y.R. Kamalipour (Ed.), *Images of the U.S. around the world: A multicultural perspective* (pp. 295–308). New York: State University of New York Press.

Lemish, D. (2002). Between here and there: Israeli children living cultural globalization. In C. von Feilitzen & U. Carlsson (Eds.), *Children, young people and media globalization* (pp. 125–134). Sweden: Göteborg University, Sweden: The International Clearinghouse on Children, Youth and Media.

Lemish, D. (2002a). Gender at the forefront: Feminist perspectives on action theoretical approaches in communication research. *Communications: The European Journal of Communication Research, 27*(1), 63–78.

Lemish, D. (2002b). *Growing up with television: The little screen in the lives of children and youth.* Tel-Aviv: The Open University (in Hebrew).

Lemish, D. (2002c). Normalizing inequality: Portrayals of women in Israeli media *The Journal of Israeli History, 21*(1–2), 110–125. Reprinted in H. Naveh (Ed.). (2003). *Israeli family and community: Women's time* (pp. 110–125). London: Vallentine Mitchelle.

Lemish, D. (2007). *Children and television: A global perspective.* Malden, MA: Blackwell.

Lemish, D. (2010). *Screening gender on children's television: The views of producers around the world.* London: Routledge.

Lemish, D. (2011). "Can't talk about sex:" Producers of children's television around the world speak out. *Sex Education Journal, 11*(3), 267–278.

Lemish, D. (Ed.). (2013). *Growing-up with television and the internet: The screens in the lives of children and youth: A reader.* Tel Aviv: The Open University of Israel (in Hebrew and English).

Lemish, D. (2014). Audience transformations and social integration: Building bridges and making a real difference in the world – Report of the WG4 dialogue with stakeholders. In G. Patriarche, H. Bilandzic, N. Carpentier, C. Ponte, K.C. Schrøder *et al.* (Eds.), *Building bridges: Pathways to a greater societal significance for audience research* (pp. 131–136). EU: COST. http://www.cost.eu. Retrieved July 25, 2014.

Lemish, D. & Alon-Tirosh, M. (forthcoming). "I was really scared": A cross-cultural comparison of reconstructing childhood fearful viewing experiences. In M. Moshe (Ed.), *The emotion industry*. New York: Science Publishers, Inc.

Lemish, D., Damari, A., Limor, Y., and Segal, Z. (2009). Convention on Television Broadcasting for Children and Youth: A case study of academic-professional collaboration in Israel. *Communication Research Trends, 28*(3), 31–32.

Lemish, D., Drotner, K., Liebes, T., Maigret, E., & Stald, G. (1998). Global culture in practice: A look at children and adolescents in Denmark, France and Israel. *European Journal of Communication, 13*, 539–556.

Lemish, D. & Götz, M. (2007). *Children and media in times of war and conflict*. Cresskill, NJ: Hampton Press.

Lemish, D. & Götz, M. (2014). Conflict, media and child well-being. In A. Ben-Aryeh, I. Frønes, F. Casas, & J.E. Korbin (Eds.), *Handbook of child well-being: Theories, methods and policies in global perspective*. (Vol. 4, pp. 2013–2029) Dordrecht: Springer.

Lemish, D. & Kolucki, B. (2013). Media and early childhood development. In P. Britto, P. Engle, C. Super, & N. Ulkuer (Eds.), *Handbook of early childhood development research and its impact on global policy*. (pp. 329–347). Oxford: Oxford University Press.

Lemish, D. & Lemish, P. (1997). A much debated consensus: Media literacy in Israel. In R. Kubey (Ed.), *Media literacy in the information age* (pp. 213–228). New Brunswick, NJ: Transaction.

Lemish, D., Liebes, T., & Seidmann, V. (2001). Gendered media meanings and uses. In S. Livingstone & M. Bovill (Eds.), *Children and their changing media environment: A European comparative study* (pp. 263–282). Mahwah, NJ: Lawrence Erlbaum.

Lemish, D., Ribak, R., & Alony, R. (2009). Israeli children online: From moral panic to responsible parenthood. *Megamot, 46*(1–2), 137–163 (in Hebrew).

Lemish D. & Rice, M. (1986). Television as a talking picture book: A prop for language acquisition. *Journal of Child Language 13*, 251–274.

Lemish, D. & Tidhar, C.E. (1999). Mothers close to life: An Israeli case study. *TelevIZIon, 12*(2), 39–46.

Lemish, P. (2008). Peacebuilding contributions of Northern Ireland producers of children and youth-oriented media. *Journal of Children and Media, 2*(3), 282–299.

Lemish, P. (2011). Facilitating the social reality challenge with youth filmmakers. In J. Fisherkeller (Ed.), *International perspectives on youth media: Cultures of production and education* (pp. 283–300). New York: Peter Lang.

Lemish, P. & Schlote, E. (2009). Media portrayals of youth involvement in social change: the roles of agency, praxis, and conflict resolution processes in TV programs. In T. Tufte & F. Enghel (Eds.), *Youth engaging with the world* (pp. 193–214). Göteborg University, Sweden: The International Clearinghouse on Children, Youth and Media.

Lesser, G.S. (1996). Programmes for young children. Paper presented at the EBU workshop, Montreal.

Levine, D.E. & J. Kilbourne (2008). *So sexy so soon: The new sexualized childhood and what parents can do to protect their kids*. New York: Ballantine Books.

Liebert, R.M. & Sprafkin, J. (1988). *The early window*. New York: Pergamon.

Liebes, T. & Ribak, R. (1992). The contribution of family culture to political participation, political outlook, and its reproduction. *Communication Research, 19*(5), 618–641.

Lim, S.S. (2012). Regulatory initiatives for managing online risks and opportunities for youths – the East Asian experience. In M. Wakrave (Ed.), *e-Youth: Balancing between opportunities and risks?* (pp. 271–290). Brussels: Peter Lang.

Lim, S.S., Basnyat, I., Vadrevu, S., & Chan, Y.H. (2013). Critical literacy, self-protection and delinquency: The challenges of participatory media for youths at-risk. *Leaning, Media and Technology, 38*(2), 145-160.

Lim, S.S. & Soon, C. (2010). The influence of social and cultural factors on mothers' domestication of household ICTS – Experiences of Chinese and Korean women. *Telematics and Informatics, 27*(3), 205–216.

Lin, W-Y., Zhang, X., Jung, J-Y, & Kim, Y-C. (2013). From the wired to wireless generation? Investigating teens' internet use through the mobile phone. *Telecommunication Policy, 37,* 651–661.

Linebarger, D.L. (2001). *Summative evaluation of* Dora the Explorer, *Part 1: Learning outcomes.* Kansas City, KS: Media and Technology Projects, ABCD Ventures, Inc.

Linebarger, D.L. & Walker, D. (2005). Infants' and toddlers' television viewing and language outcomes. *American Behavioral Scientist, 48*(5), 624–645.

Ling, R. & Bertel, T. (2013). Mobile communication culture among children and adolescents. In D. Lemish (Ed.), *The Routledge international handbook of children, adolescents, and media* (pp. 127–133). New York: Routledge.

Lisosky, J.M. (1997). Controlling children's channels: Comparing children's television policies in Australia, Canada, and the United States. PhD dissertation. University of Washington.

Livingstone, S. (1992). The meaning of domestic technologies: A personal construct analysis of familial gender relations. In R. Silverstone & E. Hirsch (Eds.), *Consuming technologies: Media and information in domestic spaces* (pp. 113–30). London: Routledge.

Livingstone, S. (2005). Assessing the research base for the policy debate over the effects of food advertising to children. *International Journal of Advertising, 24*(3), 273–93.

Livingstone, S. (2007). Strategies of parental regulation in the media-rich home. *Computers in Human Behavior, 23*(3), 920–941.

Livingstone, S. (2008). Taking risky opportunities in youthful content creating: Teenagers' use of social networking sites for intimacy, privacy and self-expression. *New Media& Society, 10*(3), 393–411.

Livingstone, S. (2009). *Children and the internet.* Cambridge, UK: Polity.

Livingstone, S. (2011). Digital learning and participation among youth: Critical reflections on future research priorities. *International Journal of Learning and Media, 2*(2–3), 1–13.

Livingstone, S. (2013). Children's internet culture: Power, change and vulnerability in twenty-first century childhood. In D. Lemish (Ed.), *The Routledge international handbook of children, adolescents, and media* (pp. 111–119). New York: Routledge.

Livingstone, S. (2014). What does good content look like? Developing great online content for kids. In L. Whitaker (Ed.), *Children's media yearbook 2014* (pp. 66-71). London, UK: Milton Keynes – The Children's Media Foundation.

Livingstone, S. & Bober, M. (2006). Regulating the internet at home: Contrasting the perspectives of children and parents. In D. Buckingham & R. Willett (Eds.), *Digital generations* (pp. 93–113). Mahwah, NJ: Lawrence Erlbaum Associates.

Livingstone, S. & Bovill, M. (2001). *Children and their changing media environment: A European comparative study.* Mahwah, NJ: Lawrence Erlbaum.

Livingstone, S. & Bulger, M. (2013). A global agenda for children's rights in the digital age: Recommendations for developing UNICEF's research strategy. New York: UNICEF.

Livingstone, S., Haddon, L., Görzig, A., & Ólafsson, K. (2011). *EU Kids Online II: Final report.* LSE, London: EU Kids Online. www.eukidsonline.net. Retrieved July 25, 2014.

Lonner, W.J., Thorndike, R.M., Forbes, N.E., & Ashworth, C. (1985). The influence of television on measured cognitive abilities: A study with Native Alaskan children. *Journal of Cross-Cultural Psychology, 16*(3), 355–380.

Lull, J. (1980a). The social uses of television. *Human Communication Research, 6*(3): 197–209.

Lull, J. (1980b). Family communication patterns and the social uses of television. *Communication Research, 7*(3), 319–334.

Lustyik, K. (2013). Media regulation: The protection and promotion of home-grown children's television. In D. Lemish (Ed.), *The Routledge international handbook of children, adolescents, and media* (pp. 378–385). New York: Routledge.

Lustyik, K. & Zanker, R. (2013). Is there local content on television for children today? In A.N. Valdivia & S.R. Mazzarella (Eds.), *The international encyclopedia of media studies: Vol. 3: content and representation* (pp. 179–202). Oxford, UK: Blackwell.

Lyons, J.S., Anderson, R.L., & Larson, D.B. (1994). A systematic review of the effects of aggressive and nonaggressive pornography. In D. Zillman, J. Bryant, & A.C. Huston (Eds.), *Media, children and the family: Social scientific, psychodynamic and clinical perspectives* (pp. 271–310). Hillsdale, NJ: Lawrence Erlbaum Associates.

MacBeth, T.M. (Ed.). (1996). *Tuning in to young viewers: Social science perspectives on television*. Thousand Oaks, CA: Sage.

Macklin, M.C. & Carlson, L. (Eds.). (1999). *Advertising to children: Concepts and controversies*. Thousand Oaks, CA: Sage.

Mander, J. (1978). *Four arguments for the elimination of television*. New York: Quill.

Marciano, A. (2009). The role of newspapers in coping with the coming-out process of gay male youth. *Media Frames, 4*, 1–28 (in Hebrew).

Mares, M., Palmer, E., & Sullivan, T. (2008). Prosocial effects of media exposure. In S.L. Calvert & B.J. Wilson (Eds.), *The handbook of children, media, and development* (pp. 268–289).

Mares, M.L. & Woodard, E.H. (2012). Effects of prosocial media content on children's social interactions. In D.G. Singer & J.L. Singer (Eds.), *Handbook of children and the media* (pp. 197–214). Thousand Oaks, CA: Sage Publications.

Mazzarella, S. (2010). (Ed.). *Girl Wide Web2.0: Revisting girls, the internet, and the negotiation of identity*. New York: Peter Lang.

Mazzarella, S. & Pecora, N. (Eds.). (1999). *Growing up girls: Popular culture and the construction of identity*. New York: Peter Lang.

Mazzarella, S.R. (2013). Media and gender identities: Learning and performing femininity and masculinity. In D. Lemish (Ed.), *The Routledge international handbook of children, adolescents, and media* (pp. 279–286). New York: Routledge.

McChesney, R.W. (2013). Digital disconnect: How capitalism is turning the internet against democracy. New York: New Press.

McKee, N., Aghi, M., & Shahzadi, N. (2004). Cartoons and comic books for changing social norms: *Meena*, the South Asian girl. In A. Singhal, M.J. Cody, E.M. Rogers, & M. Sabido (Eds.), *Entertainment-education and social change: History, research, and practice* (pp. 331–349). Mahwah, NJ: Lawrence Erlbaum.

McLuhan, M. (1964). *Understanding media: The extensions of man*. New York: McGraw-Hill.

McMillin, D. & Fisherkeller, J. (2009). Local identities in globalized regions: Teens, everyday life, and television. *Popular Communication: The International Journal of Media and Culture, 7*(4), 231–251.

McMillin, D. (2009). *Mediated identities: Television, youth, and globalization*. New York: Peter Lang.

Mendel, T. & Salomon, E. (2011). *The regulatory environment for broadcasting: An international best practice survey for Brazilian stakeholders*. Brasília, Brazil: UNESCO & Ford Foundation. http://unesdoc.unesco.org/images/0019/001916/191622e.pdf. Retrieved July 25, 2014.

Mesch, G. (2013). Internet media and peer sociability. In D. Lemish (Ed.), *The Routledge international handbook of children, adolescents, and media* (pp. 287–294). New York: Routledge.

Mesch, G.S. & Talmud, I. (2007). Privacy and networking: Ethnic differences in the use of cell phones and IM in Israel. In James Katz (Ed.), *Mobile communication and social change in a global context* (pp. 313–335). Boston: MIT Press.

Mesch, G.S. & Talmud, I. (2010). *Wired youth: The social world of adolescence in the information age*. London & New York: Routledge.

Messaris, P. (1983). Family conversations about television. *Journal of Family Issues, 4*(2), 293–308.

Messaris, P. (1994). *Visual literacy: Image, mind and reality*. Boulder, CO: Westview Press.

Messenger Davies, M. (1989). *Television is good for your kids*. London: Hilary Shipman.

Messenger Davies, M. (1997). *Fake, fact, and fantasy: Children's interpretations of television reality*. Mahwah, NJ: Lawrence Erlbaum.

Meyrowitz, J. (1996). Taking McLuhan and "medium theory" seriously: Technological change and the evolution of education. In S.T. Kerr (Ed.), *Technology and the future of schooling* (pp. 73–110). Chicago, IL: The University of Chicago Press.

Montgomery, K.C. (2012). Safeguards for youth in the digital marketing ecosystem. In D.G. Singer & J.L. Singer (Eds.), *Handbook of children and the media* (pp. 631–648). Thousand Oaks, CA: Sage Publications.

Moran, Kristin C. (2011). *Listening to Latina/o youth television consumption within families*. New York: Peter Lang.

Morgan, M. (1987). Television, sex-role attitudes and sex-role behavior. *Journal of Early Adolescence, 7*(3), 269–282.

Morley, D. (1986). *Family television: Cultural power and domestic leisure*. London: Comedia Publishing.

Murrow, E. (15 October, 1958). RTNDA Convention Speech *(Radio-Television News Directors Association and Foundation)* http://www.pbs.org/wnet/americanmasters/education/lesson39_organizer1.html. Retrieved February 13, 2014.

Naigels, L.R. & Mayeux, L. (2001). Television as incidental language teacher. In D.G. Singer & J.L. Singer (Eds.), *Handbook of children and the media* (pp. 135–152). Thousand Oaks, CA: Sage.

Naim, A. (2014). Advertising and child well-being In A. Ben-Aieh, F. Casas, I. Fornes, & J.E. Korbin (Eds.), *Handbook of child well-being: Theories, methods and policies in global perspective* (Vol. 4, pp. 2031–2055). Dordrecht, Netherlands: Springer.

Nathanson, A. (2013). Media and the family context. In D. Lemish (Ed.), *The Routledge international handbook of children, adolescents, and media* (pp. 299–306). New York: Routledge.

National Television Violence Study (1996). *National television violence study, 1*. Thousand Oaks, CA: Sage.

Neubauer, G. & Winter, R. (2008). Cool heroes or funny freaks? *TelevIZIon, 21E*.

Neuman, S.B. (1991). *Literacy in the television age*. Norwood, NJ: Ablex.

O'Bryan, K.C. (1980). The teaching face: A historical perspective. In E.L. Palmer & A. Dorr (Eds.), *Children and the faces of television: Teaching, violence, selling* (pp. 5–17). New York: Academic Press.

O'Neill, B. (2013). Internet policies: Online child protection and empowerment in a global context. In D. Lemish (Ed.), *The Routledge international handbook of children, adolescents, and media* (pp. 395–402). New York: Routledge.

Opree, S.J., Buijzen, M., van Reijmersdal, E.A., & Valkenburg, P.M. (2013). Children's advertising exposure and materialistic orientations: A longitudinal study into direct and mediated effects. *Communication Research.* Advance Online Publication. Doi: 10.1177/0093650213479129

Orr Vered, K. (2008). *Children and media outside the home: Playing and learning in after-school care.* New York: Palgrave McMillan.

Owens, E.W., Behun, R.J., Manning, J.C., & Reid, R.C. (2012). The impact of internet pornography on adolescents: A review of the research. *Sexual Addiction & Compulsivity: The Journal of Treatment & Prevention, 19*(1–2), 99–122.

Paik, H. & Comstock, G. (1994). The effects of television violence on antisocial behavior: A meta-analysis. *Communication Research, 21*(4), 516–546.

Palmer, A.W. & Hafen, T. (1999). American TV through the eyes of German teenagers. In Y.R. Kamalipour (Ed.), *Images of the US around the world: A multicultural perspective* (pp. 135–146). New York: State University of New York Press.

Papaioannou, T. (2013). Media and civic engagement: The role of Web 2.0 technologies in fostering youth participation. In D. Lemish (Ed.), *The Routledge international handbook of children, adolescents, and media* (pp. 351–358). New York: Routledge.

Parameswaran, R. (2013). Media culture and childhood in the age of globalization. In D. Lemish (Ed.), *The Routledge international handbook of children, adolescents, and media* (pp. 75–82). New York: Routledge.

Park, J. (forthcoming). (Re)Constructing Ethnic identities: New media as an important platform among Korean American adolescents in the United States. PhD dissertation. Carbondale, IL: Southern Illinois University.

Pecora, N. (2013). Media policies for children: Issues and histories in the US. In D. Lemish (Ed.), *The Routledge international handbook of children, adolescents, and media* (pp. 371–377). New York: Routledge.

Pecora, N., Osei-Hwere, E., & Carlsson, U. (Eds.). (2008). *African media, African children.* Göteborg University, Sweden: The International Clearinghouse on Children, Youth and Media.

Peppler, K. (2013). Social media and creativity. In D. Lemish (Ed.), *The Routledge international handbook of children, adolescents, and media* (pp. 193–200). New York: Routledge.

Peter, J. (2013). Media and sexual development. In D. Lemish (Ed.), *The Routledge international handbook of children, adolescents, and media* (pp. 217–223). New York: Routledge.

Peter, J. & Valkenberg, P.M. (2006). Adolescents exposure to sexually explicit material on the Internet. *Communication Research, 33*(2), 178–204.

Peter, J. & Valkenberg, P.M. (2009). Adolescents exposure to sexually explicit internet material and notions of women as sex objects: Assessing causality and underlying processes. *Journal of Communication, 59,* 407–433.

Peterson, E.E. (1987). Media consumption and girls who want to have fun. *Critical Studies in Mass Communication, 4*(1), 37–50.

Pew Internet, Pew Internet Center (2013). http://pewinternet org/Presentations/2012/Apr/ Digital-Divides-and-Bridges-Technology-Use-Among-Youth.aspx. Retrieved January 20, 2014.

Piaget, J. (1969). *The origins of intelligence in the child.* New York: International University Press.

Piaget, J. & Inhelder, B. (1969). *The psychology of the child*. New York: Basic Books.

Pingree, S. (1978). The effects of nonsexist commercials and perceptions of reality on children's attitudes about women. *Psychology of Women Quarterly, 2*, 262–277.

Pinkleton, B.E., Weintraub, E., Cohen, M., Chen, Y-C., & Fitzgerald, E. (2008). Effects of peer-led media literacy curriculum on adolescents' knowledge and attitudes toward sexual behavior and media portrayals of sex. *Health Communication, 23*, 462–472.

Pollack, W. (1998). *Real boys: Rescuing our sons from the myths of boyhood*. New York: Henry Holt and Co.

Postman, N. (1979). The first curriculum: Comparing school and television. *Phi Delta Kappan, November*, 163–168.

Price, M.E. (Ed.). (1998). *The V-Chip debate: Content filtering from television to the Internet*. Mahwah, NJ: Lawrence Erlbaum.

Price, M.E. & Verhulst, S.G. (Eds.). (2002). *Parental control of television broadcasting*. Mahwah, NJ: Lawrence Erlbaum.

Prinsloo, J. & Criticos, C. (Eds.). (1991). *Media matters in South Africa*. Durban, South Africa: University of Natal.

Raviv, A., Bar-Tal, D., Raviv, A., & Ben-Horin, A. (1996). Adolescent idolization of pop singers: Causes, expressions, and reliance. *Journal of Youth and Adolescence, 25*(5), 631–750.

Reznik, S. (2014). All you need is love. *TelevIZIon, 26E*.

Reznik, S. & Lemish, D. (2011). Falling in love with "High School Musical": Girls' talk about romantic perceptions. In M.C. Kearney (Ed.), *Mediated Girlhoods* (pp. 151–170). New York: Peter Lang.

Ribak, R. (1997). Socialization as and through conversation: Political discourse in Israeli families. *Comparative Education Review, 41*(1), 71–96.

Ribak, R. (2009). Remote control, umbilical cord and beyond: The mobile phone as a transitional object. *British Journal of Developmental Psychology, 27*(1), 183–196.

Ribak, R. (2013). Media and spaces: The mobile phone in the geographies of young people. In D. Lemish (Ed.), *The Routledge international handbook of children, adolescents, and media* (pp. 307–314). New York: Routledge.

Rice, M.L., Buhr, J., & Oetting, J.B. (1992). Specific language-impaired children's quick incidental learning of words: The effect of a pause. *Journal of Speech and Hearing Research, 35*, 1040–1048.

Rice, M.L., Huston, A.C., Truglio, R., & Wright, J. (1990). Words from "Sesame Street": Learning vocabulary while viewing. *Developmental Psychology, 26*(3), 421–428.

Rice, M.L., Oetting, J.B., Marquis, J., Bode, J., & Pase, S. (1994). Frequency of input effects on word comprehension of children with specific language impairment. *Journal of Speech and Hearing Research, 37*, 106–22.

Rice, M.L. & Woodsmall, L. (1988). Lessons from television: Children's word learning when viewing. *Child development, 59*, 420–429.

Rideout, V., Foehr, U.G., & Roberts, D.F. (2010). Generation M^2: Media in the lives of 8 to 18-year-olds: A Kaiser Family Foundation Study January 2010. Menlo Park, CA: Henry J. Kaiser Family Foundation.

Ritzer, G. (2013). *The McDonaldization of society: 20th anniversary edition*. Los Angeles: Sage.

Rolandelli, D.R. (1989). Children and television: The visual superiority effect reconsidered. *Journal of Broadcasting and Electronic Media, 33*(1), 69–81.

Rosenkoetter, L.I. (2001). Television and morality. In D.G. Singer & J.L. Singer (Eds.), *Handbook of children and the media* (pp. 463–473). Thousand Oaks, CA: Sage.

Rosenthal, M. & Ribak, R. (in progress). *Media ambivalence in everyday life.* Boston: MIT (under contract).

Rosin, H. (April, 2013). The touch-screen generation. *The Atlantic.* http://www.theatlantic.com/magazine/archive/2013/04/the-touch-screen-generation/309250/. Retrieved July 25, 2014.

Salomon, G. (1981). Introducing AIME: The assessment of children's mental involvement with television. In H. Kelly & H. Gardner (Eds.), *Viewing children through television: New directions for child development* (pp. 89–102). San Francisco, CA: Jossey-Bass.

Salomon, G. (1983). Television watching and mental effort: A social psychological view. In J. Bryant & D.R. Anderson (Eds.), *Children's understanding of television: Research on attention and comprehension* (pp. 181–198). New York: Academic Press.

Salomon, G. (1984). Investing effort in television viewing. In J.P. Murray & G. Salomon (Eds.), *The future of children's television* (pp. 125–133). Boys Town, NE: Father Flanagan's Boys' Home.

Salomon, G. (1994 [1979]). *Interaction of media, cognition, and learning.* San Francisco, CA: Jossey-Bass.

Salomon, G. & Leigh, T. (1984). Predispositions about learning from print and television. *Journal of Communication, 34,* 119–135.

Savage, J. & Yancery, C. (2008). The effects of media violence exposure on criminal aggression: A meta-analysis. *Criminal Justice and Behavior, 35*(6), 772–791.

Scharrer, E. (2007). Closer than you think: Bridging the gap between media effects and cultural studies in media education theory and practice. In A. Nowak, S. Abel, & K. Ross (Eds.), *Rethinking media education: Critical pedagogy and identity politics* (pp. 17–35). Cresskill, NJ: Hampton Press.

Schmidt, M.E. & Anderson, D.R. (2006). The impact of television on cognitive development and educational achievement. In N. Pecora, J.O. Murray, & E. Wartella (Eds.), *Children and television: 50 years of research* (pp. 65–87). Mahwah, NJ: Lawrence Erlbaum.

Schofield Clark, L. (2012). Digital media and the generation gap. *Information, Communication & Society, 12*(3), 388–407.

Schofield Clark, L. (2013). *The parent app: Understanding families in the digital age.* Oxford, UK: Oxford University Press.

Schramm, W., Lyle, J., & Parker, E.B. (1961). *Television in the lives of our children.* Stanford, CA: Stanford University Press.

Seidler, V.J. (1997). *Man enough: Embodying masculinities.* London: Sage.

Selnow, G.W. & Bettinghuas, E.P. (1982). Television exposure and language development. *Journal of Broadcasting, 26*(1), 469–479.

Shafer, A., Bobkowski, P., & Brown, J.D. (2013). Sexual media practice: How adolescents select, engage with, and are affected by sexual media. In K.E. Dill (Ed.), *Oxford handbook of media psychology* (pp. 223–251). Oxford, UK: Oxford University Press.

Shakuntala, B. & Buckingham, D. (2010). Young people, the internet, and civic participation: An overview of key findings from the CivicWeb project. *International Journal of Learning and media, 2*(1), 15–24.

Shakuntala, B. & Buckingham, D. (2013). *The civic web: Young people, the internet, and civic participation.* Cambridge, MA: The MIT Press.

Sherry, J.L. (1997). Pro-social soap operas for development: A review of research and theory. *The Journal of International Communication, 4*(2), 75–102.

Shipard, S. (2003). A brief look at the regulation in Australia: A co-regulatory approach. In C. von Feilitzen & U. Carlsson (Eds.), *Promote or protect? Perspectives on media literacy and media regulations* (pp. 237–241). Göteborg University, Sweden: The International Clearinghouse on Children, Youth and Media.

Shochat, L. (2003). Our neighborhood: Using entertaining children's television to promote interethnic understanding in Macedonia. *Conflict Resolution Quarterly, 21*(1), 79–93.

Signorielli, N. (1990). Television's mean and dangerous world: A continuation of the cultural indicators perspective. In N. Signorielli & M. Morgan (Eds.), *Cultivation analysis: New directions in media effects research* (pp. 85–106). Newbury Park, CA: Sage.

Signorielli, N. (2012). Television's gender role images and contribution to stereotyping: Past, present, future. In D.G. Singer & J.L. Singer (Eds.), *Handbook of children and the media* (pp. 321–340). Thousand Oaks, CA: Sage Publications.

Signorielli, N. & Lears, M. (1992). Children, television and conceptions about chores: Attitudes and behaviors. *Sex Roles, 27*(3/4), 157–170.

Silverstone, R., Hirsch, E., & Morley, D. (1992). Information and communication technologies and the moral economy of the household. In R. Silverstone & E. Hirsch (Eds.), *Consuming technologies: Media and information in domestic spaces* (pp. 15–31). London: Routledge.

Simpson, B. (2004). *Children and television.* New York: Continuum.

Singer, D.G. (1993). Creativity of children in a television world. In G.L. Berry & J.K. Asamen (Eds.), *Children and television: Images in a changing sociocultural world* (pp. 73–86). Newbury Park, CA: Sage.

Singer, D.G. & Singer, J.L. (1998). Developing critical viewing skills and media literacy in children. *The Annals of the American Academy of Political and Social Science Special Issue: Children and Television 557,* 164–179.

Singer, J.L. & Singer, D.G. (1976). Can TV stimulate imaginative play? *Journal of Communication, 26,* 74–80.

Singer, J.L. & Singer, D.G. (1981). *Television, imagination, and aggression: A study of preschoolers.* Hillsdale, NJ: Lawrence Erlbaum.

Singer, J.L. & Singer, D.G. (1983). Implications of childhood television viewing of cognition, imagination and emotion. In J. Bryant & D.R. Anderson (Eds.), *Children's understanding of television: Research on attention and comprehension* (pp. 265–295). New York: Academic Press.

Singhal, A., Cody, C.J., Rogers, E.M., & Sabido, M. (Eds.). (2004). *Entertainment-education and social change: History, research and practice.* Mahwah, NJ: Lawrence Erlbaum.

Slater, M.D., Henry, K.L., Swaim, R.C., & Anderson, L.L. (2003). Violent media content and aggressiveness in adolescents: A downward spiral model. *Communication Research, 30*(6), 713–736.

Smith, R. (1986). Television addiction. In J. Bryant & D. Zillman (Eds.), *Perspectives on media effects* (pp. 109–28). Hillsdale, NJ: Lawrence Erlbaum.

Smith, R. (2004). Yizo Yizo: This is it? A critical analysis of reality-based drama series. In C. von Feilitzen (Ed.), *Young people, soap operas and reality TV* (pp. 241–251). Göteborg University, Sweden: The international Clearinghouse on Children, Youth and Media.

Smith, S.L. & Moyer-Guse, E. (2006). Children and the war on Iraq: Developmental differences in fear responses to TV news coverage. *Media Psychology, 8*(3), 213–237.

Smith, S.L., Moyer-Guse, E., Boyson, A.R., & Pieper, K.M. (2002). Parents' perceptions of children's fear responses. In B.S. Greenberg (Ed.), *Communication and terrorism* (pp. 193–208). Cresskill, NJ: Hampton.

Smith, S.L. & Wilson, B.J. (2000). Children's reactions to a television news story: The impact of video footage and proximity of the crime. *Communication Research, 27*(5), 641–673.

Smith, S.L. & Wilson, B.J. (2002). Children's comprehension of and fear reactions to television news. *Media Psychology, 4*, 1–26.

Sparrman, A., Sandin, B., & Sjöberg, J. (2012). *Situating child consumption: Rethinking values and notions of children, childhood and consumption*. Lund: Nordic Academic Press.

Stein, A.H. & Freidrich. L.K. (1972). Television content and young children's behavior. In J.P. Murray, E.A. Rubinstein, & G.A. Comstock (Eds.), *Television and social behavior* vol 2: *Television and social learning (Surgeon General Report)* (pp. 203–317). Washington, DC: US Government Printing Office.

Strasburger, V.C. (2012). Children, adolescents, drugs, and the media. In D.G. Singer & J.L. Singer (Eds.), *Handbook of children and the media* (pp. 419–454). Thousand Oaks, CA: Sage Publications.

Stuart, J. & Mitchell, C. (2013). Media, paerticipation, and social change: Working withing a 'youth as knowledge producers' framework. In D. Lemish (Ed.), *The Routledge international handbook of children, adolescents, and media* (pp. 359–365). New York: Routledge.

Sveningsson Elm, M. (2009). Exploring and negotiating femininity: Young women's creation of style in a Swedish internet community. *Young: Nordic Journal of Youth Research, 17*(3), 241–264.

Talmud, I. & Mesch, G.. (2010). *Wired youth: The social world of adolescence in the information age*. Taylor & Francis.

The Teletubbies (1999). *TelevIZIon, 12*(2).

Tidhar, C.E. (1996). Enhancing television literacy skills among preschool children through an intervention program in the kindergarten. *Journal of Educational Media, 22*(2), 97–110.

Tilley, C.L. (2013). Children's print culture: tradition and innovation. In D. Lemish (Ed.), *The Routledge international handbook of children, adolescents, and media* (pp. 87–94). New York: Routledge.

Tobin, J. (2000). *"Good guys don't wear hats"*: *Children's talk about the media*. New York: Columbia University, Teachers College Press.

Tobin J. (Ed.). (2004). *Pikachu's global adventure: Making sense of the rise and fall of Pokémon* (pp. 165–186). Durham, NC: Duke University Press.

Tokunaga, R.S. (2010). Following you home from school: A critical review and synthesis of research on cyberbullying victimization. *Computers in Human Behavior, 26*(3), 277–287.

Trawick-Smith, J. (2006). *Early child development: A multicultural perspective*. Pearson Education, Inc.

Trotta, L. (2012). Children's advocacy groups: A history and analysis. In D.G. Singer & J.L. Singer (Eds.), *Handbook of children and the media* (pp. 697–714). Thousand Oaks, CA: Sage Publications.

Tufte, T. (2003). Entertainment-education in HIV-AIDS communication. Beyond marketing, towards empowerment. In C. von Feilitzen & U. Carlsson (Eds.), *Promote or protect? Perspectives on media literacy and media regulations* (pp. 85–97). Göteborg University, Sweden: The international Clearinghouse on Children, Youth and Media.

Tufte, T. (2013). *Speaking up and talking back? Media, empowerment and civic engagement among East and Southern African youth*. Göteborg University, Sweden: The international Clearinghouse on Children, Youth and Media.

Tufte, T. & Enghel, F. (2009). *Youth engaging with the world: Media, communication and social change*. Göteborg University, Sweden: The international Clearinghouse on Children, Youth and Media.

UNESCO International Clearinghouse on Children and Violence on the Screen, & Nordicom. (1998). *Children and media violence: Yearbook from the UNESCO International Clearinghouse on Children and Violence on the Screen at Nordicom*. Göteborg: UNESCO International Clearinghouse on Children and Violence on the Screen.

UNICEF (2005). The media and children's rights. http://www.unicef.org/ceecis/The_Media_ and_Children_Rights_2005.pdf. Retrieved September 1, 2013.

United Nations (1989). Text of the UN Convention on the Rights of the Child. http://www. un.org/documents/ga/res/44/a44r025.htm. Retrieved July 25, 2014.

Valdivia, A.N. (2008). Mixed race on Disney Channel: From *Johnnie Tsunami* through *Lizzie McGuire* and ending with the *Cheetah Girls*. In M. Beltran & C. Fojas (Eds.), *Mixed race Hollywood: Multiraciality in film and media culture* (pp. 269–289). New York: New York University Press.

Valkenburg, P.M. (2001). Television and the child's developing imagination. In D.G. Singer & J.L. Singer (Eds.), *Handbook of children and the media* (pp. 121–134). Thousand Oaks, CA: Sage.

Valkenburg, P.M. (2004). *Children's responses to the screen: A Media psychological approach*. Mahwah, NJ: Lawrence Erlbaum.

Valkenburg, P.M. & Calvert, S.L. (2012). Media and the child's developing imagination. In D.G., Singer & J.L. Singer (Eds.), *Handbook of children and the media* (pp. 157–170). Thousand Oaks, CA: Sage.

Valkenburg, P.M. & Cantor, J. (2002). The development of a child into a consumer. In S.L. Calvert, A.B. Jordan, & R.R. Cocking (Eds.), *Children in the digital age: Influences of electronic media on development* (pp. 201–214). Westport, CT: Praeger.

Valkenburg, P.M., Krcmar, M., Peetrs, A.L., & Marseille, N.M. (1999). Developing a scale to assess three styles of television mediation: "Instructive mediation," "restrictive mediation," and "social coviewing." *Journal of Broadcasting and Electronic Media, 43*(1), 52–66.

Valkenburg, P. M. & Peter, J. (2007). Preadolescents' and adolescents' online communication and their closeness to friends. *Developmental Psychology, 43*(2), 267–277.

Valkenburg, P.M. & Peter, J. (2009). Social consequences of the internet for adolescents: A decade of research. *Current Directions in Psychological Science, 18*, 1–5.

Valkenberg, P.M. & van der Voort, T.H.A (1994). Influence of TV on daydreaming and creative imagination: A review of research. *Psychological Bulletin, 116*, 316–339.

Van der Voort, T.H.A. (1986). *Television violence: A child's-eye view*. Amsterdam: North-Holland.

Van der Voort, T.H.A. & Valkenburg, P.M. (1994). Television's impact on fantasy play: A review of research. *Developmental Review, 14*, 27–51.

Van Evra, J. (2004). *Television and child development* (3rd Ed.). Mahwah, NJ: Lawrence Erlbaum.

Vandewater, E.A. (2013). Ecological approaches to the study of media and children. In D. Lemish (Ed.), *The Routledge international handbook of children, adolescents, and media* (pp. 46–53). New York: Routledge.

Vandewater, E.A., Barr, R.F., Park, S.E., & Lee, S.J. (2010). A US study of transfer of learning from video to books in toddlers. *Journal of Children and Media, 4*(4) 451–467.

Vandewater, E.A. & Cummings, H.M. (2008). Media use and childhood obesity. In S. Calvert and B. Wilson (Eds.). *The handbook of media and child development* (pp. 355–380). New York: Blackwell.

Vidanava, I. (2011). On disc and online: Expanding digital activism in Belarus. In C. von Feilitzen, U. Carlsson, & C. Bucht (Eds.), *New questions, new insights, new approaches:*

Contributions to the research forum at the World Summit on Media for Children and Youth 2010 (pp. 227–240). Göteborg University, Sweden: The international Clearinghouse on Children, Youth and Media.

Von Feilitzen, C. & Bucht, C. (2001). *Outlooks on children and media.* Göteborg University, Sweden: The International Clearinghouse on Children, Youth and Media.

Von Feilitzen, C. & Carlsson, U. (Eds.). (2003). *Promote or protect? Perspectives on media literacy and media regulations.* Göteborg University, Sweden: The International Clearinghouse on Children, Youth and Media.

Vooijs, M.W., van der Voort, T.H.A., & Hoogeweij, J. (1995). Critical viewing of television news: The impact of a Dutch schools television project. *Journal of Educational Television, 21,* 23–36.

Walker, A.J. & Bellamy, R.V. (2001). Remote control devices and family viewing. In J. Bryant & J.A. Bryant (Eds.), *Television and the American family* (2nd Ed.), (pp. 75–89). Hillsdale, NJ: Lawrence Erlbaum.

Walma van der Molen, J.H. (2004). Violence and suffering in television news: Toward a broader conception of harmful television content for children. *Pediatrics, 113,* 1771–1775.

Walma van der Molen, J.H. & Konjin, E.A. (2007). Dutch children's emotional reactions to news about the Second Gulf War: Influence of media exposure, identification, and empathy. In D. Lemish & M. Götz (Eds.), *Children and media in times of conflict and war* (pp. 75–97). Cresskill, NJ: Hampton.

Walma van der Molen, J.H., Valkenburg, P.M., & Peeters, A.L. (2002) Television news and fear: A child survey. *Communication: The European Journal of Communication Research, 27*(3), 303–317.

Walsh, K., Sekarasih, L., & Scharrer, E. (2014). Mean girls and tough boys: Children's meaning making and media literacy lessons on gender and bullying in the US. *Journal of Children and Media, 8*(3), 223–239.

Ward, S., Wackman, D.B., & Wartella, E. (1977). *How children learn to buy: The development of consumer information-processing skills.* Beverly Hills, CA: Sage.

Warren, R. (2003). Parental mediation of preschool children's television viewing. *Journal of Broadcasting and Electronic Media, 47*(3), 394–417.

Wartella, E. & Reeves, B. (1985). Historical trends in research on children and the media: 1900–1960. *Journal of Communication, 35*(2), 118–133.

Wasko, J., Phillips, M., & Meehan, E.R. (Eds.). (2001). *Dazzled by Disney?: A global Disney audiences project.* London: Leicester University Press.

Weaver, J.B. (1994). Pornography and sexual callousness: The perceptual and behavioral consequences of exposure to pornography. In D. Zillman, J. Bryant, & A.C. Huston (Eds.), *Media, children and the family: Social scientific, psychodynamic and clinical perspectives* (pp. 215–228). Hillsdale, NJ: Lawrence Erlbaum.

Webb, T. & Martin, K. (2012). Evaluation of a U.S. school-based media literacy violence prevention curriculum on changes in knowledge and critical thinking among adolescents. *Journal of Children and Media, 6*(4), 430–449.

Weber, R., Ritterfield, U., & Mathiak, K. (2006). Does playing violent videogames induce aggression? Empirical evidence of a functional magnetic resonance imagery study. *Media Psychology, 8,* 39–60.

Weimann, G. (2000). *Communicating unreality: Modern media and the construction of reality* (pp. 79–121). Thousand Oaks, CA: Sage.

Wilksch, S.M. & Wade, T.D. (2009). Reduction of shape and weight concern in young adolescents: A 30-month controlled evaluation of a media literacy program. *Journal of American Academy of child and adolescent Psychiatry, 48*(6), 652–661.

Williams, T.M. (1986). *The impact of television: A natural experiment in three communities* (pp. 361–93). Orlando, FL: Academic Press.

Wilson, B., Kunkel, D., Kintz, D., Potter, J., Donnerstein, E. *et al.* (1996). *National television violence study*. Thousand Oaks, CA: Sage.

Winn, M. (1977). *The Plug in Drug*. New York: Viking.

Wober, M. & Young, B.M. (1993). British children's knowledge of, emotional reactions to, and ways of making sense of the war. In B.S. Greenberg & W. Gantz (Eds.), *Desert Storm and the mass media* (pp. 381–394). Cresskill, NJ: Hampton.

Wolf, N. (1992). *The beauty myth: How images of beauty are used against women*. New York: Doubleday.

Wong, T.C. (2012). Cyber-parenting: Internet benefits, risks and parenting issues *Journal of Technology in Human Services, 28*(4), 252–273.

Zaharoponlous, T. (1999). Television viewing and the perception of the United States by Greek teenagers. In Y.R. Kamalipour (Ed.), *Images of the U.S. around the world: A multi-cultural perspective* (pp. 279–294). New York: State University of New York Press.

Zanotti, A. (2009). Views in progress, views in process. A participatory video experience with young people in a space of borderlands. In T. Tufte & F. Enghel (Eds.), *Youth engaging with the world: Media, communication and social change* (pp. 283–300). Göteborg University, Sweden: The International Clearinghouse on Children, Youth and Media.

Zaslow, E. (2011). *Feminism, Inc: Coming of age in girl power media culture*. New York: Palgrave Macmillan.

Zhao, Y., Qiu, W., & Xie, N. (2012). Social networking, social gaming, texting. In D.G. Singer & J.L. Singer (Eds.), *Handbook of children and the media* (pp. 97–112). Los Angeles: Sage.

Zillman, D. (1994). Erotica and family values. In D. Zillman, J. Bryant, & A.C. Huston (Eds.), *Media, children and the family: Social scientific, psychodynamic and clinical perspectives* (pp. 199–213). Hillsdale, NJ: Lawrence Erlbaum.

Zohoori, A.R. (1988). A cross-cultural analysis of children's television use. *Journal of Broadcasting and Electronic Media, 32*(1), 105–113.

Zuckerman, P., Ziegler, M., & Stevenson, H.W. (1978). Children's viewing of television and recognition memory of commercials. *Child Development, 49*(1), 96–104.

Index